The Property Issue
Politics of Space and Data

ARNO BRANDLHUBER,
OLAF GRAWERT,
ANH-LINH NGO

T0339046

"Philosophers have only interpreted the world in various ways; but what matters is to transform it." The famous Eleventh Thesis on Feuerbach by Karl Marx suggests that there is a clear difference between abstract theorizing and revolutionary action. The apparent opposition between reflection and action, between theory and practice, was retroactively reinforced in the version edited by Friedrich Engels, in which he added the word "but" to the sentence. Through an interpretive intervention he thus underscores the merit of action.

But is Marx truly concerned with the difference between philosophizing about the world and changing it? Or is he rather hinting that we should take philosophers at their word if we want to achieve the objectives they show us with their analyses? If our ultimate aim is the emancipation of all humanity, then we must try to find the inherent potential for liberation within the societal conditions, however difficult they may be at present, and "force them to dance," as Marx writes elsewhere.

And that is what this publication is about—with regard to a fundamental contradiction in contemporary society: the contradiction between the social character of production and the private appropriation of the results of this production. Specifically, it deals with the question of ownership of land and data, and the effects of these ownership relations on the production of space.

Who owns the land? This question is of crucial importance for all societies and their coexistence. This is because the availability of land and property controls the production of space and the social order. The fact that land (space) is as vital to life as air and water means that its use should not succumb to the unmistakable play of free (market) forces and individual whims.

Who owns data? For urban planning, the issue of data ownership has become just as relevant as land ownership. In this issue we therefore discuss the politics of space and the politics of data, the real and virtual capital of the city of the future. The debate is guided by two main questions: How do we deal with space and data as planning resources? And what role do architects and urban planners play in the digital society?

The intertwining of land ownership and finance is by no means a recent invention. On the contrary, as the philosopher Wolfgang Scheppe explains in this issue using Venice as an example, it has

Editorial

always been part of the city's feudal reality: "The limited space available for building in the city area, together with the huge and unprecedented concentration of consumers, gave the small number of aristocratic families—who had succeeded in transplanting liege conditions into the urbs—a likewise unprecedented monopolist position to increase the value of their real property. For this reason, Sombart sees ground rent as the 'mother of the city'. [...] He identifies the city's major landowners, who divided up the city among themselves, as the real creators of the city."

However, the example of Venice also shows that despite historical continuity, a radical change has occurred. Whereas landowners were once dependent on the population for generating ground rents, today the opposite holds true for the urban centers that draw tourists: the local inhabitants are an obstacle for those who seek to exploit the lands. Living space is seen as "unproductive" because it yields less than the income generated by festivals, biennials, and tourism. The consequence: the marketing of cities means the disappearing of city residents, who "underperform" in the global run on space as a resource.

What can we do about this? Not much, because there is no alternative but to politicize land. A lot, because so far everybody has failed to do so. But if we define the city as a commons for the whole of society, there is no way around comprehensive reform. It must begin with changing our conceptual orientation by denaturalizing land through a philosophy of land—by strengthening the understanding that land is always a cultural and social product, and therefore a political product (see the contribution by Milica Topalović). We must find sound arguments against the dogma of privatization! The idea of land ownership based on natural rights put forth by John Locke in the seventeenth century offers a point of attack. By linking property rights to the amount of work invested, Locke linked economic theory with political theory. This line of argumentation can be used to develop a political economy of the city, and to show that the current situation is anything but "natural." The contributions in this issue reveal the prevailing lines of conflict, but also possible potentials to redefine property in order to make the city conceivable as a public good in the long term.

Despite financialization, digitalization, and virtualization, the use of space, an increasingly scarce resource, is becoming more critical than ever. Tech companies such as Google, Microsoft, Airbnb, and Uber have long since stopped contenting themselves with the commercialization of all social activities; now they are investing their stock market gains in real estate and land. Following their respective corporate logic, they have also begun to plan their own cities of the future. Take, for example, the Sidewalk Toronto project by the Alphabet/Google start-up Sidewalk Labs, which treats residents as sources of data. In the future, artificial intelligence will be used to regulate the distribution of space.

For architecture in particular, this development has far-reaching consequences. With the smart city discourse, algorithm-based planning methods, and massive investments in infrastructure, the tech industry is penetrating far into the field of architects and planners. Their technocratic visions turn citizens into users, says Christian von Borries in this publication: "First, architecture becomes an instrument of statistics and then provides information about user behavior. The role of the architect no longer exists in this scenario, or it is limited to the design of unconnected buildings in the urban space that are predetermined by algorithms." Have architects in post-planning, as Deane Simpson calls this development, become obsolete?

This issue clearly demonstrates the radicalization of economic thinking, with which the city is conceived of and produced as an exclusive space. Cities are becoming the tech industry's central line of business, and their target group is the urban elite. This development is based on (user) data collected by the billions from mobile applications, from delivery and mobility services, and increasingly, from smart cities. The penetration of major tech companies into the physical space presents us with new challenges. After all, big data also enables new planning and design tools. However, the algorithms, equations, and conclusions behind these tools and applications are not unquestionable truths. They are neither neutral nor objective. Behind them are people—data analysts, programmers, and business people—whose decisions and interests shape our imaginations and our daily lives.

What does it mean for urban society when private companies increasingly assume the tasks of the public sector? What happens if cities thereby increasingly follow an entrepreneurial logic and the associated technocratic ideals of datafication? "Quantifying humans and habitats transforms them into biometric entities and street-scores," warns anthropologist Shannon Mattern in her article. In this vision, Mattern continues, the city, society, and people are nothing more than "algorithmic assemblages." The implications are thus not only to be found in our social interactions, but also in our self-image as human beings. The digitally produced, synthetic portraits of non-real people by the company Generated Photos on the cover are a dramatic demonstration of this insight. They are the result of machine learning in generative adversarial networks. These "random unreal people" are, in a sense, our avatars in an era of post-politics and post-planning. So the story is about us. *De te fabula narratur!*

How can architects react to the unstoppable advance of the smart city and datafication? Not only in the gesture of resistance, as Hannes Grassegger impressively reports by example of the urban struggles in Hong Kong, but by making the phenomena, in all their contradictions, the subject of design and planning for an emancipated urban society. After all, if we Marx's theory of self-creation seriously—that we create ourselves by being productive in society—architects and planners are in a key position to shape the social realm. We don't have any other choice, either. We cannot rely on the fact that the system will destroy itself through its inner contradictions. Rather, like everything else, it evolves by actually playing out these conflicts and contradictions. It's called dialectics.

This publication was produced in collaboration with guest editors Arno Brandlhuber and Olaf Grawert (station+, D-ARCH, ETH Zurich) and ties in with the films Legislating Architecture: The Property Drama *(2017) and* Architecting After Politics *(2018) by Brandlhuber+ and Christopher Roth. It summarizes the two German editions ARCH+ 231 The Property Issue (see original cover on the facing page) and ARCH+ 236 Posthuman Architecture and supplements them with new articles.*

Page 102

"In this issue we discuss the politics of space and data, the real and virtual capital of the city of the future."

Page 164

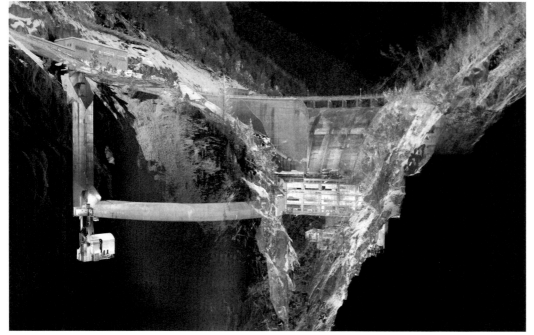

Page 174

Editorial team ARCH+:
Anh-Linh Ngo, Mirko Gatti, Christine Rüb
Guest editors: Arno Brandlhuber,
Olaf Grawert, Angelika Hinterbrandner
Contributing editors and editorial assistants:
Nora Dünser, Nils Fröhling, Christian Hiller,
Max Kaldenhoff, Melissa Koch,
Alexandra Nehmer, Alexander Stumm

Cover: Digitally produced, synthetic portraits of
non-real people by the company Generated Photos
© Generated Media Inc.

The Disappearance of Architecture and Society in the Algorithm

CHRISTIAN VON BORRIES IN CONVERSATION
WITH OLAF GRAWERT AND ARNO BRANDLHUBER

Christian von Borries works as a conductor, composer, filmmaker, and producer of site-specific installations. In his work, he appropriates existing music and images and re-samples them. In doing so, he highlights their reception and appropriation as tools and reflections of social, political, and economic control. He is a visiting professor for Intermedia Art at the China Academy of Art in Hangzhou. He recently completed his latest film, *AI is the Answer—What was the Question?*. Stills from this film are included here.

If Artificial Intelligence (AI) is truly communist (as the libertarian Silicon Valley entrepreneur Peter Thiel claims), then this statistic-based technology might actually compound centralized monopoly capitalism and the pending crisis of inequality, as described by Deleuze's notion of the control society. But it could also be seen and heard as a prototype—a new measure of beauty, redistribution of wealth, and solidarity. In times of Covid–19, we are now seeing machine learning technologies used as a state-imposed tool for surveillance. While the public debate about a data-driven approach to limit the freedom of movement of entire populations is only concerned with visible opt-in fitness tracking apps, Germany, France, Switzerland, Austria and Great Britain are now considering teaming up with the US data analytics company Palantir, which is notoriously shrouded in mystery.

Profit versus the common good

OLAF GRAWERT: *You collaborated with the Future Division of Daimler Inc. as part of the* Drehmomente *production art festival in Stuttgart. What kind of ideas were colliding with each other in such a collaboration?*
CHRISTIAN VON BORRIES: The automotive group has been expanding its product range for a while now, moving away from producing cars towards becoming a developer and provider of mobility concepts. According to Dieter Zetsche, Daimler's long-serving, recently retired CEO, this change in thinking is crucial in the race to dominate the mobility sector, which the company wants to win. Whenever a company like Daimler talks about mobility, it automatically speaks about public space and who is in charge. At this point, private and public interests are blurred, and that is what interests me as an artist: the relationship between social and corporate interests, the common good, and profit motivation. The failure of the state regulatory power became apparent when Stuttgart's Mayor, Fritz Kuhn, sent mixed messages during a Smart City conference. On the one hand, he called for reducing inner-city

and leasing division, expressed his vision of work and mobility for the future of Stuttgart with the idea of offering a single source for everything from the app to the automobile to the service itself. Images by Daimler's Future Division illustrated this vision with renderings of traffic junctions in Stuttgart, flying cars, people walking on green strips, and two men pushing a stroller. I question this narrative of an "old future" in my practice, which is highly associative.

Data instead of taxes

ARNO BRANDLHUBER: *At the same time, Daimler's idea is limited to changing the mechanical world. It replaces workers: products are no longer produced by hand but by robotic arms. This does not really rethink the notion of mobility; the transition to a different reality seems unthinkable. An artist talk you gave at the Garage Museum of Contemporary Art in Moscow was titled "Algorithms of a Smart City and the Disappearance of the Architect." Let's consider the first part of the title: what does this shift from mechanical to digital algorithmic logic mean for the city, and what role does big data play?*
CVB: Two aspects are especially important here: who is collect-

individual traffic, but then maintained that jobs in the automotive industry are more important to the region than any sort of mobility concept. Immediately afterwards, the head of Daimler Financial Services, the rental

ing which data and who is evaluating it? It might be that the user is society, represented by the state, for example with censuses. But in fact, data generated by the smart city is mostly amassed by private companies. China is an exception. We all leave our mark on the city whenever we use public transportation, shop at the grocery store, and so on; we are followed by surveillance cameras. So far, our actions are not being directly correlated. What we buy at the store, or how many cigarettes we smoke, goes unnoticed without a Payback card—unlike our virtual behavior, which leads to personalized advertising, a circumstance that we are largely aware of and that we seem to have accepted.

In the United States and China, we can observe a clear tendency to cross-reference the protocols of real actions and relate them to one another. The key question is: Who is interested in what regarding the evaluation of this data on daily and public life? With tax authorities, for instance, it might help to make things more fair, and ideally, public health insurance would also be driven by good motives. But when it comes to private corporations, profit is inevitably the key driver. The

field of self-driving cars is a good example of how the change from the mechanical to the virtual world has been accompanied by a change in power. Besides Chinese developers, Google is the world leader in navigation technology, without even producing vehicles. There is a clear separation between software and hardware, whereby the crucial added value lies in the implementation of the operating system, thus with Google and not with the car manufacturer.

OG: And in the same way, the city is being economized by evaluating and analyzing user behavior. For example, one of the most successful investment funds in the US bases its forecasts in urban areas on the parking lot monitoring system of the American hypermarket chain Walmart. Car brands and sizes, as well as how long and how often people park there, shed light on an area's economic and purchasing power and development prospects, and help to confirm the value of financial assets. This location

information is one of the largest and least expensive data sets.
AB: *But there was no intention to give data access to third parties when the parking lot cameras were first installed. The information is collected and, in some ways, interchangeable. The rise of self-learning software has revealed the importance of data and its availability. And with that, the question of interpretation becomes relevant: Where does this qualitative transition happen? What happens if this data—be it random, generated by Google or, in the case of China, government-managed—affect the analogue city and urban planning?*
CVB: This example shows the successful correlation of data. At the same time, we can observe that the key role lies not with the software developer but with the data analyst. Data analysts do not program applications, but use data patterns to establish correlations between the behavior of people and objects. Do I take the car, the bike, or do I walk? Do I leave the house at all? To whom

do I talk when riding the bus? In the past, urban planning, and with it a sense of responsibility, has been centralized without consideration for the actual residents. For example, where homes and roads are built, or how much real estate is available for public housing or private ownership. Future planning might be based on population data—a diverse data set that could help shape how the city of the future might look.

At the same time, our role is shifting from that of citizen to user. We are no longer part of a society, but a community, a homogeneous bubble. The development of Toronto's waterfront shows quite clearly that this economization of the environment by private companies is not being perceived as a threat. Sidewalk Labs, a subsidiary of Alphabet and sister company of Google, is developing a whole neighborhood there (see Bianca Wylie, p. 124–129). We need to consider where the line is between Alphabet's interests (apart from profit) and an idealistic urban development concept.

161

Data as power

OG: *Public-private partnerships like those at the Toronto waterfront are on the rise. Ever more infrastructure and urban development projects are conceived and implemented according to this model. In Germany, a similar tool exists: urban planning contracts. What do these alliances of elected representatives with private companies mean for the city? The withdrawal of the state as we know it?*

CVB: It would be too easy to say that it's bad just because it's Google. Google makes life easier—that's a fact. And now Google is building an entire city neighborhood. This step from the virtual to the real world is absolutely logical. For me, the physical presence of the large technology companies at the World Economic Forum 2018 in Davos was a crystal clear signal. For the first time, Google, Facebook, and Palantir have their own buildings in prime inner-city locations. This was a self-confident spatial expression of power and influence: the companies took their place alongside the nation-states, with the difference that access to their representative offices is

limited. If you want to visit them "at their home," you needed an invitation.

It's interesting to compare this with China, where there is no moral and political differentiation between the private enterprise and the centralized state. Although the big internet companies are managed privately and traded on stock exchanges, the state has direct rights of access. This leads to state-controlled information and data centralization. The state has contributed considerably to the development of new technologies such as AI through targeted financial support or participation. Since state structures were often perceived in the past as acting in ways that were arbitrary, unauthorized, or corrupt, today there is less the fear of Big Brother than the hope for a new, more objective approach.

AI is communist

AB: *In your film,* AI is the Answer—What was the Question? *Peter Thiel, founder of PayPal and Palantir, says that "crypto is libertarian and AI is communist." What does he mean by that?*

CVB: Of course, he is arguing from a libertarian perspective and advocates cryptocurrency as the ideal decentralized system. For him, the idea of central intelligence, as in China, is per se authoritarian and therefore communist. This would make an AI-based and controlled smart city à la Google authori-

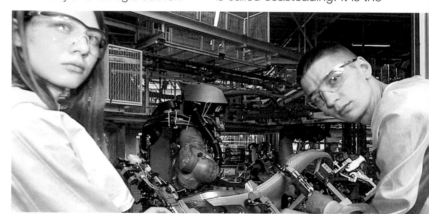

tarian, too. At the same time, there are hints of a new Cold War, not least over resources, because both technologies consume vast amounts of energy. This has a direct impact on the states involved.

But for Thiel it is also about an idea of the physical society. Its advocates speak of decentralized database-based technology and always refer to Milton Friedman, Ronald Reagan's economist and con-

fidant, and his liberal-market approaches that seek to remove all forms of state regulation. In his view, the role of governments should be limited to protecting private property. Logically, the next step would be to withdraw to islands outside national territories. This new business idea is called seasteading. It is the epitome of a libertarian society, where any variant of social system is possible: it could be a socialist state, but it could also be an authoritarian one.

OG: Algorithms are represented by people who pursue their own ideologies, prejudices, and agendas. Among other things, James Bridle writes about the influence of developers and analysts in his book *New Dark Age: Technology and the End of*

All images:
Christian von Borries: *AI is the Answer—What was the Question?*, 2019
77 min, color, 5.1 surround sound.

the Future. It explores the agency of coders and codes (see James Bridle, p. 184–191). <u>AB</u>: *In this context, Wendy Chun uses the sociological concept of homophily to explain the effects of algorithms such as those of Facebook. People are divided into homogeneous groups because they are easier to address. Is the smart city homogenous per se?*

<u>CVB</u>: Machine learning is based on statistics. Statistics of user data, existing spaces, situations, environments. However, statistics in market logic also mean that the largest group will and must always get larger. Minorities therefore become marginalized, which poses a danger, as does the lack of accountability. Although we know which algorithms AI is based on, the levels of decision-making and potential influences remain opaque. Coders can influence the behavior of machine learning (ML) by exposing the algorithm to specific training stimuli. For example, many image- and text-classification algorithms are trained by optimizing the accuracy of a particular record using data that has been manually labeled by humans (labeled data

in supervised learning). The selection of the data set and the characteristics it depicts have a significant influence on this. We can neither intervene nor disagree, which further contributes to the homogenization of groups and society.

The question is how Facebook would think and understand the city. It is highly speculative to maintain that the smart city is homogenous per se. Perhaps we should look at the physical spaces that Facebook has built for itself and their logic. Frank Gehry's corporate headquarters design is so interesting because, although the company hired one of the best-known trademark architects, Gehry didn't deliver his iconic architectural language in this case. This project is completely untypical for Gehry, but one could argue that he understood Facebook—almost in the same way that Mark Zuckerberg dresses—according to the norm-core principle: architectural indeterminacy. It's about the lowest common denominator that works globally and can be reproduced, similar to an IKEA lamp or a T-shirt by H&M. A degree of ambiguity

similar to Facebook's can be observed at the Toronto waterfront. Canada represents a business-friendly middle course between regulatory Europe and the private capitalism of the United States, a hybrid testing ground that works globally while anticipating a high degree of participation. In Canada, a different type of data generation than in the US is possible: one that is voluntary, proactive, and bilateral. This leads to architectures that, on the one hand, do not disturb anyone, and on the other hand, are generated for different and rapidly changing uses. The focus on function in ML helps us to understand why some behavioral mechanisms of algorithms are spreading and continuing, while others are

decreasing and disappearing. The function highly depends on adapting the behavior to the environment data, not the other way around, as Google's Sidewalk Labs claims. Successful behaviors (improving the multi-functionality of architecture, for example) are copied by developers of other software and hardware, or further developed to spread on ML algorithms. This dynamic is ultimately determined by the success of institutions such as corporations, hospitals, municipalities, and universities—Foucault's spaces of enclosure—which program and use AI to homogenize human behavior.

<u>AB</u>: *If we assume that the images of architecture in this case*

serve to generate resonances, which then are used as data in urban planning, architecture becomes an instrument while at the same time losing its social functions.

CVB: Exactly! First, architecture becomes an instrument of statistics and then provides information about user behavior. The role of the architect no longer exists in this scenario, or it is limited to the design of unconnected buildings in the urban space that are predetermined by algorithms.

Users and providers

OG: *In addition to Orit Halpern, you refer in your lectures to Keller Easterling. You all agree that there is a marginalization of certain undesirable populations, usually the working class. Your film also shows the Louvre Abu Dhabi, where workers are standing and waiting almost invisibly. What do these pictures tell us?*

CVB: For years, I've been collecting footage of cleaning staff in apparently senseless cleaning situations. These clips reveal something that is usually hidden: that even though we all use mobility sharing services, nobody knows who cleans, refuels, or services the cars. And if you change your computer chip or repair your smartwatch, again, the repair worker will remain unseen—invisible and underpaid. Given such structural conditions, our class system and the neoliberal politics behind it cannot last much longer. In already uncertain times, in which society is becoming increasingly polarized—here the rich, there the poor—we are now being confronted with new ideas and forms of living. But how will established companies and start-ups respond to the displacement of the middle class from the city centers? Google, Amazon, or Baidu may have no interest in this and ideally prevent ghettos of any kind. Might it be possible to use an algo-rithm to counteract this current development?

Big data as public space

AB: *What kinds of attempts are already being made to influence the public space?*

CVB: Until not so long ago, we lived under the impression that public space belonged to everyone. An intermediate step away from this was marked by the creation of commercialized, semi-public spaces such as the Mercedes Benz Plaza in front of the Mercedes Benz Arena (previously the O2 Arena), in Berlin. The square was opened by Ramona Pop, the Green Party's Senator for Economy, Energy, and Enterprises, with the words: "This is a typical Berlin district as we envision it." Police standing on a nearby street confirmed what was already apparent: that public servants don't have jurisdiction over the premises because it is a private space, where safety is privately addressed and regulated.

The World Cup in Russia in 2018 clearly shows the direction this development is taking. There, a facial recognition software called FindFace was used nationwide, with a recognition rate of 97 percent. Everyone who visited the FIFA World Cup had an RFID chip in their tickets that had to be carried outside the stadiums as well. This may sound like old technology, but it already anticipates a future in which people identified through chips can cross borders or pay for their groceries at the supermarket without waiting in line—in short, life without friction or limitations. This form of space and its acceptance marks the intersection of big data and public space .Critics of this technology are countered with the argument that the technology fosters public safety by enabling cross-references with the data of well-known hooligans. China makes a similar argument in defense of its social credit system. There, big data is already part of everyday life: those who behave inappropriately are prohibited from using the express train, for instance. The policies are often justified by using examples of people from marginalized groups. These are just a few examples illustrating how data affects public space.

AB: *Sidewalk Labs uses a self-developed, open source software called Replica to simulate and plan entire cities. They offer it to municipalities and city planners and, in return, receive labeled data to verify their algorithmic forecasts based on real-time database systems. Keller Easterling calls these unseen powers that govern the space of everyday life "extra-statecraft." Does that mean that European nation-states cannot compete with the superior power of global tech companies?*

CVB: Exactly, state administrations have no similar spheres of influence or comparable resources. We need to think about treating and controlling technology companies as supra-state structures. So far, China is the exception, because this one-party state is organized top-down by default. While this is not the rule in politics, this tendency is inscribed in technologies. Now you might ask: What then is the task for architects in China?

Society and its architecture as an algorithm

AB: *The Sidewalk Labs CEO, Daniel Doctoroff, was Deputy Mayor of New York and responsible for implementing the communications network LinkNYC, which replaced all phone booths in New York with free Wi-Fi (see Michaela Friedberg, p. 204–209). LinkNYC also belongs primarily to the Alphabet group. This drew sharp criticism from the population. How can one still have a dialogue at eye level in the face of this overwhelming economic power?*

CVB: To understand the complexity of this business and its reach, you have to consider a second level and ask: What social functions do Alphabet's technologies and offerings correspond to? These would be state responsibilities such as public transport, public hospitals, and public health insurance. At the planned Quayside district by Sidewalk Labs along the Toronto waterfront, these tasks are to be performed by private companies. But this is not about traditional privatization, it is about full access to our habitats and the subcutaneous control of our behavior. You have to understand their business model. In Google's exploitation logic, all city and state functions will seem to be free of charge, like a search query. The privatized service is just the tool to get data in return. So it might be too simple to ask what tasks architects can still fulfill in this scenario. Shouldn't we be asking where and how society is actually operating? You cannot act independently of the system; without Alphabet, Amazon, and the like, the situation can hardly be changed. We have to use their tools and think about what we can do with them and what our role should be. You are architects with the software at your disposal: use it and see what comes out of it, and what that means to you! We are certainly embedded, and there is probably no alternative. At best, it expands our utopian horizon. To look at it positively, the Quayside district might ultimately be the architecture that wins the Pritzker Prize because no architect could ever imagine it. Maybe big data will give us a vision of society that we never would have come up with ourselves.

Land Ownership

"Land, and the way it is available and accessible as private property, has become the hegemonic type of access in our society."

— Raquel Rolnik

The Ground-Rent of Art and Exclusion from the City

The Exemplary Quality of Venice's Singularity

WOLFGANG SCHEPPE

FIG. 1 Business: Theatres to tourist markets! Churches to galleries! Living rooms to tourist accomodations! The rededication of an emptied city.

Venice is an instructive model for the—literally—exclusive re-dedication of urban space in accordance with a totalitarian rationality of revenue per square meter. The reason for this is its physically exposed location on the lagoon, which separates its historic center from its agglomeration on the mainland, thus revealing the two parts to be, by nature, quantitatively and qualitatively distinct. What the prominent situation reveals is this: the running of the iconic art city is inimicable to the life of its inhabitants. Their exclusion from the city obeys the rationale of an exploitation that makes its own area of dominion uninhabitable.

The post-city city

Precisely what makes Venice exemplary as a place and hence an illuminating model for reflection on the city in general stands, paradoxically, in the way of any rational discourse, because what is happening in Venice is, at first glimpse, nothing extraordinary: it is just the regular routine of business taking its course. As always, this follows the principle—as common as it is unconditional—of property, its appropriation, and exploitation. However, to follow this generally uncontested rule in the ossified, pre-modern structures of *La Serenissima* wreaks, in a far shorter time, precisely those life-incapacitating processes of destruction, which, in usual cities that are capable of expansion and change, make themselves felt only slowly, and are mediated by compensatory factors. In Venice, displacement is necessarily, at one and the same time, exclusion. That expresses the process with all conceptual clarity. In contrast to developments in the "generic city" of the global economy, Venice's metropolitan periphery, separated by a water barrier, has the effect that the historic center associated with it suddenly becomes an uninhabitable zone, a condition incompatible with living inside it. Because its growth cannot be directed outwards, it has to take place in the form of intensification: it is subject to the unconditional rationale of the optimization of turnover per square meter.

When it comes to Venice—a city unremittingly traded as a site of global yearning—any judgement on the effects of the profitable management of land in its designated form of real estate property immediately takes on a shrill, strident note. Because who wouldn't, without the slightest hesitation, be prepared to espouse the cause that this place must be preserved for the uplifting and edification of future generations? This very site, which John Ruskin held on any scale of appreciation to be the "paradise of cities," and whose most important man-made monument he even dignified as the "central building of the world." Passions for the preservation of Venice are two-a-penny. It leads customarily to hollow rhetoric—notably the epithet "fragile" for the allegedly endangered walls of this city. Unfortunately, all the indignation and outrage, expressed almost invariably in a tone of concerned pathos, disregards one thing—namely the universally acknowledged, and hence uncontested nature of the business whose methods of exploitation of real estate as the original incarnation of property encompass each and every thing. This business is spatially expansive and, in its fateful logic, encroaches on what constituted for centuries the specific vitality of this improbable urban ensemble on the lagoon. The ensemble is in the process of being reduced to its mere transfer copy—diminished into a theme park vaguely inspired by the atmosphere of its original spatial feel. This trivialization embodies a unique selling proposition, in which the essence of the brand seems to be captured, differentiating it from its rivals as a trading commodity fostering prosperity.

The idea is straightforward and therefore sounds orthodox: for as long as the laws of the *one* economic system are in force—a system that grounds all freedom for the exploitation of private property in the genuine freedom of owning realty—the soon-to-be-completed exodus of all everyday life from the waterside settlement will be an inevitability. Conversely, it would be as idealistic as it is senseless to demand that territorially limited special regulations should be established as an exclave in the otherwise hegemonic dominion of the private control of land, so that Venice is bracketed off as an island in the *mare magnum* of globalized capitalism in order to embalm it for posterity.

Equally absurd is the reverse argument: there are scant grounds for assuming that the norms of the world economy would be overthrown simply for the sake of the wellbeing of one idyllic little spot. After all, the latter is only one-third of the size of Disneyland Paris and has a total population lower than the staff of Disney World in Orlando, Florida. That would hardly be grounds for a world revolution—even for its supporters.

Scandalization is a vicious circle, and intellectually improper since it is made up of consternation and affirmation, coating controversial political certainties in the plausibility of common sense. In scandal, it is easy to reach agreement. In what remains to be said here, therefore, one thing is always to be taken for granted: for Venice, it's already "game over."

Ground-Rent

Everything that persists in making life difficult for its last inhabitants is "business as usual." This sober fact—in contrast to the reasons for it—is thus not worth getting het up about. The arrival of this state of affairs is noted only by those final residents who are compelled to witness the death of a form of existence that was once the day-to-day life of a city. Until a few years ago, it was preserved in its autochthonous particularity as something that was as special as it was exemplary. Venice's early medieval and Byzantine structures, which have remained preserved in its isolated, waterside position, simultaneously make this city a singular and general capital; the very epitome of a "city." Consequently, along with this epitome, the city as hitherto practiced —in line with the mediaeval legal statute of the "city air that makes people free"— must perish in terms of being a concentration of interrelationships at the place in which a multiplicity of human beings have their dwelling. They do so in order to encounter one another, within the parameters of work and free time, in the spatial unity of a context that can be created only by a city neighborhood on its streets and squares. The former local residents now find the center of this unity disputed by real estate owners at every point where income can be expected in the form of a lucrative demand generated by massed and—in the literal sense—*ephemeral*, i.e. fleeting, consumers of tourist boards and lodging offers.

Society will have to come to terms with a post-city city—and this holds true far beyond the paradigm of Venice, which has monument-like status in this regard. It holds true for every iconic form of urban life that—more because of its narrative and atmospheric marketing potential than because of its historic reputation—makes itself a compliant object of marketing dynamics by becoming a destination. The deregulatory forces concomitant with this dynamic inevitably set in motion a self-propelling regime of exclusion. The means of achieving this exclusion, which is always implicit in the concept of the owner's power of disposition over real estate property, is the price that is paid for the use of space.

Among the canonical conceptions of Venice is the conviction that its lagoon-side location is an ecosystem forever endangered by anthropogenic influences and which the ancient Republic, with great technical and political skill, took upon itself to preserve as a sacred good for the generality. This commonplace view is in need of correction. The lagoon should be considered less as a fixed geological formation than as a continuously liquid field of interaction between the forces of sedimentation and erosion. In a precarious system of movement and counter-movement, it is the ever-threatening poles of antagonistic development—silting up or opening up into a bay—that determine its constitution. Contrary to what environmentalists and nature-lovers believe, Venice's lagoon owes its continued existence to a social order. The wish to forever fix as such a geological state reached in the Middle Ages transforms the natural space into a cultural landscape created wilfully by the authorities—a landscape which is dependent on a strict policy of water control, and which seeks to influence the natural water flow on a grand scale. The lagoon is therefore a highly artificial construct. It consequently requires a state power of utmost resolve which, in order to preserve its extraordinary physical location, has to resort to equally extraordinary societal efforts and to wondrous technological innovations.

When in the year 1152, following a prolonged period of rain, the Po broke its dykes in the *rotta di Ficarolo*, the ensuing flood not only depopulated the surrounding plain for a generation, but also deprived the powerful and wealthy Pomposa Abbey of its characteristic position as an island washed on all sides by diverse arms of a delta. Nervously watched by the ruling class in Venice, this catastrophic development ultimately laid the foundation for a momentous decision—the all-powerful resolution to preserve the lagoon situation of the island at all costs. In 1327, under the command of the already 100-year-old institution of the *Magistrato alle Acque*, the attempt began to stem and arrest natural changes—an attempt that reached its engineering culmination in 1488. Where they flowed into the bay with its promontories and sandbanks, the sediment- and gravel-bearing rivers were forced by an artificial bed to take a course which made the utmost endeavors to petrify what was in fact a process of continuous flow.

> Society will have to come to terms with a post-city city— and this holds true for every iconic form of urban life that makes itself a compliant object of marketing dynamics by becoming a destination.

Fortifications, fisheries, and seafaring were subordinate elements in the geopolitical status of a Maritime Republic that was to be eternalized. For in the center of this development stood the doctrine of an identity-conferring topography. This dogma uses the island situation as a token that serves a solely political purpose—the endeavor to preserve in Venice's geographical exceptionalism the raw material for a naturalizing foundation myth for its state construct. Its exceptional physical situation continued to vouch for the patriciate's claim to power. Using its distinguished territorial situation as a symbolic magnitude, Venice was intent on the quality of an essentialized historical image. That is precisely what mystification achieves: turning history into nature so as to surround the hagiography of hegemonic authority with the nimbus of necessity and incontestability. In this way, when it comes to nature, dominion appears to be a given.

The resolve to reshape territorial formations on the scale of geological coastlines and the natural forces at work in them was necessary to preserve Venice's "urban alterity."[01] In its stylization of geographical exceptionalism, the stupendously singular location is a spatial legitimization of dominion fortified by despotism and hydro-geological measures. There is probably no better evidence for the analytical capacity of Henri Lefèbvre's idea of the politics of space (whose popularity has been rewarded by its dilution into a rhetorical husk) than the sovereignty narrative—derived from its isolation on the lagoon and reified into landscape—of Venice's long-enduring power. The incomparable location advantage has thus been speculated upon far longer than the formulae of the tourism industry lead one to expect. They just continue this destination's success story. Yet it can also be recognized that the authorities in this sea-bound city not only passively accepted the limitations imposed by topography but also actively intended them.

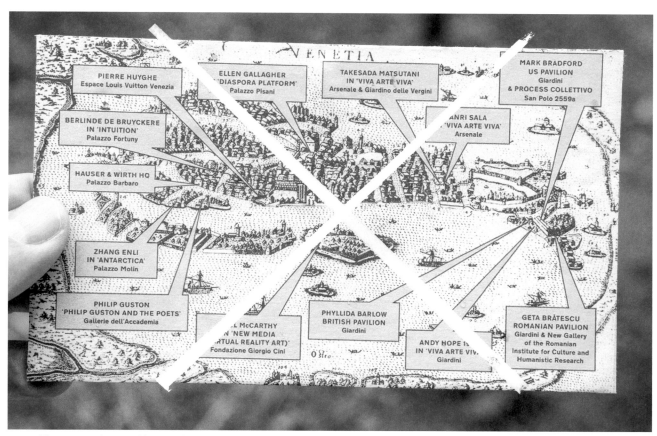

FIG. 2 The art market and its spatial requirements: battle plan for the capture of the city. Flyer of a globally operative gallery for the 2017 Biennale.

In *Der moderne Kapitalismus* [*Modern Capitalism*] (1902), his voluminous major work from the start of the twentieth century, Werner Sombart included something that he considered to be absent in academic work to date—a theory of the city.[02] In an attempt to supply the latter, he uses the special case of Venice as a fundamental pattern for his conceptualization. He sees the developed monetary economy and the emergence of merchant capital as originating in the municipal ground rent—the expression used by classical national economics for the yield from real estate property. Under the title "Ground Rent Theory," this has become the subject of major controversies because, in contrast to the prevailing doctrine on Venice, Sombart does not explain the rise of a modern capitalist economy as resulting from the sudden inception of trade prosperity, which then grew until it had uncontested superiority in the Mediterranean area. It was, Sombart argues, precisely the other way around: it was not because it was a trading city that Venice grew rich, but rather because it was rich that it could become a profitable trading city. "In economic terms, the cities of the Middle Ages are the product of the recipients of ground rent; only through it can the 'merchants' exist."[03] The use of land as the source of monetary wealth first generated the credit upon which trade was based—not vice versa, as Sombart's critics would have it.

Sombart understood not only the beginnings of bourgeois wealth-production but also the basis for the very existence of the city as motivated by the logic of ground rent, which he terms "primordial wealth." Monetary riches, this line of thought argues, grow from the "development of city culture," which occurs in the interest of a few land-owning families. They divided up among themselves the land bounded by the city's perimeters—land which, with the enormous growth of the population after the eleventh century, experienced an extraordinary rise in value and brought its owners a corresponding increase in rent revenues. As accumulated capital, he argues, these latter formed a surplus that called for re-investment, which was provided in the form of credit granted for trade undertakings. With these additional funds they could subsequently cope with a continuing growth in large-scale and long-distance trade. The limited space available for building in the city area, together with the huge and unprecedented concentration of consumers, gave the small number of aristocratic families—who had succeeded in transplanting liege conditions into the *urbs*—a likewise unprecedented monopolist position to increase the value of their real property. For this reason, Sombart sees ground rent as the "mother of the city."[04]

With reference to Venice, Sombart concludes that a good deal depended on the special characteristics of the city's location and its restriction: "The more cramped the space into which a population had to be squeezed, the higher the surplus value rate extracted from the population in the form of ground rent."[05] He identifies the city's major landowners, who divided up the city among themselves, as the real creators of the city. Among the richest land-owning families in Venice were the Ziani family, several members of which held the office of Doge. There were at least 13 densely built

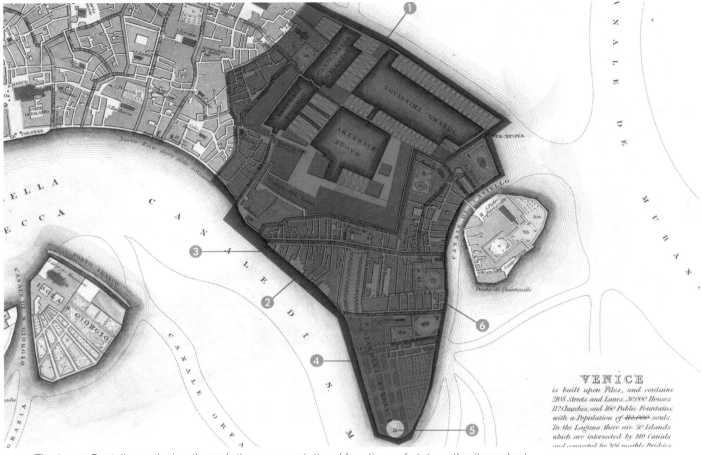

FIG. 3 The lower Castello: exclusion through the representational functions of state authority and art.

1 Arsenale [Biennale grounds since 1999]
2 Rio Sant'Anna [Boulevard Via Eugenia, 1807; Via Garibaldi since 1866]
3 Riva dell'Impero, Mussolini, 1941 [Riva Sette Martiri since 1946]
4 Giardini, Napoleonic Gardens [Biennale grounds since 1895]

5 Napoleonic Café, 1812 [British Pavilion since 1909]
6 Arsenale policing jurisdiction, 1600 [Castello Basso]

city parishes in which they owned considerable land. In several of these, the entire land surface was in their hands. In addition, the real estate empire of this long-dominant family included more than 80 salt works, but also vineyards, extensive and continually increasing agricultural lands on the mainland, and finally, extensive water rights in the lagoon.[06]

Therefore, with the rank of nobleman and privileged landowner, one could live from the rents yielded by the land on which all other city-dwellers depended. And not only that: when the feudal class began to derive revenue from the Republic's colonial conquests in addition to the rents, this income was so high that the owners were often unable to consume it on their own. The surplus capital deriving from accumulated ground rent demanded to be utilized. Lending it on interest to those who required it to fund their businesses—among whom the state itself is to be numbered—constituted the credit industry, which first emerged in Venice and subsequently assumed institutional form there.[07] With the entry of the aristocracy into the business transactions involved in trade, however, the reverse case, in which landed estates are

used as security for the receipt of credits, emerged as the historically decisive form.[08]

In the dual meaning of the "ground of the city" inherent in the spatially concentrated management of ground rent by an elite with the privilege of levying it, two historical factors essential for the modern era need to be distinguished. On the one hand, the value of land comes into the hands of money owners by means of credit. Through the granting of loans feudal wealth was transformed into bourgeois wealth. This transfer of capital, in the form of mortgages from landowners to money merchants, functioned as a decisive precondition for capital accumulation in cities. While under the conditions of feudalism (under which the urban aristocracy of the Venetian *Signoria* can be subsumed) land was firmly associated with the personal union of aristocracy and *dominum terrae*, in which hereditary nobility was like an *accidens*, an appendage, of landownership, and fiefdom and liege lord were thus inseparably bound together. Land lost this bond at the very moment in which it was transformed into a commodity. "This bartering away of land property, the transformation of land into a commodity, is the final overthrow of the old aristocracy and the final establishment of the monied aristocracy."[09] As the control of space became a banal matter of monetary demand, so it freed itself from ennobled land-ownership to be handed over to lords of money ownership. This appropriation, however, delivered the verdict on a dividing line that was destined henceforth to run right through society. With the criterion of the profitable possession of space it monopolized a foundation of life and livelihood that separated the proprietors from the unpropertied. The existential wish to make use of space forces some into the service of the others. The question "Who owns the city?" is thus not about reducing the land share for the many; it amounts to their essential expropriation.

Segregation

The distribution of estates, strata, and classes in the social geography that is always woven into the structure of any urban expanse finds its architectural reification in accordance with the economic laws prevalent there. The latter again owe their existence to the political regime the power of which guarantees them. The circumstances of Venice's primordial society, for which scarcely any written documents survive—in contrast to the ensuing half-millenium of the unbroken constitutional history of a patrician oligarchy and its excessive bureaucratization—remain recognizably inscribed in the particular spatial order and the walls of Venice right down to the present day. The social form prevalent in the early Middle Ages was dominated by an idea of community under the mantle of religion. This found its political expression in an inclusive sovereign: pre-eminence in all political decisions was enjoyed by the spontaneous institution of a gathering of the populace, known first as the *concio* and later as the *arengo*. The proclamation of the will of the entire citizenry (which the coming together of all adult male members, or at least the heads of family, in the community understood itself to be) took place in turbulently conducted plenary sessions, in which the noise generated by applause was the decisive factor for acclamation. Without any distinction, this assembly included all *maiores, mediocres et minores*, those of higher estate, those with average income and those of lower rank. Thus, the participation of persons—equal in principle to the process of exerting political influence—still resembled the archaic polis of the ancient world. For a period of four centuries, up to the election of Vitale II, the thirty-eighth Doge, in the year 1156, this popular assembly had the right to determine the incumbent from among its midst and to watch over his exercise of office.

With the increasing wealth of the Republic as it rose to be the leading trading metropolis, hegemonic political endeavors began, directed at the formation of a privileged political elite, whose noble rank was based on merchant success. Henceforth, Venetian historiography was to be the history of the increasing empowerment of a bio-politically rooted, and hence hereditary, patrician class in contradistinction to the former immediate plenary gathering, whose vote hitherto encompassed all sectors of the populace and which had the full right not only of the general election of the Doge from among its number but also of determining his mandate. On the one hand, this hereditary nobility strove to close itself off, refusing to admit socially mobile parvenus from among its fellow citizens and, on the other hand, it was increasingly concerned with reducing the office of Doge to a formal representational figure, whom it sought to keep under its control. In a protracted, conflict-ridden process, the ruling nobility managed to gain the sole supervision of policy, of the upper administration, of warfare and of command of the fleet. This occurred in the framework of a feudal, estates-based structure, which, without any distinction made, consigned both the well-to-do *cittadini* involved in trade and production and the majority of the population, known as *popolani*, to the class of those excluded from political influence. The latter were dependent on their labor as their sole source of wealth and maintained their livelihood as workers, sailors, or soldiers.

In 1172, the first Doge whose election required only formal assent from the disempowered council of citizens was the 39th Doge Sebastiano from the house of the Ziani. Their prosperity was founded in exemplary fashion on their outstanding land wealth, from which derived, alongside their credit business, their share in the pepper-handling trade monopolized in Venice. Sebastiano's inauguration, at which for the first time a specially installed council of aristocrats rose to its feet, was decreed to the populace with the laconic words, "This is the Lord Doge, whether you like it or not." The self-empowerment of the aristocracy to the exclusive exercise of political sovereignty reached its apogee in 1297 in the act of *serrata*, or lock-out, of the Grand Council, a body which combined the competences of the quorum of the community and the Doge. The demands of this leadership elite were codified in the *Golden Book*, the *Libro d'Oro*. As a birth register, it listed the legitimate descendants of the families who, with a seat and voting rights in the *maggior consiglio*, were henceforth exclusively to embody conciliar authority. With this caesura—the constitution of power in a plutocratic organ of Venetian *nobilhòmini*, which permanently excluded the populace from sharing power—the nomenclature of the city also underwent a remarkable change. It was no longer apostrophized as a *comune*, as something held in common, but now figured under the attribute of the circle of most elevated feudal representatives who held the presidential function over the council—the *Serenissima Signoria*, i.e. the superlative of most serene majesty. Finally, in the plague year of 1423, as the conclusion of these constitutional developments, the popular assembly of the *arengo*, which had been reduced to a symbolic instance of appeal, was struck out of the constitution once and for all by force of law. The leading role of the aristocracy, which excluded the overwhelming part of the populace from all political decision-making, continued for 500 years, until the Republic fell to Napoleon.

It is revealing that the social strata in this mighty center of world trade, whose prosperity, in contrast to other Italian towns of this period, fed so much on imperialist land acquisition, colonial territories and representative real estate property, and whose physical foundations rested at the same time on the unsecured, and thus especially treasured, situation of raised land, should be separated from one another in the political order, but not in terms of space and urban design.

Other towns have urban districts, *quartiers*, as the mediaeval Latinism has it that has been applied to the smallest administrative unit in the French capital since the late eighteenth century. Venice, on the other hand, was divided under the rule of precisely the first Doge (Ziani) not to be appointed by the direct consensus of communal will, into *sestieri*, or sixths. Since this was considered to be one secret of its preeminent prosperity, other Italian city-states even copied Venice's territorial numerological organisation—Ascoli Piceno, Rapallo, and even the arch-enemy Genoa arranged themselves likewise in sixths.

However, what characterizes Venice's six city districts is the absence of any socio-spatial structure determined by separation into functional spaces of societal rank or the singling out of class hierarchies in line with income level. The groups and strata that constituted the Republic's otherwise strict estate-based society were precisely not segregated from one another in terms of housing, but lived in a convergent proximity, which made families of note neighbors of the "little" people, the craftsmen and small tradesmen. Magnificent grand mansions stood cheek-to-cheek with workshops and wretched hovels. Cottagers lived in the immediate vicinity of city palaces built by merchants of renown. Rich beside poor, privileged beside lowly. Overlap was the principle behind the permanent propinquity of divergent typologies of buildings and inhabitants.

The contrast between good and bad areas did not exist. Even alignment to the canal and the presence of the ever-important water frontage was at first no evidence of an ennobling preferential situation. Almost every building in the urban ensemble, which only grew together slowly from the elevated areas of the marshlands, naturally bordered a water course. Within its walls, the city was constituted as a juxtaposition following the ideal of equality; if Ruskin is to be believed, this can be attributed to the lack of distinctions in the original, Christian-imbued spirituality that determined the cohesion of the settlement as a community of faith in ancient times. The original role of the popular assembly practiced in ostentatious social unanimity has been conserved within these walls precisely in the city's construction and design as a concerted endeavor to achieve the equality of its citizens. In line with its origins, Venice is architecturally a homogeneous heterogeneity, whose topographic conformance was emulated in self-assured manner. This is documented in many provisions elucidated in architectural history and the cultural sciences, beginning with the fact that the *palazzo* of the better-off was explicitly permitted to be called only *casa*, just like all the others, however much pomp and showiness it exhibited in its facade, and that precisely for members of the upper class it was considered morally reprehensible right up into the fifteenth century to allow the roof ridge of one's own house to tower above others. And just as among all the *campi,* only the square of San Marco was allowed to be a *piazza*, so the honorific term "palace" is, strictly speaking, reserved for the seat of the Doge in the *Palazzo Ducale*.

Only with the foundation and development of the commercial and military "hothouse" of Venetian power—to use Nietzsche's term[10] for the shipyards, naval base, and weapon store of the *Arsenale*, which had existed since the beginning of the twelfth century and was mushrooming into a huge bastion—did there develop in the shadow of its fortification walls a territorially separate zone for the lower orders. This was a ghetto reserved for those of inferior social status, a zone whose character of topographic segregation corresponded to the isolation of the Jewish minority in the

late Middle Ages, for which the term was originally coined in the *veneziano* vocabulary. The Republic-owned factory of the Arsenale created the most colossal conglomeration of manpower in pre-modern European history, with tens of thousands of laborers employed in a machinery designed for their utilization. Many methods of modern production increase were anticipated here, from processes of serial production up to stages of production arranged in an assembly line. At the zenith of its output, this Moloch, which on today's measurements occupied one-tenth of the city's total area, was capable of producing up to 50 warships or trading vessels within one week.

Beyond this facility, which spread out at the eastern periphery of the urban area, the army of inflowing workers that the state shipyards kept in its employ settled on sparse swampy islands and salt meadows scarcely above the water level. The productivity of these *arsenalotti* gave the Republic such a decisive engine for its dominion over the Mediterranean and the economic strength which this bestowed that they were granted privileges such as the exercise of self-administered policing powers, and even a limited competence for local jurisdiction. These two things, admittedly, served to reinforce the segregated character of the area, the architecture of which also bore traits of *venezia minore,* a form of building indicative of poverty. It was no coincidence that the territory became the trial site for what is likely to have been the first council dwellings and modular forms of construction in European architectural history—buildings that the city authorities arranged to be designed for deserving foremen and that are still preserved today, for example in the Marinarezza complex. To distinguish it from the Sestiere Castello, this remote district, which right up into the eighteenth century could only be reached on foot from the city center via a rarely functional drawbridge, was commonly known as the Castello Basso on account of its lower house numbers, but also its marginal social status.

This city planning policy of segregation based on the category of subdivision, which came about in the course of the architectural objectification of state power, was destined to be repeated, both for the urban structure of Venice as a whole and for the particular situation of the Castello Basso within it. After 1797, the programmatic construction measures of the Napoleonic administration reinforced the isolation of the district, making severe incursions into the autopoietic growth of the slum. These were city planning measures in the form of deictic gestures, for the sake of which part of the poor housing was demolished to make way for the municipal park that was to become the Biennale grounds from 1895 onwards. Many of the almost 100 churches and monasteries that fell victim to the imperial masterplan for the secularization of Venice stood in this area. Their loss was customarily also the loss of the essential public space of the squares that lay in front of them. But the characteristic water economy of the peripheral living area was also endangered by the filling of canals to create showpiece boulevards. The former had been the vital arteries of day-to-day supplies. The reinforcement of the embankment promenade as a parade ground for Mussolini's regime followed a comparable propaganda purpose. Its destruction of the established customs of the local economy with their dependence on watercraft went one step further in the cessation of a traditional way of living.

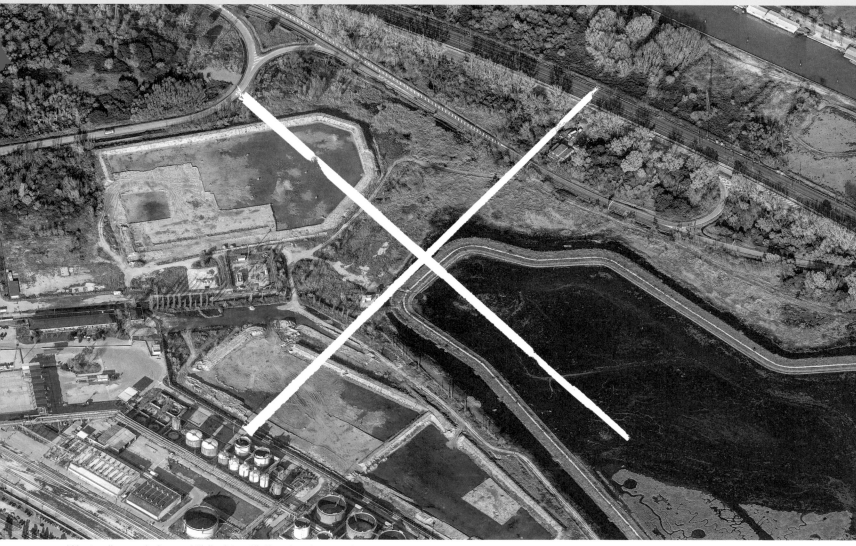

FIG. 4 Waste disposal site and "blind trust": the development of a coastal facility through the personal union of real estate speculator and local politician.

The real historical revenant of urban segregation, however, must surely be the workers' city erected in the years of Italian fascism in Marghera on the lagoon's coastline. Inhabited by former agricultural workers from the expropriated land which Conte Volpi, Mussolini's finance minister, re-invented as Europe's largest industrial facility—the former agrarian population providing the necessary workforce, a submissive Catholic proletariat—in the 1970s it became the theatre of one of the largest environmental disasters of the post-war era. Synthetically held together by a centrally sited church—designed in the fascist *Razionalismo* style and dedicated to the "Jesus of the Workers"—the layout of the dormitory suburb is just a lifeless counterpart to the gigantic, life- and ecology-threatening factory site that it serves. While Marghera is itself already a monument erected to the social exclusion of population groups defined by precarious income and bestowing spatial marginalization upon them as the very condition of their existence, its urban area also includes a neighborhood in which the rationale of separation as objectified in city planning has been taken to an

excess: a complex of social dwellings known as *Vaschette*, designed very much on the cheap, was so hermetically enclosed by the manufacturing plant of the petrochemical industry that it could be reached only through tunnels running underneath the cooling water basins that totally isolated the site. At the end of the past century, this housing, totally sealed off and lacking any structure of supply and utilities, became a flash-point of drug crime and drug-related sex work. The de-industrialization of the commercial surroundings also led to the removal of what the city authorities saw as a problem zone, a *banlieue* in need of upgrading.[11] In the jargon of the developers, this process is dubbed an opportunity for investment in so-called "urban re-qualification."

One of the representatives of this class of real estate developers is the current mayor of the municipality, which comprises not only the much-lauded old city but also the conurbations of Mestre and Marghera, with their far higher number of voters. In addition, however, the politician, who rules in an autocratic style in keeping with the times, is also president of the *area metropolitana* and has

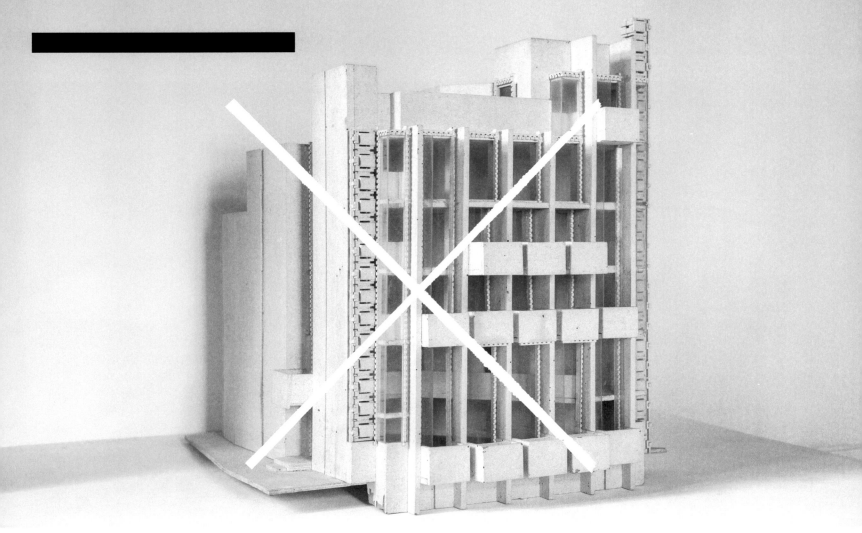

FIG. 5 Rejected as aesthetically incompatible:
modernism as social housing by Frank Lloyd Wright –
"Masieri Memorial," 1953.

furthermore awarded himself the office of Municipal Culture Assessor, in which he arrogates every decision to himself. The man—who goes by the name of Luigi Brugnaro—has emerged as the runaway winner of competition in the private sector: exploiting all forms of clientele lobbyism, which is the commonly accepted course of events in Italy, he has established Italy's largest part-time and subcontract work company providing cheap and readily available labor for the national economy.

More recently, his means of capital accumulation has been his skill in gaining possession, at the right time and under favorable conditions, of real estate whose strategic development was the subject of special speculative interest. One of these objects was by far the largest *scuola* in Venice—at some 26,000 cubic meters, the Scuola nuova di Santa Maria della Misericordia is a mighty piece of imposing architecture designed by the Renaissance architect Jacopo Sansovino—which for all its pomp, had served as the sports hall of the local basketball team during decades of neglect. Brugnaro acquired the lease of this impressive landmark for 40 years, solely on the assurance that he would restore its building substance in line with established principles of conservation. After the basketball team, of which he was now the owner, had left the field, he immediately proceeded (not entirely in the spirit of the contractual clauses) to market the property as an event

location. Restoration work seems to have only started six years later, on the day before the mayoral elections. Among the luxurious functions for which the *Scuola* was rented out, were the extraordinarily expansive presence of the German car manufacturer Audi at the Architecture Biennale in 2010, but also the weddings of Indian princes and a commercial, entertainment-oriented exhibition on Giotto showing only reproductions of his works and—remarkably enough—advertised on the municipality's own website. The show's elegant homepages suggest its potent possibilities as a source of rich takings.

More ambitious is another foresighted investment of Brugnaro's. He purchased from the state a 40-hectare piece of wasteland in the Area dei Pili, in order to—as he announced—protect the green belt from the grasp of a Roman speculator. The favorable purchasing price of 12 euros per square meter was justified by the contractual package deal linking it to the concession of freeing the area from residual waste. In Greenpeace reports from the 1990s, the Brentella industrial canal, which joins up with the former illegal toxic waste disposal site, figures as the most heavily contaminated body of water in the world. In its sludge, dioxins have been found up to two meters below ground level.[12] Up until today, the owner has yet to conduct any decontamination of the pollution in the land he purchased so favorably. However, the municipal council, domi-

The city as a resource for the cultivation of tourism is a means to a different end from that of living in the city, and it is this other end that it exclusively serves.

nated by Brugnaro's party, is considering agreeing to a repurposing of the municipal planning so as to allow a futuristic mixed development of the former waste disposal site with a sports stadium, a marina, a casino, hotels, luxury apartments, multi-storey car parks, and high-end offices—all ideally located for traffic and transport at the foot of the bridge and enjoying a panoramic view over the lagoon-side city. The talk is of a development covering one million cubic meters. As if blessed with the power of the keys to access the island city, the construction project presents itself under the visionary self-appellation of a gateway into Venice, or *Porta di Venezia* (so the corporate name of Brugnaro's owner company).

As the financier of his project, with which the local press attempts to come to terms in the epithets "pharaonic" and "stratospheric", Brugnaro was able to win the construction magnate Ching Chiat Kwong from Singapore, who has already achieved similar things with the Royal Wharf project in London, and who is himself an aggressive player on Venice's real estate market with the transformation of municipal property into hotels. Implicitly conceding the conflict of interests, Brugnaro—in an act similar to the endeavor of the US President to force legal incompatibilities into a juridical process—passed his business into the hands of a "blind trust". As a legal institution unique to Anglo-Saxon jurisprudence, this trust is run by a New York law office. This safeguard will certainly allow him to vote unencumbered in favour of his own interests in the respective committees. Should the project come about, establishing a new city district on the water's edge between Venice and Mestre, the rise in value of the land involved would be exorbitant. It would exceed every other business transaction that has ever been made with property along the lagoon.[13]

All of this is worth mentioning for only one reason: in the current constellation of political power, the prevailing standards of an—one is inclined to say: residue-free—exploitation of urban space have achieved exemplary clarity. They are present in naked conceptual form and hence give scant grounds for idealistic hopes. The city as a resource for the cultivation of tourism is a means to a different end from that of living in the city, and it is this other end that it exclusively serves. This exclusiveness has, unquestionably, congealed into a different quality and a different insistence than the classic segregation via expulsion into the *banlieue* was ever capable of.

The professional standpoint of the exploitation of land, which, beneath Brugnaro's character mask, is prototypically the attitude held by politicians towards the city, is beginning to leave its tracks in the sand, which it considers as city territory in its absolute availability and fluidity. It sounds grotesque, but the same world capital that John Ruskin valued as something of peerlessly exemplary nature, has no representative worthy of the rank of mayor. Instead, it

is governed by a mere administrator, who, from the mainland, sees the historic island ensemble as a unit of management, whose living inhabitants are more harmful than useful. It is not only the case that he does not take their side: he contests their right to be there at all. A few weeks ago, the simulated regeneration of the carnival for the benefit of tourism—the carnival which Napoleon's enlightened regime once abolished as decadent—again raised Venice's saturation level up to the pain threshold for its inhabitants. When the attempt to control the level broke the pain barrier, because inhabitants could no longer get to the front doors of their houses, he gave them the official viewpoint in the form of an imprecation: "If you live on the Rialto, you must be able to cope with tourists: those who don't like it can move to the countryside." [14]

It is the political authorities themselves who, while making the living space uninhabitable, suggest that the last remaining residents make an imperative change of position: they should withdraw completely to make way for a clientele with fatter wallets. The maxim whereby a qualitatively limited space should be utilized in a quantitatively unlimited manner calls for the unrestricted effectivization, intensification and maximization of the unit turnover per square meter.

Exploitation

On the real estate market, where the residential requirements of the normal populace also have to be met, equal deals with equal: the players are, exclusively, persons acting as proprietors. Some offer the use of the land to which they have legal title in exchange for a payment which they view as the interest on their invested capital. The others present themselves equally as owners of money, which they are compelled to expend in order to cover the costs of their existential need for dwelling space. This formal equality, in which proprietors meet as freely acting subjects in a customary transaction, conceals the difference with which they enter into the latter.

For the one party, a dwelling is a comestible, a means of life. The protection offered by permanent housing serves not only to maintain body temperature against the inclemency of weather but is also the elementary precondition and necessity of bourgeois existence. The latter is forever distancing itself from the basic threat of homelessness, which consists in the loss of such protection. On the other hand, for the other party–that of the real estate owners–dwellings are profitable investments, which like every other investment, must be continually scrutinized as to their most lucrative utilization—not least for reasons of economic good sense. In the course of their pursuit, these two opposing interests—the freedom of some and the necessity of others—must collide. The process in which this systemic conflict is enacted changes and intensifies with the historic achievements of one side in expanding its business. Once again, the territory of Venice proves to be a paradigm of escalation, and here too the reason for this is that under the conditions of island-bound limitations of space, quantitative circumstances are carried to such an extreme that they reveal themselves to be qualitative in nature.

It is a commonly known fact that, in descending order, Paris, London, and Manhattan are the numerically largest fields of activity for the business model of the booking platform Airbnb, which began life as a "sharing community." And it is equally known that its actions go hand in hand with a dramatic displacement, an ousting of the established resident population, which does irreparable harm to the urban substance of entire inner-city districts. And just as this is happening elsewhere, so too, as one might expect, it is occurring in Berlin, Germany's largest market for short-term internet-brokered housing: increasingly, streets, shops, and infrastructural elements prove now to be nothing more than stage props addressing the transitory visitor and offering them a mix of products tailored to their needs. The "non-traditional hosting industry," as these rivals to the hotel business are euphemistically labelled by sociologists and protagonists alike, has established a structurally consolidated and inescapable rack-rent system as a habitual condition of the market. In its sheer impact and speed, this method of pressing forward the mutation of the city outstrips by far the now customary business practices of real estate development known as "gentrification."

Airbnb company data reveals the following: in the metropolitan region of Berlin, there are currently 20,576 Airbnb accommodation units, creating a 292:1 ratio of inhabitants to guest apartments, which conventionally accommodate two beds. In Manhattan/New York this ratio is 85:1 and in Paris, already 40:1. In Berlin, as in many other cities, the local authorities are countering the daily bookings and the massive loss of housing with new rules and regulations, the strict enforcement of which is often assisted by controls and fines. In Venice, however, this test laboratory of mass tourism, where the foreign vacationer is considered the prime source of income, and the city with its diffuse promise of urban extraordinariness is held to be a consumer good to be marketed as a totality, legislative curbs seem to be an entirely unwanted restriction. At the present time, there are 6,027 Airbnb offers against only 54,000 inhabitants in the historic center. In this particular place, therefore, the local statistics reveal the absurd ratio of 9:1. For every nine local inhabitants there is, on average, one holiday flat used by two people—and nobody doubts that this quotient can further deteriorate.

This figure, moreover, dissolves into an even more frightening surfeit if one replaces the bureaucratic, administrative, on-paper statistic of those formally registered as resident in Venice by the empiric number of apartments on the island, for which de facto electricity bills are paid, and which are accordingly actually being used. If one subtracts from the 24,000 dwellings for which this is the case the more than 6,000 misappropriated via Airbnb for commercial offer, then this more realistic estimate gives the ratio of 3:1—for every three apartments remaining available for local inhabitants, there is now one, whose rate of return is henceforth comparable with the daily yield of a hotel room. It is this yield that sets the yardstick of expectation for the profit margin of the few remaining dwellings which are currently tied to long since obsolete rental contracts and are now waiting for the leverage pressure of re-possession or termination of occupancy.

One look at the countless window displays of real estate agents reveals this in absolutely unmistakable form: their offers are not directed at the local inhabitants. For the latter's plight, for their attempt to find a roof to go over their heads, there is no mediator.

Their predicament doesn't promise any business. Apart from current rents, there are no affordable offers to suit so-called average earners, i.e. the representatives of those typical income brackets who in the competitor-free and omnipresent tourism sector are employed as auxiliaries.

For the traditional majority of the city's population, especially the inhabitants in the previously proletarian and densely populated urban districts of Castello and Cannaregio, for students and for the many employees in subordinate positions in all trades associated with tourism, who in their own existential interest need to be close to their places of work, just living at an address in the island-bound centro storico has become a luxury. Almost any of the offers available on the market is likely to prove unaffordable. In point of fact, however, the conflict has already led to a more radical elimination of bidders: the liberalization of the transformation of residential property into pieds-à-terre has brought about such colossal increases in possible rent revenues that offers are explicitly and on principle no longer directed to long-term renters.

This state of affairs does at least enjoy recognition as a "social problem"—under the honorific title of "housing shortage." Apart from the acknowledgement of the dilemma in political rhetoric, to the effect that "excessive financial demands on tenants due to disproportionate rent increases are to be avoided,"[15] those affected receive no assistance. On the contrary: not only in Venice—but here to an escalating degree—the local authorities, as the agents of the escalation, continue to press on with the rededication of the use of the city, transferring municipal real estate to the international hotel industry and at the same time deregulating municipal land-use plans. It is as if all of Venice had room only for the one hotel, with which it would finally be coextensive. In view of the limitation of the territory, however, every local inhabitant is viewed as a deduction from the numbers of paying visitors.

Among those things in the world which come onto the market as commodities and come into existence only in that form—on account of their salability and realizable exchange value—land, the premise and substructure of all architecture and all dwelling, is the only product that itself is not produced. No one manufactured it. It can therefore belong to a proprietor as his real estate holding only in the legal form of the forcible exclusion of all others from using something that is, after all, the common condition of existence on Earth—spatial extension. Something that, like the air, is part of life and, like movement, is part of human nature. Something that in the philosophy of Immanuel Kant is discussed alongside time as the condition of empiricism altogether in the rank of a transcendental a priori, can become a traded commodity only by means of this exclusion. The exclusion denies access, so does opening up the opportunity of a business field by dint of the price that is set in front of the permission to use this fenced-in space. It is only the attribute of a barrier around his property thus accorded to the real estate owner—a barrier to the perpetuation of which all relations of force in state and society are directed— that temporarily and against payment allows the suspension of excluding and exclusive rights to cultivated or uncultivated land to be granted to a third-party non-owner. This right takes the form of rent, lease or real estate transaction and its enactment takes the

FIG. 6 Project aborted: 255 meters high and costing two billion euros. Palais Lumière by Pierre Cardin: "It should stand in Venice, or nowhere."

form of exchange. In emotional diction unusual in the work of his maturity, a renowned but little-appreciated nineteenth-century national economist calls this license to charge an entry fee for the space a "tributary right to exploit the preservation and development of life."[16]

Although in this payment of tribute the natural resource of land seems to assume the character of a usual source of income, that is not what it is by nature. In contrast to all other commodities, which come into being as the result of production, land as a spatial particle of the Earth's surface is a business resource that cannot be multiplied at will. This characteristic makes it stand out from all other traded articles—a distinctive commodity within a market economy rationale founded on ongoing quantitative increase. For the qualitative physical limits of this good are initially also those of its quantitative growth. The escalating process of building upwards, the skyscraper, is the still limited attempt to escape from this constraint. At least in the current historical phase of development, the legal restrictions imposed by heritage conservation in Venice stand in the way of any intention to increase the exploitation of ground-plan by tower-like above-ground construction. This has led to the fantasies of all the local governments that have held office over the past decades and their investors—the wish to expand the nearby mainland on the shore of the lagoon into a kind of futuristic skyline à la Dubai. Examples of this are Frank Gehry's

mammoth project Venice Gateway, whose prospects came to nothing, and the monumental Palais Lumière of the couturier and real estate developer Pierre Cardin, which was likewise to be built on the lagoon shoreline. The latter's hypertrophic design modelled on a flower vase of Murano glass blown up to gigantic proportions, would have smashed all superlatives—with more than 44,000 square meters of hanging gardens, lakes, swimming baths, five-star hotels with 500 rooms, restaurants with aircraft-like views over the historic city, a theatre seating 7,000, 10 cinemas as well as fitness and wellness centers, its own emergency services, bars, office spaces, and parking for 6,000 vehicles. In the 2015 price list, an average, medium-sized apartment was to cost two million euros. While these endeavors to cash in on Venice's location advantage on an unprecedented scale were broken off, in part after massive investment (also on the side of the local authorities), many other large-scale projects in the agglomeration have actually been realized or, as the above-mentioned development of a new city district, are close to receiving planning permission.

Given that the extension of surface by means of growth in the vertical plane is not an option, the provisionally insurmountable limit to commercially usable ground in the historic center sets in motion a dynamic that must naturally be concerned with achieving maximum intensification in the utilization of the horizontal surface available.

FIG.7 Città ideale: sightseeing 40 km away in the Noventa di Piave Outlet Centre. Venice's most popular attraction lies outside the city.

Consequently, the management of the tourist masses takes the form of a calculation of the turnover per square meter, which then dominates all use of space. This computation became absolutely binding also for the public museums, which once held an educational remit in a Venice to which travelers came because it was supposedly a site of art. In one case, the public authorities simply place the entire management of exhibitions in the hands of private and commercial contractors, who independently work on the conception and realization of major crowd-pulling events and share the entrance money harvested with the municipal or state corporations.[17] In another case, the former educational institutions are without further ado abandoned to commercial interests and serve directly as the showcase for their products. For 10 years, one of the most attractive buildings of the *Musei Civici*, the Palazzo Fortuny, was used as an exclusive showroom during every Art Biennale by an art and antiques dealer globally active as an interior decoration company. The both tasteful and much-admired object ensembles

attracted common visitors, who in contrast to the targeted elite and moneyed clientele failed to notice the commercial character of this shop window. Thus, this kind of use of space paid off for the organizer and at the same time pleased the city with its highly presentable attendance figures—a win-win constellation that soon found its emulators. A more subtle but no less general strategy is the involvement of the major galleries and auction houses in the exhibition policy of the public-sector institutions. This, however, follows the same basic pattern, providing evidence for the state of affairs in the privatization of their functionalization: public art events can now no longer do without the financial leverage and input of a handful of industry leaders among the galleries and can hence hardly conceal the impact of the galleries' interests.

In order to best satisfy the standard requirement that art should at any event pay its way,[18] art should be promoted to achieve a high degree of resonance and appear attractive to high numbers of international visitors. Therefore, Venice authorities have liberated their municipal museum network from bureaucratic obstacles and decision processes and, in a contemporary act of outsourcing, placed it in the hands of a foundation that meets the standards of "lean management." Regardless of this increase in the productivity of culture and regardless of the national successes of the past years, in which not only in Venice but all over Italy the sheer numbers of tourists flocking to behold the cultural heritage reached spectacular heights, the full data here reveal that attractions in the field of art history hold a surprising position on a comparative scale of civilizational relevance.

The 57th Art Biennale, held in 2017, attracted 615,152 visitors—a record that outstripped the previous event by more than 100,000. Since the first biennale of this millennium, the numbers of attendees have risen two-and-a-half-fold, but to date never with such a mighty difference from the foregoing occasion. The conclusions drawn by the real estate business from the presence of more than half a million guests and the economic activities involved in their servicing is impressive: the Biennale organizers maintain an internet platform known as a "noticeboard," which offers facilities on lease for all the collateral events and fringe offers, tailored to the needs of the vast passing clientele. The scope of these offers, currently encompassing 247 individual advertisements, is mind-spinning: a total of 472,867 square meters, almost 50 hectares, and thus one-sixth of the expanse of the historic heart of Venice is on offer. This means that, per head of the remaining population, there are some nine square meters being made available for activities that spread out alongside and beyond the actual Biennale, in the Giardini and the Arsenale. It comes as no surprise that the many small shops, *magazzini*, and workshops—redefined as display cases for the art market and hence rendered unprofitable in their everyday purpose—have contributed to the ousting of the essential supply services for the resident population. Among the bargains on offer for the expansion of art, there are some that involve entire islands in the lagoon, but others are just tiny leftover bits and pieces, the dregs of the exploitation campaign. These latter are to be reckoned among the residues of the real estate market, which Gordon Matta-Clark's 1970s project *Reality Properties* documented as "fake estates" and "gutterspaces," so as to show how not even the slightest and most useless fragment can escape the notice of the property owners. In the up-valuing of land taken to its uttermost extreme, which is force-fed by the collision of the art market and the struggle for a share of the island's volume, even the four square meters of embankment in front of a hotel have their price.

Symptomatically, the Accademia itself, one of the most important museums for Renaissance painting, appears in this list of hirelings—albeit with no details of price and square meters. In the past year, it achieved an 83 percent increase in visitor figures up to 570,000—presumably also because of its cooperation with a leading gallery, which proved as strategic as extraneous to the Accademia's real role. However, the crown for the most popular among the cultural sites goes to the Palazzo Ducale, which with its marketing mix made up of narrative motifs, such as Casanova's lead chambers in the adjoining prison, its monumental feudal interiors, and its use as a function location, leaves all rivals far behind in absolute visitor figures. It consolidated its position at a level of 1.34 million tickets sold.

Although this quantitative success of the museums went hand in hand with all kinds of long since customary measures of privatization and liberalization of the formerly non-profitmaking educational ideal, it appears comparatively inconsequential when measured against its competition from the seemingly art-hostile field of consumerdom and commerce. What the real estate investor Benetton (among other things, the world's largest owner of motorway networks) did to the old post office in the Fondaco dei Tedeschi, one of the formerly most-treasured incarnations of public space in Venice—namely, to turn its historic substance into the faceless anonymity of a shopping mall—attracts more than twice the number of interested parties as Ruskin's hallowed site, the Doge's Palace. As planned, more than three million consumers annually seek out the market-place of this luxury shopping center, most of them taking the shortest route directly from their own landing stages. They shun contact with the particularity of the *genius loci* even where it consists only of the indeterminate romanticism of the old townscape. That seems to be no loss: the completely interchangeable stock of goods from internationally ubiquitous brands cannot supply a specific, let alone a singular, reason and occasion for the trip anyway.

What, if anything, is noteworthy here is that even this storehouse of banalization cannot, for the sake of its self-justification, do without the celebration of art. Integrated into the shopping center is an indifferently curated showroom for contemporary art, situated on the way to the viewing platform cut into the roof which opens up an ahistorical picture-postcard view of the Rialto Bridge. The connotation of higher significance supplied by the artistic and cultural context is something valued and appreciated. As a latent consensus of the presence of an always implicit sense it can be attributed to both—to the work of contemporary art and the fetishized brand-name article. Formal permission for the demolition of the cultural monument was acquired through the promise, pretentiously formulated in the rhetoric of social responsibility, to reintegrate culture and public space in an architectural conception. The one was reduced to a decorated corridor, the other to the supply of public toilets. Despite all the uncouthness of the economic purpose here, behind which the historic building substance including the ambitions of Rem Koolhaas' OMA disappeared in their entirety, the apogee of the alienation of the city itself in this manner of space utilization has not yet been reached.

Cast in the concrete of brutalist classicism, and surrounded by its own walls, the ideal city of the Noventa di Piave Outlet Center specializes in the attraction of a few more million visitors. Part of the administrative unit of the metropolitan region, it stands some 40 km outside of Venice, directly beside a motorway exit in the midst of a soulless, abandoned provincial landscape. Given that there is no sight that attracts a larger horde of admirers, one must concede that this singular place, an intimate union of cheapness, fetishization, sale bargains and brand value in a muzak-permeated, oppressively unrelenting celebration atmosphere, embodies the real center, and the true foundation of Venice as a destination. If one subtracts all those things that have become matters of indifference in dealings with the city, then it is this that remains: lucrative selling space.

In four phases of expansion, the developer and proprietor McArthurGlen, the market leader in this sector, has expanded the Potemkin-like pseudo-village to a size of 32,000 square meters, with 200 stores, mostly taken by reputed luxury labels, and parking space for 3,100 vehicles, often filled to the last bay. In 2017, the company operated 24 such shopping centers, whose "unique selling proposition" consists in the fact that they are illustrations of urban spatial feelings, customarily crudely built in the manner of an architectural city metaphor. The mini-sized historicizing facades fronting colossal sales halls mean that the latter weigh down on one with a leaden heaviness. The company rates the Venice outpost among its outstanding successes, not only because over the past three years turnover has increased by 70 percent hand in hand with almost a doubling of client inflow, but because the facility has been awarded the title "Best European Shopping Mall."

Once again, the obligatory presence of art is remarkable—an established ingredient in a calculated entertainment mix accompanying the shopping experience and geared to a generic public. In this place too, it becomes fully evident that art and fashion have come to intermingle in their peculiar field of interference. Here, in this site of histrionic cheapness, the blend contains far less intellect and dignity than in the hallowed halls of ancient architecture along the Canal Grande, where the same producers and their private museums—Gucci, Prada, Louis Vuitton, etc.—line up side by side in the same formation and the same dutiful must-be-there presence as in the arcades of the consumer village. In this stage of their ambition for spirituality, cultural heritage, and commodity fetishes, work of art and handbag have together, presumably because of their cognate nature, groundlessly taken a liking to demanding from their admirers a veneration and solemnity which cannot get by without representational magic. To their mutual advantage they exploit the prestige of their reciprocal mirror image, in which performances copy fashion shows and fashion shows, performances.

Practiced as a co-operation between art galleries and the Venice Opera House, the Fenice, the *mélange* of fashion and art in Venice, like elsewhere, has become synonymous with an entertainment of higher significance. In the parlance of the designer outlet's market-listed operator the reference sounds as follows: "We don't just build shopping centers, we build architecturally designed retail environments strategically located near Europe's most iconic city destinations that elevate the shopping experience, making art accessible to all our visitors."[19] Does this not concede, with welcome frankness, everything that remains to be said about Venice? Its highly charged literary and museum atmosphere accoutres commerce with the aura of cultivation, thus becoming a factor in sales promotion. It now seems significant only as an auxiliary topos in revenue growth. Venice as instrument is no more than the metaphor of its own self.

Exclusion

In the first two decades of the twenty-first century, the great majority of countries in the Western world pursued a money market policy of low interest rates. This produced credit available on the cheap and hence enormously proliferated amounts of money looking for investment opportunities and so in turn provoking a bloated array of complex derivative products on the part of the credit sector. When in 2008 this development led to the infamous financial crisis, the strategy of the central banks was paradoxically to respond with the supposed remedy of renewed interest rate cuts. Not only the American FED, but also its European counterpart, the ECB, reacted to a manifest over-accumulation of capital by, of all things, further expansion.

It is worth considering here the particular nature of the fictive economic goods on the finance markets that went into crisis. What was being speculatively traded here were derived paper titles that referred to liabilities, namely the mortgages held by high numbers of American home-buyers who—without being substantially able to afford it—had hoped to benefit from a political crediting scheme without co-payment launched under the Clinton and Bush administrations. From the point of view of finance capital and the banks issuing the titles, it was the interest in mortgages as a commodity for capital investment that had made these building loans available at all in the first place. Since potential profitability increases when risks are incurred, the logic of participating in market opportunities enables precisely questionable prospects to be certain of receiving risk capital on account of their leverage effect. Such securities, which went hand in hand with the acceptance of poor credit ratings, accordingly circulated under the condescending appellation "subprime."

At precisely the moment, however, when it turned out that a large number of the underlying liabilities could not be met, the titles traded as financial capital lost their value. The rights of those who were no longer in a position to service their loans so as to cover their elementary need for a roof over their heads were unavoidably exhausted once they could no longer meet the financer's interest demands, and compulsory eviction was the impending result. The fact that the capital market created financial products which sold the debts of home-buyers as a source of growth for wealth going out in search of profit means just that there is no living space for some that is not a business for others. The former's right to a home elapses when the contractor's calculations no longer add up. In the crisis year 2008, it was just such a shortfall that brought the entire construction of a sphere of investment crashing down, without whose reckoning on debt as a source of profit many people were left without the necessity of a place to live.

The course of this crisis makes clear how things begin to blur when viewed under the aspect of being a form of investment: land now exists not only in the form of derivatives—the entire system of real estate speculation has turned it into a financial instrument. From the point of view of trading, land assets–or just the key indicators of land assets–looked in equal measure like underlying values whose price could be relied on. Ground rent commodities have become just that: one financial asset among others. As a result, land and buildings become indistinguishable from stocks and shares, and from the relative investment strategies such as options and futures contracts. Things were no different on the art market, whose historic boom correlated with the possibility of likewise offering itself to the flush of money on the market as one component in a portfolio of speculative and high frequency shares. In this period of

FIG. 8 Point of sale: traditional shops become galleries.
The former electrical appliance shopkeeper George Kunstlinger
and the new tenant, the gallerist Michele Maccarone, New York.
Christian Jankowski, 2002.

low interest rates, the management of real estate and the management of art and shares came together in the general principle of capital investment.

Before and after the crisis, cheap money—in its intended existence as accumulating capital—flowed into investment on the diversely specialized markets for real estate, art, and equities. There they are all, with no distinction between them, tradeable entitlements to future price hikes. In the abstract form of being themselves marketable and sellable hopes for potential future profits, they became virtually interchangeable as forms of investment. On account of the sheer economic potency of the protagonists involved, this has consequences for the territory on which they are active.

First of all, in accordance with the law of economy of scale, it is only major economic figures who require correspondingly high investment volumes for their capital and who thus occupy positions here. Often there are fewer than a handful of players in the arenas which these sectors open up. To name only three of them who are prominently present in the Venice arena: firstly, the half-dozen galleries that have become industries, concentrating their turnover on two dozen artists, of whom one alone states sales of 330 million US dollars for his 2017 Venice exhibition,[20] and that are matched by a scarcely larger number of decisive, big-time collectors. Secondly, in the cruise ship sector, whose four group holdings command more than 90 percent of the market; the largest among them, with its 110 ships, holds approximately half of the overall capacity of this entire line of business. And finally, there are just five globally active hotel companies whose market positions each assemble more than half a million rooms worldwide.

Just one decade ago, the number of hotel rooms now present in Venice and the number of takeovers of aristocratic palaces to provide more of the same would have seemed a far-fetched dystopia. This escalation of a requirement that is still continuing to rise has now exceeded the volume available in the old city. Consequently, even in the area around the Mestre railway station, a monstrous number of 16,000 rooms are said to be in the planning stage. Well above 1,000 of them have already been built over the past two years, above all in connection with major individual developments. The daily newspapers report that the saturation point in this development has yet to be reached and that consideration is being given to a further regional expansion of the provision of mass overnight accommodation.

The cruise industry also plays its part in this devouring of land, and does so in a complex manner: just like other powerful actors in the global tourist business, it is interested in achieving the vertical integration of its activities. The shipping companies are thus eager to concentrate within themselves all the components involved in the supply and value-creation chain of their particular profession. Recently, for example, the vast ship terminal jointly built a few years ago by the public authorities of the region, the City of Venice and the harbor authorities, passed into the hands of a consortium of those companies for whom it was originally intended as infrastructure. When the cruise lines themselves became owners of the

FIG. 9 Unhappy consciousness:
the last local in Venice – Martin Kippenberger, 1996,
photographed by Elfie Semotan.

harbor, however, they immediately gained a crucial involvement in the imminent political decisions concerning the rights of movement of the huge ships that have become, in ecological terms, a question of the city's very survival. As landowners, the ship operators and their business interests now have a voice in the decision-making process.

Another effect of the concentration of capital in the acquisition of key functions that live parasitically from the profits of the cruise industry is not so visible. When it became noticeable that the turnover from trip bookings was lower than that from consumer spending over the duration of the voyage, the shipowners began not only to extend their onboard retail business but also to take over the sales points that they themselves recommended for shopping on land. For the port of Venice, the leading destination during "shore leave" is the aforementioned shopping center for luxury articles in Noventa di Piave. It necessarily matches the expansionist drive of the cruise lines more than the stores for glassware and Chinese produced carnival masks, in which they already have holdings. In every corner of the territory, one can see this process in action: the city as place is being shared out among a few—and always the same—major actors.

Unprecedented dimensions and magnitudes of invested capital have set out to divide up the physical, spatial area of the city among themselves. And even in the field of the seemingly small-time internet business of renting out accommodation—where one imagines a large number of small profit-takers—ways and means of merging the invested money can be observed: in the city, there are increasingly powerful providers of land who have many apartments on their books. Substantially more than two-thirds of advertisers on the Airbnb transaction system have a multiple number of overnight places on offer. These pacemakers act as *multi-listing hosts* and despite their marketing practices, which are often in the black economy, are at times identical with big hotel operators. More than a dozen of the offers originate from real estate owners who have between 20 and 70 overnight options for clients to choose from. The largest among them, even with a modest occupancy rate, generates a monthly turnover of more than 100,000 euros.[21]

The fact that small-time activity, intensively practiced, can also be run as a major industry has led to a boom of new business models even in the prototypical use of Venice as a cultivation area for art—to which its exterior, rich in architectural history and manifold fictionalizations, lends itself *par excellence*. A particularly unpleasant example is a segment of the art market that has remained largely hidden from the public eye and caters for providing the sediment of artists living in precarious circumstances. This pitiable majority of art producers forms the structural substratum of the production of relevance, all the more so because the attributes of importance, significance and resonance logically require a level of mediocrity from which alone they can necessarily stand out. Here, consequently, is a reserve army of authorship and creativity, which bestows sublimity to the pedestal on which genius stands. The habitually disappointed career hopes of all these representatives of third-rate artistic activity are directed, in line with their expectations, to the magical aura of the place. They believe that with the status of Biennale participants they can ensure themselves the capital that grants them entry to the privilege of excellence—and hence to all the ostensibly associated market opportunities. For this hollow hope of acquiring the semblance of the chosen, the curated, without having been the object of curation, they are prepared to pay hard cash—presumably in the confident hope that it might pay off. No passerby, no idler among the day-to-day life of Venice can fail to note the presence of the impresarios who have milked from the management of this mass desire a further expansive industry in the artification of the city.

The three most agile representatives of this line of business, who present themselves in a respectable and semi-official light by means of self-awarded honorary titles, currently command at least 10 large city palaces or building complexes and three parks, in which, literally by the square meter, they "flog" a supposed warranty of cultural distinction for horrendous sums. Characteristically presenting themselves as European organizations with the stamp of being "non-profit" or even an "initiative," these companies contact large numbers of artists, praise their work and gently hint at the possibility of an international breakthrough on the big stage. Only in an advanced stage of the correspondence with those interested is the unvarnished figure of the price dropped that is to be paid for their appearance: typically, it is a highish five-figure sum corresponding to a small exhibiting space—sometimes in the vicinity of the only showpiece of the one well-known figure in the field, the name of which one's own name may appear alongside on the banner, sometimes in the context of an official collateral function of the world-famous art show, sometimes not. Whereas it used to be left to a conceptional decision of the leading curator whether a show applying for the status of an accompanying event suitably fitted the spirit of the whole, for many years now the sum to be paid for permission to use the logo has simply been an irreplaceable part of the fundraising, which none of the major events can do without.

When the curator of documenta 14 saw himself compelled to produce arguments against the reproach that his expenditure had brought the event to the brink of bankruptcy, he combined two remarkably incompatible platitudes: on the one hand, his provocative statement maintained that the "expectations of ever-increasing success and economic growth […] jeopardize the possibility of the exhibition remaining a site of critical action and artistic experiment," only to confirm in almost the following sentence that all the investments in art had paid off, since "the money flowing into the city through the making of documenta greatly exceeds the amount the city and region spend on the exhibition."[22] The idea that this has to be the case is thus familiar also to the idealists of a practice of artistic freedom different from that of the art market. It is evidently uncontested.

The asset that is put to good account here, as in all other investment areas, is always the same: the sheer mass audience that frequents the spatially limited theatre of the artificial island, which is still identified as a city of art. The figure of one million visitors with appropriate interests who actually attended the Biennale spectacle and Damien Hirst's populist one-man exhibition amounts, however, to at most a fraction of the entire audience—a fraction relevant

to the pretention of being a *città d'arte*. The overwhelming majority of those who come to consume the city of Venice feed only in a highly distanced manner on culture as a good: culture is enjoyed at most as an omnipresent and hence extremely thin symbolism inherent in an atmospheric environment. Instead of education being drawn from the actually educative material, an educational character is merely imputed and assumed, in lapidary manner, as a characteristic of the walls.

Although it forms the basis of all economic calculations, the factual number of consumers of the city *qua* city remains a matter of speculation. Not without reason, the city refuses to put a figure to the number of day tourists—in contrast to the calculable number of overnight stays—and so the overall figure is considered to be unknowable. Yet it wouldn't be so difficult to arrive at; in order to get from the coach parks to the landing jetty on the *Riva*, the trippers are dependent on transfer boats, whose passenger capacity, number, and frequency of crossing are known. The therefore only estimated, obscene number of 40 million visitors on average per year who flood into the city center has become a taboo, which no one has any intention of confirming officially, because the authorities themselves set a limit years ago. An academic study conducted in 1998 by a research body engaged by the local authorities calculated a daily capacity limit for the inflow of visitors from outside the city, precise to the nearest 10. One wonders which academic disciplines and methods were behind the precision and conclusiveness of this determination. But, however that may be, the "objective" threshold limit for the daily influx was stated to be 20,750. There is no way this can be communicated alongside the real daily influx of 120,000 outside visitors that has—with some certainty—now been reached.[23] On the other hand, it has long been beyond dispute that the profits from these throngs of people allow the beneficiaries to reap stately revenues. In 1993, then Mayor Massimo Cacciari, stated that the annual revenue generated by activities connected with mass tourism to Venice matched the entire gross national tourist product of Greece or was four times as high as the total assets of Fiat, at that time Italy's largest multicorporate enterprise. In 2017, the rate of foreign visitors coming to the seven square kilometers of Venice exceeded that of the entire holiday-oriented country beside the Aegean by well over a third.

It is scarcely any wonder that such a densely aggregated locational advantage enabled the market for the rent and purchase of real estate to emancipate itself from the national offer and to take its place alongside it as a wholly extra-national, globally traded real estate market. Its internationally advertised offers are totally immune to the crises and fluctuations of its domestic counterpart. Venice is, by a long way, Italy's most expensive city, not only because in Venice—in view of its historical building stock and iconic sites—purchase decisions are made that are quite singular in nature and hence comparable with the art market, based on incomparable individual goods whose price levels lie wholly outside any normal competition, but above all because every single room offers the possibility of business with occupancy rates and profit levels guaranteed.

For this reason, this place of yearning's unusual terrain, advertised around the globe like a commodity brand, summons up an equally unusual demand for space that matches the solvency of the industrially operating companies who cultivate the clientele of mass pleasure travel as their line of business. It is their monetary power that vies with the habitual existential needs of the residents for possession of the place. It comes as no surprise that in this asymmetrical confrontation the latter are the losers. Their claim on space—in their case an existential need—is dismissed as a comparatively non-lucrative use. The fact that the local residents have no place in the old city any more expresses itself as a demographic change. It is tantamount to expulsion out beyond a demarcation line into the agglomeration. The enforced move into an anonymous conurbation often devoid of infrastructure amounts, however, to nothing less than contesting the right of a populace degraded to pariahs in terms of the politics of space to the historically evolved quality of city life. If global tourism—which has absolutely mushroomed over the past few decades with the emergence of new countries of origin—and the comparatively modest local housing market confront one another on the urban projection surface of Venice, then there are two characteristics which separate the unequal rivals for space in the heart of the city: the sheer dimensions of this demand and its well-moneyed readiness to pay.

The economic clout of these armies of visitors employed as a source of revenue for globally operative industries makes the living conditions of the remaining city-dwellers seem a negligible circumstance. Their mere presence impairs sales opportunities because they mean a reduction in the one profitable economic good—space. With their existential dependence on a place to live they thus fall victim to the utilization demands of real estate capital, which is able to take richer pickings from a better off and more numerous alternative clientele.

Just as the old city made way for the staged *simulacrum* of itself, so its inhabitants have made way for the more profitably manageable figure of the spectator. The latter is available in abundance. This development, however, merely demonstrates again the nature of private appropriation of land; it is in its character to oust, to drive out, because in its rationale it is founded *per se* on exclusion.

Those who, in the performance of their everyday lives, are dependent on participating in land although they cannot call it their own, are consequently always in a tight corner: rivals emerge who are able to do more with this sphere of extension, real estate, than just to simply let someone live there. The productive use of a physical place for a utility interest that recruits its clients worldwide and *en masse*, always has the upper hand over the unproductive consumption of living space in which it is the mere user value of space that counts.

The city is the ground rent machine and has been so from the very beginning. Nobody wants to admit this necessary connection, and hence moral outrage over its unlovely consequences is a dime a dozen. The shelf life of its emotive effect is short. For it continues to be the case that, with the iron laws of bourgeois society, the utilization of land as a commodity remains inviolable.

"The bartered Earth is an Earth alienated from Man and hence encountering him in the form of a few major landlords."[24]

FIG. 1 DeSpar supermarket, Teatro Italia
       Photo: © Enrico Maria Vernì, 2018
FIG. 2 Hauser & Wirth flyer, Venice 2017
       Photo: © Eleonora Sovrani, 2018
FIG. 3 Map of Castello Basso,
       © the author
FIG. 4 © Google map data, 2018
FIG. 5 Recently re-discovered model by
       Carlo Scarpa, Courtesy Giorgio
       Mastinu, Venezia.
       Photo: © Eleonora Sovrani, 2018
FIG. 6 Rendering of Palais Lumière,
       © Unit Studio

FIG. 7 Courtesy Designer Outlet
       McArthurGlen
FIG. 8 © *Point of Sale*,
       Christian Jankowski, 2002
FIG. 9 © Elfie Semotan,
       Martin Kippenberger
       in Venice, 1996

The author would like to express his thanks to all those who discussed this topic with him, in particular to Peter Kammerer, Paolo Lanapoppi, Hanns Letz, Giorgio Mastinu, Marco de Michelis and Roberto Ohrt.

01 cf. Christian Mathieu, *Inselstadt Venedig: Umweltgeschichte eines Mythos in der Frühen Neuzeit* (Cologne/Weimar: Böhlau Verlag, 2007).
02 Werner Sombart, *Der Moderne Kapitalismus*, Vol. 1 (Munich/Leipzig: Duncker & Humblot, 1916) 124 ff.
03 Ibid., 175; cf. also ibid., Vol. 1, first edition, Leipzig 1902, 315 [translation: RH].
04 Thus paraphrased in Max Weber, *Wirtschaftsgeschichte* (1923; Berlin: Mohr Siebeck, 2011) 288.
05 Sombart 1916, 649 [translation: RH].
06 cf. Irmgard Fees, *Reichtum und Macht im mittelalterlichen Venedig: Die Familie Ziani* (Tübingen: Niemeyer, 1988). The author of this volume is one of Sombart's critics.
07 cf. Heinrich Kretschmayr, *Geschichte von Venedig*, Vol. 2: Die Blüte (Gotha, 1920), 462; "Without any difficulty, simply with the stroke of a pen, by commanding two lines to be written in their books, the banks can create large sums of money. If the banks had not granted credit, the merchants would not be well-disposed to them beyond the limits of their wealth, and the great sums would not be available with which, all over Europe, useful business transactions have been conducted." [translation: RH]
08 cf. Sombart 1916, 255.
09 Karl Marx, *Ökonomisch-philosophische Manuskripte aus dem Jahre 1844*, Marx Engels Werke (= MEW), Supplementary Volume, Part 1 (Berlin: Dietz Verlag 1968), 505 [translation: RH].
10 Friedrich Nietzsche, "Streifzüge eines Unzeitgemässen," in Nietzsche, *Zur Genealogie der Moral—Götzen-Dämmerung* (1889; Hamburg: Meiner 2013, § 38): 255 [translation: RH].
11 cf. Wolfgang Scheppe, *Migropolis* (Ostfildern: Hatje Cantz Verlag 2009), 1076 ff.
12 cf. Ufficio di Piano, Rapporto Tematico, *La gestione dei sedimenti contaminati nella Laguna di Venezia* (Venice, 2010).
13 cf. "Brugnaro, ecco tutti i conti", *Il Gazzettino*, February 2, 2018.
14 "Chi abita a Rialto deve fare i conti con i turisti: se non gli sta bene, si può trasferire in campagna," *Il Gazzettino*, January 30, 2018 [translation: RH].

15 See the Exploratory Paper for the Coalition Agreement between the CDU/CSU and the SPD, January 2018: www.epochtimes.de/politik/deutschland/sondierungspapier-von-union-und-spd-im-wortlaut-teil-2-a2319740.html (accessed February 28, 2018) [translation: RH].
16 Karl Marx, *Das Kapital. Kritik der politischen Ökonomie, Dritter Band, Der Gesamtprozeß der kapitalistischen Produktion*, MEW, Vol. 25, Berlin 1964, 782 [translation: RH].
17 cf. for example the exhibitions on Manet (2013) and "Douanier" Rousseau (2015) conceived by the media group Gruppo 24 ORE in the Doge's Palace, on Klimt (2012) and "Splendours of the Renaissance" (2015) in the Museo Correr etc.
18 Investment is put into museum shops and cafés. While longer opening times for the latter are under discussion, the exhibitions themselves are to close earlier, so as to facilitate the marketing of exclusive and highly-priced evening access, not least for corporate clients—cf. "*Musei civici, visite fuori orario e ingressi esclusivi per aziende,*" *La Nuova di Venezia e Mestre*, November 16, 2017.
19 cf. www.mcarthurglengroup.com (accessed March 5, 2018).
20 These figures refer to revenue up to November 2017. See David Colman's interview with Damien Hirst, "Colossus of Rogues—Damien Hirst recaps his polarizing show," *New York Magazine*, December 11, 2017.
21 insideairbnb.com/venice (accessed March 5, 2018).
22 Statement by the Artistic Director and the curatorial team of documenta 14, September 14, 2017.
23 Paolo Costa, Jan van der Borg, "Un modello lineare per la programmazione del turismo. Sulla capacità massima di accoglienza turistica del Centro Storico di Venezia," *COSES informazioni*, No. 32–33, 1988.
24 Karl Marx, MEW Vol. 25, 505 [translation: RH].

Land as Project
On Territorial Construction

MILICA TOPALOVIĆ

When Chinese military ships and warplanes took position in the South China Sea in 2014 in order to ensure the undisturbed realization of an infrastructural project, the earthworks filling the shallow waters and coral reefs of Spratly Islands suddenly found themselves at the center of worldwide media attention.[01] It was fascinating to see photographs of the typically overlooked land reclamation that emerged—sandy islands growing in the sea, surrounded by batteries of dredgers and sand barges—garnering so much attention. Of course, these new patches of terra firma are more than infrastructure: the newly built sites for Chinese bases controlling the maritime basin constitute a territorial encroachment, in "violation of the United Nations Convention on the Law of the Sea" and "causing 'irreparable harm' to the marine environment."[02] (FIG. 1) Apart from provoking an international uproar by disturbing the global geostrategic hierarchies, this case also speaks in a clear, even spectacular, manner about the nature of earthworks. This example helps lift infrastructure and land construction out of the mundane world of engineering and muddy building pits in order to remind of what philosophers of land or territory have long since established: that land (and infrastructure) are never neutral, or purely technical and utilitarian, but always strategic, political and ecological.

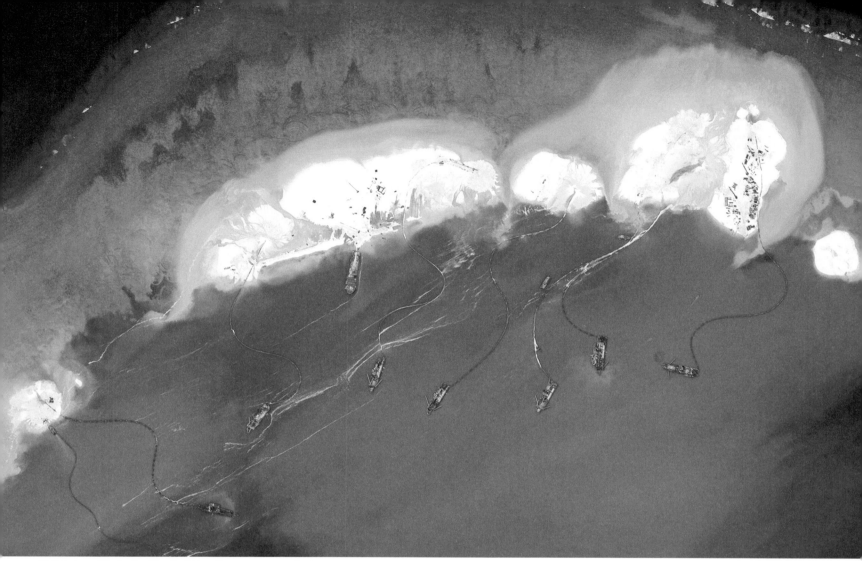

FIG. 1 Landfills in the South China Sea are connected
to China's ongoing expansion policy.

What has taken place in the South China Sea illustrates that ecology and politics of land are intertwined in ways that lead to fundamental questions about the nature of governance in the globalized world, capitalist urbanization, and urban sustainability. For example, new land construction often involves increasing the scale and complexity of resource politics. A growing patch of new land is frequently linked to long-distance resource extraction and transport, to networks of sand trade and geopolitical games in transnational sand hinterlands: "sand wars" among governments and other entities, corporate, local, and international.[03] This case also shows that new land construction exceeds the commercial motivations behind, for example, Dubai's Palm Islands or the purpose of environmental engineering for transport or industry, as seen in Chinese and South Korean ports, such as Shenzhen and Saemangeum. Land construction is also a tool of territorial appropriation and even of encroachment on sovereign borders. Importantly, the South China Sea case also helps as a reminder that earthworks, and infrastructure in general, still constitute an activity lacking public visibility and critical study, in particular from social sciences and design disciplines. But to study a city or an urban territory and to neglect its sewers, power supplies, or reclaimed lands and landfills, is to miss essential aspects of aesthetics, of change, of distributional justice and of planning power.[04]

In one of his seminal essays on philosophy of land, French-Swiss urban historian André Corboz describes land as a multidimensional entity, not solely physical in nature. Land, according to Corboz, originates from culture and politics as much as it is shaped by direct human intervention, and by 'nature's forces' deriving from climate or geology. In other words, land is a *process,* a *product,* and a *project at the same time.*[05] There is no doubt then that land can be understood as a problem of critical research, and of design. But how can we elevate earthworks out of the realm of the utilitarian, and rethink them in the domain of the political and the ecological? How can we approach land as project?

Land Construction: A Lexical Entry

A great many concepts are used to describe human interaction with the surface of the earth, its transformation, exploitation, structuring: *land, landscape,* and *territory* are the most essential. None of them connote "nature" alone, but always imply some degree of "construction"—of "the transformation of earth into land."[06] Herein are phenomena both physical (natural and man-made) and social. *Land construction* describes extensive morphological alterations of the earth's surface by displacing large quantities of material—soil, gravel, rock, etc.—in order to create a buildable or inhabitable land, often in shallow water or swamp, where no land

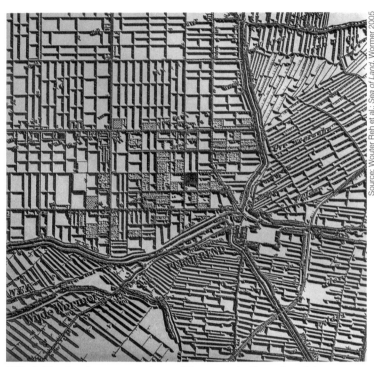

Source: Wouter Reh et al.: *Sea of Land*, Wormer 2005

FIG. 2 The landscape as mirror of the organization of society:
This reconstruction of the "polder" landscape form near Purmerend,
North Holland, at the beginning of the seventeenth century reveals
one of Holland's oldest state institutions—the water boards. The
landscape lost its clear structure in the twentieth century due to urban
growth, modern irrigation technology and transport infrastructure.

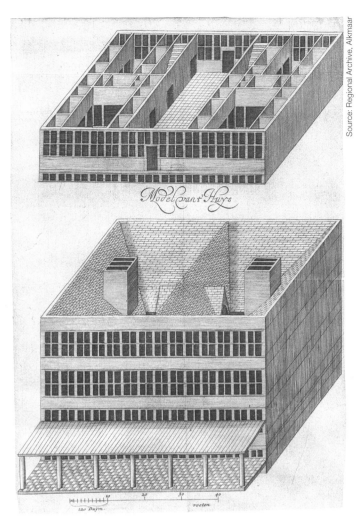

Source: Regional Archive, Alkmaar

FIG. 3 This townhouse model from ca. 1600 refers to
the coevolution of land, city, and society. Polders were
considered ideal for both cities and buildings.

existed previously. Terms such as *man-made land, artificial land,*
and *artificial landscape* are used interchangeably, while expressions such as *earthworks* and *terraforming* point to techniques and
technologies of land construction, such as cutting and filling, leveling, dredging sand, and stabilizing and compressing soil. All of
them relate to various types of modified landscapes, including polders, reclaimed lands, and landfills. Land construction abounds
throughout history—notable projects are never seen as purely
technical achievements, but as reflections of social-cultural value
systems and of political priorities. Distinctive cultures developed
around the problem of constructing an interface between the sea
and the land in naval states and cities—the water-and-land matri-
ces of Venice and Amsterdam are remarkable works of engineering. While being a cultural and technical artifact, man-made land is
also understood as a means of expression of power—absolutist
rulers intervened in a territory to bestow upon it royal or imperial
authority. In the eleventh century, Dutch polder landscapes of
drained wetlands, sea inlets, and lakes were associated with

evolving social structure and governance—a society here has a
physical image in the form of its territory. The "water board"—*het
waterschap*—the first democratic form of Dutch society, corresponded precisely to the organization of water management in the
landscape, and inversely, the metrics of agricultural polder land
was seen as an ideal measure for the organization of cities and
buildings (FIG. 2–3). Unlike today's infrastructures, which are commonly understood only as systems of substrates, merely forming a
background for other kinds of activity, in the sophisticated pol-
der-making practice, the water network is open and visible and it
structures the land—the technical (the infrastructural), the ecological, and the social are interwoven with each other to create an
aesthetic (land) form.

With polders and other intricate sociocultural landscapes in
mind, André Corboz wrote of "land as palimpsest"—this is the
land (or territory, or landscape), seen not as a passive object of
construction, but as an entity evolving through social practice.
Land bears a name; it can be parsed, semanticized, projections of

all kinds are attached to it. It therefore transforms from a passive *object* of construction, into an active *subject* that exerts its own will—and that may contribute to the stability and the reproduction of social relations.[07]

During the nineteenth century, the industrial revolution, the rise of industrial capitalism, and the creation of modern nation states gave rise to new conceptions of land, and greatly increased human ability to transform land. The laying of infrastructures and shaping of land became conjoined operations with enormous physical impact—de facto able to set new topographic laws for modern times. For railway lines or any infrastructural system to achieve optimal performance with minimum expenditure of energy, a considerable leveling of terrain must take place. These new conditions of flatness and horizontality, coupled with the space-time compression engendered by the resulting acceleration of movement, shaped the new space-time topology of industrial modernity (FIG. 4).[08] Mediated via technology and the machine, perceptions of "Nature"— and of land—began to oscillate between the views of Positivism and Romanticism—between the land seen as an *object* available to humanity for industrial exploitation and extraction of profit, and the land seen as a divine *subject* with whom a relationship has been lost and needs to be restored. Similarly, American cultural historian Leo Marx, in *The Machine in the Garden* (1964), observed that spatial ideologies of modernity have a dual, contradictory character that produces a new kind of hybridity in the landscape. Marx observed that: "the free economic competition and technological progress are valued equally with the tradition of landscape pastoralism"; thus, "in our landscape the machine is accommodated in the garden." Today it is fair to say that machine has become "indistinguishable from the garden" since the land is "inextricably intertwined" with technology.[09] Infrastructures and soils blend with human and other ecologies in hybrid, engineered systems; the planet's second skin.

Scientists have pointed out that, at the onset of the Anthropocene, with population numbers and the use of modern machinery growing, "our ability and motivation to modify the landscape by moving earth in construction and mining activities have also increased dramatically. As a consequence, we have now become arguably the premier geomorphic agent sculpting the landscape, and the rate at which we are moving earth is increasing exponentially."[10]

Land and the City:
Promiscuous Stories of Tabula Rasa

In the realm of architectural and urban design, the concept of land (or territory) does not appear as part of modern architecture's repertoire during the twentieth century, save for the intermittent interest during the period of critical reappraisal of the modern movement in the 1960s, '70s, and '80s, for example in the work of Vittorio Gregotti (*Il territorio dell'architettura*, 1966) and Aldo Rossi *(Costruzione del territorio*, 1979).[11] Rather, it appears that for much of the twentieth century, the land as concept disappeared in the "blind spots" of modern architecture and urbanism. Instead, modern technology gave architecture the instruments to revolutionize its relationship with the land and reinvent it as an artifact, disengaged from nature. This new relationship can be traced through the idea of the ground. In modern architecture, ground is not in any measure an external natural given, but a fully controlled surface, an object of conception and construction.

The romantic current of architectural modernism cultivated a reverent relationship with the idea of ground, emphasizing efforts to 'liberate' it, in order to minimize the impact of buildings and cities. In Villa Savoye, Le Corbusier described the first of five modern canons as the "recovery of building ground" by lifting the house on pilotis. The ground that would have been lost to building is in this manner "recovered"; a garden or a landscape can pass under the house, and the same ground can be doubled on the roof.[12]

> Lifted and detached from the ground, the modern building also embraced its newfound emancipation from the physical site.

Now lifted and detached from the ground, the modern building also embraced its newfound emancipation from the physical site, the metaphor of "weightlessness," and the levitation on the bel étage.[13] The consequence of this conceptual and factual detachment from the ground has been the removal of context. The (natural) conditions of the site—topography, soil, water, vegetation—generally ceased to define the building. Instead, modern architecture can presuppose and construct a quasi-abstract site or context, which corresponds to the vision of a non-specific, universal

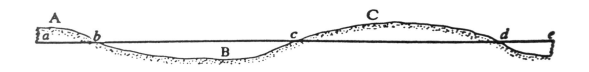

FIG. 4 Flatness and horizontality—diagram of urbanization and modernization: modern infrastructures, such as railways, require the leveling of terrain.

Source: Nicholas Wood: *A Practical Treatise on Rail-Roads*, London 1838

FIG. 5 Leveling: in some parts of Seattle, the ground level was lowered by nearly 90 feet (30 meters) and the removed surface used to fill up sea, swamplands, or other low-lying areas.

Photo: Asahel Curtis, *The Leveling of the Hills to Make Seattle*, 1910

FIG. 6 The example of the Chongqing Nail House (2007) and similar cases illustrate both
China's ruthless urban growth strategies and its residents' resistance to authoritarian planning policies.

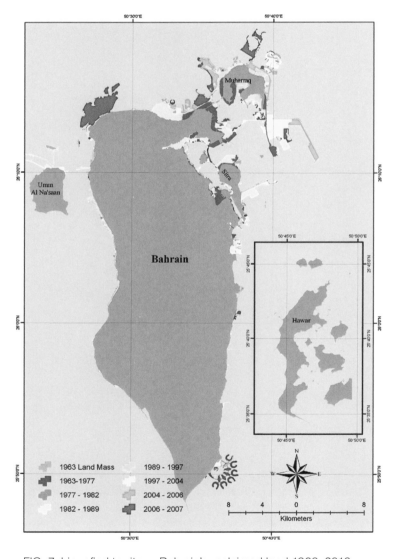

FIG. 7 Liquefied territory: Bahrain's reclaimed land 1963–2016.
In forty years, the area of Bahrain has been increased
by 108 square kilometers—almost a sixth of its original area.

© Khadija Zainal et al., 2012, updated by the author

architecture. Throughout the twentieth century, the idea of the ground appears in modern architecture in many different forms, their common horizon being the building of an artificial plane or construction of a more complex system of surfaces and infrastructures often completely detached from the actual ground level. In the process, the artificial ground develops as a refined technological instrument for organizing all elements of urban life.

There is thus a deep and uneasy affinity between modern architecture and (artificial) land. The idea of land in its long-term dimension, as a result of slow processes of stratification of human and natural traces, a palimpsest, generally stays in architecture's blind spot. Instead, it could be said that in modern architecture and the modern city, all land is constructed land—a product of urbanization and urban mentality that creates land surface as a projection of its desires, goals, and needs. These are governed by different sets of relationships than in traditional societies. The effort that bound rural inhabitants to the land has dissolved; the city-dweller has assumed a more emancipated and arbitrary relation to the land. Artificial urban land—a *tabula rasa, a clean slate*, an *unscripted tablet*—is thus not an exception; it is the central concept of the modern city: the product and the habitat of urban culture.

In cities across the globe, tabula rasa was often deployed as urban strategy in the hands of state and other protagonists, for different symbolic and political purposes. In Seattle, a staggering work of erasure, the so-called "regrading" of the city, was portrayed in the photographic work *The Leveling of the Hills to make Seattle,* by Asahel Curtis in 1910 (FIG. 5). Arguably one of the largest physical alterations of terrain ever performed—outside natural disaster and wartime destruction—it utilized America's tremendous technological capabilities and can-do spirit in a fervor of to modernize the city's infrastructures and buildings as a response to the gold rush and rising real estate values. In some places the ground level in the city was lowered by nearly 90 feet (approximately 30 meters), with the help of steam shovels and hydraulic mining techniques.[14]

A few decades later, in post–World War II Belgrade, land was reclaimed from the marshes of the river Sava to become a site for the building of the new capital of socialist Yugoslavia. Over 100,000 youth brigadiers from all over the country filled the marshes with a layer of sand six meters high. Their different religions, languages, and origins represented "brotherhood and unity," the key ideological program of the newly unified country. The constructed virgin land took on the symbolic connotations of a site of cultivation of a new socialist society that should rise beyond the history of ethnic conflicts and separations. In recent examples, the idea of land as an unscripted tablet was also connected with neoliberal forms of urban development radicalism, for example in the cases of the "flattening of Riyadh" to build villas[15] and the Chongqing nail house in 2007.[16] Here, cut hills and leveled terrain surfaced as synonyms of state-organized destruction and appropriation of land and property for the benefit of political-economic elites (FIG. 6).

Many other cities today—including highly visible cases of terraforming spectacle from Bahrain and Dubai to Hong Kong and Shanghai—have embraced tabula rasa and land construction as key elements of their development repertoire. The generic character of reclaimed land projects—their oft-repeated forms (palms, islands, and other protrusions) found all over the world—may seem surprising. The urbanistic logic of reclaimed land is equally generic and widely shared. The basic programmatic ingredients are the same—large-scale facilities involving logistics, oil, and gas, and extravagant real estate for investment—only the relative amounts can vary. These resonances are in part due to long-distance sharing of experiences and know-how in the field, disseminated by the multinational dredging industry. Dutch dredging company Van Oord, for instance, has taken part in every major land-reclamation project of the past few decades from Singapore's Tuas and Changi to Palm Jumeirah.[17]

But, there are other affinities: most of the leading land reclamation cities are coastal cities (or city-states), sharing high population density, strong economic growth, and scarcity of coastal land—these characteristics make them prone to land reclamation. Ultimately however, it is their common political feature of entrepreneurially minded and authoritarian state governments with unrestricted authority that are able and willing to push territorial expansion forward.

State governments and agencies exploit—legitimately or not—the economy of the reclaimed-land prototype, which offers remarkably low prices for building land. The total reclamation costs are usually below 250 euros per square meter (by comparison, the seafront land prices in Singapore are more than 20 times higher; in Hong Kong even 100 times higher).[18] Additional revenues from activities at those sites can further multiply the profits. Thus, for a select group of cities where politics and geography come together in the right formula, land reclamation amounts to a form of alchemy for creating prime sites and exorbitant returns "out of nothing."

The case of Bahrain, where more than 90 percent of the reclaimed land (315 square kilometers in total, half of the original land area) is in the hands of private investors,[19] also illustrates a shameless affinity that has developed between terraforming and private security. Private estates on reclaimed land, protruding into the sea like castles surrounded by defensive ditches, speak of the fact that exclusive access has become a bon ton of the real estate business, in which the high-security regime functions as a business compliment paid by the government to the private entities and multinationals residing and operating in their territory. As a result, less than 10 percent of Bahrain's coastline is now accessible to the public (FIG. 7–9).[20]

The indiscriminate land reclamation here has also been linked with wide-ranging cultural and ecological destruction, from the depletion of marine life and the demise of local fishery, to the erasure of cultural heritage sites and the lack of drinking water. Ironically, it appears that, in the process of the territorial overhaul, the ruling class and economic elites have appropriated some of those same resources. But this is not a surprise: tabula rasa and the new land routinely bring about the erasure of local history and ecology, and, in exchange, they open space for construction of new historical narratives and ecological imaginaries, reinforcing the given social order. For example, the private estates occupying Bahrain's new coastal areas also have access to an abundant water supply, insuring their verdant oasis experience against the conditions of the water-scarce city.[21] By contrast to Bahrain, Singapore's new land is not identifiable as a spectacle of image urbanism in the littoral zone. Singapore shows tabula rasa as a long-term strategic project of "nation-building"[22]—an all encompassing three-dimensional transformation of both old and new land and landscape, used as fundamental tool of social, political and economic transformation, following post-colonial independence in 1965 (FIG. 10–11). The process of change from a backwater colonial port, predominantly rural, to the new nation of the industrial middle class housed in public high-rises, was dubbed "territorial revolution"[23] with many layers: the social, political, and economic dimensions of the national territory have been sculpted by the hand of state, using topography as the main medium.

Singapore also shows that construction of urban land usually doesn't come without a (vast) hinterland. The city-state is known as the world's largest importer of sand for construction, having come to lay at the center of the sand trade region whose radius extends to South China, Cambodia, and Myanmar. With around 140 square kilometers added over the years, it has been estimated that nearly a quarter of Singapore is "built on foreign soil."[24]

> For a select group of cities where politics and geography come together in the right formula, land reclamation amounts to a form of alchemy for creating exorbitant returns "out of nothing."

Up until the 1970s, the material for construction of land and buildings used to come from the island's granite quarries, leveled land, and clay pits, but in the 1980s, the flows of sand, gravel, and rock to the city-state began to extend across the border to Malaysia and Indonesia, and further afield—in other words, Singapore's sand hinterland had begun to "disintegrate,"[25] and assume geopolitical scale.

The shifting sands and the liquefied territorial contours in the region have also exposed national tensions and older colonial and postcolonial borders that continue to problematize the current geography of governance. For example, land reclamation and dredging in the Singapore Straits led to national border disputes (Singapore-Indonesia and Singapore-Malaysia) in front of international arbitrage, and at huge collateral costs. This and other similar reasons were cited by Indonesia and Malaysia when they introduced successive bans on sand trade with Singapore, followed by Cambodia and Vietnam.[26] In the unstable political geography of the region, sand trade and reclaimed lands have become themes of war (gaming exercises and conflict simulations).

Proponents of globalization have argued that the world is becoming "flat": a level playing field in terms of commerce where all competitors have equal opportunity, and where historical and geographical divisions are being neutralized due to communication technologies, transport, and the worldwide synchronization of various systems of rules.[27] This has been coupled with more lamentable

FIG. 8 Bahrain, Durrat Marina, 2016: state-organized speculation. The ruling elite personally profited from land reclamation. Private investors own more than 90 percent of the reclaimed land.

FIG. 9 Bahrain Investment Gateway, 2016: the reclaimed land offers the elite security and seclusion. Less than 10 percent of Bahrain's artificial coastline is open to the public.

Photos: Bas Princen

manifestations of cultural flattening: a widespread acceptance of generic cultural production and consumption at the expense of any authentic form of culture. This discussion can gain unexpectedly when approached from the angle of physical geography: if not economically or culturally flatter, the world is becoming flatter, literally.

In Bahrain, Singapore and other cities attached to flatland production, economic and technical rationalities have often taken precedence over other values in urban space; the priorities of speed, efficiency, and profit have brushed other concerns aside. Heritage, ecology, and social equality have been assigned lower priorities, but the cases show that the shortage of gravitas can also help liberate the city's identity from restrictions. The preference for artificiality and newness, and the untroubled pursuit for more, also constitutes a specific flatness.

The question is, do these choices matter? Does twenty-first-century culture permit, or possibly even favor, the innocent charm and frivolity of instant history, ready-made identity, do-it-yourself nature, and topography on demand? Ultimately, can design make a difference in these decisions?

Epilogue: Designing Land Better?

Cities inevitably modify their surroundings—their actual sites and their hinterlands. Over the last century, despite the extraordinary increase in our ability to transform land and topography through the construction of urban structures and infrastructures, both land and infrastructure as problems of design—as "willful configuration[s]"[28]—have barely been articulated. Neither architecture and urbanism nor landscape architecture seems to have firm grip on the problem; among the three disciplines, the (under) world of the messy earthworks, machines, cables and pipes, exists largely unnoticed.

No doubt, land does invite opportunities for design—precedents abound. Sensibility to a territorial form goes back to the Italian Renaissance, which invented landscape as a pictorial genre and looked for ways to "reconcile the necessities of production and the 'beautiful landscape'."[29] Agrarian landscapes grown over time became cultural artifacts of great value and are sometimes protected as such. For expressionist architect Bruno Taut, who envisioned the reconstruction of Alpine summits into crystalline cities, land was a medium in which human society can shape itself—the

work of art by the state and the people. For land artists such as Robert Smithson or Michael Heizer, land became the medium of artistic protest against the perceived artificiality, plastic aesthetics, and commercialization of urban life.

Inevitably, land is always a project, a made entity. "This necessity for a collective relation to be experienced between a topographic surface and a population established in its folds permits drawing the conclusion that there is no land without imagining a land."[30] The value attributed to the land and landscape, its form and configuration—its design—is and can only be cultural. Culture supplies the program, the underlying vision to any design.

The question of the city's relation to the land is essentially the question of its relation to its place, its geographical and cultural setting. The choices with which the city approaches these specific limitations are political. It may seem that these choices are indifferent, but this would be a simplification—cities are always forms of their politics, the signs of their collective will.[31]

Land (or territory) is not merely a utility or a product, part of the invisible infrastructural (under)world we have created, but an entity with highly complex performance and function, and an object of relations of appropriation that involve geo-strategic, economic, symbolical, and other intentions. Instead of maintaining the distance between infrastructure as a problem of engineering, and city or urban space as domains of landscape architecture and urban design, these areas need to be brought together. In addition to the currently simplified conception of (urban) land as an abstract surface with technological character, land has to be recovered in terms of its stabilizing ideologies[32] —soil, fertility, history, place, permanence. Conversely, infrastructure is not a neutral technical apparatus, but a political, ecological, and ethnographic entity.

FIG. 10 Oil cavern, Jurong Island, 2013: despite the landfills, Singapore's territorial expansion is increasingly subterranean, as these artificial crude oil reservoirs on Jurong Island show.

FIG. 11 Semakau landfill, 2014: most of the Singapore coastline has been secured with retaining walls since the 1950s. In Pulau Semakau these walls were backfilled with ashes from Singapore's incineration plants.

Photos: Bas Princen

01 Rupert Wingfield-Hayes, "China's Island Factory," *BBC News*, September 9, 2014, www.bbc.co.uk/news/resources/idt-1446c419-fc55-4a07-9527-a6199f5dc0e2 (accessed February 23, 2018).

02 Jane Perlez, "Tribunal Rejects Beijing's Claims in South China Sea," *The New York Times*, July 12, 2016.

03 Peter Dupont, "Sand Wars," trans. Rafael Njotea, working grant proposal for the Pascal Decroos Fund, 2013/995, www.fondspascaldecroos.org/en/inhoud/werkbeurs/sand-wars (accessed February 23, 2018).

04 Susan Leigh Star, "The Ethnography of Infrastructure," *American Behavioral Scientist,* no. 43 (1999): 377–91.

05 André Corboz, "The Land as Palimpsest," *Diogenes* 31, no. 121 (1983): 12–34.

06 Ibid., 13.

07 Ibid., 18–19.

08 Wolfgang Schivelbusch, *The Railway Journey: The Industrialization of Time and Space in the 19th Century* (University of California Press, 1986), 22.

09 See Gary L. Strang, "Infrastructure as Landscape," *Places* 10, no 3 (1996): 8–15 and Leo Marx, "The Machine in the Garden. Technology and the Pastoral Ideal in America" (Oxford University Press, 1964).

10 Roger LeB. Hooke, "On the history of humans as geomorphic agents," *Geology* 28, no. 9 (2000): 843–46.

11 See Vittorio Gregotti, *Il territorio dell'architettura* (Milano: Feltrinelli, 1966) and Aldo Rossi, Fabio Reinhart, Bruno Reichlin et al., *Costruzione del territorio e spazio urbano nel cantone Ticino* (Lugano: Fondazione Ticino Nostro, 1979).

12 Werner Oechslin and Wilfred Wang, "Les Cinq Points d'une Architecture Nouvelle," *Assemblage*, no. 4 (1987): 82–93.

13 Ilka Ruby and Andreas Ruby, *Groundscapes: The rediscovery of the ground in contemporary architecture* (Barcelona: Editorial Gustavo Gili, 2006), 11.

14 V. V. Tarbill, "Mountain-moving in Seattle," *Harvard Business Review* 8 (1930): 482–89.

15 Joumana al Jabri, "The Flattening of Riyadh," *Volume* 23, "Al Manakh Gulf Continued," ed. AMO, Archis, Pink Tank et al. (Amsterdam: Stichting Archis, 2010): 430–431.

16 "Demolition ends China house row," *BBC News*, April 3, 2007, news.bbc.co.uk/2/hi/asia-pacific/6520317.stm (accessed February 23, 2018).

17 Jan Schaart, "Mega Reclamations: Opportunities and Challenges," presentation at the CEDA Conference on Dredging and Reclamation, Doha, May 2008, www.cedaconferences.org/documents/dredgingconference/downloads/2/qatar2008_2008-18-05_41_schaart.pdf (accessed February 23, 2018).

18 Ibid.

19 Cynthia O'Murchu, Simeon Kerr, Russel Birkett and Aleksandra Wisniewska, "Explaining Bahrain's land reclamation controversy," *Financial Times*, November 27, 2014 and Mohammad Noor Al-Nabi, *The History of Land use and Development in Bahrain* (Bahrain: Kingdom of Bahrain Information Affairs Authority, 2012), www.housing.gov.bh/en/PublicationsLibrary/6681%20book%20resized.pdf (accessed February 23, 2018).

20 Ibid.

21 Gareth Doherty, "Bahrain's Polyvocality and Landscape as a Medium," in *The Right to Landscape: Contesting Landscape and Human Rights*, ed. Shelley Egoz, Jala Makhzoumi and Gloria Pungetti (Farnham: Ashgate Publishing, Ltd., 2011), 185–96.

22 Peggy Teo, Brenda S. A. Yeoh, Ooi Giok Ling and Karen P.Y. Lai, *Changing Landscapes of Singapore* (Singapore: National University of Singapore, McGraw-Hill Education, 2004).

23 Rodolphe De Koninck, "Singapore or the Revolution of Territory. Part One: the Hypothesis," *Cahiers de géographie du Quebec* 34, no.92 (1990): 209–216.

24 S.L. Lee et al., "Layered Clay-Sand Scheme of Land Reclamation," *Journal of Geotechnical Engineering* 113, no. 9 (1987): 984–995.

25 Neil Brenner and Christian Schmid, "Planetary urbanisation," in *Urban Constellations*, ed. M. Gandy (Berlin: Jovis Verlag, 2011), 10–13.

26 "Singapore's sand shortage: The hourglass effect," *The Economist*, October 8, 2009, www.economist.com/node/14588255 (accessed February 23, 2018).

27 Thomas L. Friedman, *The World is Flat* (New York: Farrar, Straus and Giroux, 2005).

28 Corboz, "The Land as Palimpsest," 19.

29 Ibid., 21.

30 Ibid., 18.

31 Peter Eisenman, "The Houses of Memory: The Texts of Analogue," introduction to *The Architecture of the City*, by Aldo Rossi (1966; Cambridge, Mass: MIT Press, 1982), 3–10, 10.

32 Joshua Comaroff, "Built on Sand: Singapore and the New State of Risk," *Harvard Design Magazine*, no. 39 (2014): 138–143.

Land Policy Glossary

COMPILED BY
ILKIN AKPINAR AND LORENZ SEIDL

Germany's constitution, the *Grundgesetz*, or GG (Basic Law), protects the right to own property like few others; however, it also gives cities and municipalities important tools for action. Article 14 section 2 GG states: "Property entails obligations. Its use shall also serve the public good." This Land Policy Glossary provides an overview of the control options available to the public sector, focusing on the following three areas:

§ Active land policy by the public sector: What immediate control mechanisms do municipalities have for urban development oriented toward the public good?

$ Passive land policy through taxes and compensation: How can gains that are earned through development and investments by the public sector, without any effort on the owner's part, be absorbed for the general public?

 Collective development models: What alternative models are there for collective urban production?

Cooperative

Besides owner-occupied housing and rentals, with around six percent, cooperative living constitutes the third pillar of the housing supply in Germany. The legal form of the *eingetragene Genossenschaft* (eG, registered cooperative) is based on the principles of self-help, self-determination, and self-management.[1] The reserve assets and the paid membership fees constitute the equity capital of the cooperative, which together guarantee the financing of the business operations, renovation measures, new buildings, and further services for the support of its members.[2] Whereas in the case of other corporate forms the right to vote is dependent on capital investment, in cooperatives each member has the same right to vote. In housing co-ops, with the purchase of shares in the cooperative each member receives a lifelong right to use a cooperative apartment. They are at once tenant and shareholder of the housing co-op.

Community Land Trust

A Community Land Trust (CLT) is a nonprofit organization that buys parcels of land for the purpose of developing, building, and managing low-cost housing and other community assets. Through the separation into landownership—which remains with the CLT, as only the right of use is transferred in the (→) building lease—and residential property, land shall be made available for financially weak social groups. The sale of real estate on CLT property is subject to a resale formula that is fixed and gives the CLT the right of preemption. The sales price is capped in order to prevent speculation. There are CLTs in the United States as well as Australia, Belgium, England, Canada, Kenya, New Zealand, and Wales.

§

Concept Tendering Procedure

Usually, pieces of property held by the public sector are sold to the highest bidder (best price procedure). But the municipality also has the option to sell them according to the best-suited concept for the realization of predetermined goals based on a set of criteria. The concept qualities with respect to architecture and urban inclusion, energetic and social standards, etc., affect the acceptance of a tender, not the purchase price alone. The agreements reached become part of the property sale contract or are included in an (→) urban development contract.[5]

§

Expropriation

In German Basic Law, article 14 section 1 protects the right to own property, yet limits it in section 3: for example, "Expropriation shall only be permissible for the public good," in the course of (→) urban development measures. Expropriation rights that concern pieces of property are regulated in the *Baugesetzbuch* (Federal Building Code) (sections 85 BauGB) and coupled with the corresponding compensation in the form of payments or compensatory land. An expropriation constitutes the *ultima ratio* according to the principle of proportionality.

§

Federal Land Foundation

A federal land foundation would make an active real estate policy possible on a federal level and work according to the principles of a (→) <u>land fund</u>. The assets of the federal land foundation would consist of federally owned real estate that has been dedicated to the fund. The aim here is also to actively shape urban development that is oriented toward the public good.[6]

Foundation

A foundation with legal capacity under civil law serves noncommercial purposes and enjoys tax-related privileges.[7] In the context of land issues, there are foundations that oppose land speculation and specifically devote themselves to the sustainable use of property as well as innovative, collective living models. The aim is to remove land from the flow of commodities and the inheritance cycle and make it permanently available for projects oriented toward the public good. Beyond that, they often play an advisory role in the development of alternative legal forms and financing models as well as the setting up of self-managing structures.[8]
The former premises of the printing machine manufacturer Rotaprint in Berlin were bought by the Edith Maryon Stiftung and Stiftung Trias foundations, and by means of a leasehold awarded to the ExRotaprint gGmbH for a period of 99 years. The one-third parity representation laid down in the user contract—labor, art, and social affairs—guarantees its noncommercial status, with which the site and the buildings are developed and operated in the possession of the ExRotaprint gGmbH.[9]

§

Land Fund

By means of land provisioning, a land fund creates long-term resources for an active real estate policy. The public sector continuously acquires pieces of property for the purpose of managing them in a land pool. The fund therefore also serves municipalities as an instrument for exercising their (→) <u>right of preemption</u>. Thus the municipality can regulate sustainable and social urban development by awarding the right of use according to specific criteria and in the form of (→) <u>heritable building rights (leaseholds)</u>. On a revolving basis, the revenue yielded through ground rents finances the development of land as well as the purchase of additional pieces of property in the long term.[10]
With the Sondervermögen für Daseinsvorsorge *(SODA, Special Assets for Public Services), in which unused property from the real estate fund and additional pieces of property are parked for strategic reasons, Berlin possesses a basic stock that could be developed into a revolving land fund.*[11]

§

Land Reserve Policy

The provision of land by municipalities in a basic stock guarantees long-term urban development. Moreover, added planning value can, for example, be generated through rezoning: suburban sites are bought at an early stage for the purpose of regulating superordinate goals in the areas of housing or industry. See: (→) <u>land fund</u> and (→) <u>federal land foundation</u>.

Land Value Increment Tax

Property owners benefit from rezoning measures or improvement of the surroundings. The value of their property rises without any active investments on their part. Since the 1970s, attempts have been made to impose taxes on such land price increases. A first step toward a new land value increment tax has been made in the *Städtebauförderungsgesetz* (Law Promoting Urban Development), which allows the public sector to have a share in the profits arising from planning measures.[12] Zoning law itself provides insufficient regulations in terms of the building code to absorb increment value that can be attributed to urban development, so-called unearned gains from property owners. See also (→) <u>planning value adjustment</u>.
From 1972 on, several attempts on the part of the Social Democratic Party of Germany to legally incorporate a land value increment tax have failed, due to constitutional concerns, among other things. Because it is a matter of taxation of unrealized gains, an owner could be forced to liquidate their property. This would be incompatible with article 14 GG.

Land Value Tax

One of the most well-known proponents of land value tax is the American land reformer Henry George (1839–1897).[13] The land value tax was intended to replace other forms of taxes and be imposed exclusively on "natural" (i.e., without taking into account the added value created by the owner) property value.

The aim is the best possible exploitation of property within the scope of planning requirements, as the owner aspires to compensate the tax burden. As a result, unused or insufficiently used pieces of property are mobilized and the lack of available building land, which promotes land speculation, is counteracted.[14] Land value tax is imposed in parts of New Zealand and Australia as well as in Denmark and Estonia. The two city-states Hong Kong and Singapore also, for the most part, collect their taxes by way of a land value tax, whereas labor and capital taxes are kept as low as possible.[15] In Germany, a land value tax could replace the (→) <u>property tax</u>.[16]

Heritable Building Rights (Leaseholds)

Based on the *Erbbaurechtsgesetz* (section 1 ErbbauRG), a law introduced in 1919 that regulates heritable building rights in the form of leaseholds, against payment of ground rent a builder obtains the right to erect or maintain a structure on or under the surface of a piece of property.[3] While the land remains the property of the lessor, the structure is the property of the leaseholder for a certain period of time, normally 99 years. Leaseholds are entered into both the land register as well as in a building lease register and can be sold, inherited, and burdened; it also remains valid in the case of forced sale of the property. As a right equivalent to real property, the lessee must also pay (→) property tax. The ground rent is based on the land value at the beginning of term of the contract or, in the case of commercial use, on revenues, and is laid down in the leasehold contract. Should it come to a so-called reversion—the transfer of the granted right to the original right holder, due to breaches of contract or bankruptcy—the lessor must repay the value of the building, at least proportionally. With the termination of the leasehold, the property and structures again merge to become an economic unit.[4]

Mietshäuser Syndikat (Tenement Syndicate)

As a noncommercial holding company, the Mietshäuser Syndikat GmbH (Tenement Syndicate, Inc.), founded in 1999, purchases real estate for the purpose of converting it into public property, creating affordable housing in the long term and initiatives oriented toward the public good. The advantage lies in the reciprocal control of the shareholders. The buildings are owned by Hausbesitz GmbH (Home Ownership, Inc.) with two shareholders: the *Hausverein* (building association), which is made up of all of the occupants and is self-managed, as well as the superordinate Mietshäuser Syndikat GmbH, which prevents privatization of the buildings. Both of them have equal votes in the Hausbesitz GmbH, so that sale or conversion into marketable assets are only possible by mutual agreement. All other decisions (e.g., rent amount, financing, apartment allocation) reside with the Hausverein.[17] The Mietshäuser Syndikat, which originated in the squatter and activist scene, grew into a nationwide network in the '90s.[18] Today it participates in 17 project initiatives and 128 building projects throughout Germany, of which 24 are in Berlin and Potsdam.[19]

Planning Value Adjustment

Planning value adjustment involves absorption of the land value increase as a result of municipal planning activity, and corresponds with the compensation of losses in land value in tax law. Today it is a one-time compensation payment by property owners for urban planning redevelopment measures and (→) urban development measures to the municipality according to section 154 paragraph 1 sentence 1 BauGB.[20]
In Berlin, the municipality designates areas that will undergo targeted upgrading within the next 15 years through investments in the infrastructure and in public institutions as redevelopment areas. This procedure is a prerequisite for the municipality to ask property owners to pay compensation for increased land value after the conclusion of redevelopment.

Property Tax

Property tax is a tax that is levied on the ownership of a piece of property, including its development. The *Grundsteuergesetz* (GrStG, Property Tax Law) from 1973 constitutes the foundation, whereby a distinction is made between property tax A for agricultural and silvicultural assets and property tax B for developed or developable pieces of property and buildings. Netting approximately 13 billion euros annually in the whole of Germany, the latter is one of the most important sources of income for municipalities.[21] Only nonprofit organizations such as (→) foundations and societies are exempt from paying property tax. Landlords generally divide the tax proportionately among tenants by way of the incidental rental expenses statement.
The assessment basis for property tax is the standard land value. In the western states of Germany, this continues to be based on land values from 1964, whereas in the eastern states, on those from 1935. The standard land values ascertained in this way bear no relation to real land values and result in an unfairly distributed tax burden. Because of the considerable expenses for municipalities, the planned adjustment of the standard land values in six-year cycles was never carried out. *The Constitutional Court is currently reviewing whether property tax in its current form is unconstitutional, since the value distortions are in violation of the principle of equality (article 3 section 1 GG).*22

§

Right of Preemption

Under certain conditions, the municipality has a legal right of preemption of pieces of property in order to safeguard its urban land-use planning. A distinction is made between the "general" (section 24 BauGB) and the "particular" (section 25 BauGB) right of preemption. Whereas the particular right of preemption becomes effective, among other things, in the case of an (→) urban development measure, the general right of preemption applies, among others, in (→) social environment protection areas. Instead of exercising its right of preemption, however, the city can reach an agreement with private project developers interested in purchasing the property to contract into the preservation of social environment protection. In special cases, the municipality can exercise the right of preemption at the limited market value.

Social Environment Protection Area

Based on section 172 paragraph 1 sentence 1 number 2 BauGB, structural alterations or changes in use in defined areas are subject to prior approval. On the one hand, the aim is the preservation of the urban character of the area, for instance due to its particular importance in terms of architectural history (*städtebauliche Erhaltungsverordnung* [Urban Development Preservation Act]), and on the other hand the preservation of the social composition of the resident population (*soziale Erhaltungsverordnung* [Social Preservation Act]), or *Milieuschutzverordnung* [Social Environment Protection Act]).[23] In areas with a social preservation act, the district has the (→) right of preemption.

Urban Development Contract

According to section 11 BauGB, municipalities can transfer the preparation and implementation of urban development measures to investors and project developers and lay down framework conditions. This applies, in particular, to the restructuring of property relations under private law, land reclamation, and the clearance of plots of land. In connection with urban land-use planning or other planning procedures according to municipal by-laws, urban development contracts can serve, among other things, the urgent need for housing in the local population. Parties willing to develop the land pledge to assume costs and other expenditures vis-à-vis the municipality that the latter incurs, for instance, due to urban development plans (so-called follow-up cost agreements), in particular the creation of the social and technical infrastructure. The origination of development rights hinges on the willingness to cooperate.[24]

The Berlin Model *of cooperative building land development provides a uniform municipal regulation for the conclusion of urban development contracts. In 2017, the model was aligned with the* Munich *Model, theoretically increasing the share of eligible housing to 30 percent of the floor space; investors were involved in the creation of additional capacities in primary schools and daycare facilities as well as in the technical infrastructure.[25] According to section 34 BauGB, building projects in inlying areas are permitted even if a land-use plan does not exist, as long as the construction conforms "to the character of the existing context." Because this code applies in most cases in Berlin, developers do not have an incentive to enter urban development contracts in exchange for a building permit. The result is that the percentage of such contracts is actually single-digit.[26]*

Urban Development Measure

The urban development measure, an instrument introduced by sections 165ff BauGB, enables a uniform overall measure, for example for meeting an increased demand for dwellings and workplaces in outlying and inlying development areas. The municipality has a (→) right of preemption in the designated area and can carry out the (→) expropriation of pieces of property without a land-use plan. The property value is set before the development measure, as the prices are frozen at the beginning of the measure. The municipality absorbs the increased market value due to the rezoning into building land. Owners also have to pay this difference as compensation (see (→) planning value adjustment) if they do not sell their property and the municipality refrains from an expropriation process.

01 Information page of the Federal Ministry for the Environment, Nature Conservation, Building, and Nuclear Safety, www.bmub.bund.de/themen/stadt-wohnen/wohnungswirtschaft/genossenschaftlich-wohnen/genossenschaftlich-wohnen-in-deutschland (accessed February 15, 2018).

02 Cf. Detlef Maaßen (March 19, 2017), www.wir-leben-genossenschaft.de/de/ein-rechtsformvergleich-zwischen-eg-e-v-und-gmbh-349.htm (accessed February 15, 2018).

03 Springer Fachmedien Wiesbaden, ed., *Gabler Wirtschaftslexikon* (Wiesbaden: Springer Gabler, 2013), www.wirtschaftslexikon.gabler.de/Archiv/5353/bodenwertzuwachssteuer-v10.html (accessed February 15, 2018).

04 Cf. Wikipedia, isa, www.juraforum.de/lexikon/erbbaurecht und www.exrotaprint.de/erbbaurecht (accessed February 15, 2018).

05 Cf. Deutscher Verband für Wohnungswesen, Städtebau und Raumordnung e.V., *Mehr Bauland für bezahlbaren Wohnungsbau* (2016), www.deutscher-verband.org/fileadmin/user_upload/documents/Brosch%C3%BCren/Mehr_Bauland_bezahlbarer_Wohnungsbau_DV.pdf (accessed February 15, 2018).

06 Frauke Burgdorff and Jochen Lang, and Stefan Rettich, *Mehr Boden für Wohnen: Vorschlag für die Gründung einer Bodenstiftung des Bundes als Fundament für dauerhaft bezahlbare Wohnungen* (December 5, 2017), www.marlowes.de/mehr-boden-fuer-wohnen (accessed February 15, 2018).

07 Cf. www.stiftungen.org/stiftungen/basiswissen-stiftungen (accessed February 15, 2018).

08 Cf. www.maryon.ch und www.stiftung-trias.de (accessed February 15, 2018).

09 Cf. www.exrotaprint.de/erbbaurecht (accessed February 15, 2018).

10 vhw—Bundesverband für Wohnen und Stadtentwicklung e.V., *Bodenpolitische Agenda 2020–2030: Warum wir für eine nachhaltige und sozial gerechte Stadtentwicklungs- und Wohnungspolitik eine andere Bodenpolitik brauchen* (2017).

11 Cf. Katrin Lompscher im Interview mit Arno Brandlhuber, December 2017, unpublished transcript.

12 Wiesbaden 2013 (see note 3), www.wirtschaftslexikon.gabler.de/Archiv/5353/bodenwertzuwachssteuer-v10.html (accessed February 15, 2018).

13 Cf. Henry George, *Progress and Poverty—An Inquiry into the Cause of Industrial Depressions and of Increase of Want with Increase of Wealth: The Remedy* (1879) (New York: AMS Press, 1973).

14 Beate Dieterich and Hartmut Dieterich, eds., *Boden—Wem nutzt er? Wen stützt er?—Neue Perspektiven des Bodenrechts* (Basel: Birkhauser Verlag, 2000).

15 Thomas Trares, "Der Boden und die Bodenrente—die Verteilungsfrage des 21. Jahrhunderts?" (November 27, 2017), www.nachdenkseiten.de/?p=41285 (accessed February 15, 2018).

16 Caspar Dohmen, "Modell Bodensteuer: Wundermittel gegen Wohnungsnot?" *Deutschlandfunk* (January 15, 2018), www.deutschlandfunk.de/reform-der-grundsteuer-modell-bodensteuer-wundermittel.724.de.html?dram:article_id=408360 (accessed February 15, 2018).

17 nika.haus/index.php/about/das-mietshauser-syndikat (accessed February 15, 2018).

18 Cf. Bernhard Hummel, "Das Mietshäuser Syndikat—Eine Alternative zum Eigentumsprinzip," *ARCH+* 201/202, *Berlin* (March 2011), p. 124

19 Cf. www.syndikat.org (accessed February 15, 2018).

20 Wiesbaden 2013 (see note 3), www.wirtschafts-lexikon.gabler.de/Archiv/937/planungswertausgleich-v10.html (accessed February 15, 2018).

21 Cf. Claudia Kornmeier, "Wie gerecht ist die Grundsteuer?" *Tagesschau* (January 16, 2018), www.tagesschau.de/inland/grundsteuer-101.html (accessed February 15, 2018).

22 Decision from October 22, 2014, file number II R 16/13, www.juris.bundes-finanzhof.de/cgi-bin/rechtsprechung/document.py?Gericht=bfh&Art=en&sid=0dd1b4bacac64e10971a88e085d9bdeb&nWhenr=30850&linked=pm (accessed February 15, 2018).

23 Cf. Topp Andreas, "Soziale Erhaltungsgebiete (Milieuschutz)," information page of the IHK Berlin (July 5, 2017) www.ihk-berlin.de/produktmarken/branchen/bauwirt/news/Karte_der_Milieuschutzgebiete/2271754 (accessed February 15, 2018).

24 Ibid., www.wirtschafts-lexikon.gabler.de/Archiv/13811/staedtebaulicher-vertrag-v9.html (accessed February 15, 2018).

25 Cf. www.stadtentwicklung.berlin.de/wohnen/wohnungsbau/de/vertraege/ (accessed February 15, 2018).

26 Cf. Lompscher 2017 (see note 11).

The Value of Land

How Community Land Trusts Maintain Housing Affordability

OKSANA MIRONOVA

In 1969, Charles Sherrod and his wife Shirley, together with other civil rights activists, founded the New Communities agricultural collective in Albany, Georgia. It is considered a pioneer project of the Community Land Trust. Photo: Dawn Makarios © Equity Trust, Inc.

A combination of stagnating wages and rising rents has left more than half of New York City dwellers economically burdened.[01] The scale of the city's housing crisis is pushing advocates, policymakers, academics, and average New Yorkers to seek out new ways to build and preserve affordable housing. One model that is gaining traction among some of the city's housing advocates is the community land trust (CLT). CLTs have a dual tenure structure, where the ownership of land and the ownership of property are separated. Urban CLTs frequently operate on a community-wide scale and seek to address broader issues beyond housing affordability, ranging from neighborhood stabilization to environmental sustainability. While New York City has a few existing CLTs, many challenges limit broader implementation, especially the high cost of land. The multifaceted nature of the CLT model is nonetheless pertinent to the city's housing crisis, a structural problem that cannot be addressed on the individual unit or building scale.

History and National Landscape

The CLT model is rooted in the civil rights movement of the 1960s. Activists established the first CLT—New Communities Land Trust in Albany, Georgia—to provide landownership opportunities to African-American farmers. The experiment eventually led to the founding of the Institute for Community Economics (ICE), which today is one of the key funders of CLTs across the US. In 2012, there were 258 CLTs, with 9,000 units of housing, distributed across 46 states.[02] There is a smaller sub-group of CLTs that function in urban areas like New York City, where city- and state-subsidized Mitchell-Lama limited equity cooperatives are the most prevalent form of shared equity housing.[03]

The CLT model falls into the shared equity category of tenure, which operates in a zone between homeownership and renting. This category—which includes CLTs along with limited equity cooperatives, mutual housing associations, and deed-restricted housing—ensures property affordability through sale-restriction mechanisms. In *Shared Equity Homeownership,* John Emmeus Davis defines CLTs as "a dual ownership model" where "the owner of the *land* is a nonprofit, community-based corporation, committed to acquiring multiple parcels of land throughout a targeted geographic area with the intention of retaining ownership of these parcels forever."[04] Buildings on CLT land may include single-family homes, rental buildings, condos, co-ops, and mixed-use structures with commercial or office spaces. CLTs lease land to property owners through long-term ground leases, which typically run for 99 years. The sale of property on CLT land is governed by a resale formula outlined in the ground lease, which usually gives the CLT the first right of purchase. When the CLT resells the property, for a below-market price to a buyer who meets agreed-upon income eligibility requirements, the deed to the building is conveyed to a new owner. The deed to the land remains with the CLT.

Like the first community land trust in Georgia, many urban CLTs today have also responded to the particular needs of different neighborhoods. Larger, well-established CLTs function like community development corporations, with a range of programs and professional staff. A prominent example is the Sawmill Community Land Trust, which grew out of a protest against a particleboard manufacturing plant in Albuquerque, New Mexico. The

> CLTs emerged in the Lower East Side, as extreme disinvestment and neighborhood abandonment in the 1970s gave way to aggressive real estate speculation in the 1980s.

polluted land was eventually acquired by the city for Superfund remediation. The Sawmill Community Development Corporation successfully petitioned the city to turn the land into a CLT.

The CLT model was chosen "to protect low-income residents from gentrification," said Chavez, "and to enable them to make decisions about and benefit from the redevelopment of the area … Sawmill is adjacent to the downtown business district and the historic Old Town area, one of New Mexico's biggest tourist attractions. The encroachment of these interests has caused real estate values in the surrounding neighborhoods to spiral upwards, pushing land and housing costs beyond the affordability of most families that have lived here for decades." The Sawmill CLT remediated 27 acres of land into Arbolera de Vida, which includes housing, a park, a community center, offices, retail space, manufacturing, senior apartments, and live/work spaces for home businesses.

Historical Context for CLTs in NYC

The Cooper Square and Rehabilitation in Action to Improve Neighborhoods (RAIN) CLTs both emerged during a turning point on the Lower East Side, as extreme disinvestment and neighborhood abandonment in the 1970s gave way to aggressive real estate speculation in the 1980s. While many CLTs focus on producing new housing units, both New York City cases emerged out of broader community organizing efforts focused on preserving the affordability of existing units.

In an in-depth study[05] of the Cooper Square CLT, Tom Angotti, Professor Emeritus of Urban Affairs and Planning at Hunter College and Cooper Square CLT board member, explains its roots in a community organizing effort against a 1959 urban renewal project initiated by Robert Moses, which would have demolished 11 blocks on the Lower East Side between the Bowery and Second Avenue. Community opposition formalized into the Cooper Square Committee (CSC) and developed an alternative plan for the area in 1961.

The 50-year saga of this alternative plan's implementation is described in *It Took 50 Years: Frances Goldin and the Struggle for Cooper Sq.* This unreleased documentary focuses on the plan's evolution in response to neighborhood change, and on Frances Goldin, one of the main driving forces behind its implementation. When the city finally accepted the alternative plan in the early 1970s, the Cooper Square Committee was "the first to confront the basic reality of retracting government" said Dave Powell, a housing activist and one of the film's documentarians. In 1973, the federal government put a moratorium on any new federally subsidized housing programs, making a key feature of the alternative plan—the development of new permanently and deeply affordable housing—unachievable. In the following years, the Cooper Square Committee shifted their focus to residential displacement due to fires and property neglect. By the late 1970s, the neighborhood was awash with tenant-occupied properties that were abandoned by their landlords and taken over by the city due to the non-payment of taxes. The Cooper Square Committee was aware of the Tenant Interim Lease (TIL) program that allowed tenants to turn their buildings into limited-equity cooperatives, according to Powell. However, the CSC also knew that affordability restrictions under the TIL program only lasted 15 to 20 years and realized that real estate speculation was beginning to put pressure on affordability restrictions in some newly formed cooperatives on the Lower East Side.

Therefore, the group settled on the CLT model after looking for "a limited-equity cooperative model that did not sacrifice permanent affordability," as stated by Powell. In 1991, the CSC created the Cooper Square CLT and the Cooper Square Mutual Housing Association (MHA), for 356 apartments in 22 formerly city-owned buildings. A few years ago, Cooper Square received State approval to turn the residential units into a limited-equity cooperative, which will remain a permanently affordable leaseholder of the Cooper Square CLT.

Cooper Square's multi-layered governance structure—with two distinct boards of directors—balances community control with permanent affordability. The MHA board—on which residents have a controlling stake—oversees the day-to-day management of the multi-family buildings that are on CLT land, acting as the property manager, developer, and owner. The CLT board acts as an affordability steward, by giving the control to members who "don't have a financial stake in the MHA," according to Harriet Putterman, the former chair of the Cooper Square CLT.

At the same time, the Cooper Square Committee continues to serve the broader Lower East Side community with a wide spectrum of programs like tenant counseling and social service referrals, the Senior Health, Advocacy and Recreation Program (SHARP), and a Streetscape Project on East Fourth Street.

The RAIN CLT is located a little bit further east on the Lower East Side. RAIN began as a coalition of homesteading groups, funded by the Lower East Side Catholic Area Conference (LESCAC), which itself was supported by Catholic Charities. RAIN was one of a myriad of grassroots groups that addressed the incongruence of a large stock of vacant city-owned buildings and a large population of people in need of housing, through homesteading[06] and squatting[07] in the 1970s and 1980s.

Like the Cooper Square Committee, LESCAC was also aware that many buildings converted into limited-equity co-ops through a range of city programs—including the short-lived homesteading program and TIL—were losing their affordability. Howard Brandstein, who at the time was working for LESCAC and now heads the Sixth Street Community Center, wrote in a 1984 position paper that "the land trust is a means for neighborhood residents to withstand the challenge of market forces entering the Lower East Side by bridging the separation between ownership as an expression of self-interest, on the one hand, and community empowerment on the other."[08]

Brandstein views CLTs as a "synthesis of anarchist and socialist thought." CLTs incorporate the anarchist perspective on self-help and mutual aid with one of the philosophies behind European social housing and American public housing, which holds the ownership of affordable housing for the greater public good.

Brandstein believes that the RAIN CLT ended up being "too weak in the community domain." The homesteading effort itself—claiming ownership of and rehabilitating buildings that were in legal limbo and deep physical distress—was monumental. The group did not have the capacity to create a fully developed CLT at the same time. Out of the 15 buildings homesteaded by RAIN, nine joined the CLT. However, each building functions as an independent cooperative, without the cohesion that is present at Sawmill or Cooper Square. Getting buy-in from homesteaders, who did not want to give up their autonomy, was difficult. RAIN granted homesteaders the controlling stake on the board, which is an uncommon setup for the landowning entity of CLTs. Nevertheless, the RAIN CLT still exists today, and has preserved the affordability of the nine cooperatives on its land.

CLTs in NYC today

In the past few years, interest in CLTs has spiked, promoted by housing and urban policy organizations like the National Housing Institute,[09] the Lincoln Institute of Land Policy, and the Cornerstone Partnership, large philanthropy groups like the Ford Foundation and the MacArthur Foundation, CLT-focused groups like the CLT

> CLTs incorporate the anarchist perspective on self-help and mutual aid with the philosophies behind European social housing and American public housing.

Community Land Trust

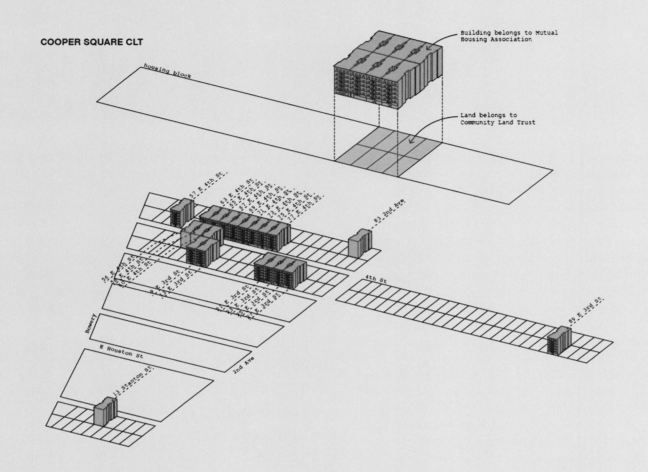

COOPER SQUARE CLT

The dual governance structure of Cooper Square MHA and Cooper Square CLT reflects the separation of land and property ownership. This is to ensure balance between the control of cooperative members and a permanent anchoring of the principle of affordability.

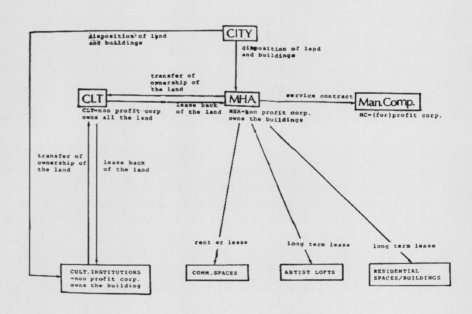

Scheme of the legal structure, property distribution, and relationship with the city as well as the tenants and leaseholders of Cooper Square MHA, 1990.

56

Banner on East 9th Street in 1984. The committee pushed for the renovation of buildings and the land trust model to counteract the pressure of the real estate market.

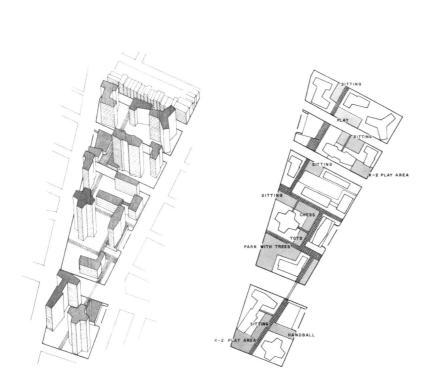

Aerial view and scheme of the counterproposal by Walter Thabit, which was approved by the city in the early 1970s. The preservation of about half of the blocks was significant, alongside various new buildings in a park landscape.

THE COOPER SQUARE AREA

Map of the Cooper Square urban renewal area. Robert Moses planned the demolition and redevelopment of 12 blocks on the Lower East Side. The Cooper Square Committee was formed in 1959.

Community Land Trust

Network and Burlington Associates, as well as the Federal Reserve. The CLT model's flexibility and adaptability to local conditions make it an appealing solution to a range of problems affecting communities across the country, including disinvestment, gentrification and displacement, foreclosure, loss of affordability due to expiring public subsidy, housing discrimination, and decreasing social capital.

In New York City, Picture the Homeless (PTH)—an organization founded and led by homeless and formerly homeless New Yorkers—identified the CLT model as a potential tool for addressing the severe shortage of permanently affordable housing within reach of people with extremely low incomes. Like activists on the Lower East Side in the 1980s, PTH wanted to highlight the disconnect between the city's vacant property and skyrocketing population of under-housed, homeless, and doubled-up New Yorkers. In 2011, PTH counted vacant lots and buildings in one third of the city's community boards. According to Arvernetta Henry, a member of PTH, "after the vacancy count, we started talking about CLTs. We took a tour of Cooper Square and saw how the model can benefit people in the shelter system."

The New York City Community Land Initiative (NYCCLI) grew out of several parallel efforts.[10] NYCCLI has four working groups: education and outreach, which facilitates discourse about the CLT model in the city; policy and legislation, which defines a legislative and policy agenda for CLTs; governance, which develops the governing structure framework for equitable and sustainable CLTs; and a pilot project group, which is actively working to start a CLT in East Harlem.

For Picture the Homeless, East Harlem seemed like a natural place for establishing a CLT, because the neighborhood "has a lot of buildings with expiring subsidies and gentrification pressure," according to Althea Yorke, another member of PTH active in NYCCLI. There is interest in the CLT model from Community Board 11, which recently co-produced a report with the Regional Plan Association that brought attention to the fact that one third of the neighborhood's affordable housing stock is set to expire by 2040. The report recommended CLTs as a potential strategy for preserving affordable units.

The East Harlem pilot project aims to bring city-owned properties, distressed low-income co-ops, and buildings preserved through the TIL or ANCP programs into the newly created CLT. The properties identified by NYCCLI for the pilot have a concrete reason for joining the CLT, which will provide financial relief and stability of tenure. In the 1970s, when the Cooper Square CLT and RAIN took shape, New York was awash in city-owned, tax-foreclosed property. Today, this is no longer the case. However, East Harlem still has a significant number of city-owned properties, due to municipal programs that addressed the problem of landlord abandonment.

Broader application of the CLT model

The problem of affordability loss due to expiring subsidies compounded by mounting gentrification pressure is not limited to East Harlem. Most subsidized housing constructed by private developers are affordable only for a set period of time, usually 20 years. The city experienced a wave of opt-outs during the height of the housing bubble, which has since subsided. However, "As long as the city retains a growing economy, the real estate market will exert a strong pressure toward rising private rents and the removal of subsidized housing from the at-risk affordable stock," according to a report by the Community Service Society.[11]

A diversion of even a portion of subsidized properties into a CLT would go a long way towards preserving the city's highly vulnerable affordable housing stock in perpetuity. Further, it would conserve the tax dollars that were spent on the construction and operation of these developments. The difficulty comes from finding a way to incentivize private landowners to join a CLT, and give up control over the disposition of land under their properties.

> A diversion of a portion of subsidized properties into a CLT would go a long way towards preserving the city's highly vulnerable affordable housing stock in perpetuity.

CLTs become more palatable when they offer the landowners or co-op shareholders something in return for transferring control over the land to the broader community (however it may be defined), beyond the knowledge that their property will serve as a resource to future generations of low- and moderate-income New Yorkers.

Today New York City has a sizable stock of privately owned, multi-family rental buildings in extreme physical distress and facing looming foreclosure. At the height of the housing bubble, some investors used the availability of cheap credit to overleverage[12] these buildings, with disastrous consequences for their tenants. While the problem of predatory equity is fairly unique to overheated housing markets in rapidly gentrifying cities like New York, the national foreclosure crisis affecting single-family homes had a severe effect on neighborhoods[13] with high rates of African-American homeownership, like St. Albans, Hollis, and Queens Village in southeast Queens. The CLT model could help single-family homeowners and tenants in multi-family buildings facing foreclosure to stay in their homes, and in the process create units affordable in perpetuity. Land acquisition is the key challenge for CLTs everywhere. According to Emily Thaden of the CLT Network, most CLTs use federal funding by the Department of Housing and Urban Development (HUD)[14] to purchase land.

Some have collaborative municipalities that funnel city- or state-owned land to CLTs, while others receive private land grants.

The transfer of city- or state-owned land to a CLT is generally the cheapest and easiest option. High real estate costs and changes to the city's tax policy in 1996 have decreased the number of buildings and lots the city controls. During their 2011 vacancy count, Picture the Homeless found 3,551 vacant buildings and 2,489 vacant lots in the 20 Community Boards they surveyed,[15] which is a significant number. However, only 10 percent of that property was city-owned. Of course, as Powell put it, "the lesson going forward is that the city should bank some of this land for community resources, as part of a citywide CLT. That way, when communities step forward with a plan for their own salvation, as Cooper Square did, the cost of land doesn't hold them back."

Future CLT projects in New York will have to look beyond city-owned properties, both because the city-owned property pool has shrunk significantly, and because our current housing crisis is rooted in an aggressive real estate market, rather than disinvestment. In order to take the CLT model to scale in New York City, the current administration would have to make a significant financial and political commitment to the idea. The administration's involvement is necessary for any group that may want to unravel the complex debt burdens carried by rental buildings affected by predatory equity or find a way to transfer privately held land into a CLT.

While the administration has not shown any inclinations toward a citywide or multi-neighborhood CLT yet, cities as varied as Chicago, Austin, Las Vegas, and Chaska, MN, have created their own CLTs, as highlighted in a 2007 article in *Shelterforce*.[16] Municipalities are increasingly initiating CLTs at a larger scale, usually as a means for preserving public subsidy and public land long-term across a range of neighborhoods. Some municipally initiated CLTs have governance structures that are different from community-initiated ones. The Chicago CLT's board is appointed by the Mayor, for example. A CLT's governance structure will reflect whether its main goal is to address the problem of expiring affordability or the issue of community control of its housing.

The model, if applied in tandem with a range of other policies, could be a step towards addressing New York City's growing crisis of inequality, by stabilizing the cost of land and "decommodifying property," as Hillary Caldwell, a researcher actively involved with NYCCLI, puts it. The heightened interest in CLTs from organizations as diverse as Picture the Homeless, the Ford Foundation, and the Federal Reserve may open new opportunities for the model's application. NYC's future CLT projects are likely to be very different from those that have been undertaken in the past, because the city has changed so much in the last 40 years. Two vital facets of CLT sustainability that should be cultivated within any future endeavor are active community participation, as well as a strong stewardship framework that will maintain the CLT well into the future.

This article is a revised version of a text, originally published on Urban Omnibus, *April 29, 2014, urbanomnibus.net/2014/04/the-value-of-land-how-community-land-trusts-maintain-housing-affordability.*

01 The Furman Center for Real Estate and Urban Policy, *#NYChousing. 10 Issues for NYC's Next Mayor* (2013), furmancenter.org/files/fact-sheets/NYChousingIntro.pdf (accessed February 16, 2018).
02 The Federal Reserve Bank of Richmond, "Community Land Trusts: An Alternative Approach to Affordable Homeownership and Neighborhood Revitalization," *MarketWise Community* 3, no. 1 (2012), housinglandtrust.org/pdf/MarketWise_vol03_issue01.pdf (accessed February 16, 2018).
03 Mitchell Lama was an affordable housing program created by New York State in 1955 to incentivize the development of limited equity cooperatives and rentals for moderate-income residents. The Mitchell-Lama program is no longer producing new housing units, but there are 33,000 rental and 61,000 cooperative Mitchell Lama units in NYC today, which serve low and moderate-income residents.
04 John Emmeus Davis, *Shared Equity Homeownership. The Changing Landscape of Resale-Restricted, Owner-Occupied Housing* (Montclair, NJ: National Housing Institute, 2008), 18, shelterforce.org/wp-content/uploads/2008/04/SharedEquityHome.pdf (accessed February 16, 2018).
05 Tom Angotti, *Community Land Trusts and Low-Income Multifamily Rental Housing. The Case of Cooper Square, New York City* (Lincoln Institute of Land Policy, 2007), www.lincolninst.edu/publications/working-papers/community-land-trusts-low-income-multifamily-rental-housing (accessed February 16, 2018).
06 See John Curl, *The Cooperative Movement in Century 21*, July 10, 2010, trustcurrency.blogspot.de/2010/07/cooperative-movement-in-century-21.html (accessed February 16, 2018).
07 See Cari Luna, "Squatters of the Lower East Side," *Jacobin*, April 3, 2014, www.jacobinmag.com/2014/04/squatters-of-the-lower-east-side (accessed February 16, 2018).
08 Howard Brandstein, "Toward a sheltering community: Developing a land trust for the Lower East Side,"*LESCAC Position Paper,* 1984.

09 See Miriam Axel-Lute, "Investing in Community Land Trusts. A Conversation with Funders of CLTs," presented at the Neighborhood Funders Group Annual Meeting, Minneapolis, September 2010, shelterforce.org/2010/12/21/investing_in_community_land_trusts_a_conversation_with_clt_funders (accessed February 16, 2018).
10 Representatives of Picture the Homeless, along with the New Economy Project, Community Board 11 (East Harlem), and the Housing Environments Research Group (HERG) at the CUNY Graduate Center convened at the Ford Foundation in 2012 to identify ways to promote the CLT model in New York City.
11 Tom Waters and Victor Bach, "Good Place to Work, Hard Place to Live," Community Service Society (New York, 2013), 2, b.3cdn.net/nycss/1c9817fd6343bf9c88_lkm6va7t8.pdf (accessed February 16, 2018).
12 See *Predatory Equity. A Survival Guide*, Making Policy Public (New York, 2009), www.welcometocup.org/file_columns/0000/0021/pepdffinal.pdf (accessed February 16, 2018).
13 See Amanda Fung, "Southeast Queens is foreclosure central," *Crain's New York Business*, October 3, 2010, www.crainsnewyork.com/article/20101003/REAL_ESTATE/310039983/southeast-queens-is-foreclosure-central (accessed February 16, 2018).
14 The United States Department of Housing and Urban Development (HUD) is the country's federal housing agency. It provides funding for the operation of public and subsidized housing for low-income people; enforces federal laws against housing discrimination; and conducts research about national housing needs and market conditions.
15 Picture the Homeless, *Banking on Vacancy. Homelessness and Real Estate Speculation*, 2011, picturethehomeless.org/project/banking-on-vacancy-homelessness-real-estate-speculation (accessed February 16, 2018).
16 Michael Brown, "City Hall Steps In", *Shelterforce* 149, 2007, shelterforce.org/2007/04/23/city_hall_steps_in (accessed February 16, 2018).

"Property Entails Obligations"[01]

Hans-Jochen Vogel explains the first urban development plan for Munich in 1963. Film stills from the TV report *München. Großstadt mit Tradition und Zukunft* (Bayerisches Fernsehen, 1963).

HANS-JOCHEN VOGEL
IN CONVERSATION WITH
ARNO BRANDLHUBER
AND CHRISTOPHER ROTH

ARNO BRANDLHUBER: *Mr. Vogel, you made a major effort[02] to reform land law in the 1970s. Playing an important role in this effort was the German Association of Cities in 1971, where the then-President of the Federal Republic, Gustav Heinemann, addressed land law reform in his welcoming address.[03] Can you describe the political context that made such an initiative possible?*
HANS-JOCHEN VOGEL: The motto of the 1971 Annual Meeting of the German Association of Cities in Munich was "Save Our Cities Now!" I remember that very well. Issues regarding land prices and land legislation played a key role in this context. The main focus was on the financing of municipalities, and municipal tax revenues. Federal President Heinemann's welcoming address dealt mainly with the issue of land prices.

The problem was blatantly apparent in Munich, where the cost of land had risen by 372 percent between 1950 and 1970. As a result, there were already considerable increases in rents at that time, although the share of social housing was still higher than it is today. This increase also meant that the city had to spend additional millions on land that it needed for public infrastructure. Gustav Heinemann recognized all of these problems and articulated them in his appeal.

That set things rolling. The Urban Development Promotion Act was passed that same year, in 1971. Although it didn't include concrete regulations on land prices, it provided the municipalities with additional tools to develop new districts or districts in need of rehabilitation. For example, it gave public authorities the right to issue building orders, demolition orders, and other possibilities for intervention. My tenure as mayor of Munich ended in December 1972, after the Olympic Games. Then I became federal minister for Regional Planning, Building, and Urban Development. One of my central tasks was to amend the Federal Building Code by introducing the planning gains tax as a key issue. I wasn't the only one

who thought it was a great injustice that if a municipality had to compensate a landowner, it had to factor in the actual high land prices, which were partly due to planning decisions, yet if a landowner sold land, all the planning gains remained with him. Although Article 14 of the Basic Law is sometimes quoted ("property entails obligations"), I would also like to draw attention to the Bavarian Constitution. It specifies that effortless land gains are to be used for the common good. The Bavarian state governments have hardly—or not at all—complied with this mandate of their constitution.[04] Instead, they claimed it was made obsolete by the Basic Law, which came into force later on.
AB: *Can you explain the term "effortless land gain?"*
HJV: Land gains are increases in value resulting from the fact that a landowner, for example, develops a piece of land or changes its use. The landowner provides a service and takes risks, by taking out a loan, for example. When owners provide benefits and take risks, they should also be entitled to the profits made from them. But if an owner doesn't invest, and instead leaves the property to lie unused or continues to use it as before, and the

land price rises, then this isn't due to the owner's efforts, but because the city is growing and demand is accordingly increasing, or because surrounding areas have been made available for development. Owners can skim off these land gains when selling or renting, even when they aren't responsible for them.

The key element in my proposal for the Federal Building Code was that the municipalities should receive 100 percent of effortless planning gains. In addition to this law, there were ideas about laying claim to the steadily increasing gains through income tax or a special property tax arrangement. But at the time, the Ministry of Finance wasn't interested in such a radical overhaul of the existing legislation.

Before I moved to the Ministry of Justice in May 1974, when Willy Brandt resigned and Helmut Schmidt formed the government, I presented my revised draft to the cabinet. It no longer provided for a 100 percent levy on planning gains, but only 50 percent, in response to objections by the FDP. But it was better than nothing. The draft was debated for two years, first in the Bundestag, then in the Bundesrat, then again in the Bundestag, and in various committees and parliaments. When it finally came into force, the planning gains tax had completely disappeared.

AB: *In 1972, your article "Land Law and Urban Development" was published in the journal* Neue Juristische Wochenschrift.[05] *In it, you go into detail about regulations such as the planning value adjustment[06] and the land value supplemental tax.[07] These fiscal instruments aimed to reform legislation on expropriation and compensation.[08]*
HJV: Yes, one of my suggestions was to address the land valuation issue, which continues to be the subject of debate even today. Taxation of real estate in the former GDR is still based on values calculated according to the status of 1935, and in the former Federal Republic according to the status of 1964.

Today the main question should be: What must be done to slow down price increases? Prices have been rising continuously, by up to 12 percent annually in recent years. On average, the increase is more than five or six percent per year in the whole of Germany, although lower price increases and

decreases in the new federal states are taken into account.

In Munich—and I hardly dare say the figures—the price of land rose by 352 percent between 1950 and 1972, and has increased by about 36,000 percent to date! How can society remain silent about this? Why isn't this issue on the agenda? Why doesn't society put up a fight?

This deserves a small footnote: In the early 1990s, there was actually an amendment to the Federal Building Code, allowing municipalities to draw up contracts with building permit applicants. That's practicable social land management. But only a few cities, Munich included, made use of it. It gave investors a certain amount of security for going through complicated procedures, and in return they provided the city with part of their planning gain, which was used for needed infrastructure construction. It's such a simple approach, and easy to implement. And in individual cases, Munich has received considerable sums of money from investors as a result.

AB: *You made an explicit reform proposal in 1972. The reorganization you proposed would change the existing landownership concept by distinguishing between the right of use and right of disposal[09]—a rather radical approach. What made that discussion possible at that time? And how did you envisage its implementation?*
HJV: Before addressing the issue of distinguishing between land and property ownership and rights of use and disposal, I want to mention the political situation surrounding the planning gains tax. It wasn't only the SPD, but almost the whole political spectrum that was dealing with the issue at that time, between 1970 and 1972. At its party congress in 1973, the CSU also voiced its support of the planning gains tax and, at my suggestion, compiled suggestions in the Munich City Council. A commission then elaborated on these proposals, an approach that also received strong support from Oswald von Nell-Breuning, a main proponent of the Catholic social doctrine. The CDU executive committee supported the planning gains tax as well, but then it was rejected at its party congress in autumn 1973. The FDP's Freiburg Program reflects some similar ideas. I just wanted to mention enough to make it clear that, at the time, the issue was being addressed across the board.

Spiegel cover from June 1971, presenting outdated land laws as a problem for the community and impediment to thriving urbanity.
© Der Spiegel 24/1971

Now, back to your question. At the time, I wasn't alone in the opinion that we couldn't solve the problem merely by levying a tax on planning gains. We had learned how in Stockholm, the city was the primary landowner, and only granted leaseholds. In the case of leasehold rights, the building owner is in possession of the building, but the land remains in the ownership of the municipality. In 1973, the SPD's party congress accepted our suggestion to apply this model more frequently in Germany. Unfortunately, and I have to criticize my party in this as well, although the topic was pursued for a while, it was then more or less implicitly buried.

In 1989, I again took a step in this direction with a proposal to amend my party's Berlin Program so that the municipalities, as landowners, would benefit from increases in the value of their land assets. The building owner, as the user, would benefit from the building's value increase, but this wouldn't grow as much as the land price. This partial expropriation wasn't intended for the entire nation but was limited to certain problem areas and property that the municipalities already owned; after all, most municipalities had a certain inventory of land. It was then decided not to speak in terms of use and disposal rights, meaning a new ownership construct, but in terms of leasehold rights, which would essentially lead to the same results.

However, conservative circles succeeded in raising fears among owners of single-family homes and owner-occupied

Land Policy

Prices for residential land in Munich
by district in 2016.

*Prices for individual residential land in Munich increased
by an average of 29.8% from 2014 to 2016.*

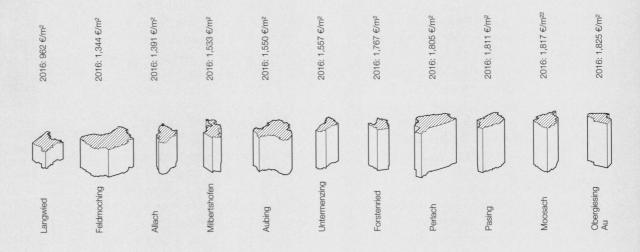

2016: 962 €/m²	2016: 1,344 €/m²	2016: 1,391 €/m²	2016: 1,533 €/m²	2016: 1,550 €/m²	2016: 1,557 €/m²	2016: 1,767 €/m²	2016: 1,805 €/m²	2016: 1,811 €/m²	2016: 1,817 €/m²²	2016: 1,825 €/m²
Langwied	Feldmoching	Allach	Milbertshofen	Aubing	Untermenzing	Forstenried	Perlach	Pasing	Moosach	Obergiesing Au

Price development of residential land in Munich.

This real estate market report from 2016
does not indicate details for the
inner city districts Altstadt, Haidhausen,
Lehel, Maxvorstadt, Sendling,
or for Ludwigsfeld und Schwabing.

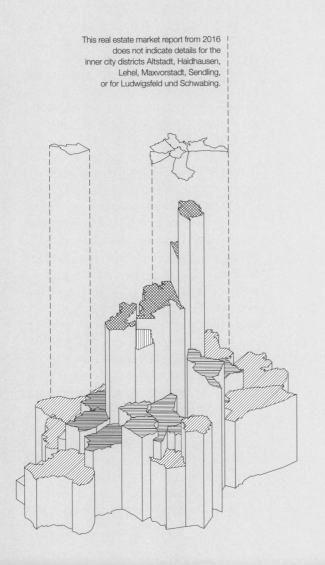

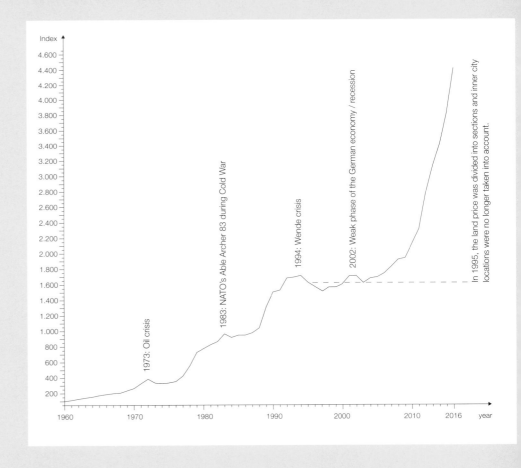

In 1995, the land price was divided into sections and inner city locations were no longer taken into account.

1973: Oil crisis

1983: NATO's Able Archer 83 during Cold War

1994: Wende crisis

2002: Weak phase of the German economy / recession

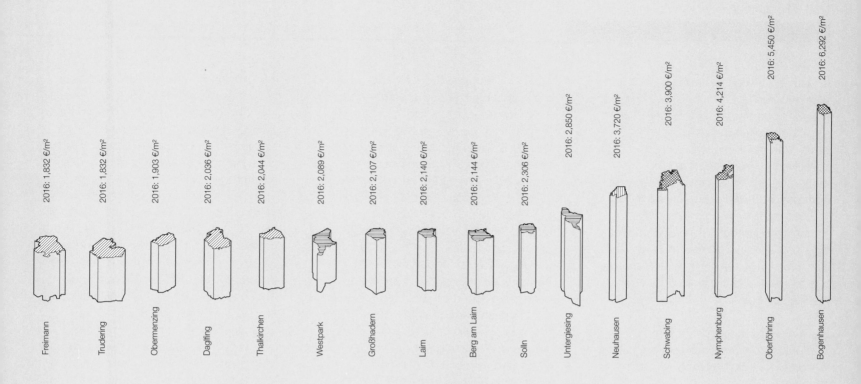

2016: 1,832 €/m² — Freimann
2016: 1,832 €/m² — Trudering
2016: 1,903 €/m² — Obermenzing
2016: 2,036 €/m² — Daglfing
2016: 2,044 €/m² — Thalkirchen
2016: 2,089 €/m² — Westpark
2016: 2,107 €/m² — Großhadern
2016: 2,140 €/m² — Laim
2016: 2,144 €/m² — Berg am Laim
2016: 2,306 €/m² — Solln
2016: 2,850 €/m² — Untergiesing
2016: 3,720 €/m² — Neuhausen
2016: 3,900 €/m² — Schwabing
2016: 4,214 €/m² — Nymphenburg
2016: 5,450 €/m² — Oberföhring
2016: 6,292 €/m² — Bogenhausen

Development of residential land prices, construction prices, consumer prices, and household disposable incomes per inhabitant in Munich.

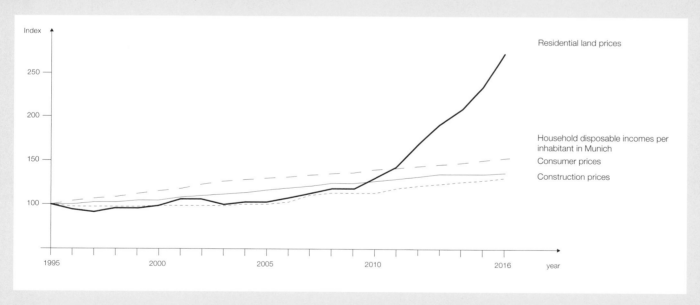

Residential land prices

Household disposable incomes per inhabitant in Munich

Consumer prices

Construction prices

All graphics: Annalena Morra © Brandlhuber+
Sources: Geschäftsstelle des Gutachterausschusses für Grundstückswerte im Bereich der Landeshauptstadt München: Der Immobilienmarktbericht in München: Jahresberichte 1980, 1995, 2016; Duken & V. Wangenheim (2017): "Münchener Grundstückspreise haben sich verdoppelt. Amtliche Bodenrichtwerte München", www.wangenheim.de/de/unternehmen/news/muenchner_grundstueckspreise_ haben_ sich_verdoppelt (accessed February 28, 2018).

apartments—meaning millions of citizens, whose potential protest plays a significant role for all parties—that this reform was targeted against them. But it was never planned in the way that the public perceived it. From the beginning, the ownership of single-family homes and condominiums was explicitly excluded!

And there were no general rules for farmland, either. The provision would only take effect when the property was converted into a building plot. Because it is precisely this conversion that brings the highest gains.

AB: *So was it a populist argument that prevented further debate about land law at various points, including within the SPD?*

HJV: The fear of being accused of expropriation indeed prevented the SPD from pursuing the land issue. And I'm not denying that there were more urgent problems at the time: East-West tensions, the NATO Double-Track decision, German unification, and growing concerns about nuclear energy. To be fair, I must admit

1980–81, brought about by squatting and the loss of the majority in parliament. It led my predecessor, Dietrich Stobbe, to announce his resignation. In order to avoid a political impasse, I agreed to stand for election and was elected governing mayor at the end of January 1981. At the beginning of February, I delivered the policy speech that you quoted. In it, I articulated what I had always drawn attention to: that land is not an arbitrary commercial object. On the contrary, no human being can live for even one second without the use of land. I put land on par with water and air. By that analogy, we would have to differentiate the rules of the market (and the market does have its merits, in the form of the social market economy) according to goods that can and cannot be multiplied arbitrarily. You can live without the use of a car, but not without land. That's what my Berlin policy statement says.

AB: *You also made a very nice comparison at the Bergedorf Round Table in 1981: "As far as non-violent offenses are*

tax evasion is rated significantly higher than the non-violent offense of trespassing. One would expect that the amount of public uproar, particularly in the media, would reflect the gravity of the violation." Why did you emphasize proportionality so strongly?

HJV: There was also cause for the comparison in Berlin, because the public reaction to non-violent trespassing in the form of squatting, on the one hand, and to tax evasion, on the other hand, were drastically different. Tax evasion received little attention. Today this is different: the uproar about tax evasion is now stronger than it is about non-violent trespassing. Back then, we were busy addressing the squatting situation and the violence that accompanied it. It was in this context that I proposed a Berlin Line of proportionality, as I did after the Schwabing riots in Munich in 1962. Proportionality means that for the police to intervene, simple facts alone were not enough, and other factors had to be considered. In particular, what to do with the vacated buildings and the people

that those pressing issues made it difficult for other topics to catch on.

AB: *In the early 1980s, you moved from federal politics to the state level, and became the governing mayor of West Berlin. In that role, you continued to deal with the land issue, articulating in your policy statement: "Had we a land law that would treat property not as a commodity that can be arbitrarily multiplied, but as an elementary basic need, like water or bread, decisive focal points for the latent readiness to use force would disappear." What was the situation you found yourself in, as you formulated this sentence?*

HJV: The city, and especially my party, were in a crisis at the turn of the year

concerned, they must also be dealt with by means of the law. But in doing so, it is important to maintain credibility in both directions and to consider proportionality. I have personally learned profound lessons about the extent to which our sense of justice is affected by trespassing, for example, and what negative consequences this can have. I take such lessons quite seriously. Yet I sometimes wonder why this kind of violation attracts such sustained and emotional attention, while tax evasion, economic crimes, and fiscal issues, which are common to all democratic parties, provoke a far lower degree of emotional response. According to the penal code, the non-violent offense of

involved had to be clarified. The Berlin Line was also recognized by the public prosecutor's office in specific cases, and was essentially adopted by my successor, Richard von Weizsäcker.

AB: *You again managed to include the land issue in the Berlin Declaration of 1989. How could it be put back on the agenda today?*

HJV: The land issue is a national responsibility and can therefore only be addressed at federal level. Nowadays, you must always keep in mind whether something might fall under the jurisdiction of the European Union, but that's not the case here.

Unfortunately, other problems are pushing their way to the fore again. I think it's worth considering including Article 14 of the Basic Law and Article 168 of the Bavarian Constitution as a topic in the election campaign platforms. I can understand that my party is prioritizing other issues at the moment, especially since they aren't being pressured about it by the municipalities or, as before, by the Association of Cities. I would like to see the land issue put back on the agenda. If I can still contribute to this objective, then I will give it serious consideration. At least I would ask the responsible bodies, mayors, or associations why this challenge is being met with so much passivity.

AB: *What is the relevance of this issue today?*
HJV: Rents are rising continuously. Cities must spend ever-increasing amounts on the land they need to build schools, hospitals, roads, and infrastructure for growing urban districts. Amounts that God knows could be better used for something more meaningful. In my view, there's still no justification today for the enormous windfalls going to incidental landowners.

AB: *It's really a systemic issue that gains are privatized yet costs are socialized. For example, land gains are tax-free after 10 years. Why isn't it possible to overhaul this system?*
HJV: I find this criticism too general. Our tax system actually does skim off considerable gains. It's not the case that gains are not taxed, and in fact, the current government is trying to close the loopholes. Your mention of the tax exemption of property gains after the 10-year period brings us back to the land issue. This is indeed a problem, but I don't accept that it's because of a problem with the system as a whole. Incidentally, there's a lot of talk about raising the top tax rates, and there's a ruling on inheritance

tax by the Federal Constitutional Court. Meanwhile, precautions have also been taken to ensure that, in the event of future bank failures, the bank's shareholders are called to task first, so it can't be said that gains aren't taxed while losses are socialized in Germany.

CHRISTOPHER ROTH: *You mentioned the distinction between the building and the property with regard to ownership. Where would you start in addressing the land issue today?*
HJV: If I do address this again, then it won't be in order to focus on the question of use and disposal rights, but primarily on the issue of planning gains. I would build on what the SPD and CSU agreed on in 1973. I wouldn't blame anyone— that would be the normal route, and too easy. No, I wouldn't blame, but ask questions. And I would ask—since we

have tackled and solved other big problems, our Eastern policy to name just one—whether we shouldn't put the issue of the planning gains tax back on the agenda. Or whether we should discuss the reasons why this won't happen in future, despite the dramatic increases and despite the fact that land is something indispensable that everyone needs in order to live.

CR: *Won't it be too late at some point?*
HJV: Forgive me, but now that all this has been on the table for nearly 40 years, a delay of one or two years is probably not too late. You've only recently taken up the issue, haven't you?

Our special thanks go to Stephan Trüby, Chair of Architectural and Cultural Theory at the Technical University of Munich, for organizing the discussion.

01 *Basic Law for the Federal Republic of Germany*, Art. 14: (1) Property and the right of inheritance shall be guaranteed. Their content and limits shall be defined by the laws. (2) Property entails obligations. Its use shall also serve the common good. (3) Expropriation shall only be permissible for the benefit of the common good. It may only be ordered by or pursuant to a law that determines the nature and extent of compensation. Such compensation shall be determined by establishing an equitable balance between the public interest and the interests of those affected. In case of dispute concerning the amount of compensation, recourse may be had to the ordinary courts.
02 Hans-Jochen Vogel, "Bodenrechtsreform. Ein Modellfall für gesellschaftliche Reformprozesse," in Heinrich Böll, Helmut Gollwitzer, Carlo Schmid (eds.), *Anstoß und Ermutigung. Gustav W. Heinemann Bundespräsident*

1969–1974 (Frankfurt: Suhrkamp, 1974), 21.
03 More on the German Association of Cities in Munich, 1971, in "Rettet unsere Städte jetzt! Vorträge, Aussprachen und Ergebnisse der 16. Hauptversammlung des Deutschen Städtetages vom 25. bis 27. Mai 1971 in München," in *Neue Schriften des Deutschen Städtetages*, 28 (Stuttgart: W. Kohlhammer, 1971).
04 Art. 161 of the Constitution of the Free State of Bavaria: (on land distribution and use): (1) The distribution and use of land shall be supervised by the state. Any misuse must be ended. (2) Any increase of the value of the land which arises without special effort or capital expenditure of the owner shall be utilised for the general public.
05 Hans-Jochen Vogel, "Bodenrecht und Stadtentwicklung," in *Neue Juristische Wochenschrift* 35 (1972), 1544ff. Reprinted in Arno Brandlhuber, Florian Hertweck, Thomas Mayfried

(eds.), *The Dialogic City— Berlin wird Berlin* (Cologne: Walther König 2015), 651ff.
06 Vogel, ibid.: "The following measures seem to be necessary for this purpose from a municipal point of view […] The planning value equalization as a counterpart to planning compensation. Under the principle of equal treatment, there is no reason why a landowner can pass on losses resulting from reclassifications to the public, yet fully benefit from value increases resulting from reclassification or upzoning."
07 Vogel, ibid.: "A land value supplemental tax on extraordinary value increases that are not the result of reclassifications or own contributions (e.g. development) and which go beyond an appropriate return on the capital invested in the land. The tax should not be levied on building value increases but only on land value increases, irrespective of whether they have already occurred through sale or are unrea-

lized gains. Limiting the tax to realized gains would reduce the inclination to sell and act as an additional market barrier."
08 Vogel, ibid.: "A reform of expropriation and compensation legislation that facilitates expropriation, separates the compensation procedures, and introduces a price-limited right of first refusal. If this right is exercised, the agreed purchase price shall be replaced by the amount which would have to be granted in the event of compensation."
09 Vogel, ibid.: "The previous ownership of land shall be divided into the right of use and the right of disposal. The right of disposal shall be transferred to the community. It establishes terminable or limited-use ownership of individual areas by means of contracts that stipulate the type of use, the usage fee, and the duration of the use. If this is not contrary to community interests, the right of use shall be granted by means of a public invitation to tender."

Toward a New Land Policy

EGBERT DRANSFELD
IN CONVERSATION WITH
ARNO BRANDLHUBER

ARNO BRANDLHUBER: *Why does the housing problem hinge on the question of landownership and land policy?*
EGBERT DRANSFELD: It's essentially a simple observation: *no housing without land.* And yet, strikingly, large parts of society—be it politicians, experts, or civil society at large—look at land policy and housing policy as separate issues. Once we recognize that the land market is upstream from the residential real estate market, the need for action becomes clear: *we need a steady supply of buildable land that actually reaches the market!* When the supply of buildable land dwindles or dries up, economic effects come into play. Prices rise and real estate speculation ensues.

AB: *That's an issue I'd like to discuss with you on several levels—global and European, and especially with a view to the situation in Germany—in order to find out what the best course of action might be. Let's start with Raquel Rolnik, the former UN Special Rapporteur on adequate housing as a basic right. Her report very quickly turns to the issue of land use and property policies* (see Raquel Rolnik, p. 110–111).
ED: Land and its development are basic prerequisites for housing, and providing housing is a universal goal. All over the world, what's needed is access to land. The question, then, is whether land is available and who holds the right to determine its use, or in other words, how property and its distribution are organized. The legal structure of property is a fundamental determinant, but also a reflection, of the prevailing conception of land policy in different societies. So when we talk about land and its availability, we're ultimately also talking about questions of power. Who controls and allocates land and real property?

If the availability of buildable land is the primary prerequisite for more housing, what we need first and foremost is land that's connected to the necessary infrastructures. It must be ready for building in accordance with the applicable construction planning laws, which is to say, the requisite planning and technical development measures must have been implemented. But how can buildable land be made available in a society that has organized its land policies by instituting a particular set of property rights?

This is where, in my mind, a fundamental dilemma seems to loom around the world that is connected to the various legal structures governing landownership. Although most countries have laws that reflect a political will to organize land use with a view to the common good, the land is often already divided up between owners. So how do you strike a balance between safeguarding the public interest in controlling land use and protecting existing real property rights? That's the crucial question.

The public interest in controlling land use often necessitates infringements on the private right to determine the uses made of land. Such interventions can be quite beneficial to owners: when urban planning and infrastructure construction turn unzoned and undeveloped land into fully-developed, buildable land, property values rise considerably. Especially when cities and municipalities implement these measures, landowners often effectively profit at the public expense without lifting a finger. The alternative is that private owners are excluded from the urban planning process, and the result may be that, economically speaking, nothing ever changes.

Organizing the actual process of making buildable land available in a way that doesn't sufficiently take the common good into account and leaves it largely or entirely to private developers and other private owners or investors often leads to major problems in the land market. Ensuring a supply of buildable land should be seen as a basic public service whose primary objective is the common good, not much different from the demand-driven construction and operation of, say, preschools, schools, and transportation infrastructures. That, in a nutshell, is my basic proposition, which I've derived primarily from a study of the situation in Germany; but the problem may well be a global one.

AB: *So there's a link between property rights—whether or not land is a freely tradable asset—and questions of how to promote the common good. Societies deal with these questions in very different ways. In Amsterdam, for instance, where the leasing of heritable building rights is a widely used tool.*
ED: This concerns the question of how fully developed buildable land is allocated to third parties for use. Now we're talking about the instrumental level, meaning, for example, which legal constructs and particular stipulations we use to organize the allocation of land, for instance when cities and municipalities have already developed land at their own expense. Another concept that comes up in such cases is interim acquisition by the municipality. This is where the different legal property structures are crucial. Once the land has been developed—once good urban planning is in place and the actual work of development has been done—are the plots reprivatized right away or are they allocated using other forms of ownership such as heritable building rights?

Leasing heritable building rights is an established practice in some countries. It's widespread in the Netherlands, a country where, because of the tradition of land reclamation and the associated cultural understanding of landownership, the state doesn't sell all buildable land to private owners and real estate developers; some is retained as municipal public property. What is sold are rights of use. Israel, I believe, is another country that has allocated significant parts of its territory through rights of use. The British leasehold system, also, is not altogether unlike the German *Erbbaurecht* or heritable building rights (see glossary, p. 48–51).

The upside to allocating rights of use is that, from the long-term perspective, the public, the state, retains potential control of the land, which makes it easier to avoid misuse, and any increase in land values accrues to the public rather than being siphoned off by private owners. The advantages for the municipalities are considerable. Unfortunately, over the past two decades, municipalities have sold off much of the land they owned, almost like a fire sale. They moved in exactly the wrong direction.

AB: *Champions of "small government" often argue that the public sector is bad at managing property. This neoliberal reasoning dominated the discourse in the 1990s and shaped government policies. The consequence was a privatization campaign that ultimately left the public sector incapable of exerting any control. One of your studies refers to Hamburg as an example of an active land policy in which the municipality retains ownership of a* basic *property portfolio.*
ED: Hamburg, and some other cities such as Ulm, have pursued long-term land supply policies for decades, even centuries. These cities and towns are aware that ensuring a supply of developed land ready for building is a basic public service they need to take into their own hands, and so they plan for the long term. We're not talking about project-related land development proposals to be implemented in three to five years; this is a matter of decades—20 to 50 years or more.

These are policies that need to be organized: you need public authorities and financial structures that enable the city to continually acquire undeveloped land before planning for it begins. By buying land early on, cities and municipalities build sizable portfolios and implement an active property policy focused on the community's interests. This lets the municipalities realize and harness the

profits generated by land appreciation due to planning decisions. And when they confront specific urban development challenges, such as an urgent housing shortage, they have an inventory of suitable plots ready. That's without doubt a key strategy.

AB: *But many municipalities are already strapped for cash. Doesn't that mean that an active land policy isn't widely feasible? Critics would ask: how can you buy land when you don't have money? Might a revolving fund be a solution, one that would not only buy land but also reinvest the surplus value generated by its utilization? Would it be possible to set up such a fund without subsidizing it in perpetuity?*
ED: Municipalities that have pursued this strategy over the long term have demonstrated that it's possible to build a self-sustaining revolving municipal land fund. So it's not a money-losing proposition. Of course, the initial establishment of a land fund—as the first step of a strategic land supply policy, as it were—requires financial support from public coffers. But that's ultimately a more general question of distribution: where or into what is public money invested and what are the priorities behind these decisions? Even cities and municipalities that have not pursued land supply policies in the past usually already own properties they acquired at some point. These properties are assets that can be used as seed capital for a fund.

An alternative would be to transfer the fund to a municipal corporation. This often becomes necessary when municipalities have serious budget imbalances and are already largely barred from making investments of any kind without the approval of higher-level authorities. These municipalities, which are subject to strict budget consolidation regulations, can regain control of their finances by, as it were, moving the land fund off their books and transferring it to a separate municipal real estate corporation, which can be organized, for example, as a limited liability company. The municipal development companies that set up and manage such land funds are then enterprises but still fully controlled by the public.

AB: *When there is land at the public's disposal, these questions arise: who gets to build on it, and how to attach conditions that are in the social interest. Berlin, for example, has been struggling with a housing shortage for years. So the city-owned residential development companies—luckily they still have properties—could do the building. But there's the question of financing construction. Might we imagine a mixed model in which more expensive apartments cross-subsidize below-market rents for low-income tenants? Might this also be a way to achieve socially mixed neighborhoods?*
ED: Let's assume that thanks to a long-term land supply policy, municipally owned plots are available. What we now need is a functioning system on the municipal level to provide buildable land. It's my firm belief that the *development of buildable land*—the regulatory processes and infrastructure construction—should be increasingly, even exclusively, a municipal responsibility; it should not be in the hands even of municipally-owned development companies. By contrast, *developing the actual buildings* should still be left to municipally and privately owned builders, which is to say, the market.

A crucial aspect of this strategy is that it lets the municipalities exert control over their own fully developed land, or in other words, plots that are ready to build. Private law then gives them virtually complete discretion over whom to sell these plots to and at which price, largely bypassing the time-consuming complications of public law.

In recent years, we've had some positive experiences in Germany with so-called concept tendering procedures (see glossary). Tendering criteria can stipulate a whole host of things, such as the standards according to which buildable land developed by the municipality is allocated, and at which prices, or deductions for low-cost housing or mandatory quotas of rentals reserved for low-income tenants. All these things are very easy to stipulate in the property purchase agreement.

AB: *Should the public actually sell land it owns or merely lease rights of use, such as heritable building rights? What are the advantages of the latter model for the municipalities?*

ED: There are different aspects to this question: on the one hand, there's the public interest in exerting control over land use; on the other hand, there's the fiscal side. Let's talk about the land-use issue first. From the perspective of urban planning, leasing heritable building rights allows municipalities to orchestrate a long-term urban development strategy, by allocating the right plots in the right place at the right time. The land remains publicly owned, and if the need arises one day to use it for a different purpose, or during periods of high structural vacancy rates, the municipality has leeway to revise its land use strategy.

As for the financial aspect: unfortunately, municipalities that struggle with liquidity problems still try to sell properties in which third parties have leaseholds. Given today's high land prices, such sales sometimes bring in considerable revenues that help balance municipal budgets. But when you look at it more closely, this approach and the argument behind it are unpersuasive. When you lease heritable building rights instead of selling the land outright, you earn consistent ground rents of generally between two and five percent of the property's value, depending on the use. These revenues are usually guaranteed to grow over time because the rents rise, for example because they're indexed to the cost of living. You'd think that would be a solid investment, also in times of uncertainty. But—and this is a useful argument to have ready when you're dealing with treasurers, some of whom are still critical of this model—municipalities are now required by law to switch from the old fiscal accounting to the standard double-entry bookkeeping system practiced by corporations. In this system, land on which others have leaseholds is part of a municipality's land fund, and as long as it's not sold, it stays in the credit column, as it were, and with its full value, so on the balance sheet there's no outflow of assets. Then, it's important to understand that the ground rent payments amount to an additional consistent revenue source.

In the medium and long term, cities and municipalities stand to derive not inconsiderable additional fiscal advantages from this steady revenue, as model calculations demonstrate very clearly.

What's more, assuming that the real estate market will remain somewhat tight, land values will generally rise. The appreciation is taken into account in value adjustments—at some point a plot's value is, say, 500 instead of 300 euros per square meter. These gains, which may accrue over years and decades, are an additional accounting profit for the municipalities. Leasing heritable building rights is a shrewd way to operationalize these gains to the municipalities' benefit. So from a fiscal perspective, there are no longer any good arguments against leaseholds.

One problem we currently have is that due to the persistently low interest rates of the past several years—which are in part a product of political decisions—real estate buyers can get very cheap financing. If you charge ground rents of between two and five percent while a prospective buyer could finance the purchase at 1.5 or 1.8 percent interest, leaseholds are *prima facie* the less attractive option for those who want to build on a plot. Therefore the municipalities are under pressure because it makes better economic sense right now for users to buy the land outright.

AB: *We might also turn the argument on its head. Especially in very tight markets—where access to buildable plots is the main concern—it's better to have building rights to a plot than to have no land at all.*

ED: That's exactly my view. If municipalities were more actively involved in or even entirely in charge of developing buildable land, the question or problem wouldn't even come up. Land would be allocated—when and where desirable—solely by leasing heritable building rights, putting developers in a bit of a bind, given the lack of alternative markets.

AB: *This argument has been made for decades; one prominent proponent is the Social Democratic politician Hans-Jochen Vogel* (see Hans-Jochen Vogel, p. 60–65). *Like Vogel, you've pointed to a 1967 Federal Constitutional Court decision, from which I'd like to quote a short passage:*

> "Contrary to the complainant's view, there is no constitutional requirement that the trade in rural land be as unrestricted as the trade in any other 'capital.' The fact that land cannot be increased and is indispensable forbids leaving its use entirely to the incalculable free play of market forces and the discretion of the individual; a just legal and social order necessitates instead that the interests of the public be asserted much more forcefully with regard to land than with other assets. The economic and social significance of land is not neatly comparable to that of other assets; it cannot be treated in legal practice as a movable commodity."[1]

Why does it remain so immensely difficult, a full 50 years later, to translate this finding of the highest court of the land into general practice? Sure, the next election is always coming up, and the polemical buzzword expropriation is an easy way to scare voters. What would an agitprop-style political argument look like that would appeal to the general public as well as to municipal treasurers?

ED: That's a tough question: why is it that these fundamental issues have been raised repeatedly over the decades but in the end remain unresolved? You've mentioned one stumbling block: upcoming elections. But the primary problem, I think, has to do with a certain self-conception and sense of entitlement: the belief that increases in value that result from planning decisions automatically and unquestionably accrue to the landowner. In reality these are in part unearned gains, often generated by zoning decisions, which is to say, actions of the authorities, the community. The prevailing idea in our society is that there is no such thing as unearned profits in real estate. But then why does the Constitution of Bavaria, for example—I think it's in article 161—state that any appreciation due to planning shall be recaptured for the benefit of the community?

This raises the question of a levy on increases in land value arising from planning decisions. Several attempts have been made to institute such a levy, especially starting in the 1960s and most recently in 1987/89. The idea of a levy on development gains is very difficult to cast into unambiguous law. I'm no legal expert, but conversations with colleagues have taught me that the proposal raises constitutional concerns. There are well-founded objections and views that, as I understand it, make an implementation that will stand up to legal scrutiny seem elusive.

AB: *Another strategy to socialize planning-related value increases that has been around for a long time is urban development contracts. What's your view of this land policy instrument? Would you describe it as part of a neoliberal trend?*
ED: Urban development contracts have been used in Germany since the early 1990s, and in some areas they've fundamentally changed the prevailing planning practice. Whether they're also a manifestation of neoliberalism doesn't seem to me to be the key question. Their objective is to establish cooperative relations between municipalities and investors, and an empirical study has shown that they're a helpful way for the public to recapture some of the value gains arising from planning decisions. They're a legal instrument that has been established practice for decades. Still, when some say that urban development contracts obviate the need for a more comprehensive legislative solution, that strikes me as a bit shortsighted.

Several cities have adopted general resolutions on this issue; Munich, for example, has one on "socially fair land use," that dates from 1994. But when you examine these resolutions more closely, you realize that their purpose is limited to ensuring uniformity and accountability in the use of urban development contracts and preventing legal challenges. Of course, they're also an attempt to refinance some of the expenses for the production of buildable land by making investors pass some of the land value gains on to the municipalities. But such contracts are an insufficient tool to reverse the trend and enable the municipalities to do what Münster did in exemplary fashion: the city exercises additional control over the implementation of planning decisions by participating in the real estate market on its own account, collects a significantly greater share of the land value generated by its actions, and retains greater influence by carefully managing the allocation of land to users. Absent this more activist strategy, it's not surprising that the problem of high land prices continues to bedevil municipalities.

AB: *Interestingly, the question of land-ownership was always a Social Democratic issue, although attempts to revive the discussion now fall on deaf ears. But isn't it ultimately a conservative issue as well? How might we instigate a cultural and social debate today that avoids the whole technical terminology of supply policy, revolving funds, and planning-related land value gain levies?*
ED: That's a tricky one. You're right—at its core, the question of landownership also touches on deeply held conservative tenets, and one would think that it should be easy to get voters, including those in the much-coveted political center, to pay attention to the issue.

Approaching it from different angles over time, I came across Catholic social teaching, for example, Oswald von Nell-Breuning, whose writings on these questions I highly recommend. All this goes to show that the subject really has deep roots in society.

Who profits from appreciation? Who profits from speculation? I'd argue that these are ultimately also questions of social justice. For the time being, a measure that would achieve a great deal and bring a lasting solution to many problems would be to replace the current property tax, which is outdated and unfair, with a pure land value tax.

AB: *Are you referring to a land value tax of the kind envisioned by the American economist Henry George? It's interesting to note that neoliberals—such as, most recently, Patrik Schumacher—refer to his work as well* (see Patrik Schumacher, p. 78–83).

ED: Henry George's proposal of a single tax on land is of course part of the discussion. In theory, his model would make all other kinds of taxes, even taxes on labor, obsolete. George's basic idea is to subject the real value of land to taxation. The leading thinker of land reform in Germany, Adolf Damaschke, took up this idea, and it still has its champions. Deservedly, I think.

AB: *With an eye to the next elections: how would you frame a land value tax proposal in positive terms to communicate the idea to the public?*
ED: One should point out first and foremost that the introduction of a pure land value tax would enable the public to exert wide-ranging control, also over spatial and architectural planning. This is crucial. Debates over rent control, new depreciation models, or first-home buyer allowances, I think, ultimately miss the point. If we want to make progress on the issue, we need to associate the land value tax with questions of social justice more than anything else. Focusing solely on the tax revenues it would generate would be a mistake. Tactically speaking, the way to advocate for it right now would be to point to the housing shortage. There's a pressing need for action! The pure land value tax has a mobilizing effect on land; it's a way to significantly increase the supply of buildable land. Again: no housing without land. In particular, it cuts the proverbial "ground" from under the pernicious speculative strategy of keeping fully developed but unbuilt land out of the market.

And although we're still going to need to have a debate over the right instruments, a long-term municipal land supply policy in conjunction with a pure land value tax and significantly wider use of heritable building rights—these are the crucial keys or building blocks on the way to a new and socially just land policy. That's basically all it would take!

01 Bundesverfassungsgericht, January 12, 1967. 1 BvR 169/63, opinioiuris.de/entscheidung/ 1436 (accessed January 8, 2018).

Capital Home

HARALD TRAPP

"The rooms are growing,
the house stretches out."
– Friedrich Schiller, *Song of the Bell*

Margaret Thatcher (front right) visiting the Parker family in London's Northolt district. They were one of the first to buy their home from social housing stock after the 1979 "Right to Buy" law initiative

In the original house—*oikos*, as the Greeks called it—production and reproduction were grouped together. While *oikos*, the root of the word economy, referred to the house as well as the paterfamilias, his family, the slaves, and all activities and property of the household, the other Greek term for house, *domos*, was also used as a verb. It described the tutelage of the spouse, the education of the slaves, the discipline of the children, and even the physical training of the body. Mark Cousins sees therein a clear description of the nature of domestication: *domos* is a place of mastery, and it is therefore likely that the complementary term "home" came into existence.[01] Thus, from the outset, the house has had a twofold character: as the basic unit of the economy and as a locus of identity; as a household and as a home. According to Heidegger, dwelling is our being-in-the-world; it generates the innermost, the intimate, both spatially and mentally: "The way in which you are and I am, the manner in which we humans are on the earth, is *Buan*, dwelling. To be a human being means to be on the earth as a mortal. It means to dwell."[02] The United Nations derives its stipulation for a right to adequate housing from this fundamental distinction: "Housing is the basis of stability and security for an individual or family. The center of our social, emotional and sometimes economic lives, a home should be a sanctuary; a place to live in peace, security and dignity. Increasingly viewed as a commodity, housing is most importantly a human right."[03]

The capitalization of space

With the development of the capitalist mode of production, the house and the apartment became commodities—as homes and emotionally owned refuges of the self—that are produced and traded by the construction industry, but were still not considered as capital or a means for its multiplication. Moreover, in many cases, the municipality, city, or state was the owner, and they would provide affordable housing for the socially disadvantaged. At the level of the individual and the family, the core of society and identity, the home as private homestead initially remained a place of residence and fixed locus of identity. This changed with the aggressive ideology of neoliberalism that took off in the US and the UK before asserting itself across the world from the 1970s onwards.

Neoliberal hegemony arises from the generalization of the principle of market and capital through the entire social corpus, including the areas of reproduction not governed by money. A prerequisite for this is the infiltration of capital into all areas of life and social relationships. It is not about how the individual is subjugated by power, but how subjectivity can be actively produced.[04] At the same time, what Henri Lefebvre emphasized still applies: while commodities, money, and capital are concrete abstractions, they require substance to be relevant in society. They achieve this relevance in the production of space: "Not only has capitalism laid hold of pre-existing space, of the Earth, but it also tends to produce a space of its own."[05] Beyond this production of space, the neoliberal capitalization of space eventually subsumes the home and, as a result, not only the production of subjectivity, but the reproduction of the self.

Essentially, the expansion of the capitalist form of production into the realm of space is marked by the conflict between its social character and the private ownership of its location.[06] Land and architecture then become commodities, both primarily defined by their exchange value and not their use value. According to Marx, "the mysteriousness of the commodity" also lies in the fact that the producers experience the social character of their work as an object, because they compare their work with the value of the commodities they produce, and "because the relation of the producers to the sum total of their own labor is presented to them as a social relation, existing not between themselves, but between the products of their labor. This is the reason why the products of labor become commodities, social things whose qualities are at the same time perceptible and imperceptible by the senses."[07] As long as commodities are exchanged in the cycle of "commodity–money–commodity", i.e. selling in order to buy, Marx says this represents a normal circulation. If these signifiers are inverted, however—buying commodities only to later convert them back into money—then this commodity becomes capital.

Expropriation of land as a prerequisite for capitalist accumulation

To describe the "economic sin" that made this historically possible, Marx used the term "primitive accumulation"[08]: a historical process in which the producers are divested of their means of production. Because of this, Marx later believes a more fitting term would have been "primitive expropriation."[09]

Before primitive accumulation, two types of production characterized the European economy: the rural peasant economy and the guild organizations of the city. Whereas the guilds of tradespeople obstructed the rise of modern capitalists by protecting their work, Marx stated that the feudal lords in the countryside were "in possession of the sources of wealth,"[10] as large swathes of land there could be acquired relatively easily. Besides the expropriation of the Catholic Church and a large amount of publicly held domains, from the eighteenth century onward, based on an outdated legal status, this appropriation concentrated on land managed in the common interest, the so-called commons. Between 1725 and 1825, the ruling landowners in Great Britain appropriated more than six million acres of common land using almost 4,000 *Enclosure Acts*.[11] "Fences, ditches, walls, hedges, razor wire, and the like demark the boundaries of private property. They were built 'lawfully' by Act of Parliament when the Parliament was composed exclusively of landlords. They called it 'improvement', and today they call it 'development' or 'progress'."[12] This enclosure of the commons—the annexing of common land for private use—meant that most peasants were deprived of their means of subsistence. From that point on they were forced to take on work as laborers. Thus, in contrast to medieval merchant and monetary capital, the origins of capital in the modern sense can be found in arable farmland. According to Marx, the expropriation of land from the masses was a prerequisite for capitalist accumulation.[13]

Capitalist accumulation is therefore based on the production of space—that is, on shifting the control of land use and the (loosely understood) architectural act of enclosure using hedges and fences. As the forceful expropriation of peasants and the destruction of their dwellings unleashed more proletariat than the cities and the emergent manufacturing economy could absorb, the result was large-scale unemployment, vagrancy, and criminality, which led to a second, parallel system of enclosure: the birth of the modern prison in the form of work- and jailhouses, whose inmates consisted largely of beggars and vagrants.[14] "In this way, through grotesque and terroristic laws, the peasantry, forcefully expropriated of their land, displaced and made into vagabonds, were whipped, branded, and tortured into the discipline necessary for the system of wage labor."[15] Although the enclosures of the commons were related to historical events, according to Marxist theoreticians such as Massimo De Angelis and Pier Vittorio Aureli, it is a mistake to reduce them to a specific historical moment. Instead, these processes will be continually repeated, like the processes of en- and decoding and re- and deterritorialization were also repeated. "What appears to us as territory is not just the given environment in which we live but also a 'machine' whose goal is to extract surplus value from the totality of social relationships."[16]

The conservative revolution

The major *caesurae* of the two world wars resulted in a massive strengthening of the state; not least, as Thomas Piketty believes, because there was more damage to the stock of capital than to the stock of labor,[17] and therefore most of the urgently needed investments had to be organized communally. But after this reconstruction,

Photo: © Sandra Lousada, The Smithson Family Collection

the crisis of the resulting centralized economy in the UK in the late 1970s led to a conservative revolution[18] of neoliberalism, which also had decisive consequences for the production of space. According to Piketty, since the turn of the twenty-first century there has been an unprecedented prevalence of different forms of capital accumulation: "By 2010, and despite the crisis that began in 2007–2008, capital was prospering as it had not done since 1913."[19]

The market's claim to unlimited authority, something neoliberalism seeks to impose, permeates every aspect of life: "Here we can't lose sight of the 'neo' in neoliberalism. We need to distinguish, for example, between the colonization of everyday life by the commodity, a feature of liberal capitalism, and the saturation of every part of existence and the construction of the human subject itself by contemporary economic metrics of value, and especially the gutting of democracy and justice with market values. We are in a different kind of struggle today over what constitutes a livable world than was imagined by older Leftist critiques of capital."[20] Capitalism thus attains a new quality. According to Douglas Spencer, as it is no longer content with the implementation of a profit-oriented market economy, it encroaches on the production of subjectivity itself: the market exerts control over its subjects; over their development, formation, and status; and over the conditions of a corporate environment that reproduces these very subjects. At the same time, the market economy is safeguarded by state interventions, which ensure its continuing survival.[21] For the production of space, this not only means dominance of "Big Capital" (also the title of Anna Minton's book about the real estate market in London[22]), but the acquisition and accumulation of individual, intimate space. The private house, the home—personal territory—is thereby capitalized. The neoliberal subject isn't a tenant but an owner, and no longer acquires its place of residence according to a use or asset value, but as capital that needs to generate return. Reflecting Piketty's hypothesis that returns from capital are always greater than those from work, nowadays homes earn more than their inhabitants: "Homes in the south-east of England earn more money than most of the people who live in them. Even the Prime Minister of Great Britain [David Cameron] experiences this. As shown in his recent tax return, since he became PM, his house in Notting Hill earned comfortably more money than his salary."[23]

The Marxist definition of the capitalist mode of production differentiates production—the accumulation of capital through work—from reproduction of labor—care, education, leisure, etc.—which is not primarily organized in a capitalist way and thus wasn't considered in detail by Marx. Sociologists such as Massimo De Angelis view reproduction as the most important field of commoning: "Here I build on the feminist debates of the 1970s criticizing Marx

Robin Hood Gardens (foreground) with the Canary Wharf office complex
rising into the sky in the background.

Robin Hood Gardens was
built in 1972 by Alison and
Peter Smithson as public
housing in London.
The brutalist building with
two crossed blocks was
their first and only council
housing project. The
demolition plan decided
in 2012 was justified as
a "regeneration" measure
for the Blackwall Reach
district and was carried out,
despite strong protests,
in 2017.

The Smithsons' "streets in the sky" concept was intended
to allow neighborhood life in the building.

Demolition of the Robin Hood Gardens residential complex designed by Alison and Peter Smithson, London, August 2017. Photo: © dezeen

Capital Home

███████████████████████

for disregarding the circuit of reproduction of labor power. I reproduce this circuit of reproduction of labor power and argue that itself it is but a moment of a broader circuit, that of the (re)production of commons."[24] The apartment block and the apartment, especially as homes, belong to the architecture of reproduction. Capitalism increasingly exploits this resource for its own objectives: reproduction is produced, industrialized, and commercialized. Colonizing—or the enclosure of—the areas of life not organized in monetary terms is the overarching project of capital. The production of reproduction now encroaches on the last reserves of commoning and has reached its ultimate goal: the reproduction of the self.

Right to buy

Before 1865, the housing demands of the low-income population in the UK were met almost exclusively by private providers, which led to poor living conditions and exorbitant rental rates. Following the Public Health Act of 1875, social (council) housing was built for people in need, war veterans, and, as part of later slum clearances, for the working class. In the 1950s, a large-scale public building program was implemented, with the result that in 1980 almost 42 percent of the population still lived in social housing. With the 1980 Housing Act and the "Right to Buy" scheme, Margaret Thatcher's Conservative government enabled council house residents to purchase their homes at a discount of 33 to 50 percent of their market value. In selling its own housing stock, society effectively expropriated itself. In this way, there are parallels between the house hunters released onto the housing market at the end of the twentieth century and the masses of workers unleashed by the *enclosures* in the eighteenth and nineteenth centuries. To defend this absurdity politically, the housing stock—public property—was not offered to the housing market but to its residents. At the same time, with a proviso that stated the revenues raised by the local councils couldn't be used to construct new housing, the expropriation was made irreversible. The percentage of the UK population living in council housing has fallen from 42 percent in 1980 to 8 percent today.[25] The abrupt cessation of public or cooperative housing production resulted in a housing shortage, entailing enormous price increases. Accompanied by political measures such as the curtailment of social benefits, the increasing privatization of pensions, and amendments in tax laws, welfare provisions are increasingly dependent on the individual speculating with their own home.

At the end of this process is the capitalization of the private dwelling: the home is transformed into capital. The private home is no longer bought primarily to live in, rather to resell. Through the objectification of living as a commodity, treating the home as capital brings speculation, a fixation on returns, and the necessity of yield increase into the individual's own four walls. Ubiquitous in the UK, the term "property ladder"—getting onto which is deemed imperative in the property market—highlights two things: the hierarchical division of society in upper and lower, winners and losers, as well as the necessity of climbing it. Tenants, who haven't even reached the ladder's first rung, are considered losers. "In such markets, the value of housing is no longer based on its social use. Properties are equally valuable regardless of whether they are vacant

Advertisement for a new building in Canary Wharf, designed by Herzog & de Meuron.

or occupied, so there is no pressure to ensure properties are lived in. They are built with the intention of lying empty and accumulating value."[26] The capitalization of the housing market leads to a total abstraction and reduction of the idea of dwelling, or, as a UN report from 2017 sums it up: "dehumanized housing."[27] In the London district of Chelsea and Kensington alone, the amount of empty residential units increased by 40 percent between 2013 and 2014. Apartments are no longer homes, they are now "safety deposit boxes in the sky."[28]

Help to buy

Assisted by supply-oriented neoliberal politics, the purchase of property is promoted as the only economically meaningful kind of dwelling. Yet the resources necessary for this are usually beyond the financial capabilities of the individual, leaving only borrowing as an option. Labor is no longer merely exploited through the added value it generates, but also through the level of debt it makes possible. The borrower is the operative of speculative capitalism. The deregulated housing market gives investors the idea that prices are constantly rising and is thus a source of continually increasing returns. Therefore, home ownership is not only an alternative to renting, it is an investment.

Political measures are also facilitating this development, for example the "Help to Buy" program introduced in the UK in 2013, which the government promotes in the following way: "With a Help to Buy: Equity Loan the Government lends you up to 20 percent of the cost of your newly built home, so you'll only need a 5 percent cash deposit and a 75 percent mortgage to make up the rest. You won't be charged loan fees on the 20 percent loan for the first five years of owning your home."[29] This implies that for 10,000 GBP an individual can buy a house with a value of 200,000 GBP. In this way, the home owner is doubly indebted: as a private person for the house they have bought and as a taxpayer—through all the other state-sponsored guaranties paid by the Help to Buy program. If prices keep rising, the houses purchased in this way can be sold at a profit before the mortgage is paid off. If prices fall, as they have since 2017, property bought at an inflated level can lead to financial ruin. The amounts of money being redistributed from the public to the private hand by such a policy are reflected in the scandal surrounding the payment of 128 million GBP to the chief executive of the construction company Persimmon, one of the main beneficiaries of the Help to Buy program.[30]

Neoliberal politics sees it as the function of the state to guarantee that market activity proceeds in an unhindered manner. Besides restricting, reducing, or removing regulation, this also implies the state retreating as far as possible from the provision of welfare for its citizens. According to a study by the Swiss bank UBS, basic state pensions in the UK are among the lowest in the developed nations of the world.[31] As a result, retirement provision is heavily reliant on the security provided by property ownership. This means, however, that a property that might have only just been paid off has to be mortgaged again. The financial market has developed tools to ensure indebtedness remains an almost uninterrupted, lifelong process. These "products," referred to as equity release by banks, are in principle nothing other than asset reduction, as part of the property is sold. According to the *Guardian*, in the UK over eight million GBP a day is withdrawn from home ownership in this way.[32]

The UN claims that global real estate represents almost 60 percent of all assets, of which 75 percent is residential property—more than twice the world's gross domestic product.[33] By bundling mortgages, huge returns can be achieved through highly speculative financial products. The trade in so-called "sub-prime credits" was the cause of the 2008 financial crisis: deregulation and a lack of supervision in the market enabled banks to grant risky credit and lower lending standards, and in turn stipulate higher or variable interest rates, thereby increasing their profits. Through this bundling, the speeding up of trade, and the use of complex strategies to conceal the volatility of these financial constructs, small mortgages attained an enormous leverage effect.

The debt subject

The expropriation that Marx termed primitive accumulation created an expropriated class, who were forced to sell their labor. In neoliberalism, on the other hand, the state expropriates itself by privatizing common property. The individuals unleashed by this privatization are to the market what the landless peasants of the eighteenth and nineteenth centuries were: a necessary prerequisite for the accumulation of capital. But, through inversion, the neoliberal variant of accumulation impacts those affected more thoroughly than the "primitive" one. This applies especially to the property market: as a borrower, the expropriated is turned into a property owner. The neoliberal subject becomes pseudo-capitalist; it produces and reproduces itself as capital. This "debt subject," as Joseph Vogl calls it, is exploited twofold: through the added value of their labor and the added value—the interest—of their debts. "The economic reality of debt subjects represents an elementary financial resource; there can be no better example of what Walter Benjamin referred to as capitalism's 'cult of blame/debt' [*verschuldender Kultus*]. Contemporary politics appropriates this cultish dimension and, citing financial emergency, demands a 'sacrifice' from its subjects."[34] Financial capital is more intelligent than industrial capital; it has created new workers who, as borrowers, produce added value. The dialectic of capital and labor, which should have led to new forms of coexistence, has become obsolete. State intervention has been reduced to promoting the market economy and compensating the losses it incurs in its regular crises: "The combination of global capital, government policies designed to kill off social housing and failures in housing benefit are reconfiguring the city. The politics of space is replacing the traditional politics of class." [35]

01 Mark Cousins, "The House-Home," in *Home Economics,* ed. Shumi Bose, Jack Self, Finn Williams [Catalogue of the British Pavilion, Biennale di Venezia] (London: The Spaces, 2016), 39.
02 Martin Heidegger, "Bauen, Wohnen, Denken," in *Vorträge und Aufsätze* (Pfullingen: Günther Neske, 1954), 20. Translation: ssbothwell.com/documents/ebooksclub.org__Poetry__Language__Thought__Perennial_Classics_.pdf (accessed May 7, 2018).
03 www.ohchr.org/EN/Issues/Housing/Pages/HousingIndex.aspx (accessed May 7, 2018).
04 Douglas Spencer, *The Architecture of Neoliberalism* (London: Bloomsbury Academic, 2016), 12.
05 Henri Lefebvre, *The Production of Space* (1974; Oxford: Wiley-Blackwell, 1991), 326.
06 Ibid., p. 88f.
07 Karl Marx, *Das Kapital* (1872; Frankfurt a. Main/Berlin/Wien, 1978), 51. Translation: www.marxists.org/archive/marx/works/download/pdf/Capital-Volume-I.pdf
08 *Marx-Engels-Werke,* Bd. 23: *Das Kapital.* Bd. I (Berlin/DDR: Dietz Verlag, 1968), 741.
09 Karl Marx, "Lohn, Preis und Profit," in *Marx-Engels-Werke,* Bd. 16, 131.
10 Ibid., 743.
11 Peter Linebaugh, *Stop, Thief!, The Commons, Enclosures, and Resistance* (Oakland: PM Press, 2014), 144.
12 Ibid., 1f.
13 *Marx-Engels-Werke,* 1968 (as footnote 8), 789.
14 Cf. Michel Foucault, *Überwachen und Strafen, Die Geburt des Gefängnisses* (Suhrkamp: Frankfurt a. Main, 1994).
15 *Marx-Engels-Werke,* 1968 (as footnote 8), 765.
16 Pier Vittorio Aureli, "unit 14 brief 2016/17," AA London, 2017.

17 Thomas Piketty, *Capital in the 21st Century* (Cambridge MA/London: Harvard University Press, 2014).
18 Ibid., 41f.
19 Ibid., 42.
20 Wendy Brown, "The End of the World as We Know It," *Artforum*, December 2016: 246f.
21 Spencer, 2016 (as footnote 4), 2.
22 Anna Minton, *Big Capital. Who is London For?* (London: Penguin, 2017).
23 Eddie Blake, "Homesickness" in *Home Economics* (as footnote 1), 23.
24 Massimo De Angelis, *Omnia Sunt Communia*, (London: Zed Books, 2017), 22.
25 Lisa Mckenzie, "People shouldn't have to feel grateful for social housing – it's a basic human right," *The Guardian*, August 11, 2017.
26 Dawn Foster, "UN report lays bare the waste of treating homes as commodities," *The Guardian*, February 28, 2017.
27 Ibid.
28 Cf. Peter Wynne Rees, "London needs homes, not towers of 'safe-deposit boxes'," *The Guardian*, January 25, 2015.
29 www.helptobuy.gov.uk/equity-loan/equity-loans (accessed May 7, 2018).
30 Cf. Rupert Neate, "Persimmon chair resigns over chief executive's 'obscene' £128m bonus," *The Guardian*, December 15, 2017.
31 Patrick Collinson, "UK pensions among the worst in the developed world, study finds," *The Guardian*, September 21, 2017.
32 Rupert Jones, "Over-55s take £8m a day out of their homes," *The Guardian*, September 16, 2017.
33 Cf. www.ohchr.org (as footnote 3).
34 Joseph Vogl, "The Ascendancy of Finance," *Artforum*, Summer 2017: 331.
35 Minton, 2017 (as footnote 22), 111.

Land of the Free Forces

PATRIK SCHUMACHER
IN CONVERSATION WITH
ARNO BRANDLHUBER

The black and gold flag is the symbol of anarcho-capitalists. Gold stands for the precious metal or supranational capital, black for anarchy.

At the 2016 World Architecture Festival (WAF) in Berlin, Patrik Schumacher, the Principal of Zaha Hadid Architects, presented an eight-point urban policy manifesto calling for the withdrawal of government from all fields related to architecture and planning, as well as the abolition of public spaces and social housing. His polarizing speech drew international outrage from many fellow architects, but at the same time, Schumacher's call for radically abolishing building regulations also resonated with many colleagues who increasingly feel burdened by an over-regulated profession. Schumacher takes advantage of widespread professional yearning for more creative freedom to disseminate political views, which are based on a strictly entrepreneurial society of anarcho-capitalism. Such a populist strategy has become quite common among politicians who exploit latent anxieties and discontent within the populace in order to achieve hegemony in the political discourse. Because of the degree of sympathy he attracted from some parts of the profession, and in the interest of open debate, we decided to let Patrik Schumacher elucidate his political ideas in the following interview with Berlin-based architect Arno Brandlhuber. We have also invited Manuel Shvartzberg Carrió, who runs the Architecture Thesis for the Masters of Science in Critical, Curatorial, and Conceptual Practices in Architecture (CCCP) at Columbia GSAPP, to critically examine these arguments in an accompanying essay. ALN

PATRIK SCHUMACHER'S EIGHT-POINT URBAN POLICY MANIFESTO

1. Regulate the Planners: Development rights must be the starting point, then tightly define and circumscribe the planners' scope and legitimate reasons for constraining development rights: access/traffic constraints, infringements of neighbors' property utilization (rights of light), historic heritage preservation, pollution limits. Nothing else can be brought to bear—no social engineering agendas!

2. Abolish all land use prescriptions: The market should perhaps also allocate land uses, so that more residences can come in until the right balance with work and entertainment spaces is discovered. Only the market has a chance to calibrate this intricate balance.

3. Stop all vain and unproductive attempts at "milieu protection."

4. Abolish all prescriptive housing standards: Planners and politicians should also stay away from housing standards in terms of unit sizes, unit mixes, etc. Here too the market has the best chance to discover the most useful, productive and life/prosperity-enhancing mix. The imposition of housing standards protects nobody, it only eliminates choices and thus makes all of us poorer. Stop all interventions and distortions of the (residential) real estate market. (All subsidized goods are oversupplied and thus partially wasted.)

5. Abolish all forms of social and affordable housing: No more imposition of quota of various types of affordable housing, phase out and privatize all council housing, phase out the housing benefit system (and substitute with monetary support without specific purpose allocation).

6. Abolish all government subsidies for home ownership like Help to Buy: This distorts real housing preferences and biases against mobility.

7. Abolish all forms of rent control and one-fits-all regulation of tenancies: Instead allow for free contracting on tenancy terms and let a thousand flowers bloom. Here is a recipe for the creation of the dense, urban fabric that delivers the stimulating urbanity many of us desire and know to be a key condition of further productivity gains within our post-Fordist network society.

8. Privatize all streets, squares, public spaces and parks, possibly whole urban districts.

ARNO BRANDLHUBER: *You grew up in West Germany and studied during a time of big political changes: the transformation of the consensus-driven postwar period in West Germany, nicknamed the Bonn Republic, and the revolutions in eastern Europe that eventually led to the unification of Germany. How do you remember and relate to this period today?*

PATRIK SCHUMACHER: I grew up in a diplomatic neighborhood in Bonn. My youth was not especially politically inspired—it was just normal to be around political institutions. I studied mathematics and philosophy in Bonn, before studying architecture in Stuttgart in the early '80s and moving to London in 1987. By that time, I was already politicized and increasingly interested in Marxism and the political Left. I worked with various Trotskyist organizations and became a semi-activist, debating the transformations in eastern Europe, the idea of reforming the Eastern Bloc, and market socialism. This was all before the break-up of the Soviet Union and events that were to take place in the GDR.

I was electrified by the changes in Germany. I actually happened to be in Berlin when the Wall opened and watched the eastern Europeans stream in. I had crossed over to East Berlin just a few months earlier to purchase the complete works of Marx and Engels.

After living in London for a while, I returned to Berlin because I was really fascinated by the changes and dynamism in the new Republic. I lived there for two years and was still very left-oriented at the time.

AB: *The ruptures in the late '80s and early '90s were a stark contrast to the reformist ideals of the '70s. It is unthinkable today, but back then almost all political parties, from Left to Right, agreed in principle that there needed to be some form of real estate reform to cope with the housing problem and the increasing commodification of urban development. Among others, Hans-Jochen Vogel, a leading politician of the Social Democrats, stated that land should not be privatized as it cannot be reproduced and should therefore be treated as a public resource, comparable to air and water (see Hans-Jochen Vogel, p. 60–65).*

Anarcho-Capitalism

████████████████████████████

City of London

Privately owned public spaces in the City of London (red) and unspecified open spaces (blue).

Source: Oliver Dawkins, data provided by the Office for National Statistics (GB), Crown copyright and database right 2014; *The Guardian*: www.theguardian.com/ cities/2017/jul/24/pseudo-public-space-explore-data-what-missing (accessed March 8, 2018)

PS: I would have agreed with this argument during my left period, but now I have a very different view. I don't think that land resource is a problem; we are not using most of the earth's surface and it's always a question of homesteading, taking in, elaborating, investing in, and building up the land and its uses. That's an initiative and an effort, and it will only happen in a decent way if it's being properly incentivized with strategic intelligence and sustained investment. I would suspect this could only be done sufficiently by private owners and private investors. I think that the commodification of land was a great accelerator historically. When land could be bought and sold, cities were flourishing and growing. Land was unlocked—used and reused.

AB: *Could an accelerated property development, that is free for speculation, be progressive?*
PS: I expect property owners and investors to see the potential of a site, to be very creative and forward-looking, and therefore to be at their best if they don't encounter too many planning constraints. That's the view of an optimistic progressive: I expect the ownership markets to be driving innovation.

I am sympathetic to some of the new left currents coming out of philosophy into politics—such as accelerationism. I'm an accelerationist, rather on the Left than on the Right. I consider productivity and progress the main drivers—getting barriers, restrictions, guarantees, and crutches out of the way to move forward much quicker.

AB: *You talk about the necessity of a productive society with few limitations. Still, property defines social order and our understanding of what society is. How do you envisage social order in a market of free forces?*
PS: My defense of private property rests on the idea that it is a fundamental universal aspect of human social order, which also brings architecture into play. The social order needs to cling onto, work and evolve through spatial order. The definition of property rights needs incentives hooked onto it in order to accelerate. The standard of human nature is not fixed; it is an open-ended and evolving project. I'm excited by this. I am all about risk taking. I want to be around in 20, 30 years and see something different—new dynamics—that is why I am frustrated by the stagnation coming from the idea of safeguarding everything and not allowing individual initiatives. There's this philosophy of over-politicizing everything so that we have to hold hands before anything can move forward, we all have to agree. But this is slowing us down.

In this context, ideas like universal basic income is a double-edged sword. On the one hand, it's a rationing system where individual decisions about income are taken away and everybody is infantilized; on the other hand, you would have individual empowerment and responsibility with respect to this basic allocation. Thus, you would try to work on it and top it up. To that extent, as a substitute and improvement over the welfare allocation system, I am very much in line with the new-new Left.

But I would even like to take these restraints away and let us all be set free and self-responsible. We could have charitable private initiatives to catch those who can't flourish in a more open and free society, rather than universal income. Although I prefer it to the welfare system, I see the risk of this getting entrenched and somehow taking the initiative out of too many people who might choose, what I would argue to be, the "poisoned chalice," the easy option of relaxing back and letting others charge forward. I want everybody to be on the edge and charging forward.

AB: *On the one hand you rigorously defend private initiative and ownership, on the other hand you are against the idea that people have to buy their property. How come you are against one of the most momentous legislations by Margaret Thatcher, the "right to buy," which pushed for the privatization of social housing in Great Britain?* (see Harald Trapp, p. 70–77).

PS: I'm a defender of private property but I don't want the government to interfere and subsidize certain choices, for example by encouraging people to purchase their residences as permanently owned homes. That's not what I mean by private property. There should be free choices unbiased by subsidies. That's why I am critical about Margaret Thatcher's "right to buy." Giving away collectively owned property is like giving away social housing and pushing it into private hands—that's unfair and unsustainable. What I consider to be free choice is the possibility to choose, as an individual, to *not* own any apartment or piece of land, but to have landlords instead who rent out property and curate it for more nomadic populations. I think there's too much home ownership, it immobilizes society. I think we should be cut loose as cosmopolitan citizens.

AB: *The German constitution stipulates that "property entails obligations," which means that, on the one hand, property is a tool you are free to use and, on the other hand, its use comes with certain obligations for society and the common good. What's your take on this constitutional principle?*
PS: In a free market system the owners of the means of production, including land, will only stay in charge as long as they utilize the resources for the best,

including market interests. This means, validation from the consumer side and sorting out through the profit-loss system, if they squander, waste, or misuse these resources. I think that in a truly capitalist society we would see more fluidity and shifting ownerships. The entrepreneurs who deliver would thrive and those who waste resources would disappear and maybe re-emerge as employees, no longer holding properties. Property ownership isn't something entrenched, it is rather a chance for entrepreneurs. And if others see more potential, they can come in, bid for these resources and bring them to an even more flourishing use. That represents a dynamic and fluid system.

AB: *This fluid system without moral implications seems to be a world that would be better organized by algorithms. You work a lot with algorithms in your own practice. Can you imagine a world that's not just physically defined by algorithms but also legally, such as in terms of property rights? An "antihuman" world—you use the word antihuman in a very positive reading—where questions about who is in charge of resources— such as land—and for how long, or who has the best chances, and the highest potential are answered by algorithms?*
PS: I think this is part of becoming superhuman. So my antihuman is going against what you also find in architecture. Namely, that people would like to see traditional surroundings they like— something small-scale, warm, and cozy—surrounded by nature and genuine materials. We should forget about all this and let operators try out different sensibilities: high-density, hyper-density, etc. The post-Fordist network society is characterized by high urban concentration; the city, in a way, becomes a super brain, a kind of AI, which continuously designs and redesigns the systems and products. People worry about AI taking over professional jobs and intelligence. I'm not afraid of it—I welcome it. I'm very much interested in becoming a kind of cyborg, AI-infused, new ecology, semi-organic, semi-silicone-based human. And for that we need freedom in terms of entrepreneurship and the allocation of resources and properties, such as land.

AB: *What are the consequences of this celebration of entrepreneurship? We are facing a situation, not only in Berlin,*

where square meter prices are increasing because land prices are rising. The profit you can make with a project is already accounted for in the land price, which means that to maximize the profit you have to cut the costs for architecture. This is a systemic problem we have faced for the last five to ten years, if not longer. There is no progress because of land speculation. Could we think of a better kind of landownership besides the afore-mentioned concept of the free market?
PS: I think there are problems, I would not attribute them to the free market but to the constrained market. Land values are rising in London and other cities because we are living in an era of urban concentration. If everybody wants to squeeze into central locations, resources become precious and they need to be allocated carefully. In that process, market mechanisms aren't playing a significant role. The sky-high prices are becoming a constraint and problem, but I think they have a lot to do with supply restrictions coming from the government itself: restricting higher densities, land use and unit sizes—implementing milieu protections.

Considering this criticism of rising land values in our cities, there is another potential concept one could look at, which comes from Henry George. It says that if you accidentally own a site and other people invest around it, your land value rises accidentally without you having done anything for it—these are windfalls, unearned. The Georgist idea is that you have a tax on these windfalls, which would be the only taxation in an otherwise libertarian system. There would not be any other income or corporate taxes, but also no land speculation. If you tax corporate incomes, you are actually disincentivizing production and investment. Georgists argue that the taxation of land, as you are taxing the windfalls, is not disincentivizing. It's an interesting proposal, which is certainly far more radical and libertarian than our system now. The idea of the land value tax has the advantage that there's only one arena, one resource that is constrained and drawn upon for the benefit of the public.

AB: *At the 2016 WAF you suggested that whole neighborhoods and districts should be privatized. Today, we are in a situation where the costs for public amenities, like streets and infrastructure, are covered by the public, whereas*

Anarcho-Capitalism

the profits from these investments are privatized. How would you see the balance between private and public investments?
PS: I'm still considering the Georgist idea; going back to more libertarian proposals, like those I pushed at the World Architecture Festival, with the privatization of everything. This would overcome the fact that public resources are being invested in streets, squares and infrastructure, whereas the benefits are reaped by nearby private owners. This should be overcome if all the public zones are equally privately managed. It doesn't mean that they are closed down—I wouldn't expect that—but I would expect it to allow a richer diversity for the public, who would all need to have the same restrictive law and order policing. So that it's not only safe for middle-aged couples, or the standard family. There could be a much greater diversity of cultures and rules attached to different types of streets, squares or parks, like the variety you find in restaurants, bars, cafes or clubs. They would not be equally inclusive, which I think is an illusion anyway—which space is ever an all-inclusive space?—they would be for different publics.

AB: *Pretty much all your work takes place in the "valuable centers" of the world. Would your concept work everywhere? What about, let's say, a run-down suburb somewhere in the middle of America?*
PS: I am thinking of the aforementioned milieu protection, where the government aims at keeping certain populations, certain zones, and certain milieus, and protecting them from market pressure. I am skeptical, because we treat certain cultures like reservations to be protected, or zoos where tourists can enjoy the

There's this philosophy of over-politicizing everything so that we have to hold hands before anything can move forward, we all have to agree. But this is slowing us down.

flavor of the working class district and its anachronism. What about regions like the Rust Belt, which are now less dynamic? Is it a good idea to subsidize them, to keep these communities locked in?

I think the whole suburbanization process of the twentieth century was not something the market would have delivered in the same way. It was hugely subsidized by the state through investments in infrastructure—roads, railways and electricity routes all the way to the suburbs—which is something we might now regret. This wouldn't have happened if there had been a market allocation of resources. Now we keep subsidizing these zones. We perpetuate the mistake. If these spaces are unsustainable, maybe it's a good idea if people move to the city centers, or even to other countries. I think we are locking in a lot of intelligent people. Maybe they should move to China or from western Europe to eastern Europe, instead of being left behind. So again, let these wastelands go to waste, or let entrepreneurs take over. Like those in Detroit now, where dirt-cheap space brings new initiatives and projects. That's dynamism, which is not subsidized. It's a lifeline that draws resources from elsewhere. It is self-generated, unlike the subsidizing and freezing of everything. We need to get the government out of that process.

AB: *In your market-driven model, would everything be unprotected?*
PS: Yes, otherwise you only perpetuate the waste of resources.

AB: *What do you do with people who, for whatever reason, don't deliver productivity? How would you deal with this part of society? Or do you assume they'd just disappear according to your highly entrepreneurial concept of society that seems to be some kind of social Darwinism?*
PS: Well, how do we treat human resources that seem less productive, or seem to find it harder to catch on and be thrilled with the new productive potentials? I think everybody is productive and that entrepreneurs really go out and find these human resources. But we live in

this strange situation where we are also creating this disability. I think the welfare state, with its guarantees and its minimum wage restrictions, is cutting off career potential. It's nearly irresistible for somebody who is, for one reason or another, not well positioned, to be taken care of rather than finding their niche. In the contemporary world, with the internet and so many new companies roaming the scene to find new workers—people who can work from home, who can do all sorts of things—I think there is no reason to presume that somebody's inherently unproductive. The market will find these resources and create useful mechanisms to make this happen. Yes, there is disability and tragedy but there will be plenty of non-governmental organizations and charities that would have a lot of resources to help them in a much more humane and tailored way than the state. My imagination is not only about private enterprise in terms of profit, but also private not-for-profit initiatives, which at the moment are held back by the immense amount of resources being drawn back into the state bureaucracy. If you look back at the nineteenth century you realize that, even though the world was much poorer, a much larger percentage of people's incomes was given in charitable donations and communal contributions, without the coercion of the state … I think we have learned that the existence of the welfare state actually makes society less productive, which is very tough to swallow. When welfare was introduced and ramped up in the '50s and '60s, there was a sense that what was left of poverty would be eradicated. This never happened. So maybe we have to step back and confess that we made a huge historical mistake.

AB: *It sounds like a political campaign! The eight-point manifesto that you presented at the 2016 WAF in Berlin was rebuked by many—even the mayor of London replied to it in a newspaper article. Assuming you were considering a shift into politics, what would your program be? Historically, it is mainly right-wing architects who go into politics …*

Photograph from the series *Private Public Places* by Luca Picardi showing a privatized open space in Broadgate, London, which is obviously not designed for lingering. Photo: © Luca Picardi

PS: The more I get into the topic of property—which is of course a very political topic—the more I can imagine becoming *more* political. I started becoming politicized after the 2008 crash and the following debt crisis. Then the Arab Spring and its repercussions caused a lot of our work in the Middle East to stop. The world has become much more volatile and our business potentials have been stunted and compromised. The parametricism movement has been derailed to some extent through all these processes.

I'm still an architect, and as architects we get close to mayors, to city-building, nation-building. I identify with cities and countries, as well as leaders and entrepreneurs: as an architect you see the big picture, you see how things interact and integrate. I find it a fascinating form of engagement, but it doesn't mean I will give up my professional life. I wear a different hat when I'm working within existing political and economic frameworks. I love to speculate about what's possible and what we could create. Obviously, I have an interest in radical libertarian discourse, but if one were to enter an arena, one would do it gradually, step by step: roll back the state; open up degrees of freedom; turn to employers, to communities, to individuals to be self-employed and self-contracting. There's no guarantee that what one theorizes would come to pass or would flourish, but I think it's worth trying new avenues and taking some risks for more degrees of freedom. That's what my message would be in the political domain, and I'm agitating for that from within the urban and planning arena.

This is what we are confronting right now: restrictions, where we seem to be unable to do creative work in a city, where everything is totally prescribed—the land-use, the total volume of buildings, the unit mix, the unit size… There's nothing left for us to really challenge in terms of how social relations should be structured and ordered. Architecture and spatial arrangements are very important elements in the evolution of society, and if we freeze them, we will be freezing human progress. That becomes, at a certain point, a political issue.

Defending Democracy
Against Anarcho-Capitalist Architecture

MANUEL SHVARTZBERG CARRIÓ

I have been asked by ARCH+ to write a rebuttal to Patrik Schumacher's widely disseminated claims for an "anarcho-capitalist architecture"—the latest iteration of his "parametricism" crusade (see Patrik Schumacher, p. 78–83). The risk of engaging with extreme right-wing discourses like this one is that they are so one-sided, polarizing, and in some ways, toxic, that they don't usually allow for the kind of measured and critical thinking that should accompany complex and nuanced discussions of the vitally important, indeed existential, questions they raise, namely: basic issues of justice, political life, and the distribution of resources in society that affect us all. A shouting match does not clarify such issues, it merely indexes the power of those who shout the loudest—giving an edge to the sensationalist, the bully, the sophist, the demagogue, and ultimately, the privileged. Impassioned public discourse requires a level playing field, and Mr. Schumacher's intellectual project, grounded in his de facto position as an active power player within the contemporary nexus of architecture and capital, would systematically demolish it. The stakes are high.

Let me first begin by outlining those aspects of Mr. Schumacher's position that I think ought to be welcomed in the discourse of architecture and public culture at large. At the broadest level, it is high time to reappraise architecture's role in society, not merely as an aesthetic or symbolic representation of the social but as a crucial site of production where political struggles are played out, actively constructing the categories of "architecture" and "society." This relation needs to be revisited in toto, from the politics of architecture as a profession all the way to the practices of designing, constructing, and running urban spaces, neighborhoods, cities, infrastructures, and territories.[01]

More precisely, I welcome the opportunity to discuss the need for establishing a discourse on architecture's construction of what we call "economic" matters. At its root, the issue revolves around the articulations between economics, politics, and architecture—with the latter as, perhaps, a crucial hinge that could undo the facile binary between the "normal" administration of things and processes of social change.[02] In this connection, Mr. Schumacher challenges us to address the question of what, exactly, do we understand "social change" to be, and how, exactly, does it come about? He forces us to face these questions, not simply of "change," but of change for what, by whom, where exactly, and managed in what way.

Finally, I agree with Mr. Schumacher's general dissatisfaction with the dominant modes of urban development and its attendant modes of regulation. However, I radically disagree with both his diagnosis and his prescriptions. Development is indeed over-regulated and over-prescribed, limiting possibilities for architecture and social flourishing at large. The problem, though, is that it is over-regulated to *support* capitalism at the expense of the majority of society. I would like it to be re-regulated with the help of architects as citizens; not, as he would have it, with architects as mere market-operators, which leaves the foundations of the problem intact. This means reinventing architecture by reengaging politics, not just attempting to actualize a nineteenth-century free market ideology and its related discourse regarding the architect as a singular genius-entrepreneur. Since his position entails, implicitly and explicitly, many complex consequences, I have organized my response around four main aspects: a historical argument; a political-economic, or democratic, argument; an ontological argument; and finally, an architectural argument.

I. History

At the heart of the idea of an "anarcho-capitalist architecture" lies a romanticization of the medieval and early modern European city. In its crudest expression, this fantasy today takes the form of a return to feudalistic imaginaries of independent city-states powered by futuristic technology and where the traditional monarch has been replaced by "the Great Algorithm": capital. Hence, we see the emergence of alt-right discourses like "neoreaction," an ideology subscribed by the likes of Silicon Valley billionaire Peter Thiel that seeks to undo democratic advances that started in the eighteenth century—the establishment of social, economic, civil, and political rights, variously institutionalized by different forms of democracy: parliamentary, bourgeois, constitutional (and hopefully one day,

radical). Instead, neoreactionaries advocate the rule of private contract as the exclusive instrument for organizing social relations, and the complete dismantling of the state, whereby, as Mr. Schumacher defends, those cast aside by the market will fall into the hands of private charities and philanthropy.

As mentioned above, this vision rests on an idealized image of the medieval and early modern city—like those of the Hanseatic League, a quasi-confederation of Northern European trading cities—in which the relative freedoms gained from the sovereign by artisans, merchants, and small property-holders were able to spur a dynamic of functional differentiation in society between new classes, emerging professionals, and cities themselves.[03] The narrative of "free trade" underwriting this popular view, and later eulogized by Adam Smith, has today become not only an omnipresent ideology, but also the very operating system of the institutions governing global capitalism, from the European Union to the World Bank. Yet, it is striking how such a global system—now digitally encoded—still harkens back to medieval imaginaries of organic communities, merchant self-interest, archaic instruments of trade, and alchemical mysticism.

The importance of this imaginary to the current state of affairs cannot be overestimated. It serves as a legitimating myth for the most extreme forms of neoliberal ideology. The problem is not just that it presents a romantic version of the past, an arcadia of freedom, but that the way this is expressed reproduces some of the worst forms of historical violence the world has ever seen. It is no coincidence that much of the alt-right has seized on this imaginary, because it suggests a world that is resolutely white and Judeo-Christian—celebrating (or at least minimizing) the religious crusades of medieval Europe, the oppressive nature of feudalistic and early-capitalist social relations, and the plunder of colonial conquest and subjugation that underpinned European development throughout modernity.

Thus, while ostensibly what is being celebrated is merely the idea of a society of property-holders, all trading freely with each other, the history of how such a society was in fact built is effectively obscured and mystified. By the nineteenth century, as Karl Polanyi wrote in his seminal critique of unregulated capitalism:

"Trade had become linked with peace. In the past the organization of trade had been military and warlike; it was an adjunct of the pirate, the rover, the armed caravan, the hunter and trapper, the sword-bearing merchant, the armed burgesses of the towns, the adventurers and explorers, the planters and conquistadores, the man-hunters and slave traders, the colonial armies of the chartered companies."[04]

According to Polanyi, it was not that trade created peace, but that rule-by-trade (in the form of an imperialist financial capitalism undergirded by the gold standard) demanded peace among European nations so that they could continue exploiting the rest of the world in a more orderly and systematic fashion. Indeed, right-wing ideologues like Carl Schmitt, shedding the proverbial fig leaf of liberalism, saw European colonial plunder as a necessary prerequisite to the accelerated power drive of Western modernization.[05]

A few critiques of Mr. Schumacher's position thus flow from the historical conditions implicit in his claims. At the most basic level, the history of "free market" capitalism is fraught with violence and dispossession. But even if we accepted that such violence was now in the past (which it is not), unfettered capitalism brings about its own set of problems. As Smith himself noted, competitive capitalism requires a state that will regulate markets, providing public goods like roads, ports, courts of justice, education and security so that trade can actually take place. As the world capitalist market expanded and integrated, the birth of large corporations exacerbated the need for closer cooperation between states and markets. Joseph Schumpeter, no stranger to classical liberalism, also concluded that unfettered corporate capitalism tends toward centralization, which in turn requires bureaucratization and thus ultimately, more managed modes of political economy.[06] Failure to do so leads inexorably to massive systemic crises—of overproduction, lack of effective demand, and financial bubbles—as seen in the late nineteenth century, the Great Depression of the 1930s, and the Great Recession of 2008, among many other periods of capitalist meltdown.

II. Political Economy; or, The Meaning of Democracy

The historical argument around how capitalism began, and its historical specificity as a mode of production in which a minority controls the majority of the social surplus, is key to understanding the ethics implied by Mr. Schumacher's position, and of articulating a counter-project to it.[07] As we have seen, a key aspect of the anarcho-capitalist narrative is the naturalization of a society of property-holders, and the imaginary of a society "free" from political institutions that would regulate market processes—in effect, their total dissolution in favor of private contracts. However, the emergence of private property rests not only on contracts, but on coercion, exploitation, violence, and dispossession. Two main consequences flow from this. If the "unit" of measure of modern capitalism has historically been twinned with the nation-state as the largest concrete juridical-spatial form of organization—and, more recently, supra-national institutions like the European Union—Mr. Schumacher's emphasis on private contract would ultimately entail the dissolution of these *political* mechanisms for orchestrating trade and development. In the face of historical oppressions carried out by states, in principle this might not be a bad thing. However, while a universalistic theory of private contract would undo the sovereignty of the state, it also has the inverse effect upon the sovereignty of the individual—inflating it with an undue amount of agency and authority.

A key aspect of the anarcho-capitalist narrative is the naturalization of a society of property-holders, and the imaginary of a society "free" from political institutions that would regulate market processes.

In classical liberalism, the relation between the market (as the site of private self-interest) and civil society (as the sphere of community engagement) was grounded in religious morality, the cultural mores and norms of patriarchy (organizing and reproducing the familial division of labor), and the social constructions of race associated with nation-state identitarianism. In the contemporary anarcho-capitalist ideology extolled by Mr. Schumacher, these cultural modulations become naturalized to such a degree—their historical roots and actual instantiations so obscured—that they appear not to be present anymore. As a result, the individual appears as entirely self-determined and self-realized, seeking their own further "optimization" as the main goal—what Mr. Schumacher refers to as "becoming superhuman"; an incredibly problematic terminology for multiple reasons, not least because the techno-utopian rhetoric, in its disregard for history, effectively smuggles in old liberalism's religious moralization, patriarchy, and racism.

This type of bloated hyper-individualism masks an intense authoritarianism. The self-realizing, self-determining individual, becomes the sole unit—the irreducible atom—of political sovereignty. As a consequence, the market's systematic production of winners and losers becomes a discursive truth machine for disclosing individuals' true nature (their ability to compete, to perform), obscuring the underlying socio-political conditions that determine the structure of the market in the first place. It then becomes tenable to sustain the dubious proposition that the poor and oppressed are wholly responsible for their poverty and oppression. Again, this view is only possible under a discourse that would completely disregard the historical processes that gave rise to, and continue to structure, capitalist society. In other words, the private contract is almost never a purely "free exchange" between fully self-realized and self-determined individuals. Individuals arrive at their positions historically, and history is underpinned by the oppression and exploitation of vast amounts of subjects that were violently kept from the possibility of self-determination: whether it is the domestic labor of women, the forced labor of slaves, the expropriated labor of workers, or the massacres and displacements of indigenous peoples. Pretending that this history doesn't continue to structure social relations today constitutes an illegitimate, performative claim to power.

The reality is that all forms of society are based on social contracts that are not algorithmically derived by the sole economic calculus of self-governed individuals, but through very complex social, political, and cultural mediations. In other words, legitimacy must always rest on political deliberation, not merely market transactions. If democracy makes it harder to "optimize" certain parameters, like "productivity" in Mr. Schumacher's telling, the solution isn't to curtail democracy by subordinating populations to the rule of markets; it is to subordinate markets to the rule of democracy, effectively re-signifying the meaning of "productivity" and establishing a new distribution of the social surplus. Let's not forget that democracy means the rule of the *demos*; the rule of those without any special qualifications—by birth, wealth, skill, or status—to rule.

The anarcho-capitalist tale would have us believe that the market is a natural mechanism for sorting out those who should rule, and those who should obey. This is a coercive and deeply authoritarian vision, because the history of markets itself is fraught with violence. Furthermore, since "unfettered" capitalist markets entrench power by design—leading to massive structural inequalities, the creation of monopolies and other forms of political-economic domination (such as unfair trade agreements)—anarcho-capitalism is in direct tension with the principle of democracy.

Once a minority can control the political channels by which to secure their own position—in our age, the relative minority of property-holders in the form of financial and real estate assets—democracy is critically undermined. The ethical question of how those who are cast aside by the market are treated—being "rescued" by private charities, according to Mr. Schumacher—is one of moral imperative: in my view, it is immoral, and a philosophical mistake based on the long-debunked myths of methodological individualism, to simply write off those who do not "perform" under the highly questionable rule of the free market.

But is also a question of political economy at two other levels: one concerns the expediency of different ways of governing the social surplus; another concerns its aesthetic dimensions. On the former, Mr. Schumacher's claim that privatizing all land would lead to more dynamism and intensity of use is only tenable if we consider legitimate that only those with control of property will reap the surplus of investments that are, ultimately, produced collectively. In the case of Detroit, which he brings up (and where I live), the current wave of property speculation is built upon decades of investments that were both public and private. Furthermore, Detroit's "brand value," which is a central dimension of the current commodification, was built by local people's cultural innovations: its music, arts, design, and even traditions of organized labor (such as with the enormous legacy of the unions or of legendary civil rights and anti-imperialist activists like Grace Lee and James Boggs). It is these people, disproportionately black and poor, who are now bearing the brunt of Detroit's bankruptcy, housing foreclosures, and water crises. In Mr. Schumacher's playbook, such populations should be displaced at any cost, to satisfy the needs of capitalists and entrepreneurial *innovators*; their collective assets—schools, neighborhoods, cultural traditions—seized and privatized. Only a very cynical or ignorant perspective could construe such a displacement and appropriation of public life as positive. The solution isn't to gift these spaces and cultures to private interests—it is to find ways to re-invent Detroit's industrial base in a way that fully enfranchises local communities. The solution is the opposite to that advocated by Mr. Schumacher: space should be collectively owned and managed—which does not necessarily mean bureaucratically managed by the state, but by political-economic forms of association that democratize decision-making, productivity, and distribute equitably the ensuing social surplus. Demagogues often claim that this implies a blind opposition to any "change" or mobility whatsoever. The key issue, however, is not opposing change, it is to radically transform what it means, and to radically democratize how it happens.[08]

Finally, the question of political economy involves an aesthetic dimension—it operationalizes particular *figurations* of the relation between the individual and the community. In Mr. Schumacher's position, as discussed above, the individual is construed as fully autonomous, self-realized and self-determined. His call for "everybody to be on the edge and charging forward" has distinct military connotations, evoking the technological sublime and glorification of war of the Italian Futurists, or the soaring rhetoric of other avant-garde movements of the early twentieth century. However, while many of these movements modeled their visions on nurturing communities—such as the communal housing experiments of Red Vienna, for example—Mr. Schumacher's rhetoric suggests the neo-steampunk imaginaries of a war of all against all; future cities more like the dystopia of *Blade Runner*, a cacophony of barely controlled anarchic capitalism where massive monopoly corporations determine at will not only the distributions of roles and spaces in society, but the very nature of existence: a new ontological configuration synthesizing human and machine, fully determined by capital.

III. Ontology

This curious return to an old-fashioned futuristic imaginary, a techno-enhanced Hobbesianism, is in great part also derived from Mr. Schumacher's reliance on a very ontologically old-fashioned framework of methodological individualism. While the promise of hypermobility and the challenges of what it means to be (or not be) human should indeed be very contemporary concerns, Mr. Schumacher's discourse threatens to take us back to the dangerous fiction of the sovereign individual—smuggling in everything that historically comes with the undersides of humanism; capitalist male rule in its most heteronormative, patriarchal, and racist mold.

How would a society of private individuals deal with the fact that, as contemporary thinkers of ontology suggest, what we term human "individuality" is no more than a fiction of Enlightenment thought, propped up by the violent history of European colonialism? How can the sovereignty of the individual market transaction be coded into exchanges with animals, plants, or even microbes and minerals, which have now been shown to be clearly constitutive of the modern condition, but clearly do not partake of "human" individualism? At stake here is not only the neces-

sary relinquishment of parochial models of rule by the market—which means rule by methodological individualism—but also the method of constructing much more critical and capacious forms of democracy that would account for the full complexity of the imbrications between human and non-human subjects.

It is becoming increasingly evident that the challenge of capitalist globalization is not merely between different scales of sovereignty—between, say, powerful cities and marginalized peripheries; or nation-states and supra-national institutions—but also an assault on the very survival of ecological systems. How then, can we expect private contracts and markets to adequately contain (exclusively on their own) the diversity of constituencies involved in producing the Anthropocene: humans, animal populations, seeds, waterways, etc.? At some point we're going to have to leave the provincialism of auto-poiesis and engage with the real difficulties of sym-poiesis—making-with rather than self-making—as Donna Haraway has written.[09]

Designing for such complex ontological constituencies requires an expanded cultural and critical literacy, not merely the calculations of the market, for it demands a capacity to translate across epistemologies and conditions of existential co-sustainability. The core algorithm of capital—"increase productivity" through cutthroat competition by and for human players—is too simplistic an approach for the enormity of the problem in a world where over-production, over-consumption, and extractive processes are leading the planet toward catastrophic global warming. Instead of addressing the practical and political challenges of how to engage ontological cross-constituencies, Mr. Schumacher places his faith in the unfettered market to single-handedly resolve this situation—a situation the unfettered market was instrumentally involved in bringing about to begin with. Does Mr. Schumacher really believe that climate change can be resolved without the tools of political institutions, broad cultural and social deliberation, and complex multi-organizational cooperation? Architecture has much to offer this toolkit, but in order to do so, it has to become much more intellectually and politically engaged; more ontologically curious, not less so.

IV. Architecture

At the base of Mr. Schumacher's position lies a deep romanticism masking a deep fear of open-ended curiosity: that of architecture as a fully transparent social process that can be disclosed by self-mastered individuals, all freely transacting with each other via pri-

It is immoral, and a philosophical mistake based on the long-debunked myths of methodological individualism, to simply write off those who do not "perform" under the highly questionable rule of the free market.

The city as public space provides other logics that cut across the market's supply-demand imperative. This unscripted and unpredictable quality is the richness of the city.

vate contracts. This would be a fine vision, except that it is based on a flawed figuration of the human individual, erasing the 200-year-old history enfolded within it—from the dangerous mastery over nature, to the expropriation of large portions of the world, to an ideology of ever-expanding "progress" and aimless "growth," measured, tendentiously, as capital accumulation rather than the satisfaction of basic vital needs like health, housing, or culture. Bucolic romanticisms don't need to be dressed in neo-gothic (or neoreactionary?) styles for them to be recognized as such—sometimes they emerge in the form of steampunk deliriums appropriating the rhetoric of socialist avant-gardes without paying their full price in terms of actually delivering broad-based social advancement. At the most literal level, the type of city advocated by Mr. Schumacher is one in which the logic of hyper-segmentation, compartmentalization, and social inequality coded within the very mechanism of the market (when artificially construed as "autonomous" from other social processes), becomes articulated spatially. This is the city we see today under the most extreme forms of "unfettered capitalism"—one of massive segregations, insecurity, and precariousness. Whether or not cities can be designed to accommodate more nurturing social relations—relations not of exploitation for profit, but of complex cultural literacy, translation, and exchange—depends on how the social surplus they naturally produce as a function of their accommodating different, intersecting, forms of life, can be articulated politically.

In other words, the city as public space provides other logics that cut across the market's supply-demand imperative. This unscripted and unpredictable quality—which can be purposefully designed through public modes of deliberation and design, through deliberate attempts to create spaces that cannot be totalized by any one actor or system, spaces that foster democratic enfranchisement—is the richness of the city. As Claude Lefort famously put it, in democracy, "the locus of power becomes *an empty place*"[10]— empty in the full-of-potentiality-and-possibility sense.

Understood architecturally, this raises the question of how the creativity required for designing and instituting such unruled spaces can be politicized and managed—what are its parameters, its subjects, its subjacent material conditions, and how can they be nurtured, expanded, and democratized? Not so long ago, Jean-François Lyotard attempted to sketch out an answer to this question in a way that resisted both of the universalizing spirits of modernity: "systems" and "humanism."[11] His answer, to prize creative differentiations of the particular (what he termed "paralogy") was explicitly based upon rejecting the tyrannical logic of the market—in other words, directing resources toward culture, science, and other concrete endeavors of inquiry, and away from the instrumentalizing operations of capital, like the pervasive privatization of ever-larger spheres of the lifeworld. This doesn't mean rejecting the administrative forms of capitalist modernity—like corporations, contracts, or even markets—but understanding them as socio-technical assemblages that are not merely economic, but also political and architectural, and therefore, as collective instruments that may be redesigned to defend and empower democracy against capitalism.

01 As an example of an emerging organization seeking to do just this, see the work of The Architecture Lobby: www.architecture-lobby.org (accessed March 9, 2018).

02 This, in my view, is a core shortcoming of Jacques Rancière's political philosophy—a binary he reproduces in his dichotomy between "police" (the mere protection and administration of existing social roles) and "politics" (their effective opposition and re-distribution). See: Jacques Rancière, *Disagreement: Politics and Philosophy* (Minneapolis: University of Minnesota Press, 1999).

03 The early 20th century liberal historian Henri Pirenne supplies a popular template for this narrative.

04 Karl Polanyi, *The Great Transformation* (1944; Boston: Beacon Press, 1957), 15.

05 Carl Schmitt, *The Nomos of the Earth in the International Law of the Jus Publicum Europaeum* (1950; New York: Telos Press, 2003).

06 Joseph Schumpeter, *Capitalism, Socialism and Democracy* (1942; New York: Harper Perennial, 1962).

07 See, for instance: Ellen Meiksins Wood, *Democracy Against Capitalism: Renewing Historical Materialism* (London: Verso, 2016).

08 In the context of Detroit, a number of coalitions of citizens, artists, and architects have emerged to defend and give form to this project. See, for instance: www.detroitresists.org (accessed March 9, 2018).

09 Donna J. Haraway, *Staying with the Trouble: Making Kin in the Chthulucene* (Durham: Duke University Press, 2016).

10 Claude Lefort, "The Question of Democracy," *Democracy and Political Theory* (Minneapolis: University of Minnesota Press, 1988), 17.

11 Jean-François Lyotard, *The Postmodern Condition: A Report on Knowledge* (Manchester: Manchester University Press, 1984).

"The Public Sector is a Great Source of Freedom"

RENÉE GAILHOUSTET IN CONVERSATION
WITH FLORIAN HERTWECK AND NIKLAS MAAK

In 1962, Renée Gailhoustet became chief architect of Ivry-sur-Seine, a suburb in southeastern Paris, which to this day is administrated by the Communist Party. In 1968, she brought in Jean Renaudie, who had just left Atelier de Montrouge, to work with her on Ivry's urban redevelopment. Together with Raymonde Laluque, then director of public housing in Ivry, they developed an integrated urban concept that kept property in the public hand. The buildings were not grouped into functional zones, but arranged as mixed-use complexes with integrated community facilities and often included public-use spaces on the ground floor. The apartments there have amazing, very diverse layouts, often a variation on the triangular form, with spacious green roof terraces. Gailhoustet, now 88 years old, still lives in a rental apartment in the ensemble Le Liégat, one of the buildings she designed in Ivry.

FLORIAN HERTWECK: *We are here in your apartment in Ivry-sur-Seine, a former working-class town on the southeast edge of Paris, where you and Jean Renaudie had a decisive influence in the 1960s and 1970s with a decidedly public project. Today we'd like to talk to you about the relationship between the private and public spheres. For some decades now, the public sphere seems to be shrinking or withdrawing, while isolated enclaves are forming in the cities and the real estate industry is dominating the production of space.*

RENÉE GAILHOUSTET: The issue you raise is a fundamental one in urban planning, where there are constant conflicts between the individual and the community. Here in Ivry, our guiding principle was to mix the private and the communal. Whether by car or on foot, Ivry is always easy to access. This is rather the exception in old Paris, where communal places are controlled everywhere, where you always need a key or a door code. In Ivry there is no access control, except of course at the door to the resident's apartment, but that goes without saying. The building we are in right now can be accessed day and night. I am still convinced that this is a good thing, but the trend is actually going in the opposite direction.

NIKLAS MAAK: *What was the main idea behind your buildings and how are they different from Renaudie's?*
RG: Renaudie's architecture is certainly more capitalist, but we also have many things in common, such as the basic idea of letting people circulate everywhere on the ground floor. This was achieved by establishing various public spaces, public gardens, entrance halls, and covered passages that are always accessible.

Renée Gailhoustet in front of her apartment in the ensemble Le Liégat, Ivry-sur-Seine.

Renée Gailhoustet

There is a school here that Renaudie built in the midst of the apartments. Usually schools are separate, autonomous places. Here, all of the apartment terraces face the school, so that mothers can see their children there. For Renaudie, this direct relationship between home and school—or between private life and community—was central.

FH: *In addition to the school, many of the community facilities are located on the ground floors.*
RG: That's right: the LCR—Local Collectif Résidentiel (Local Residential Collective) plays an important role here. It's a multifunctional common space that anyone can use with authorization from the municipal HLM (Habitations à Loyer Modéré—"rent-controlled housing") Office. A Muslim funeral took place here recently, and children's birthday parties are often held there as well. I myself have used the space for conferences on architecture and urban planning. Since this space is located in the middle of the residential complex, many residents will pass by and say, "Something's going on, let's take a look." This makes these spaces public, which I like very much. Anyone can organize an event, even people who don't live in the complex, and anyone can participate.

NM: *And who manages this space?*
RG: The HLM Office, which also takes care of the apartments. Apartments like this are exclusively rentals. None of the apartments in our projects are privately owned.

FH: *Was there a formula according to which one of these common spaces was allocated to a certain number of dwellings?*
RG: There was a formula, but I don't recall the exact ratio. There had to be a critical mass of apartments—not five, but rather fifty—which would then be granted a LCR of around 150 square meters.

FH: *And was there a corresponding budget for that?*
RG: There was a small budget for the construction of the common spaces.

Sometimes we managed to create quite generous spaces with it. For example, on the top floor of the residential towers I designed a common room with 300 square meters of space and direct access to a common roof terrace.

NM: *Was that only possible because there was a communist mayor that sought to do things differently?*
RG: That was certainly decisive. There were numerous public workshops where our project was discussed; but as always in France, it was the mayor that ultimately had the say. Renaudie and I never intended to create housing that was isolated from shopping and public facilities, but rather to mix these uses among the buildings, which was an idea that the mayor liked.

NM: *As for the terraces that are so important in your projects, how were they different from those of Renaudie?*
RG: In this building here, the terraces are connected, which makes the exchange among the neighbors more intensive. Renaudie's terraces are more separate, which also makes them more protected. But we put 30 centimeters of soil on all of the terraces. Have you seen the cherry tree on mine?

FH: *Impressive. One resident told me that living here was like living in the countryside and the city at the same time. Did you have an extra budget for these spacious terraces?*
RG: The first project of this kind with intensively planted terraces was the Casanova complex by Renaudie. He brought a model of it, clearly showing the terraces, to the workshops with the residents. People went wild with joy because social housing hadn't seen anything like that before. Villa Savoye has a green roof terrace, but that was for the elite. The aim here was to provide rental apartments with real gardens on each floor. At Casanova, there was no extra budget for that. Renaudie managed to install the terraces essentially as a gift to the residents. The political mood at the time also gave us a boost. When Casanova was handed over to its resi-

dents, the response was very positive. It was the revolutionary spirit of 1968. Many architects, younger ones in particular, came to Ivry and studied Casanova with enthusiasm. Some asked themselves why they shouldn't try to do the same. Since then there have been many similar approaches, especially in the communist-managed suburbs to the north and southeast of Paris. It was a real movement. And over time, the government agreed to finance such additional features.

NM: *You mentioned the political situation. Were you already a communist when you came to Paris from Algeria at the age of 18 in 1947?*
RG: No, I came to Paris to study philosophy; there was a communist cell there that I sympathized with. After a year, I got my membership card.

NM: *Were you involved in the student revolt?*
RG: Of course. We were in the streets, distributing leaflets and left-wing newspapers, and confronting our political opponent. By the way, Jean-Marie Le Pen was already around then. I studied at the Sorbonne, and he studied at the Paris Law Faculty, which was a pool for fascist students. He regularly set his troops on us as we handed out leaflets—he even broke my nose!

FH: *Why did you give up philosophy for architecture?*
RG: I wasn't a good philosopher because I was much too interested in politics. I came to architecture through a friend, enrolled at the École des Beaux-Arts, and joined the studio of Marcel Lods …

FH: *… who accepted women. That wasn't a matter of course.*
RG: That's right, no one took on women, except for Lods. After all, the ratio was 10 women to 40 men. I worked in the office of Georges Candilis on the side, mainly drawing plans for Shadrach Woods.

FH: *How did you translate your philosophical background and political commitment into architecture?*
RG: They translated themselves, into

an unconditional love for Le Corbusier! We knew all of his projects and books; we devoured them.

FH: *Unconditional? Even though you worked with Renaudie and Woods? Both were more or less involved in Team 10, but since the 1950s they had been criticizing the great master's ideas, especially the separation of functions. Renaudie himself said that Ivry was born from a rejection of the Athens Charter. And in your description of Ivry, you also support the articulation of different functions within the buildings, even spaces that are not assigned to specific functions. Wasn't it also about building on a critique of functionalist dogma?*
RG: Yes—in spite of which we shared an unconditional love for Le Corbusier. You can see his influence in my early projects, both in my diploma project and in the Raspail Tower, which features staggered half-duplexes with an integrated 300-square-meter painting studio.

NM: *How did you become chief architect of Ivry-sur-Seine?*
RG: After my studies, I worked for an architect named Roland Dubrulle, who was entrusted with Ivry's redevelopment. Since his firm already had a lot of work and he showed no active interest in this task, he offered to introduce me to the responsible authorities and hand over the job to me. Then I worked on the afore-mentioned residential tower near the town hall, the Raspail Tower. This became embroiled in a huge controversy.[01] People couldn't understand that residential towers were being built in a working-class suburb, where before there had only been small, pavilion-like detached homes. This debate helped to make Ivry somewhat popular. The city council then succeeded in convincing a factory to move from here to further outside the city, which freed up a large area for development. That's when I brought Renaudie on board. Renaudie, who as an 18-year-old in 1943, and had joined the Resistance in Limoges, had come to Paris to study painting, first with old [Auguste] Perret, and then he switched to architecture with Marcel Lods, like me. That's where I met not just him but

also his future partners at Atelier de Montrouge, which they founded shortly after graduating in the late 1950s. In 1968, however, they had a big falling-out: Renaudie refused to compromise on their project in Vaudreuil, which led to their separation, and then I brought him to Ivry. While I was working on the Spinoza complex, which included 70 apartments, a children's library, a kindergarten, a foyer for young workers, and other communal areas, he designed the Casanova terraced complex, which also included a shopping arcade. Instead of load-bearing walls, which was the norm in social housing at the time, he used a girder support system, which gave him enormous freedom in designing the floor plans.

FH: *At the time, you were working with Raymonde Laluque, who became director of the HLM Office in 1965, and who was also a young woman and a communist. Did she define the programs?*
RG: She was an impressive woman. She allowed us to dissolve the separation of functions that was customary at the time and to integrate the various activities within the buildings. That didn't always work. The residential towers, for instance, only have a few shops on the ground floor. But since the surface area of the towers is relatively small, so is the space available for public use. Renaudie, on the other hand, developed much lower and more linear buildings, which enabled much more intensive public use. This includes the many sheltered traffic areas running along the buildings, sometimes penetrating them, which were always linked to public spaces that were never located on the higher floors, but always on the ground floor to foster accessibility.

NM: *As a former communist, what do you think of the idea of the state owning land and property?*
RG: For us it was clear that we were working for communist-led communes, and our client was the HLM Office, a municipal institution. It wasn't the state that owned the land in Ivry, but the commune. And it either already owned the land that was needed for develop-ment, or would acquire it. Under no

circumstances, however, would it privatize the property. We were therefore part of an entirely public chain of urban develop-ment: from the land owner—the com-mune—to the developer and the distributor, which were both in the hands of the municipal HLM Office, which was finan-cially supported by the state. All of the apartments were rented. Everything was controlled and managed by the commune.

FH: *And this public development chain then led to this specific architecture. Do you think that these projects would have been possible, had parts of this chain been privatized?*
RG: For me, the public sector is a great source of freedom. My private clients have always been too focused on profita-bility. It shouldn't be expensive, but it should yield high gains. It was always like having a conversation with someone who was hard of hearing. The commune, on the other hand, was more accommo-dating in critical situations. It would be more like: "We're running out of money. Be careful with how you can still imple-ment your ideas." After all, it's not much more expensive to put 30 centimeters of soil on the terraces than any other kind of floor covering. But the fact that the terraces could be so large was also due to the motivation of the public developer.

FH: *This is also the case with the communal facilities on the top floor of the residential towers, which is the most profitable area in a commercial project. Would this still be possible today?*
RG: It would at least be desirable. French society was certainly shaped by the leftist sentiment after the war. And that no longer seems to be the case.

01 Also involved in the debate was Dubrulle, for whom the experiments with duplex apartments went too far, such as those in Corbusier's *Unité d'Habitation*, and even more so in the Soviet *dom kommuna* from the 1920s with its integrated com-munal facilities, which inspired Gailhoustet and Laluque. Dubrulle tried to win over some of the city councilors to his side, advocating the building of more "normal" social housing. See Bénédicte Chaljub, "Lorsque l'engagement entre maîtrise d'ouvrage et maîtres d'œuvre encourage l'innovation architecturale: le cas du centre ville d'Ivry-sur-Seine 1962–1986," in *Cahier d'Histoire. Revue d'histoire critique* 109 (2009): 77–94.

Jean Renaudie

1 Cité Spinoza, R. Gailhoustet, 1973
2 Tour Raspail, R. Gailhoustet, 1968
3 Ensemble Jean-Baptiste Clement,
   J. Renaudie, 1975
4 Ensemble Jeanne Hachette,
   J. Renaudie, 1972
5 Tour Jean-Baptiste Clement,
   Sofinin, 1973
6 Ensemble Marat, R. Gailhoustet, 1986
7 Tour Jeanne Hachette,
   R. Gailhoustet, 1976
8 Ensemble Voltaire, J. Renaudie &
   N. Schuch, 1987
9 Ensemble Le Liégat, R. Gailhoustet, 1982
10 Tour Casanova, R. Gailhoustet, 1976
11 Cité du Parc & L'École d'Albert Einstein,
   J. Renaudie & N. Schuch, 1981
12 Ensemble Danielle Casanova,
   J. Renaudie, 1972
13 Tour Lénine, R. Gailhoustet, 1970
14 Cité Maurice Thorez
15 City hall of Ivry-sur-Seine

As part of the urban renewal program initiated in 1960, 1,300 new housing units were built in Ivry-sur-Seine, mostly social housing (HLM), 30,000 m^2 of commercial space, 18,000 m^2 of office space, 3,500 parking spaces, and various public facilities. The realization of the project took about 30 years.

Jean Renaudie: city plan for Le Vaudreuil, 1968. This project illustrates Renaudie's theoretical understanding of the city as a mixed fabric with individual functions embedded in the overall context of public and private spaces. This plan thus deviates from the principles of the Athens Charter.
© Jean Renaudie

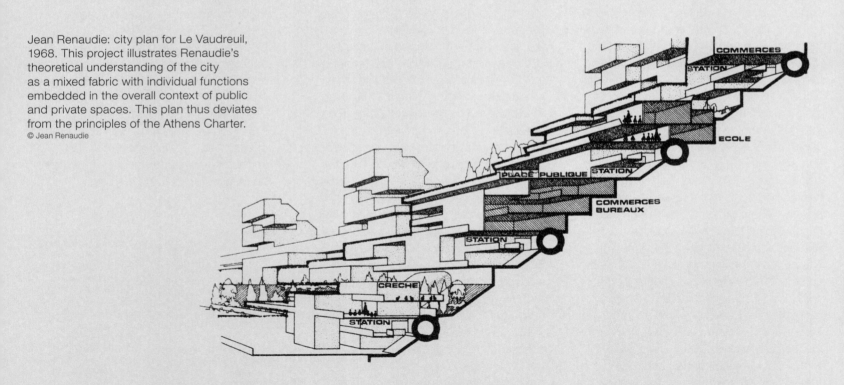

Aerial view of the ensemble Danielle Casanova, 1975.

Jean Renaudie: ensemble
Danielle Casanova,
third floor ground plan.

Jean Renaudie: Ensemble Jeanne Hachette, first floor shopping arcade.

Ensemble Voltaire and ensemble Le Liégat at Place Voltaire. © Lorenzo Zandri ZA2

Le Liégat

After completing the first residential towers and Cité Spinoza, Renée Gailhoustet worked with Jean Renaudie to revise Roland Dubrulle's master plan for Ivry-sur-Seine. The first experimental drafts for Le Liégat, the ensemble to be built in the area between the municipal post office and Renaudie and Nina Schuch's Place Voltaire, already called for a combination of public functions and social housing. The buildings were not completed until 1978; by that time Gailhoustet had realized a similar project in Aubervilliers, the residential complex La Maladrerie, in which she resolutely abandoned the modernist models she had hitherto emulated.

Le Liégat, a nine-storey building, is based on a load-bearing structure organized as a grid of numerous hexagonal cells supporting radial trusses and series of pillars. This scheme allows the building to benefit from the advantages of open-plan architecture while providing a high level of spatial complexity as the walls inserted between the pillars form variegated polygonal floor plans. The terraced upper storeys throughout the complex look out on spacious roof gardens. Several interior courtyards above the building's hexagonal centers bring natural light into the apartments around them and the publicly accessible ground floor.

At street level, an arcade with altogether seven entrances connects the complex to Rue G. Péri, Rue Danielle Casanova, and Place Voltaire. It also provides access to the courtyards and community facilities such as the Local Collectif Résidentiel (LCR), service rooms, and the community garden between the ensemble and the adjacent post office. Retailers, studios, and architecture firms occupy the commercial spaces along the arcade, turning the ground floor into a public space, with businesses, offices, and various events in the community hall bringing the wider citizenry of Ivry to the scene. By contrast, the 146 apartments above, grouped around interior court-yards and accessed via five circulation cores, convey a sheltered and neighborly atmosphere. Each unit has an individual layout and opens onto at least one terrace, conceived by Gailhoustet as an extension of the living space; each terrace abuts those of neighboring units. The residents plant the gardens to suit their individual tastes, lending the building's sloping exterior the appearance of an inhabited hill. The scenery recalls suburban gardens, with lively interaction between neighbors, a friendly ambiance that defines the complex's character. The building costs exceeded the standards in effect at the time by a mere 10 percent.

The complex marks the transition to the second phase in Gailhoustet's oeuvre that was influenced by Renaudie's understanding of architecture as a continuous fabric, his rejection of standardization, and his firm belief that spatial diversity is in itself a form of luxury. NF

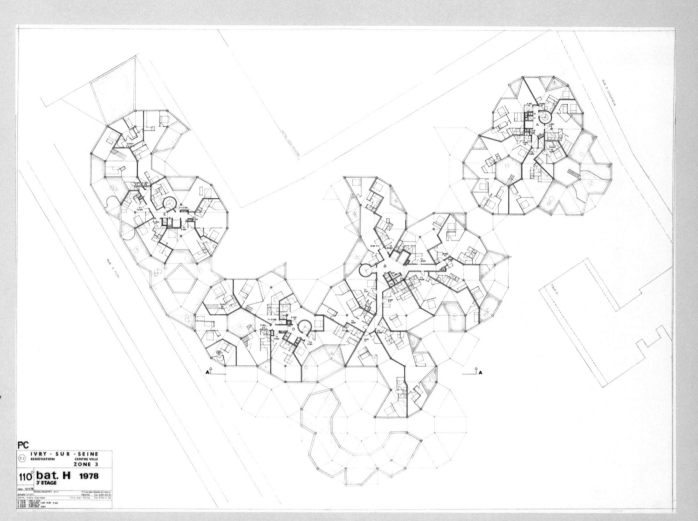

Ensemble Le Liégat: third floor ground plan, planning stage 1978. The hexagonal structure and the various orientations of the balconies and terraces create intimate neighborly connections.

Ensemble Le Liégat: ground plan of ground floor, planning stage 1978. The building is characterized by a winding passageway with retail space, offices, and communal areas.

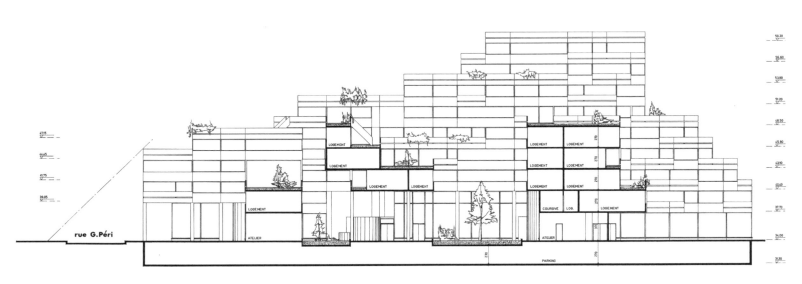

Ensemble Le Liégat: section, 1978. The terraced reduction of the volume on the upper floors allows strong external connections and generous exposure to light.

Ensemble Le Liégat: access level during construction phase in April 1980.

Patio of the ensemble Le Liégat. The hexagonal arrangement of the columns defines the center of the courtyard. The overlapping of different levels creates covered outdoor areas.

Renée Gailhoustet

Each unit has a different layout and opens onto an individual terraced garden.

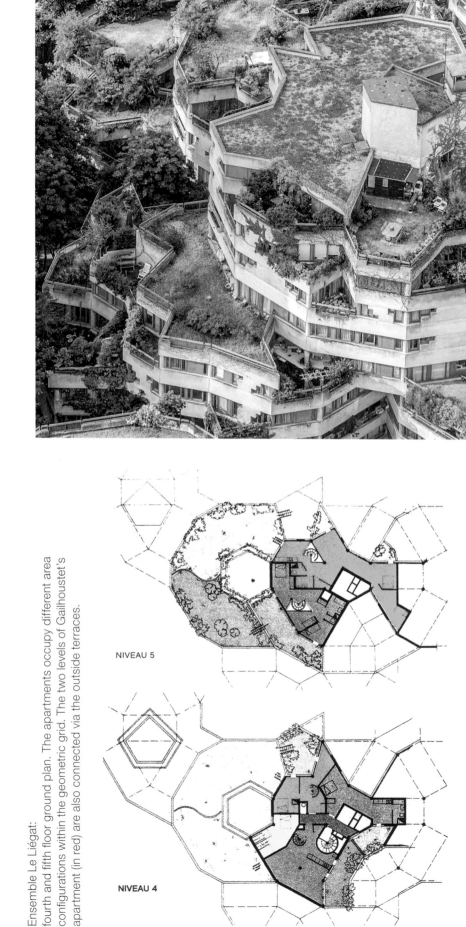

Ensemble Le Liégat: view from the north. © Alex S. MacLean

Ensemble Le Liégat: fourth and fifth floor ground plan. The apartments occupy different area configurations within the geometric grid. The two levels of Gailhoustet's apartment (in red) are also connected via the outside terraces.

NIVEAU 5

NIVEAU 4

References

Bénédicte Chaljub, *La politesses des maisons – Renée Gailhoustet, architecte* (Arles: Actes Sude Beaux Arts, 2009).
Bénédicte Chaljub, „Réinventer les modes d'habiter: L'oeuvre insolite de Renée Gailhoustet," Société suisse des ingénieurs et des architects, ed., Tracés 139, no. 7 (Zurich 2013).
Renée Gailhoustet, Des racines pour la ville (Paris: Les éditions de l'Epure, 1998).
Renée Gailhoustet, *Éloge du logement* (Paris, Sodedat 93).
Renée Gailhoustet, *Le panoramique et l'Observatoire de la ville*, (Ivry-sur-Seine: Ne pas plier, 2000).
Jean Renaudie, *La Ville est une Combinatoire* (Ivry-sur-Seine: movitcity édition, 2012).
Irénée Scalbert, *A Right to Difference* (London: Architectural Association, 2004).
Irénée Scalbert, *AA Files 23* (London: Architectural Association, 1992).
Johanna Diehl & Niklas Maak, *Eurotopians: Fragmente einer anderen Zukunft* (Munich: Hirmer, 2017).
www.johannadiehl.com

Into the Ground

How the Financialization of Property Markets and Land Use puts Cities under Pressure

MARKUS HESSE

Aerial view of Plateau Kirchberg and the European Court of Justice.

Dark deals

It is by now common knowledge that the process of globalization in recent decades has profoundly transformed the realities of life in cities, along with their prospects for development. Far-reaching political regulation fostered the emergence of a global trade and production regime in the last century, followed by the globalization of services. Technological innovations in data processing enabled current trends such as digitization and platform economics. The growing influence of the financial markets on the real economy has further intensified these trends. Traditional boundaries between economic sectors or territories are disintegrating, while global and local standards are becoming increasingly blurred. Property, as a fundamentally immovable good, is joining the global exchange economy as an active asset.

How local economic and living environments are changing under the influence of global exploitation is reflected in the case of the Büchertisch ("Book Table") in the neighborhood of Berlin-Kreuzberg in Germany. This non-profit initiative is dedicated to the promotion of reading culture, donating books to schools and many other institutions. A change in owners at the property on Mehringdamm, where the Büchertisch had been a tenant for 12 years, resulted in a drastic rent hike. Because its sponsoring association was unable to cover the added cost, the Büchertisch was forced to find a new home. So far, the plot of this story seems to follow the well-known pattern of capitalization, appreciation, and displacement. This particular case, however, entails an elaborate web of ownership structures, financial transactions, and tax benefits, which has only recently emerged. It involves the use of a complex network of companies and shareholdings, in order to lower profits for tax purposes and provide shareholders with high returns. The causal relationships in the case of the apartment building in Kreuzberg, where the Büchertisch was located, are truly global: they include a building portfolio in Berlin, financing structures in Great Britain and Germany, tax-optimized administrative offices in Luxembourg and Cyprus, and a company headquarters on the British island of Jersey.[01] Such "dark deals," the primary aim of which is tax reduction, are turning cities into playgrounds for global profit-making interests.

Political economy of the city

The era of local autonomous urban economies has long since passed. During the great age of nineteenth-century industrialization, many cities already based their economies on exchange with other locations; this so-called export base was regarded as the key to economic success. What was locally determined over the long term, on the other hand, was the political field, where decisions were made and urban development was steered towards growth and competition. To this day, alliances of important players from companies, chambers of commerce, trade unions, and political parties are still calling the shots. They view the city as a driving force for growth, a "growth machine"[02] for the prosperous development of national economies.

Land has long been a key resource for such growth policies, even before the emergence of financial capitalism. This has been evident in many countries since around 1980, when major urban projects started being built at strategically important locations, outside of traditional paths of urban expansion (outward growth). The decline of old industries and changes in port and logistics businesses opened up new land reserves within the cities, which could be used for lucrative development projects. Not only did these spaces help to localize new services—such as the Docklands in London, Battery Park in New York City, La Défense in Paris, the Kirchberg quarter in Luxembourg City, and countless urban waterfront revitalization projects. The rent gap of these high-potential, mostly undeveloped areas made it possible to skim off enormously high yields. Urban growth impulses and private profits were closely linked in these projects.

What's new?

Recent developments, due to the expansion of the financial sector, have fundamentally changed this system. The strong growth in services in the overall economy has led to high demands for office space, particularly in urban areas. As the financial economy increasingly decouples from the real economy, the real estate industry is being integrated into the financial sector. More and more investment capital is flowing into landownership, both from real estate companies and third parties within the framework of diversified investment strategies. Land has become a tradable good, and speculation determines the playing field in increasingly volatile markets.

The large influx of international investment capital into the cities is reinforcing this trend. The result is an increasing delocalization of the real estate industry. This means that a broader range of companies owns real estate, with the industry increasingly determined by anonymous investors (such as institutional investors) and investment funds, from all over the world. In times of low-cost loans, private households are also pushing to invest in real estate. The status of real estate is shifting, from being a good that is used to one that is traded. According to Susanne Heeg, professor of geographical urban research at the Institute for Human Geography in Frankfurt am Main, "In contrast to 30 years ago, today investors in financial metropolises such as Frankfurt are no longer primarily owner-occupiers, but are instead interested in real estate as an income property."[03]

This development has been accelerated by the policies of the central banks, which are flooding national economies with cheap money in an attempt to recover from the financial crisis of 2008-9. That, in turn, was a structural crisis, triggered by the granting of uninsured property loans and their trade on secondary and tertiary markets. In this respect, real estate markets no longer react primarily to the local interplay of supply and demand for space, but are increasingly determined by the abstract imperatives of money markets and the investment strategies of anonymous actors. The relationship between investors and the investment property has long since disappeared. Furthermore, in the wake of urban revitalization efforts, interest in inner-city living and home ownership has grown over the past 15 years. Initially hailed by urban planners and architects as "reurbanization," extensive waves of modernization have had near-toxic effects as they spread across entire neighborhoods. It is doubtful whether the term "gentrification" remains sufficient to aptly describe these changes.

██████████████████████

Meanwhile, the term "financialization" has established itself as an analytical concept, finding particular use in the field of urban studies to address the full scope of the impact that these changes are having on cities.[04]

The role of the state

Inspired by classical globalization discourses, the conflicts associated with this trend are often interpreted along a dichotomy of global vs. local, according to which the cities are unilaterally seen as victims. However, the different levels of scale are closely linked and interdependent, not mutually exclusive. Many cities have embarked on the risky path of "growth machine" politics, and short-sighted speculation before and during the financial crisis put some of them in great need.

The state also has its role in this discourse: ultimately, the social accountability of ownership also applies to the right to land. The unleashing of the financial sector would never have been possible without the relevant regulations and their emphasis on privatization. The same applies to the aggressive tax-saving strategies of multinational corporations, which could only grow as they have through deregulation and tax competition. The victims of these deregulatory policies are the public budgets of nation-states and local authorities, which have been deprived of funds on a grand scale. They also include small businesses and tenants, who are unable to pay property rents that are skyrocketing due to expected returns. The problematic consequences for cities have been obvious ever since average wage earners, such as bus drivers, teachers, police officers, and nursing staff, started being forced out of the cities that rely on them to function.

When the mechanisms of land capitalization disrupt the polity, we must examine the conditions that could enable alternative ways of dealing with the problem. A variety of alternatives is conceivable: corrections could be made within the logic of the prevailing system, for example. From a pragmatic point of view, this is a popular option because it does not affect manifest interests. However, such approaches are not very effective—as demonstrated by the rent capping situation in major German cities. Others have tried to break out of the logic of capitalization by securing some of the profit for their users, for example in the case of increasingly active building cooperatives. However, niches risk remaining just that.[05] Another option is the introduction of new frameworks to change the balance of power, especially through regulation and an active role of the state. Under welfare state conditions, the provision of housing for the population is one of the polity's core tasks. But in times of globalization and the depletion of public budgets, this is no longer possible—according to prevailing thought. Does this thesis hold true? I would like to answer this question by examining two highly contrasting cases below. In very different ways, they represent what Anne Haila, professor of Urban Studies at the University of Helsinki, calls the "property state."[06]

Property states—crisis catalyst or strategic response?

The first case is the city-state of Singapore. As one of the "Asian Tiger" states, it has undergone dynamic development since the second half of the twentieth century and is often cited as a prototype of highly concentrated Asian urbanism. After gaining independence from the British Crown in 1965 and separating from Malaysia, the country was faced with the challenge of devising a sustainable strategy for the development of its then backward city-state. The construction of housing on a wide scale was a prerequisite for the planned population growth.

Both objectives could be achieved by actively exploiting Singapore's status as a sovereign country, which offers the small city, or city-state, far more room for manoeuver than, for example, a federal system. Singapore is a city within a state—and state within a city. This enables legal, financial, and strategic resources to be used much more effectively than is possible in large countries. At the same time, the smaller the territory and the more limited the internal market, the greater the need to become involved in higher-level, or even global, networks and associations. This is the only way to compensate for the territory's small size. It is not by chance that services, and financial activities in particular, are dominated by a domain of small states, islands, and political enclaves.[07]

This outward economic orientation corresponds to a specific way of dealing with a scarce resource: land. Land in a small state faces quite different pressures than in large territories. At the same time, how these pressures are dealt with is strategically geared toward the state's economic development goals. The founding of Singapore as an independent republic in 1965 provided an opportunity to establish a housing policy strategy in line with the country's political economy, practically under experimental conditions with full territorial and economic control. The same applies to its policy of securing industrial land reserves. The result is that the state owns most of the land—around 90 percent—and time-limited land use rights are obtained via auctions and long-term leases. Around 80 percent of the population currently lives in apartments developed by Singapore's public housing authority, the Housing and Development Board. About 90 percent of those inhabitants own their home on a time-limited basis.

According to Anne Haila, the "property state" is the main protagonist in land use, both supporting it and directly using it. At the same time, it regulates access by third parties: "The developmental state of Singapore owns land and leases it to developers in public auctions, appropriates land for private developers, makes private developers compete, provides public housing and industrial space, intervenes in the real estate market, and promotes 'good values'."[08] In this respect, it resolves the traditional dilemma of land procurement that exists in the federal system, in which local decision-makers usually act too closely to economic interests, while the state is too far removed to articulate an interest. In the Singapore city-state, land is allocated for communal uses and services, especially public housing, irrespective of social class and ethnic origin—whose diversity is promoted on a quota basis—or specific economic interests.[09] In her case study, Haila argues that this approach allows land distribution issues to be treated on equal footing with aspects of market efficiency, and thus offers a way out of the doctrine of private landownership. Yet this acknowledgement does not mean ignoring the downsides of Singapore's autocratic political model. There is a political price for the state's unusually active

The HDB (Housing & Development Board) was founded in Singapore in 1960 to counteract housing shortage and the emergence of slums. The authority manages 80 percent of the housing stock and allows people long-term residential property ownership.

███████████████████

role in politics, business, and society. The state's paternalistic activities and social control are mechanisms that cannot be generalized.

This caveat also applies to the property state of the second small country that I would like to address: the Grand Duchy of Luxembourg. Like Singapore, Luxembourg is a small territory with rapid economic and population growth in recent decades; the per capita economic data is exceptionally high. The country is also a kind of city-state and—with its recent development strategy integrating finance, economics, and technology—is more like an Asian or Arab city-state than a central European country. Luxembourg is among the top ten European financial centers and the top 15 global financial centers. It is home to a large number of international holdings and headquarters. The home ownership rate is around 73 percent, while the share of privately owned property is around 92 percent. There is no significant home rental culture. Land prices in Luxembourg diverge greatly from those in areas close to the border in Belgium, Germany, and France.

Land is a key parameter in the country's success model. As a resource that cannot be reproduced at will, it is an absolute and relatively scarce resource, whose profit-oriented management yields maximum returns. On the one hand, the issue of land is approached here in a quite liberal and pointedly unideological manner, on the other hand, the state is also ubiquitous. Politics and administration act in a more or less recognizable coalition with private landowners, and ensure the creation of added value through calculated, if not cultivated, shortage. A kind of financialization of land resources exists in several ways: first, private households maintain their own land reserves as a form of family savings, which contributes to the scarcity of land. Second, market transactions are carried out mainly via commercial intermediaries and developers. Third, strategic investments are made in areas that promote the development of Luxembourg as a business location. Fourth, developers play a key role in this system, by strategically acquiring building land, having the best contacts in the political field, and exercising extensive control over the construction value chain.

The growth of business services and the country's role as a financial center has triggered a high demand for space, especially office space, at a rate that housing can hardly follow. As a result, employment and the resident population are growing rapidly apart. To keep pace with the population growth, available housing would need to increase by around 4,000 units per year, yet the amount of new housing actually being built is about 50 percent lower. Although the use of office space and living space is generally planned separately, these two categories of space are essentially in competition with each other, especially since the existing municipal incentive structures reward the creation of jobs far more than housing. There are two state-owned companies that oversee the construction of social housing, but they are far from closing the gap between demand and supply.

The accelerated economic development, the country's traditionally cultivated liberalist political approach, and the culture of speculation in both commercial and private circles, all help to intensify the spiral of exploitation in terms of land and property. Exorbitant property prices and corresponding displacement processes in the real estate and housing markets are a direct result of this trend. While the housing shortage might also limit economic growth, it has also caused a growing exodus from the country by members of the local population, who can no longer afford the horrendous real estate prices.

And the future for landownership?

It seems to be an irony of recent history that the perceived dominance of a market-economy with a profit-oriented governance of land and property is actually strongly determined by the nature and extent of government action. Property states can feed and intensify the problem, as the Luxembourg case demonstrates. Under certain conditions, they can also point to possible alternatives, as can be seen in Singapore—regardless of the historical specifics of the case.

These cases mark two poles in the spectrum of possible political solutions. Other pragmatic, yet by no means uncontroversial, approaches are discussed by David Madden and Peter Marcuse in their book *In Defense of Housing*. In it, they call for changes in housing policy, including de-financialization, enforced construction of social housing, and prioritization of residents' interests over landowners' interests.[10] Going even further in this direction are voices calling for new land legislation, an approach that clearly takes its cues from the 1970s.[11] This approach gives cities a central role through a policy of long-term landownership, municipal preemption rights, and inter-municipal cooperation. A property state would massively support these instruments by imposing a land value tax. On the other hand, as long as the real estate market remains a golden egg for commercial actors and private households alike, we should be under no illusions about the chances of fundamental reform.

01 See Adrian Garcia-Landa and Christoph Trautvetter, "Düstere Deals," in *Tagesspiegel*, November 15, 2016.
02 Harvey Molotch, "The Political Economy of Growth Machines," in *Journal of Urban Affairs* (March 1993): 29–53.
03 Susanne Heeg, "Was bedeutet die Integration von Finanz- und Immobilienmärkten für Finanzmetropolen? Erfahrungen aus dem anglophonen Raum," in *Wohnungs- und Büroimmobilienmärkte unter Stress. Deregulierung, Privatisierung und Ökonomisierung*, ed. Susanne Heeg and Robert Pütz (Frankfurt am Main: Institut für Humangeographie, 2009), 123–141, here 130.
04 See Ludovic Halbert and Katia Attuyer, "Introduction: The Financialisation of Urban Production: Conditions, Mediations, and Transformations," in *Urban Studies* 53 (2016), 1347–1361.
05 See Nathalie Christmann, Markus Hesse, and Christian Schulz, "Tracing the Place of Home," in *Tracing Transitions* ed. Claude Ballini, Serge Ecker, Daniel

Grünkranz and Panajota Panotopoulou (Luxemburg: LUCA, 2016), 36–50.
06 See Anne Haila, "Real Estate in Global Cities: Singapore and Hong Kong as Property States," in *Urban Studies 37* (2000): 2241–2256; Anne Haila, *Urban Land Rent. Singapore as a Property State* (Chichester: John Wiley, 2015).
07 Godfrey Baldacchino, *Island Enclaves. Offshoring Strategies, Creative Governance, and Subnational Island Jurisdictions* (Montreal: McGill-Queen's University Press, 2010).
08 Haila, *Urban Land Rent*, 113.
09 Haila, *Urban Land Rent*, 116.
10 David Madden and Peter Marcuse, *In Defense of Housing. The Politics of Crisis* (New York: Verso, 2016).
11 Deutsches Institut für Urbanistik, *Bodenpolitische Agenda 2020–2030. Warum wir für eine nachhaltige und sozial gerechte Stadtentwicklungs- und Wohnungspolitik eine andere Bodenpolitik brauchen* (Berlin: Difu, 2017).

Property without Obligations

RAQUEL ROLNIK IN CONVERSATION
WITH OLAF GRAWERT

OLAF GRAWERT: *The famous German Social Democrat Hans-Jochen Vogel compared land to air and water, in that it is finite and cannot be reproduced. Therefore, it shouldn't be a tradeable commodity and should be taken out of the economic circuit* (see Hans-Jochen Vogel, p. 60–65). *What would this non-tradability mean?*

RAQUEL ROLNIK: Over the last 250 years, land, and the specific relation between land and people, the way it is available and accessible as private property, has become the hegemonic type of access in our society. Property freehold blocks all other forms of land access, all other forms of tenure, and all other forms of tenure relationship. This hegemony of land as property clearly blocks access to land for those who don't own it. Property has an economic value and this is essential for the notion of property as the preferred form of tenure; it is related to an economic system but also to a political system.

This political system was invented during the Enlightenment, connecting property with persons and citizenship. It has its origins in the ideas of philosophers like John Locke and others of that time, and the way society decided to organize itself in order to maintain political, social, and economic ties. The result of this experiment—that started as a utopian ideal during the Enlightenment—is the hegemonic model of modern democracy. The experiment continued during the English and American revolutions and became the predominant model to be implemented globally through a very clear strategy: colonialism. Colonialism was a very specific mode of occupying and changing different territories around the world by imposing a single political system.

It is impossible to dissociate private property, which relates one specific part of land to one specific person, from the economic concept of capitalism. A necessity of capitalism is that everything becomes a commodity and circulates freely—in terms of the economic system but also in terms of the political system. Property ownership as an extension of what John Locke framed back in the seventeenth century—in regard to the relationship between tenure and labor—has become a frontier defining who is a citizen and who is not, who is allowed access and who is not. In the end, property ownership defines who can participate in the social pact, which was constructed in order to protect private property.

Today, this hegemonic system is in deep crisis. The property principle by which space is organized has influenced urban planning. All urban regulations—including zoning laws—are based on the notion of individual versus collective ownership. The idea of public space was born together with the notion of private space. Up until the nineteenth century there was a continual increase in the amount of public space and, I would say, public space became the most important private property of the state. This is also central to the practices of planning and urban management.

OG: *The way you describe it implies that property has become the main factor in how our society, and we as individuals, understand ourselves, and is therefore always related to the idea of tenure. There are very different forms of tenure: The German constitution states that "property entails obligations. Its use shall also serve the public good." The constitution of the United States, however, clearly ties property to private ownership. Whereas in former Yugoslavia, the concept of social ownership proposed a more collective model.*

RR: Yes, the big difference between the systems is how they organize collective and individual forms of tenure. As collective forms we can mention all the systems of tribal landownership related to native populations in all parts of the world, to whom the land was a common and collective good to be used collectively. There are also different modes of collective ownership in the modern world like cooperatives, the system used in former Yugoslavia you mentioned, or existing systems of social housing in Sweden and Uruguay—a Latin American example in which social housing policy is based on cooperative and collective ownership.

The financial crisis has shown that the acqusition of land and property by finance is a recent move by the capitalist system. As well as reflecting the hegemony of financial capital over the entire economy, it also adds a layer that didn't necessarily exist in capitalism's early period or in the nineteenth and early twentieth century, when productive capital was the predominant mode and land was a basic means for production. Nowadays we talk about property and location as a source of return for financial capital that is invested in it. This has had a huge influence on the way property is organized, loosening the close ties between individuals and their property. Property has become fictitious, dematerialized; we now talk about investment funds and shareholders.

The idea you mentioned ("property comes with obligations") that exists in Germany and other constitutional democracies—the idea of the social function of property and the responsibility of property holders regarding the public good and public interest—can't be managed anymore, as there is no "one" responsible. The shareholder is a very abstract entity,

Herman Moll's map of South America from ca. 1726 also records the Potosí silver mines in Bolivia, symbolizing the close integration of territorial and economic interests during the colonial era, which is in fact based on the expropriation of land belonging to indigenous peoples and launched the systematic exploitation of natural resources worldwide.

floating above us like a dark cloud of investments, papers, and assets. I think it is very important to understand that these assets are the ultimate development in this concept of property; with them the main ties between individuals and the land they use are broken.

OG: *So, in your view, this dematerialization of land and property has led to very specific forms of ownership not tied to the idea of the nation-state, or territory, as we perceive it. An example you mention in this regard is land grabbing. Oana Bogdan, a Brussels-based Romanian architect who became part of the Romanian technocratic government in 2016, dedicated her work mainly to one case of land grabbing by a Canadian mining company. Would land grabbing be one manifestation or example of this globalized understanding of landownership and property as financial assets?*
RR: Land grabbing is one way in which capitalism solves its systemic crisis—caused by the natural limits of economic growth—by continually expanding its borders. The taking over of more and more new land serves to open space and to provide a response, both to the surplus of capital and the work force. The best example I can give of this is the nineteenth century gold rush in the United States.

The colonial expansion of capital is a story of centuries, but now it is almost over. With the fall of the Iron Curtain, capital was able to go on and take over formerly blocked territories. Nowadays we are facing a scarcity of land and resources. Of course this has a lot to do with climate change and the environmental crisis. So yes, land grabbing is a way for financial capital to take over, to "reserve," the remaining places that have not yet been organized in a capitalist way or been taken for agribusiness. But reserving is very speculative in its nature. This is one thing, but you also have more acquisition of urban space by financial capital. How else can we explain the hundreds of thousands of square meters of corporate space that were built in the metropolises around the world? Dubai, London, São Paulo, Santiago—you can pick any of these. Large parts of these corporate spaces are empty and have no use. For the investors this is fine, because they exist on paper, they exist as assets and there is no need for them to be used by people.

There is a disconnection between the idea that the main driver of urban planning and urban structure should be the needs of the residents and citizens and the completely different understanding of property as being only valuable in economic terms—which I think is part of the crisis we are facing right now.

OG: *Back in 2016, Patrik Schumacher, principal of Zaha Hadid Architects, gave a speech at the World Architecture Festival in Berlin in which he proposed the privatization of public space (see Patrik Schumacher, p. 78-83). He argued that this would lead to a self-regulating system. He also spoke about accelerating the capitalist system, which would lead to new proposals and solutions, as entrepreneurs would take over building social housing, for instance, and do it in a different way, according to market needs: free competition, free forces.*
RR: If you talk about *free* market, you have to talk about *equal* conditions for the people who are competing in it. What we are seeing in the world—not just in developing countries, but also more and more in European or North American countries—is increasing inequality. The means we have with which to compete in the market are completely different. How can I compete with the oil sheikhs? How can I compete with a Russian magnate? Look at London: the global competition to attract investment is destroying any possibility for local people to survive in the city. What is going to happen is that basically all public space will be taken over by plutocrats.

Platform Urbanism

"The triumph of financialization—driving urban environments toward privatization, spatial segregation and social control—has reached its high point with the regime of the smart city."

— Deane Simpson

The Challenges of Platform Capitalism

Understanding the logic of a new business model

NICK SRNICEK

The platform business model is predicated upon a voracious appetite for data that can only be sated by disregard for privacy (and often workers' rights), and constant outward expansion. As they become ever more central to the global economy, Nick Srnicek argues that it's incumbent on us to understand how they function.

All around us, it seems that a nebulous series of entities called "platforms" are increasingly shaping our world. Facebook is blamed for perpetuating fake news and changing the US election outcome; Amazon is radically transforming logistics and creating an automated, jobless future; Google is rapidly developing new artificial intelligence techniques that are already changing how we interact with technology around us; while Uber sets out a new hyper-exploitative employment model. Yet what are these entities, and what sorts of commonalities do they share?

For the most part, critical reflection on these firms has focused on them as political and cultural actors. The uproar about fake news is only the most recent example, but the history of these firms is often laden with privacy violations and political lobbying. Similarly, when critics argue about how these firms should act, the arguments are often made in the language of values – of a Californian ideology, of libertarianism, of information wanting to be free. The appeals to act better or more humanely are made in cultural and political terms. Yet this common approach to these firms obscures the fact that they are first and foremost economic actors. Not only that, they are economic actors operating within a capitalist economy—a type of economy that imparts specific demands upon firms. By taking this into account, and looking at platforms as a new business model within capitalism, we can come to illuminate some of the more mysterious activities of these firms.

What are platforms?

Essentially, they are a newly predominant type of business model premised upon bringing different groups together. Facebook and Google connect advertisers, businesses, and everyday users; Uber connects riders and drivers; and Amazon and Siemens are building and renting the platform infrastructures that underlie the contemporary economy.

Essential to all of these platform businesses—and indicative of a wider shift in capitalism—is the centrality of data. Data is the basic resource that drives these firms, and it is data that gives them their advantage over competitors. Platforms, in turn, are designed as a mechanism for extracting and using that data: by providing the infrastructure and intermediation between different groups, platforms place themselves in a position in which they can monitor and extract all the interactions between these groups. This positioning is the source of their economic and political power.

That characteristic also helps us to understand a first mystery: why firms outside the technology sector are adopting platform elements. As data becomes a central resource for both tech and non-tech sectors in the economy, companies are having to rapidly develop ways to siphon off and aggregate this information. The platform provides a ready-made solution to this problem. The result is companies like John Deere, the largest agricultural machinery company in the world, are building a platform that links together farmers, seed producers, chemical producers, equipment sensors, tractors, and more. All the while John Deere itself extracts the data and uses it to improve its services to customers (such as making better predictions about when and where to plant a particular crop), to improve its

114

products (reducing wear and tear on its machinery, for example), and ultimately to gain an advantage and beat its competitors, as capitalism demands.

Yet this drive towards more and more data has a nefarious consequence: impingement on privacy becomes a necessary feature of platform capitalism. As Shoshana Zuboff has argued, the fact that platforms require more and more data—just as the old railroad monopolies once devoured coal—means that there is an intrinsic drive for these companies to be pushing up against the limits of what we presently consider the private realm.[01] Google has been rebuked for collecting household Wi-Fi data as its Google Street View cars drove by; Facebook has been continually criticized for pressing too far into individuals' lives; and Vizio was denounced for spying on people via their smart TVs. Rather than seeing these incidents as accidental oversteps, we must see them as necessary consequences of platform capitalism: if data is a central resource, and capitalist competition places a high premium on getting that data, then our age will inevitably be filled with privacy scandals.

Expansion, Monopolisation, Invulnerability

Platforms' appetite for data means that these businesses are also constantly expanding. Not only does this lead to privacy concerns, but it also means that these forms grow and expand according to a data-centric logic of capitalist centralisation. The surge in mergers and acquisitions by companies like Google, Facebook, and Amazon attests to the ways in which data extraction forms a novel set of structural imperatives for these companies. They cannot remain content with their core businesses; rather, they must continually extend their data extraction apparatus into new areas. Innovative start-up firms that show potential in data extraction are rapidly bought up by these companies. Even second-tier platforms, like LinkedIn or Twitter, become fodder for the insatiable data appetites of the major platforms. All of this helps us to understand why a search engine company like Google is now investing in completely unrelated ventures around self-driving cars or the consumer Internet of Things—they are simply new ways to extract data. Unlike the classic vertical integration of Fordist firms, platforms take on a rhizomatic form of integration.

The expansionary nature of these platforms means that firms that were operating in completely different areas are now converging together under the pressures of competitively extracting data. Google, originally a search engine company, is now competing with Facebook, a social networking site when it began, and they are all competing with Amazon, which was once only an e-commerce company. While overt antagonism between these major platforms is at a low ebb for now, as they expand into new areas they will increasingly come into direct competition. The consumer Internet of Things is a good example here, with Amazon and Google making major plays in an effort to dominate this arm of their data extraction empires. Online commerce forms another friction point, with Facebook aiming to bring more and more business transactions onto its platform, in more or less direct threats to Google and Amazon. As these businesses expand, we should expect them to become more aggressive towards each other as the capitalist imperative to compete takes hold.

This dynamic is balanced by a counter-trend towards monopolisation. One of the key features of platforms is their reliance on (and ability to generate) network effects. The more users are using a platform, the more valuable that platform becomes for everyone.

The result is a virtuous circle that leads to a winner-takes-all market. For example, we join Facebook simply because so many of our friends and family are already on it—but this simultaneously reinforces the centrality and monopolistic nature of Facebook in the social network domain. We are seeing this tendency towards monopolization occur across the spectrum of major platforms: Google, Facebook, and Amazon, not to mention their non-Western rivals Alibaba and Tencent. Each seeks to have absolute dominance over its core business area—and, once they are ensconced in this position, they become virtually unimpeachable by competitors ranging from state-supported platforms to worker-owned platform co-operatives.

The sharing economy's death drive

The outcome is a tendency towards monopoly-like platforms competing in increasingly aggressive ways—a path which will undoubtedly lead to some significant casualties. In fact, the most hyped-up type of platform—those associated with the sharing economy—is also the most unsustainable. These companies, like Uber, Airbnb, and Deliveroo, operate by outsourcing as much of their costs as possible. Workers take on the costs of fuel, maintenance, insurance, and so on for Uber, while hosts take on the costs of cleaning and insurance for Airbnb. For most of these companies, employees are also hyper-exploited, with low wages and no benefits. The platforms, meanwhile, simply siphon off a rent from every transaction they facilitate. Yet despite all these advantages, these firms are still unprofitable and survive only on the back of venture capital welfare. Funding from Silicon Valley (and elsewhere) flows into these companies, enabling them to continue operating at a loss for years at a time. While Uber has managed to become profitable in some cities, it was still losing US$1 billion annually while it tried to fight off an (unprofitable) Chinese competitor[02] (Uber has since given up that fight and admitted defeat).[03] More broadly, these firms have been *successful* only by leaping ahead of regulations and workers. As cities and countries catch up and start making appropriate regulations, and as workers mobilize against their exploitative practices and secure better wages, these firms will only become less rather than more financially viable. The result is that the sharing economy will be a short-lived phenomenon.

Most of these firms will go bankrupt, or turn into luxury services for the rich, or transform themselves into a different type of business model altogether (incidentally, the latter is Uber's strategy, with their efforts to develop and own a fleet of self-driving automobiles). In any case, sharing economy platforms are not long for this world.

The challenge facing us today is to grapple with these intrinsic tendencies of the data-centric platform model and their often counterintuitive consequences, and to strategize ways to counter their power. An underestimation of their dominance serves only to enshrine their position, and as they become increasingly central to the global economy, it becomes even more important to understand their functioning.

01 Shoshana Zuboff, "The Secrets of Surveillance Capitalism", in: *Frankfurter Allgemeine*, 5 March 2016, accessed December 4, 2018, http://www.faz.net/ aktuell/feuilleton/debatten/the-digital-debatte/shoshana-zuboff-secrets-of-surveillance- capitalism-14103616.html [Abrufdatum? Deutsche Version]
02 Adam Jourdan, John Ruwitch, "Uber losing $1 billion a year to compete in China", in: *Reuters*, 18 February 2016. http://www.reuters.com/ article/uber-china-idUSKCN0VR1M9
03 Brad Stone, Lulu Yilun Chen, "Uber Slayer: How China's Didi Beat the Ride-Hailing Superpower", in: *Bloomberg Businessweek*, 6 October 2016, accessed December 4, 2018, https://www.bloomberg.com/features/ 2016-didi-cheng-wei

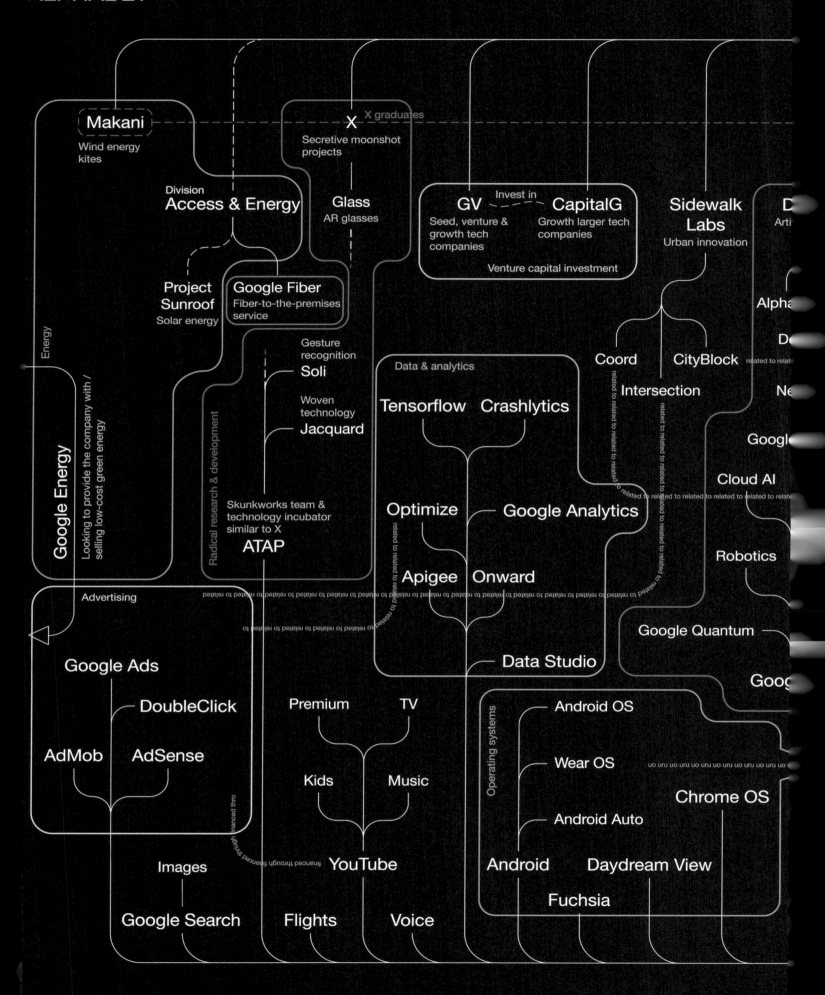

Makani
Wind energy kites

X X graduates
Secretive moonshot projects

Division
Access & Energy

Glass
AR glasses

GV Invest in **CapitalG**
Seed, venture & growth tech companies
Growth larger tech companies
Venture capital investment

Sidewalk Labs
Urban innovation

D
Arti

Project Sunroof
Solar energy

Google Fiber
Fiber-to-the-premises service

Alpha

De

Energy

Google Energy
Looking to provide the company with / selling low-cost green energy

Gesture recognition
Soli

Woven technology
Jacquard

Data & analytics

Tensorflow **Crashlytics**

Coord **CityBlock**
related to relat

Intersection

related to related to related to related to related to related to related to related to related to related to related to relate

Ne

Google

Radical research & development

Skunkworks team & technology incubator similar to X
ATAP

Optimize **Google Analytics**

Cloud AI

Apigee **Onward**

Robotics

Advertising

Google Ads

DoubleClick

AdMob **AdSense**

Premium **TV**

Kids **Music**

Data Studio

Google Quantum

Goog

Operating systems

Android OS

Wear OS

on run on run on run on run on run on run on run on run on

Chrome OS

Android Auto

Images

financed through financed through financed thro

YouTube

Android **Daydream View**

Fuchsia

Google Search **Flights** **Voice**

As of June 2019, Alphabet has made a total of 270 acquisitions (including those made under Google, before the restructuring). Most noteable are the likes of Deepmind Technologies, Android, and YouTube. Most Alphabet companies are comprised of several specialized teams and often partake in numerous partnerships, of which the list is near unexhaustive.

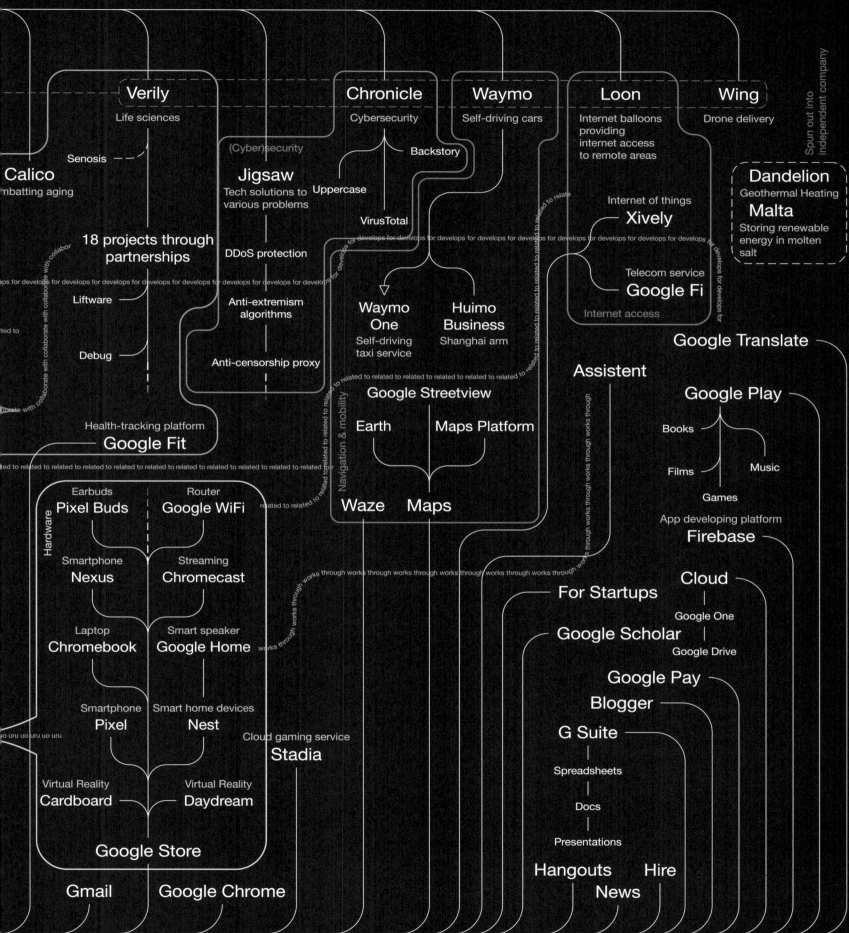

The list of Google subsidiaries, products, services, platforms and departments extends well beyond the capacity of this scheme. Therefore, a selection was made of those that are most recognizable, relevant, or interesting.

The City of Platform Capitalism

DEANE SIMPSON IN CONVERSATION
WITH ARNO BRANDLHUBER AND OLAF GRAWERT

The cities of the future are being planned by technology companies and management consultancies on the basis of algorithms; it seems the expertise of architects is becoming obsolete. The common good is being replaced by profit interests—and governments are playing along. Deane Simpson, an architect, urban planner, and professor for Urbanism & Societal Change at the Royal Danish Academy of Fine Arts (KADK) in Copenhagen, spoke with Arno Brandlhuber and Olaf Grawert about the smart city business model, continual increases in efficiency, and alternatives to this model that urgently need to be considered.

ARNO BRANDLHUBER: *In your research on the changing conditions of urban planning and the arrival of the "smart city" into our everyday lives, you mention David Harvey, who notes a shift from managerial to entrepreneurial city, ending with the vision of postpolitical, algorithmic urban planning.[01] What role do today's cities play in the economic considerations of the big tech firms that are investing in the physical space?*

DEANE SIMPSON: Harvey describes this turn regarding the role of states and municipalities in urban planning taking place since 1980s. Instead of the largely state-led managerial "predict and provide" planning of the 1960s and 1970s, from the 1980s onwards the city's role increasingly became an entrepreneurial one, promoting development through city-led public-private investment. Under the recent influence of platform-capitalism, with developments like Sidewalk Lab's Quayside in Toronto, theorists including Guy Baeten have suggested that a new type of algorithmic (post-) planning is emerging. One characterized by new kinds of public-private partnerships, led this time by big tech firms delivering a form of A-to-Z solution-based urbanism. Technology giants like the Big Five (Facebook, Alphabet, Amazon, Microsoft, and Apple)—corporate actors of a scale not seen before in history—are attempting to exploit the potential of the city as a growth model in their business plans. We are experiencing a massive shift in the balance of power between urban actors, especially with regard to urban planning. The growth strategies of these companies are expanding from a mostly digital context into a merger of the virtual and the physical worlds. This is linked to the ambition to collect data not only on our online behavior but also on our behavior in physical space, as urban infrastructures now produce data themselves.

AB: *How do these companies combine their existing knowledge of data mining with algorithm-based planning?*
DS: According to Anthony M. Townsend, the tech industry sees the city as a low-hanging fruit: there's a lot of money to be made without much effort, with the current value of roughly $1.5 trillion per year expected to triple within a decade. smart city pitches are commonly centered on the rhetoric of big data and its provision of a new set of opportunities it offers for architecture, infrastructure, and planning. This is described in terms of greater optimizations, efficiencies, feedback, and responsiveness, based on greater amounts of information. Alphabet's Sidewalk Labs project, for example, intends to achieve greater flexibility in programming based on the constant digital monitoring of space usage (see Bianca Wylie, p. 124–129). This kind of algorithmic-driven responsiveness is

In the run-up to the 2014 World Cup in Brazil, Rio de Janeiro partnered with IBM to implement real-time, area-wide monitoring of the public space.

Algorithmic Planning

promoted by its supporters as a more democratic, and post-ideological form of planning, producing a hyper-efficient and optimized urban outcome. I believe we should be extremely suspicious of such a claim to post-ideological planning. Obviously, the design of the data collection system, and the particular design of the algorithms themselves have implications that are highly political in nature, and largely informed by the agendas that drive the big tech companies, be that short-term economic performance or their longer-term business strategy.

AB: *The Sidewalk Labs Quayside project in Toronto is creating new rules and roles that the city and we architects and citizens have yet to learn to deal with. Given the hidden political and business interests, would you agree that this will lead to a more homogenous habitat, despite current promises of heterogeneity?*

DS: What is interesting is the extent to which platitudes dominate the rhetoric of Sidewalk Labs's promotional brochures and videos—describing its participatory engagement and its commitment both to locality and heterogeneity. Especially in relation to Toronto's diverse multi-cultural population. I am skeptical as to how this rhetoric will translate into reality. While Sidewalk Labs repeatedly emphasizes the project's social commitments, as researchers we know the extent to which such development projects primarily serve commercial interests and mainly target economically advantaged groups, thus playing into the hands of homogenization and gentrification. Based on the high level of investment and the expectations riding on this, one can anticipate the extent to which Sidewalk Labs will attempt to control and curate inhabitants and urban life on the site. How long could one anticipate homeless people being allowed to stay in the semi-covered public spaces of the development? Or to what extent could we predict political demonstrations being tolerated in these spaces? One of the key evaluation points in assessing the project will be the extent to which diversity, tolerance, and inclusivity are realized—or if this will remain an empty

**SECURITY
COMFORT
SUSTAINABILITY**

ÉGALITÉ
FRATERNITÉ
LIBERTÉ

advertising claim. These aspects are absolutely central in evaluating how our cities support accessibility for all citizens.

OLAF GRAWERT: *This leads us to the question of values in architecture and urban planning. In our film,* The Property Drama*, and the accompanying ARCH+ publication*, The Property Issue,*[02] it became clear that a discussion about property is always about accessibility, or rather about inclusivity and exclusivity. Whoever has property rights has the power to make decisions as well as the final say on values.*

DS: According to Rem Koolhaas, the emergence of the smart city paradigm is increasingly displacing traditional values and ambitions that have long dominated European planning—in his usual very cognizant way he speaks of a silent revolution in which *egalité*, *fraternité*, and *liberté* have been supplanted by values of comfort, security, and sustainability. I agree with his assessment. This shift in values threatens the vision of the welfare city and the ideal of the city as a collective project. The focus on comfort (or livability) and security supports an urban imaginary directed toward a techno-savvy middle- and upper-middle class audience, while actively excluding others.

Hidden behind the shift toward the smart city is a business model that focuses largely on data production through citizens in space as a new territory to exploit. What does that mean for the

future of urban values, such as the ambition for equality? For tech companies, citizens only have value when they generate data. The lack of control and transparency of the data collectors, and what happens to those members of society with whom no money can be made, pose great challenges. This has a lot to do with who has "the right to the city" and the role of architects and urban planners in a context in which space is being absorbed and colonized by a very different ideology.

These developments operate to a large extent according to techno-rationalized values native to tech companies. They are informed by the managerial sciences; with the notion that the algorithm is capable of producing a post-political, hyper-efficient, and optimized city—a reality that could hardly be more distant from previous visions of urbanity. The city as a melting pot, a space of freedom and emancipation underwritten by anonymity and privacy, is being fundamentally questioned by this new paradigm.

OG: *Given the current shift from the public to the private sector, China—where the major tech companies are under state control—is a curious exception. In this case, the smart city discourse is dominated by the state. How do Western and Chinese approaches differ with regard to the manipulative potential of big data?*

DS: From a European or North American perspective, we see recurring utopian narratives attached to the promotion of smart cities. These narratives push concepts such as the hyper-optimized, efficient, frictionless city; the utopia of the safe city or the utopian city of participatory democracy. These stories attempt to point to a sustainable, citizen-empowered vision of the city, facilitating a fairer and more responsible distribution of resources. But the reality that is emerging suggests quite a different picture. With the monopolies represented by the large tech companies and the control of information they achieve, we are seeing a growing concentration of resources in the hands of a few key actors. We have been aware of potential abuses of power at the latest since the Cambridge Analytica scandal, when it became clear that social media microtargeting had a massive impact on voter behavior in the 2016 US presidential election and the Brexit referendum. The implications of Alphabet's plans in Toronto, where an entire neighborhood is to provide the urban infrastructure for even greater levels of data collection, raises further concerns. But it has also become evident that the major tech companies and the state are not completely independent—just think of the NSA scandal concerning PRISM[03] in 2013 or the intensive cooperation between Silicon Valley and Washington, DC.

The narratives promoting the smart city in a Chinese context are framed in similar utopian terms, referring to efficiency, convenience, and safety. And as you suggested, they are influenced by far greater entwinement between the central government and tech companies than in the West. Critics have suggested that the smart city infrastructure is a pretense for introducing greater levels of state-initiated social and political control. The Social Credit System is perhaps the most emblematic and concerning of the Chinese experiments in this emerging form of authoritarian data-governance. This of course presents a highly contrasted reality to the euphoric narratives of freedom and hope connected to the global expansion of the internet in the 1990s.

AB: *Tech companies don't just formulate vague ideas, but also concrete visions on urban planning and architecture. One aim, for example, is the reinvention of the flexible loft typology, which allows all possible models of living and working. What are the implications of this openness to flexible programming?*
DS: Sidewalk Labs strives for a comprehensive understanding of human behavior. The company intends to establish a constant feedback loop between the virtual and physical space, in order to make continuous adjustments and improvements. However, this claim distracts from the massive implications the model has on the political, economic, social, and cultural dimensions of the city. The rhetoric of freedom, efficiency, and flexibility—built on large

The emergence of the smart city paradigm threatens the vision of the welfare city. The focus on comfort and security supports an urban imaginary directed toward a techno-savvy middle- and upper-middle class, while actively excluding others.

amounts of data—play out at different scales. A flexible zoning concept has been proposed, which is very different from modern urban planning. Its equivalent at the scale of architectural typology is the loft. Its flexibility points to a paradigm shift for architecture. I see Sidewalk Labs loft concept proposal pointing to two opposing poles. On the one side, it is an experiment in potentially delirious mixtures of program, activities, and life forms. While on the other hand, it presents a spatial dystopia of our late-capitalist, tech-led world, in which all distinctions between work, play and sleep are eroded.

OG: *So the loft would be the spatial manifestation of our attitude to life, always having to be productive so as not to be left behind?*
DS: The loft concept implies the concentration of our activities in a single location and demands a corresponding degree of flexibility from us. This stands in stark contrast to modern planning approaches of the post-war period, when distinct spatial zones were intended for different activities. Think of Copenhagen's Finger Plan, for example, whose zoning is strictly based on the distinction between work, leisure, and housing. This urban plan can only be understood if one takes into account the efforts of the labor movement to achieve an eight-hour work day, in response to the industrial revolution and the 24-hour operation of the factory. But it was also the intention of modern urban planning to separate the polluting

industrial workplace from the site of living. In his book *24/7: Late Capitalism and the Ends of Sleep,* Jonathan Crary argues how contemporary late capitalism has invited and pressured us in the last decades to consume and produce 24/7. This blurs the distinction between work and leisure, between consumption and surveillance, to the extent that even time for sleep, as the last affront to capitalism, is encroached upon. Because even in our sleep we generate data that is collected. The lofts of the Quayside project are ultimately just one example of a much broader tendency that can be observed in the emergence of the leisure and play—evoking workspaces of the late 1990s in Silicon Valley.

AB: *We architects have long since lost the discussion on values, programs, and aesthetics. Our role has turned into more of a side note. Why are we losing ground to other players who claim expertise in spatial issues?*
DS: Our discipline continues to suffer from the legacy of modern urban planning and its perceived failure. By the end of the twentieth century, architecture had turned its back on urban planning, which left a vacuum to be filled by other actors and agendas. Another reason for our marginalization, as suggested earlier, is the shift from a managerial to an entrepreneurial city. The most recent developments in algorithmic (post-)planning will lead architecture even further away from planning and decision-making expertise. This is also reflected in the composition of the Sidewalk Labs team, whose members have mainly technical and business expertise and hardly any urban planning expertise. Architects are degraded to window dressers; they are only consulted after most of the critical decisions have been made—not only regarding the digital layer but also the spatial aspects. The result will be a built environment that owes its existence to the technical and economic culture of big tech and management consultancies, but has little to do with urban culture.

OG: *In our latest film,* Architecting After Politics, *the architectural theorist Keller*

Algorithmic Planning

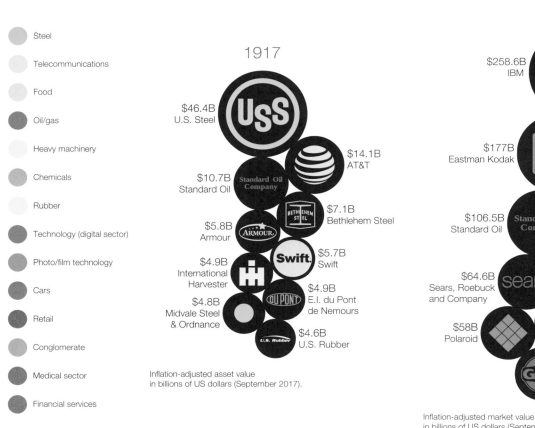

Steel

Telecommunications

Food

Oil/gas

Heavy machinery

Chemicals

Rubber

Technology (digital sector)

Photo/film technology

Cars

Retail

Conglomerate

Medical sector

Financial services

1917

$46.4B
U.S. Steel

$14.1B
AT&T

$10.7B
Standard Oil

$7.1B
Bethlehem Steel

$5.8B
Armour

$5.7B
Swift

$4.9B
International
Harvester

$4.9B
E.I. du Pont
de Nemours

$4.8B
Midvale Steel
& Ordnance

$4.6B
U.S. Rubber

Inflation-adjusted asset value
in billions of US dollars (September 2017).

1967

$258.6B
IBM

$200.5B
AT&T

$177B
Eastman Kodak

$171.2B
General Motors

$106.5B
Standard Oil

$82.3B
Texaco

$64.6B
Sears, Roebuck
and Company

$63.9B
General Electric

$58B
Polaroid

$58B
Gulf Oil

Inflation-adjusted market value
in billions of US dollars (September 2017).

The ten most valuable listed US companies
in a comparison of the years 1917, 1967, and
2017.

*Easterling notes that "some of the
greatest changes of the globalizing world
are being written in the language of
architecture and urbanism. There has to
be a chance that we know something
more about these changes than the
28-year-old McKinsey consultant who is
influencing global decisions." What
qualifies them and disqualifies us, apart
from reservations about modern
architecture?*
DS: The McKinsey consultant plays a
central role in decisions involving
politics, economics, and technology.
They approach urban development from
a purely quantitative perspective. This
offers a level of abstraction that renders
the complexity of the city and the
life forms it supports understandable for
investors and politicians. However,
important perspectives fall by the wayside:
the complex understanding that architects
have of the relationship between the
spatial and physical substance of the city
and the social life forms it enables.

We should bear in mind that projects
such as the Sidewalk Labs' Quayside are
a test case, which if successful, will be
rolled out globally. This prospect points to
the need for viable alternative visions
of urban development that can compete
with McKinsey and Alphabet's projects,
and also entail a certain moral obligation
towards the city's inhabitants. Formulating
convincing arguments and rhetorics
for such alternatives must be the task of
architecture and urban planning.

AB: *Helmut Schmidt allegedly once said,
"anyone who has visions should see a
doctor."*[04] *What if the architect as visionary
is long dead?*
DS: The view that our discipline has lost
its visionary potential is certainly related
to the frequently cited failure of modern
urban planning. However, a common
set of tendencies in European and North
American cities over the last three
decades coincides with the triumph of
financialization—driving urban environments toward extensive privatization,
unaffordable housing, inequality, spatial
segregation, gentrification, and social
control. For the time being, this development has reached its high point with
the regime of the smart city, which
focuses on innovation and technology.
In relation to Helmut Schmidt's
statement, I would probably argue that
those who do not see the urgency to
develop alternate visions should be the
ones heading to the doctor. When I
use the term visions, I am not referring to
rarefied utopias, but rather approaches
that negotiate the multiple parameters in
play—from those embedded in the

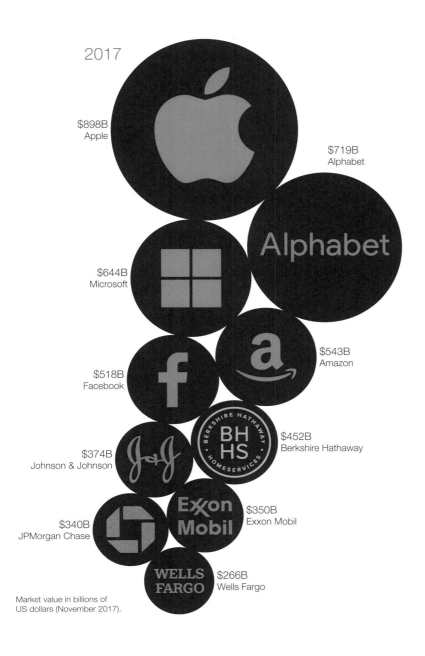

2017

$898B
Apple

$719B
Alphabet

Alphabet

$644B
Microsoft

$543B
Amazon

$518B
Facebook

$452B
Berkshire Hathaway

$374B
Johnson & Johnson

$350B
Exxon Mobil

$340B
JPMorgan Chase

$266B
Wells Fargo

Market value in billions of
US dollars (November 2017).

The triumph of financialization—driving urban environments toward privatization, unaffordable housing, inequality, spatial segregation and social control—has reached its high point with the regime of the smart city.

McKinsey brief, to those materializing the physical and social composition of the territory. If architects do not do it, which other groups are able to work creatively and spatially across the multiple fields of complexity? Our capacity involves more than just business plans, but to actually envision alternatives to the tracks that we are already on.

AB: *What could these alternative narratives look like? What is our role here and how can these stories be embedded in a wider context?*

DS: In recent decades there has been a great deal of emphasis on communication within disciplinary borders, or between limited fields, like architecture and philosophy, or architecture and geometry. I am very interested in the possibility to communicate more broadly in various ways, particularly visually. This is also something

that we are exploring a lot with our students at the Royal Danish Academy of Fine Arts. For example, we are looking for analogue and digital formats to give intellectuals or activist students a stronger voice in public debates.

It's encouraging to see that there are various actors currently looking at the relationship between architecture and media or architecture and communication, such as your explorations into storytelling and online television and their potential to increase the reach of architecture. I don't see that as following a renewed megalomania for architects as urban "saviors." A little more modesty would do us all good, and it is important that we form new alliances and work together with others to develop alternative visions— visions that take into account the complexities of the city and the need for equity in the right to access it. And just as

important, how we develop new narratives and frameworks to communicate these urgent, necessary, and pragmatic visions.

This conversation took place as part of a Master's colloquium at the Department of Architecture at ETH Zurich.

01 David Harvey, "From Managerialism to Entrepreneurialism: The Transformation in Urban Governance in Late Capitalism," *Geografiska Annaler: Series B, Human Geography* 71(1), 1989: 3–17.
02 An earlier version of *The Property Issue* titled ARCH+ 231 *The Property Issue – Von der Bodenfrage und neuen Gemeingütern* was originally published in April 2018, in German and English, to accompany the film *The Property Drama* by Arno Brandlhuber and Christopher Roth, released in 2017 as part of the Chicago Architecture Biennial.
03 PRISM is the name of a surveillance program by the United States National Security Agency (NSA) that comprehensively monitors internet communications with the help of numerous internet companies in the United States.
04 The quote was retrospectively attributed to Helmut Schmidt in an interview with Giovanni di Lorenzo. See "Verstehen Sie das, Herr Schmidt?," *ZEIT online,* March 4, 2010, accessed August 31, 2019, www.zeit.de/2010/10/Fragen-an-Helmut-Schmidt.

Searching for the Smart City's Democratic Future

BIANCA WYLIE

View from the harbor area to the Sidewalk Labs headquarters,
with the skyline of downtown Toronto in the background. © one2one Photography

In 2017, Sidewalk Labs, a subsidiary company of Alphabet, won a bid for the development of Quayside, a prototype for a smart city located on a 12-acre brownfield along the Toronto waterfront. The project was conceived as the launch pad of a much larger development comprising a vast swathe of high-value real estate in the former docklands. After much public concern arose about Sidewalk Labs's strategic goals, a realignment of the original development agreement, first made in 2018 and amended in July 2019, was discussed in October 2019 to tackle some "threshold issues." In particular these included the collection of personal data through smart technologies and the company's possible future development of the waterfront. Plans for Quayside are moving forward, but a formal comprehensive reevaluation of the master innovation and development plan (MIDP) by Sidewalk Labs is underway. If approved, the terms of the new MIDP are expected to be released to the public by June 2020.

There is a striking blue building on Toronto's eastern waterfront. Wrapped top to bottom in bright, beautiful artwork by Montreal illustrator Cecile Gariepy, the building—a former fish processing plant—stands out alongside the neighboring parking lots and a congested highway. It's been given a second life as an office for Sidewalk Labs—a sister company to Google that is proposing a smart city development in Toronto.

"Our mission is really to use technology to redefine urban life in the twenty-first century," Dan Doctoroff, CEO of Sidewalk Labs, stated in an interview with Freakonomics Radio. The phrase is a variant of the marketing language used by the smart city industry at large.

Put more simply, the term "smart city" is usually used to describe the use of technology and data in cities. No matter the words chosen to describe it, the smart city model has a flaw at its core: corporations are seeking to exert influence on urban spaces and democratic governance. And because most governments don't have the policy in place to regulate smart city development—in particular, projects driven by the fast-paced technology sector—this presents a growing global governance concern.

This is where the story usually descends into warnings of smart city dystopia or failure. Loads of recent articles have detailed the science-fiction-style city-of-the-future and speculated about the perils of mass data collection, and for good reason—these are important concepts that warrant discussion. It's time, however, to push past dystopian narratives and explore solutions for the challenges that smart cities present in Toronto, and globally. To understand the questions that Sidewalk Labs is forcing policy makers to grapple with, it's important to understand some of the context around the proposed Toronto development.

Sidewalk Toronto

Sidewalk Toronto is a joint venture smart city project created by Sidewalk Labs and Waterfront Toronto. Waterfront Toronto is a not-for-profit corporation leading the renewal of Toronto's waterfront. The three orders of the Canadian government (federal, provincial, and municipal) are equal non-equity-share sponsors and have provided the corporation with seed capital to transform 2,000 acres of brownfield waterfront land. A board of directors, appointed by the three levels of government, oversees the strategic direction of the corporation, which began seeking a partner to help develop a small 12-acre plot of land, known as Quayside, in early 2017. Later that year, Waterfront Toronto named Sidewalk Labs the winner of the request for proposal (RFP) process. An agreement was signed in July 2018, and then amended in July 2019. The agreements solidified that Sidewalk Labs will invest US$50 million to create a plan for Quayside, and to develop products and services there to sell to other cities globally.

To do this work, Sidewalk Labs and Waterfront Toronto have created a new legal entity—Sidewalk Toronto, a limited partnership. So far, no land has changed hands. Approval of the plan for this 12-acre plot will be required from the Waterfront Toronto board, Alphabet (Sidewalk Labs' parent company) and the Toronto City Council, as well as other levels of government as required.

In 2018 and 2019, Sidewalk Toronto hosted a series of public consultations focused on urban life staples, from mobility to housing. As a whole, the grand marketing vision for Toronto's neighborhood of the future is expansive and data driven, and speaks to issues of affordability, resilience, and sustainability. It features underground garbage robots, autonomous vehicles, snow-melting sidewalks, and more. While many of the features rely on the use of new technology and data to create responsive and adaptive places and spaces, other key features—modular housing and wooden buildings, for example—do not rely on new technology at all. The proposal also makes persistent mention of the need for access to more than the initial 12-acre plot of land for the innovations to be realized at scale. This nods to a possible play for a larger stake in the development of Toronto's prime waterfront real estate.

Setting the particulars of this deal aside, there is definitely a case to be made for rethinking cities. Ken Greenberg, planner, author, and adviser to Sidewalk Labs, puts it this way: "Our systems are strained; established ways of doing basic things are stretched to the limit and beyond... The Sidewalk partnership may just provide the catalyst, R&D resources, and the time and space we urgently need to help us make the leap in critical areas." But while Greenberg's definition of the problem is correct, the solution that is on the table for Toronto should be considered somewhere on the spectrum of highly contentious to full-fledged democratic emergency.

Commit to open procurement and contracting

As the public becomes more aware about the impact of technology, they also grow more alert to related dangers that privacy and surveillance experts have been ringing alarms about for decades. This

Part of the smart city company's approach is giving the impression of encouraging citizen participation. © Nick Kozak

recent awakening should give governments permission to take decisions around smart cities seriously and slowly, and to demand open information about them. Procurement is a good place to start. In Toronto, the opposite has played out: for nine months the public was kept in the dark about details of the deal, despite promises of an open and collaborative process and public pressure.

Recently, both the original and amended agreements that the organizations have signed were released. The newest agreement details the nature of the working arrangement between both organizations and some high-level language around data use. Still, the agreements are short on specifics, and they fail to impose baseline requirements around control of public data and publicly owned digital infrastructure.

Waterfront Toronto went out on a limb with this procurement in the name of innovation, asserting an unchecked assumption that Toronto residents want this type of smart city development to occur, but the report compiled by the City of Toronto reveals that six initial applicants bid in the RFP process, and that three were short-listed for the final round, and while the criteria for selection were included in the RFP, Waterfront Toronto hasn't

published any additional information about how the final decision was made. Sidewalk Labs's persistent declaration that "it chose Toronto" adds to the gray.

Think of civic data management as a government responsibility

Data collection, privacy, and surveillance are at the center of discussion around Sidewalk Toronto. Consistently, however, these discussions begin with "what will you do with my data?" rather than with "why do you need my data at all?" It's as if providing data to the private sector is required. It's not.

It is vital to find more precise language for the data used in a smart city in order to talk about it together. Personally identifiable information is one thing. Aggregate and anonymized human behavioral data about how people move around in cities is another. There is also environmental data (weather, pollution) or geospatial data (maps, facility locations), among many others. Each data type and context require a different type of conversation around how the data might be used by governments, how it might be commercialized, and how it might be made open, shared, or kept closed.

The Quayside neighbourhood

This view of the Quayside site plan looks northeast towards the Gardiner Expressway. The plan incorporates a series of innovations around transportation, social infrastructure, housing affordability, digital tools, sustainable infrastructure, building construction, and public space — with the goal of improving quality of life for Torontonians. It reflects 18 months of public engagement needed to refine these planning ideas and start to achieve Waterfront Toronto's ambitious priority outcomes.

In terms of a discussion about who owns city data, Teresa Scassa, a CIGI fellow and the Canada Research Chair in Information Law and Policy at the University of Ottawa, has recently written that the concept of legal "ownership" doesn't fit the bill when discussing data. She also describes many cases of data hand-off from residents as surrender rather than consent. Several data governance initiatives offer some guidance on how to tackle problems related to data collection and use.

In Canada, for the Sidewalk Toronto project, the idea of a data trust has been raised as a possible solution for the management of civic data. Data trusts might provide a short-term data management approach, but they also require new levels of civic participation, which are challenging to meet for residents already burdened with other realities of life. According to Renee Sieber, associate professor in the Department of Geography at McGill University, data trusts aren't likely to be a cure-all: "We grant government the right to collect very personal data about us to improve the public and personal good. This is a fundamental part of the social contract. We don't have that relationship with the private sector. We don't know what they will or could do with our data—there are no mechanisms for us to manage what they are collecting about us," she says. "This is why the idea of a data trust is attractive for the private sector, but not for the public sector—we already have a social contract with government, it includes mechanisms substantiated in law and a political process for influencing that collection and control."

Recognize smart cities as a political issue, not a technology issue

A long list of failed smart cities is often trotted out to demonstrate the folly of the techno-utopian vision—from the Songdo International Business District in South Korea, to the Epcot Center in Florida, to Masdar City in Abu Dhabi. There are, however, new approaches to technology management that stand as examples of improvement. They include the use of participatory models that engage residents in decision making and data stewardship. While most of these models are not set in the fully entrenched type of smart city real-estate development that Sidewalk Toronto represents, they make strides in defining best practices for smart cities. Francesca Bria, the chief technology officer for the city of Barcelona, is spearheading one such initiative.

In 2015, Ada Colau, a progressive candidate, won the mayoral election in Barcelona. Her campaign has been described by some as a response to the corporate smart city movement. Under her leadership, Barcelona is instituting policy to guarantee not only open technology systems as a procurement requirement, but also resident control of data and technology-driven civic participation. In another nod to civil society at the center of the smart city, Barcelona's public libraries are being brought in to support the open data program component, an approach that Canadian community technology leaders such as Mita Williams have wanted for years. Barcelona demonstrates an important distinction for smart cities: smart city development is not a technological decision, but a political one.

As Bria explains: "We must challenge the current narrative dominated by Silicon Valley's leaky surveillance capitalism and dystopian models such as China's social credit system. A New Deal on data, based on a rights-based, people-centric framework, which does not exploit personal data to pay for critical infrastructure, is long overdue."

Political will was critical to Barcelona's story. Political change—election of a progressive leader with a vision to create a resident-led technology movement—came before technological change.

Sidewalk Labs

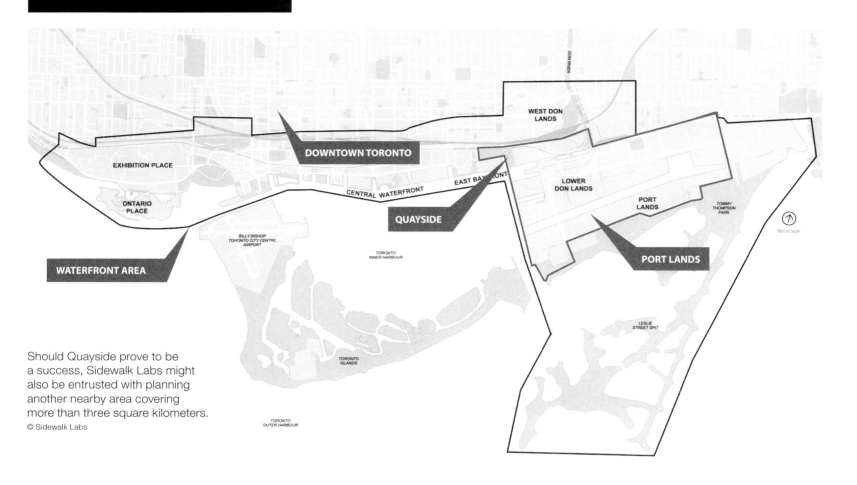

Should Quayside prove to be a success, Sidewalk Labs might also be entrusted with planning another nearby area covering more than three square kilometers.
© Sidewalk Labs

Adopt an agile policy-making process

Smart cities don't fit neatly into existing legislation or policy at any level. As a result, corporations seeking to exert their influence on urban spaces are doing so in a policy vacuum. The technology and data governance frameworks that govern most cities were created prior to the internet era and aren't designed to manage the emerging issues created by pervasive data collection and connected technology.

Laws need to be updated to protect privacy, security, sovereignty, and more. These changes tend to happen slowly, which is generally the right thing with the law. But to address the range of urgent governance challenges that smart cities pose, a set of complementary actions can be taken to create workarounds and stopgap models. If they're bad or don't work, they can be revised or dismantled entirely. Agile policy creation is something all governments will need to start getting comfortable with as technology development in the private sector continues to move faster than policy.

Anthony Townsend, author of *Smart Cities: Big Data, Civic Hackers, and the Quest for a New Utopia*,[01] explains that the baseline operational models for cities—everything from how public records are organized to information-handling principles—haven't been revisited in decades. He suggests that cities should create digital master plans to direct overarching technology policy that can support a city's general strategic planning efforts.

Within such a framework, there would also be opportunities to create collaborative approaches to share infrastructure with other cities. Software code, which is digital infrastructure, has a key difference from traditional physical infrastructure such as bridges and roads—it can be replicated and shared around the world.

Creating data standards to support this type of shared digital infrastructure and interoperability is another track of work to consider. Such efforts have been underway for years already but could be energized with a broader set of stakeholders at the table and with an increased sense of urgency. Sidewalk Toronto certainly provides that urgency.

This story is set in Canada, but it should prompt policy makers everywhere to roll back the bright, distracting wrappings and playful narratives of smart cities. Open procurement, public education and engagement, responsible data management, a focus on local democracy, and an agile policy process aren't easy, but they provide a path forward from the dystopian smart city. Technology can be well deployed in cities—not to track, monitor, profile, and profit, but to support local needs, improve urban environments, and support democratically informed policy.

This text is a shortened and updated version of an article previously published by the Centre for International Governance Innovation. Learn more at cigionline.org.

01 Anthony Townsend, *Smart Cities: Big Data, Civic Hackers, and the Quest for a New Utopia*, (New York: W.W. Norton & Company, 2013).

Sidewalk Labs is planning modular building systems made of freely programmable lofts that are virtually able to react to the changing needs of users and of the market.

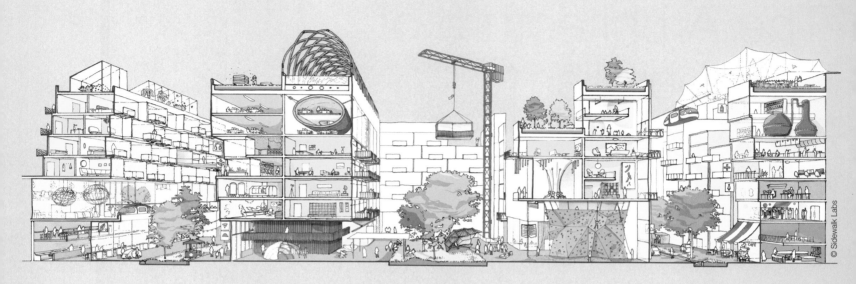

In addition to implementing new technologies, Sidewalk Labs plans to invest more than CAD$80 million in a glulam plant in the Greater Toronto area to establish a new industrial hub for mass timber and modular construction. Before doing so, the firm wants the municipality to guarantee that it will be able to expand its development plans to include Toronto's sought-after Quayside waterfront promenade. © Picture Plane for Heatherwick Studio

"The Architecture of Neoliberalism Disavows Labor"

DOUGLAS SPENCER IN CONVERSATION WITH
HARALD TRAPP AND ROBERT THUM

As a cultural theorist with a focus on architecture, urbanism, and critical theory, what is your relationship to the work of Karl Marx?

DOUGLAS SPENCER: I started reading Marx as an undergraduate back in the 1980s and then rather neglected him to some extent, but when I began working on my book *The Architecture of Neoliberalism*, the first thing I did was to go back and read *Capital* cover to cover. There are a great number of important things that one can still take from Marx, which remain relevant today. The one that really strikes me is his emphasis on critique. Marx says in his much-quoted 1843 letter to Arnold Ruge that what we must engage in is the ruthless criticism of everything that exists.

Central to my inspiration from Marx is the idea that critique is ruthless, so one shouldn't be scared or fearful about naming names—even if they are people who might seem like your allies to others. I think that this notion of critique is fundamentally important to us today, specifically in the case of architecture, neoliberalism, and of the relationship between the two. It is important in terms of architecture, because we have been undergoing a period, perhaps beginning in in the 1970s, where architecture has become increasingly distant from the political. It is increasingly wary about

making comments about society, which it sees as an abstraction, or capitalism, or, in more contemporary terms, making references to neoliberalism. It's scared of making statements on that broader totality that Marx is reaching for through his own dialectical method.

How can Marx still be useful to understand the development in architecture?

DS: It might seem rather an old-fashioned, vulgar way of understanding Marx but one of his most famous ideas is the distinction between base and superstructure, and the notion that the economic base determines the political and ideological superstructure. The relationship of base and superstructure is open to debate, in that the superstructure is determining the base as well as the other way round, yet architecture really seems to be—more than any other field—a simultaneous embodiment of both the economic base and the ideological superstructure. Because we know that nothing gets built without an economic project behind it, without investment, architecture is therefore deeply implicated in realizing the value of land and the value of property. So it is deeply implicated in that economic base. It is part of it and its reproduction. It is part of the whole valorization process of capital. At the same time, architecture, unlike financial capital, is

not merely an abstraction or something that one has to solely theorize. We can always see it. It is apparent. It is experienced. It always has some type of outer and inner appearance. It has symbols, explicit or not. It has ornaments of one type or another. So it's always simultaneously in the field of the economic base and in the realm of ideas and experience. Few other disciplines typically fall on more than one side or the other of those two modes.

The specific danger in architecture is a turn towards the pragmatic, a turn towards the post-critical, which is simultaneously a turn against theory. And what this does consciously—deliberately or otherwise—is that it effectively allows architecture off the hook in that it sidesteps critique in terms of its political, larger economic and social implications by saying those approaches, those perspectives, are no longer valid or relevant. That is something I try to challenge. Now, alongside that turn to the post-critical, there is the concurrent development of neoliberalism, which has its origins in the 1930s and '40s, but really came to prominence and power politically in the early 1970s.

Why, do you think, did this start in the Anglo-Saxon world, with Margaret Thatcher and Ronald Reagan?

130

The photo series *Private Public Places* by Luca Picardi shows casual scenes from the highly commercialized metropolis of London. Photo: © Luca Picardi

DS: I don't think it started exclusively in the Anglo-Saxon world. Because if we look at the movements that David Harvey identifies in his history of neoliberalism, we see these going on in South America, for example, or if we start to talk about political and military coups against socialist and reformist governments, those happened in many parts of the world. Neoliberalism takes this turn against the political in the aftermath of the Second World War, where, for one thing, both Stalinism and Fascism are equated as being the outcomes of planning. Most of us have no problems with condemning Stalinism and Fascism, but that's also a maneuver that neoliberal ideology takes to discredit any form of socialism, whether it be revolutionary, or even democratic, or any type of social reform. So Friedrich Hayek, the leading theorist of neoliberalism, says that whenever you plan, whenever there is any endeavor on the part of human beings to grasp or understand society and its direction and to make it more equitable, this inevitably leads to dictatorship. He's against all forms of welfare and the whole economic philosophy of Keynesianism. The premises of neoliberal theory and belief, and its so-called ideology of non-ideology, are that on moral and ethical grounds there cannot be planning, because it will lead to dictatorship.

There is also an essential understanding of the limited capacity of human beings to understand the world. This is what Hayek says as well. He says that human beings are necessarily ignorant. The world is too complex for us to understand. Therefore we have to seek some superior form of management of our world, and that comes through the inhuman calculating powers of the economy—inhuman in that it is not intentionally planned. The market will guide us. It's not simply a *laissez-faire* policy, although it might be presented as that, because only the role of government changes. It is not that government disappears—instead its function changes from having a vision of society into how the economy can best be managed and supported so that it itself provides the calculation and becomes a kind of a supercomputer that will organize society for us.

How would you distinguish between capitalism and neoliberalism? One is an ideology, the other not?
DS: One thing that distinguishes neoliberalism from capitalism is that there wasn't a group or society of people that got together and said: "Let's found capitalism" and then "Let's insert ourselves in key institutional positions and promote the idea of capitalism," but this was precisely what neoliberalism did.

Neoliberalism is quite often presented as something like a fantasy of the fevered imagination of the left, as though it doesn't really exist—but it does very much exist! It's a program: there are names, there are meetings, there are conferences, and there are organizations that set out strategically to promote neoliberalism. It is pure ideology, a form of politics that shapes our everyday lives.

131

View of Greenwich Peninsula where, with the help of well-known architects popular with the media, such as Santiago Calatrava, a new city district is developing. Foreground: residential towers by Skidmore, Owings & Merrill LLP at Upper Riverside.

The whole notion that one, on account of the very condition of being a human, is not in any position to understand or even to attempt to understand the world in which one lives is a profoundly ideological and market-serving belief.

When did this enter into architectural debate and practice? Has it ever officially entered architectural discourse or did architects just pick up elements from post-structural or postmodern theory?
DS: In my book, I discuss how the development of neoliberalism and neo-liberal thought coincide and overlap with the kind of transformations that went on in architectural practice and architectural theory from the '70s, but especially around the mid '90s. There isn't an explicit embrace of neoliberalism within architec-tural theory, with the exception of Patrik Schumacher, who has only lately begun to talk directly and explicitly about archi-tecture's role in serving the market and market economy as the indisputable base of society that every architect has to work with (see Patrik Schumacher, p. 78–83).

What neoliberalism and certain architectural practices and theories have in common lies in the opposition to critique and criticality. It lies in the oppo-sition to the political. It lies especially in theories of cybernetics, complexity theory, self-organization, and emergence, which are right at the heart of neoliberal thinking from the 1950s, and became simultaneously, or perhaps slightly later, embraced within architectural practice.

The point where architecture and neoliberalism converge, although it's not usually made explicit, is precisely in the type of projects that we've seen archi-tects finding work in over the last 10 to 15 years: the production of new transport hubs, new forms of shopping malls, new universities, where they are actually servicing new ideas about the subject. For example, the notion that the university student is not allowed to be merely a student anymore—instead they have to be simultaneously an entrepreneur.

This development coincides with the emergence of the system of "starchitects" or architecture as a commodity.
DS: You're right. If we look at the projects that for me are most characteristic of what I call the "architecture of neoliberalism,"

they tend to be by high profile architects, and very publicly visible and often quite highly publicized projects. They are projects where the clients want to have well-known architects as part of their publicity strategy.

In contrast, the condition of the architectural worker is becoming more and more precarious. Their own role in architectural production is entirely obscured, in part by the star architect name-function, which, whether architects like to use that term or not, is how they are understood by capital and neoliberal capitalism: as a name that can be attached to a product.

So the notion of labor in neoliberal architecture has changed?
DS: In most contemporary architecture, certainly with practices like Zaha Hadid Architects or Foreign Office Architects, and to some extent with OMA, we see an interesting disavowal of labor. It is as if labor can't be acknowledged to even exist and certainly cannot be represented. Of course there are many different types of labor involved in the design and in the building of architecture. We often end

up with very complex, warped and convoluted architectural forms that appear to have folded themselves and undergone their own immanent process of shape-shifting. If you took the cladding away, you would see the awkwardness of their construction. The labor itself is revealed only at the moment of construction; the role of cladding is to come in and disguise and obscure all of that production. Labor is disavowed, is hidden—much as Marx says of all commodity-production.

The programs that neoliberal architecture is interested in tell us something about the condition of labor itself. Take for example the BMW center in Leipzig: it's only the central building that's designed by Zaha Hadid Architects. This is a space of work, yes, but it's a space designed to make work disappear. Again, it is a disavowal of labor as something that is laborious, difficult, involves struggle, which is displaced with a notion of community, teamwork, togetherness, and interaction.

Further to that, we can also think of the fact that we are engaged in labor even when we're not officially at work. The constant processes of networking, of using our mobile devices to keep in touch with one another, to constantly be working on our own profile to make ourselves networked, to make us employable, is simultaneously a process of leisure and a form of work upon ourselves. And again the job of the architect is to present this as a kind of smooth, attractive landscape of experience in which we are freely engaging and interacting with one another, never en masse but always as a manageable group of individuals.

This is vital to understand, and to me it seems one of the most promising developments over the last two or three years is the emergence of groups like The Architecture Lobby in the US, or Architectural Workers in the UK, who are trying to understand what is political about architecture. But not in terms of what it can do formally—whether it can work for or against neoliberalism, or for or against globalization through form and design—but rather to understand it as a practice of labor and then to think about it. Then you can start to forge solidarity between architectural workers and other workers. This is the classic abstraction of Marx, to unite universal workers, to unite workers of the world. What we have in common is this abstract unity that we are all part of the wage system.

Which brings us to another topic that is prominent in your book: what do you mean by the "neoliberal subject"?
<u>DS</u>: This goes back to Marx as well. In the *Grundrisse* he says that capital not only produces an object for the subject, but also produces a subject for the object. So this already gives us a more sophisticated notion of the relationship between base and superstructure, between the economic and the political. Marx is saying that capitalism does not only produce commodities for consumers, but it must produce a market, it must produce desires. It must produce certain types of needs and furthermore it must effectively produce the subjects who engage with it, who could take on those needs, desires, tastes, habits etc.

More commonly, we might look to Michel Foucault for his account of the production of subjectivity. He is much more interested in this on a micro-scale, but I think we can use both Foucault and Marx together. Neoliberalism is a type of subjectivity, or the desire to produce certain types of subjects, who do not

A poster advertising luxurious new housing in the densely built-up financial center Canary Wharf. © Harald Trapp

Architectural Labor

The Architecture Lobby campaign #notmyAIA criticizes the American Institute of Architects' support of building projects by Donald Trump. The campaign motif is an alienation of Madelon Vriesendorp's *Flagrant Délit* (1975), quoting the original cover image of Rem Koolhaas' *Delirious New York*.

identify themselves as part of a class or even of an ethnic or national group, but identify themselves fundamentally as individuals, who have to invest themselves as a whole being in a personal entrepreneurial project.

Education is now an example of this. Today a student might find it difficult to think about education in terms of the opportunities I had, which was: "It will be interesting to understand the politics of aesthetics." To do that now, you have to borrow money. But then you want to have some sort of guarantee that when you are going to invest that money and become indebted, that you are going to be able to recoup that money later on and perhaps receive some sort of profit from it. There is that dimension of the neoliberal subject. It is economic and individual, rather than being a political animal; it is an economic individual entrepreneur, as Foucault said.

Another dimension of this that relates more to architectural, urban, and spatial conditions is that the relationship presented to us as being of primary importance is the relationship with our environment. So rather than relating to the state or a class or a town or a community, we have neoliberalism's own abstraction, which is "the environment." The primary type of environment is the market. The market is the immediate environment, but everything is in these abstract environmental terms, and architecture too talks about these and the subject in relationship to its environment.

Connected to subjectivity is the notion of the home. Increasingly the home is a commodity—and not only a commodity, but also something that is there to provide for you at the later stages of life. DS: Yes, property and architecture of all sorts is this condition of a two-way switching between use value and exchange value, as Marx would have said. What you're talking about is the very concrete everyday example of the rather abstract sounding notion of the production of neoliberal subjectivity. It might sound like you have the opportunity to get onto the property ladder, and this is what everyone should have the opportunity to do, but in some sense you have no choice but to pursue that, whether it's achievable or not, because—what's the alternative? The alternative in London is to rent, to find 12 months' rent in advance. It is to have your contract renewed every year for it to go up by 10 to 15, even 20 percent each year, to be paying very high rent and essentially throwing that money away. So it's where what presents itself as an opportunity in effect is, because of the conditions and because of the economic base, something that you have no choice but to engage in.

Some young architects at the moment are seeking a collective approach in architecture, working with communities, using the idea of participation from the '70s. Do you think that they are escaping the neoliberal ideology?

DS: I don't think they escape the neoliberal ideology. I think trying to pin all your hopes on notions of participation or community is problematic. They have to be approached very rigorously, carefully and critically. Participation is something that capitalism is very happy with. Participation is something that neoliberalism is very happy with. It is an abstraction itself that is not useful, unless you think about what the end of that participation is. This is similar for notions of community, especially under conditions of neoliberalism. Community and participation come to play this role in place of the state, but neoliberalism itself is trying to downplay the importance of the state. Its proponents say people should be more responsible for and look after themselves, and that the kind of support that a welfare society would provide cannot be expected. Therefore, one has to be actively involved in participating in communities. A lot of the will or enthusiasm that comes with those sorts of endeavors is well placed, but has itself to be critically reflected on as to what its actual ends are, because they can be too easily confused with an agenda that is in any case essentially neoliberal.

In one important chapter of Capital, *Marx historically tries to pin down the origin of the accumulation of capital to the enclosure of the commons in England* (see Harald Trapp, p. 70–77). *There is a whole movement in economical, as well as in political thinking, based on this idea of revitalizing the commons in a new interpretation.*
DS: Yes, again I have some sympathy for it, but it cannot simply be a kind of empty abstract slogan that people gather around. We have to think about where is this going on, what are the particular conditions in which any project takes place, and what are the kinds of outcomes being sought. If I sound very negative, it's because the problems—if not insurmountable—shouldn't be underestimated. It is not easy. Architects overestimate

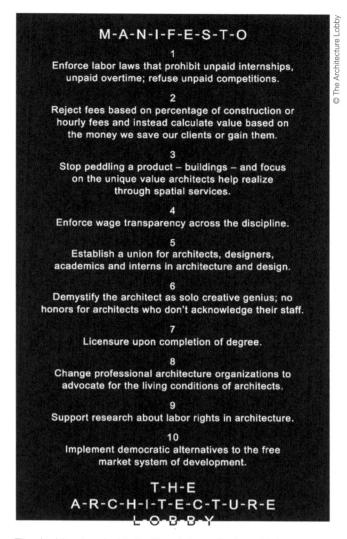

M-A-N-I-F-E-S-T-O

1
Enforce labor laws that prohibit unpaid internships, unpaid overtime; refuse unpaid competitions.

2
Reject fees based on percentage of construction or hourly fees and instead calculate value based on the money we save our clients or gain them.

3
Stop peddling a product – buildings – and focus on the unique value architects help realize through spatial services.

4
Enforce wage transparency across the discipline.

5
Establish a union for architects, designers, academics and interns in architecture and design.

6
Demystify the architect as solo creative genius; no honors for architects who don't acknowledge their staff.

7
Licensure upon completion of degree.

8
Change professional architecture organizations to advocate for the living conditions of architects.

9
Support research about labor rights in architecture.

10
Implement democratic alternatives to the free market system of development.

T-H-E
A-R-C-H-I-T-E-C-T-U-R-E
L-O-B-B-Y

The Architecture Lobby's 10-point manifesto, which calls for a labor union organization of workers in the field of architecture.

their own political agency. It is very easy for architects to be political agents of the existing status quo or of the direction it's taking—but can they direct it somewhere else? It is very difficult to find any historical examples where architecture has done that—there are notable examples that people always talk about, such as the Red Vienna. These are very contentious, isolated cases, and my most pessimistic approach to that is to become like Adorno and say: there can be no right life in the wrong one. But without being that absolutely negative, I think that if you do want to have some political effectivity or agency as an architect, you have to first think critically about what your actual agency is. The default position for architects is to think about what they're doing within their own medium, about what one can do with form. For example, if spaces seem to be too open, too connected, or too flexible in neoliberal-

ism, then the default reverse position is to provide isolated, hermetic spaces, as if that protects the individual. I don't really think that's effective politics.

But do you see in architecture at the moment any movements that are going in a positive direction? To echo Adorno: any that are able to overcome the existing trend, or to get the right life into the right architecture?
DS: I see some of the critique of the way in which architecture is used, which is coming from certain communities, to be very promising. There's the example of Detroit Resists, a group that emerged in response to the US Pavilion at the 2016 Venice Biennale, curated by Cynthia Davidson and Mónica Ponce de León, who commissioned twelve American architectural practices with "creative" projects addressing the decline of Detroit. Detroit Resists produced a very strong critique of the ways that architecture represents itself, regardless of the context or the nature of the project, so as to show off their own creativity in response to a brief. Detroit Resists presents a community-level response against the fetishization of creativity; we see this fetishization of creativity presented as the agency of the architect far too much. I'm talking about people hacking IKEA, for example, taking symbols of standardization or uniformity and using these almost as a platform to express their own seemingly subversive creativity.

I think the most promising signs that I can see on the horizon are developments of semi-clandestine unions or movements to unionize architectural workers, where architecture recognizes its agency as a form of labor, rather than as a form of creativity.

Female (Open) Space Invaders

A PHOTO ESSAY BY MARISA GONZÁLEZ

Video stills from *Ellas, filipinas* (2010–12). © Marisa González

Ellas, Filipinas

Every Sunday, the financial district of Hong Kong is invaded by hundreds of Filipino women, who temporarily occupy empty public spaces or office building plazas, including Norman Foster's famous HSBC tower. They share meals on the stone-paved squares and lobbies; they play games; they organize informal flea markets, peacefully re-claiming the otherwise deserted center of one of the world's leading financial capitals. But what makes these gatherings really peculiar is the apparent absence of any male presence. The majority of the participants are female domestic workers who have emigrated to Hong Kong to find employment in the thriving domestic service and care industries. The video documentary

Ellas, filipinas, directed by the artist Marisa González between 2010 and 2012, captures these weekly occupations and traces the personal experiences of some of these foreign women, who often leave their own families behind to work for wealthier households in Hong Kong. It is estimated that more than 150,000 Filipino women are employed as domestic helpers in the city. Their spontaneous and convivial gatherings incidentally reveal one fundamental— albeit often invisible—characteristic of the prevailing capitalist division of labor: that the current economic system relies on the systematic exploitation of huge numbers of almost exclusively female workers for the reproduction of society. But while decades of feminist struggles have taught us that

this is no novelty, what appears to be relatively new is the global scale of the phenomenon. As author and activist Silvia Federici points out in her contribution to this volume: "a restructuring of reproductive work has taken place internationally, whereby much of the reproduction of the metropolitan workforce is now performed by immigrant women coming from the Global South. [...] While governments celebrate the 'globalization of care,' which enables them to reduce investment in reproduction, it is clear that this 'solution' has a tremendous social cost, not only for the individual immigrant woman but for the communities from which they originate." MG

Gig Space

Deliveroo and the Algorithm-Based Gig Economy

CALLUM CANT, PHD CANDIDATE AND
FORMER DELIVEROO COURIER, IN
CONVERSATION WITH HARALD TRAPP
AND ROBERT THUM

PHOTO ESSAY BY IMMO KLINK

HARALD TRAPP, ROBERT THUM:
*Callum Cant, how did you become a
courier for Deliveroo?*
CALLUM CANT: I began to work as a
courier in Brighton in Summer 2016.
I primarily became involved as a militant
before I started researching Deliveroo.
There was a huge strike in London that
broke out in August 2016. It came out of
nowhere, a wildcat strike, where suddenly
hundreds of Deliveroo workers were
descending on Deliveroo HQ and shutting
it down over a proposed change to the
pay structure. Rather than being on 7
pounds an hour plus 1 pound per delivery,
they were going to be moved on a pure
piece rate, so just 3.75 pounds per order.
The dynamics of the self-organized strike
were fascinating, and I wanted to know
how it had happened. I immediately began
to find that there was a huge self-organized network of Deliveroo couriers. There
was a political consciousness that was
latent there about exploitation and conditions of labor. All employment of labor
under capitalism is exploitive but there is
something particularly biting about the
conditions at Deliveroo which demands
the response.

HT/RT: *How does a gig job differ from
other kinds of labor?*
CC: For me the primary issue is the
automation of management. I have had
other jobs in hospitality where you work in
a kitchen and have a human supervisor
who tells you, "You've got to do this. Now
you've got to do this." Your labor power
is producing value for your boss but it
is being managed by a human, whereas
in Deliveroo suddenly you don't have a
supervisor. The immediate person on your
back telling you "Go faster, go faster"
has disappeared. Instead you have an
app that issues a series of repetitive com-
mands: "Go to this restaurant. Pick up
this food. Go to this customer. Drop off
this food. Confirm. Cycle back here."
All these kinds of orders come out of the
smartphone, but there is a sense of
notional independence. You get rid of the
monkey on your back: the supervisor.
For a while I understood how this could
feel incredibly liberating.

HT/RT: *How does Deliveroo pay its
couriers?*
CC: In Brighton, I was paid 4 pounds
per delivery, and that was the flat fee.
If you did one order an hour you got 4
pounds an hour. That is before you
subtract costs, which are something like
2 pounds an hour. If you did no orders
you got zero pounds. This meant in
busy periods you were trying to make as
much money as possible. Often that
meant taking a lot of risk: "Am I going to
overtake this taxi? Am I going to undercut this bus? Am I going to go down this
hill too fast? Am I going to go out and
work when actually the conditions are
so bad that I shouldn't be working?" All
these decisions I was being forced to
manage myself. Whereas I thought I got
rid of the supervisor, in fact the supervisor was in my own head and I had to
push myself harder and harder in order
to get enough deliveries to make a
decent wage.

HT/RT: *Does Deliveroo operate a consumer rating system?*
CC: No, instead there are a number of
standards for performance that you are
meant to meet. You are meant to accept
90% of orders. You are meant to deliver
within a certain timeframe. Through a
process of machine learning, couriers
are discriminated between depending on
these metrics.If you are faster—for
instance, if you are on a moped and you
constantly break the speed limit—you are
assigned more deliveries. But performance
management was incredibly opaque. It
was not discussed. It was not negotiated.
The only way I found out that couriers
were systematically de-prioritized for being
slower was because a mutual friend who

All pwaphs: Immo Klink © Capital Architecture, London 2018

is a software engineer working at Deliveroo disclosed to my friend how this "black box" system works in the app.

HT/RT: *How many couriers are dependent on their job and how many could at least claim to be flexible, as they work part-time?*
CC: There are moped workers who are locked into hire agreements where they have purchased their mopeds and are paying it off bit by bit, month by month. They work 40, 50, 60 hours a week in order to try and make that kind of money back. They really are long-term workers and they perform the vast majority of the work for Deliveroo. The flexible minority—cyclists and students—are certainly important as part of the Deliveroo workforce, but fundamentally there is a core of hyper-exploited migrant labor at the heart of Deliveroo's process. When there are strikes, it is precisely these workers that you see on the streets. The two strikes we had in London have both been led by Brazilian migrant workers. In Brighton, it was the same thing. The cyclists started the organizing process, but it was the migrant moped workers who really took the thing forward and made it work. The exploitative use of the employment category of independent contractors is entirely about reducing labor costs and reducing workers' security. It's about disempowering workers. But there is a flip side to this that Deliveroo failed to understand when they first designed the model. British workers in general are restricted by an incredibly narrow set of trade union laws. They include restrictions on how you are allowed to picket, how many people are allowed to picket, where you are allowed to picket, and so on. But when platform companies like Deliveroo get rid of the category of worker or employee, there is a certain freedom that comes with it. Actually, all the restrictions which are forced on workers as to how you may or may not exercise your democratic right to organize are suddenly abolished. You are allowed to organize in the way you want, in the most effective mechanism of organizing. You can simply log off and go on strike. Every Deliveroo

courier knows that. They will chat to each other and say: "Oh, should we go on strike?" And they don't have to ballot and give six weeks' notice.

HT/RT: *So the couriers organize through platforms as well?*
CC: The really interesting thing is that there is a whole structure of invisible organization that goes on below the surface at Deliveroo. When I started working in Brighton I thought our Deliveroo workers were all isolated, did not know each other, and had no idea how the process works. In fact, an incredibly strong organization already existed across the city. And that scaffold was what they relied upon to build a strike. There were a few WhatsApp groups with huge numbers of workers who were constantly communicating about the weather, rates of pay, working conditions, or if they had a problem.

HT/RT: *How did you learn about this?*
CC: I got added into it at the zone center. The physical zone center is where Deliveroo stores labor, the hub where couriers must go in order to take on an order. Particularly in the winter when the pay rates were getting worse, there would be 30 to 40 workers with no work sitting in the same square talking to each other about how they had no work. These were readymade massive union meetings.

HT/RT: *Are the spaces provided actually architectural spaces?*
CC: There are both formal and informal spaces. The formal ones are specified on the app and it says "go here." In Brighton we had two. They were both in what is called North Lane, a little area with trendy bars and restaurants. The one for cyclists was a big public square outside a library and this was where we would have 30 workers waiting around talking to each other. There was one for mopeds a couple of streets up where they could park. There are also informal zones. For example, UberEats couriers often create informal zone centers outside the local McDonald's. In Brighton, the London Road McDonald's always has ten or so workers sitting outside it because that is where

the bulk of their orders come from. Both formally and informally, structures are created which allow physical communication, and through this physical communication we did things like distribute our bulletin: the *Rebel Roo* went out entirely from these zone centers.

HT/RT: *Are there problems with violence, in traffic or other situations?*
CC: This comes back to the pressured nature of work on the road on a piece rate. When you are paid 4 pounds a drop, you have to go as fast as possible. This leads you into all kinds of confrontation with other road users. When you are using the road as your means of work and other people are just using it to travel around, there is a conflict that comes into place. I am not a very angry person, but I used to get into road rage confrontations where people would shout at me and I would shout right back at them. This is bound to happen when you use public space like Deliveroo does. It uses the free good of the transport infrastructure set up within the city and actually deteriorates the quality of transportation for everyone. There is a certain lack of respect where people do not really think that Deliveroo is proper work. The situation is particularly tricky for moped couriers who have hire purchase agreements for their mopeds. Delivery drivers are often the target of attempted robberies and normally you would say, "If someone tries to steal my moped aggressively and violently I'm not going to fight back. It's not worth getting stabbed for a moped." But a lot of moped couriers have weapons with them with which they intend to fight off people who try to steal their mopeds. I didn't get the mindset, but they explained to me that if they lose the moped they would lose everything. You can decline orders from certain areas, but if you decline more than ten percent of orders you can get your contract terminated with no appeal process, no explanation—it just gets terminated straight away.

HT/RT: *Is Deliveroo a platform? How does it fit into the concept of platform capitalism?*

CC: The bosses of Deliveroo explain the system as a logistically enabled food delivery. It's fundamentally based on city environments, but as a digital platform it has an unparalleled dataset. Deliveroo has the capacity to skim data off interactions between thousands of restaurants and millions of customers and through those kinds of interactions determine how food deliveries spread across the city. What times do people order the most? What food products are in demand? What do people order when they are hungover? When do they order drinks? In short: Deliveroo knows what the customers want. This strategic advantage, that the platform knows everything about their customers—their locations and their preferences—is played out with Deliveroo Editions and the so-called Roo Kitchens. These are fully-equipped kitchen container units that Deliveroo sets up on unused sites in strategic locations around the city, to boost the reach and revenue of popular restaurants more efficiently. This is where virtual data becomes real. Now Deliveroo has also started to withhold user information from the restaurants, so that customer loyalty is exclusively based on the platform. That data set can also be employed in future business models.

HT/RT: *Deliveroo is planning to produce its own meals?*
CC: Yes, and that will be the point at which they undercut the restaurant industry. The restaurant industry knows this and are terrified of it. Your local Papa John's, Pizza Express, or McDonald's will be outcompeted by delivery apps. This is similar to what you see with the businesses dying out on the high street, because now a majority of customers buy online. The logistical enablement of distant delivery will mean the end of all that was left in city centers of vibrant public culture. However much I disagree with exploitative practices in the restaurant industry, one has to recognize they do foster a certain kind of collectivity in social spaces. That will be fundamentally stripped by something like the Roo Kitchens.

HT/RT: *What food does Deliveroo deliver mainly? Who are its customers?*
CC: It's not sushi. People order Deliveroo mostly when they are exhausted and knackered. If you want to pay restaurant prices for restaurant food and have the restaurant experience, you go to a restaurant. People use Deliveroo when they are in a crisis of reproduction. They are stressed, aren't able to go grocery shopping, or they are looking after a child and don't have any food in the house. Any of these reasons. Deliveroo essentially sells a vision to these people: "You're not exhausted and ordering cheap takeaway food—you're ordering a luxury experience and actually your crisis is not a crisis; it's a symptom of how hip and urban your life is."

HT/RT: *Is it important for the Deliveroo Editions kitchens to be close to the customers?*
CC: It's interesting to think of Deliveroo as a warehouse and transport network mapped on top of each other. But before the Roo Kitchens, it did not have a way of setting up that distribution network. It did not control where the points of production were within that network. Whereas now, with its own kitchens, it gets to set up its own hubs within the network. Here you can see the beginning of a process of centralization, which is immensely threatening to workers; it could make them redundant. But this spatial concentration also means that these can become sites of worker power. When there was a Deliveroo strike in Brighton, one of the first things the workers did was they dispatched a flying picket to the Roo Kitchens to shut them down. And they

did it immediately: the shutters were pulled down and the kitchen workers came out; it wasn't operating. Whereas the abstract digital platforms disempowered the workers, these sites actually give them back an immense amount of power.

HT/RT: *Deliveroo has offices in London with employees in administration. As a courier, did you ever encounter this side of the company?*
CC: Deliveroo has a set of incredibly skilled software workers who work at the London HQs. They are under a system of quite light control and are paid very high wage premiums. Then they have workers in the kitchens and on the streets. Fundamentally part of their structure relies on maintaining a separation between these two worlds. One of the greatest potentials for resistance is connecting those two workforces. When all of the workers can communicate with each other, when the

Deliveroo worker doing deliveries on the street can meet a software engineer, that is where you start to see how the self-organization of the workforce can become a big problem for Deliveroo. As far as in-person management goes, part of this algorithmic management structure of getting rid of the person-supervisor does mean they are very light on their feet in different cities. In Brighton, there was an office somewhere but I never saw it. What I saw was that there was a storage unit in a big yellow storage structure. You went there and there was a guy who gave you your kit, which you had to pay for. The first 300 pounds you were earning, half of that went to pay for that equipment. There was also a person who did a test to make sure you could ride a bike. Those were the only managers I ever saw and they were not really managers, they were very low-paid functionaries. All the contract signing and training occurred entirely

online. The office is liquidated and the only workplace you have left is the zone center or the kitchens where you meet other workers.

HT/RT: *Is Deliveroo a logistics company?*
CC: Deliveroo's app is, in a way, a new form of logistical software for both transport and distribution. It combines the warehouse and the transport network in one space. However, the supply chain for the base material, the groceries, is currently external and comes through more conventional channels. I think even if Deliveroo starts its own food production, the supply chain to that point will be entirely conventional. There is no advantage in having Deliveroo drivers transport base materials. What Deliveroo does is a very small part of final-stage logistics. If you go to a logistics conference, they will talk about the pavement as an under-utilized logistical infrastructure. So one of

Gig Space

the few public spaces left in any city is going to be filled with these little self-driving shopping carts with anti-tamper devices, driving burgers around the city.

HT/RT: *What is the relationship between courier and customer?*
CC: Back in the beginning, when it was a new form of work, people always tipped, but over time that has declined. Now the relationship to the customer is less friendly. But there is always a possibility for interaction and also for some kind of solidarity. I know of a number of customers who used to take our bulletin the Rebel Roo and when they ordered Deliveroo, they would hand the bulletin to the person they were ordering from.

HT/RT: *Is there a typical demographic of Deliveroo couriers?*
CC: You have the low-paid cyclist who is

getting another job, or they might be on a bad student loan. They are young. They are on the bike because it's cheap and they already had one. They are the variable workforce: some months they will work 80 hours, some months they work ten hours, some weeks they do not work at all. In Brighton, about ten percent of the city's population are students. They would prefer to work in hospitality or something easy on a market stall, but the only employment they can find is with Deliveroo. Other couriers have chosen it because they love their bikes or want to get fit. They are often quite transient, highly educated, predominantly white, and male. They are who Deliveroo wants you to think everyone is. Moped couriers tend to be older. They often have family dependents and work many more hours, often full-time. It is their primary source of income; they have no

other way of making ends meet. These workers bring with them all kinds of inherited cultural experiences. The Brazilian couriers often have a strong understanding of trade unionism through their national background. If they are first-generation immigrants, then they will often in their earlier life have experienced a very strong political culture that they imported to their new environment.

HT/RT: *Is our impression correct, that most of the couriers are male?*
CC: Yes, it is predominantly male, but I have started to observe that there is a much larger female workforce than before—though when I say much larger we are probably talking some 15 percent. Part of that was potentially down to the role of the zone center culture as well. There were loud, noisy, silly meetings where any woman who

turned up would get hit on. It was an inhospitable environment. It did not really work for female workers and they were excluded both by workers' behavior and by the structure of the company. But Deliveroo gives certain dynamics to individual competitiveness as well. It is on a piece rate structure and often workers will be a bit macho. I have talked to German workers about the distinction between Deliveroo and Foodora, where Foodora is paid on an hourly rate, and all the women work for Foodora. An hourly rate means security and you do not have to go too fast. Whereas the more competitive men work for Deliveroo.

HT/RT: *Is there anything left of the romantic image of the nomadic urban courier for you?*
CC: There is something nice about being able to self-direct your own work. But at other times you are outside in howling gales at the point where the delivery box literally starts to act like a sail and you get blown out of your lane into oncoming traffic. Immediate reality is often hyper-exploitation. But you can see a possible social use value in Deliveroo. In discussions with the workers, we talked about what Deliveroo's role in society would be if we were to change it and produce something that is good for human beings. What would we make it into? You have a delivery model of something remarkable in terms of a Meals on Wheels service and we know we have got an ageing population. We know that many people in society are struggling with loneliness and food provision, and do not have the density of community networks whereby someone will go and get their shopping for them. Deliveroo could provide an amazingly similar service. But at the moment they are neither the priority market of Deliveroo, nor even the secondary market. If you are a pensioner who can barely pay for heating, you cannot afford it. But you can well imagine these Editions Kitchens run by the NHS as part of a provision of food as a human right, part of the provision of city communities.

HT/RT: *Could Trebor Scholz's idea of platform cooperatives* (see Trebor Scholz, p. 154–161) *be a model for the future?*
CC: The capacity of companies such as Uber or Deliveroo to spend you out of a market is remarkable. For example, in the Netherlands, in Amsterdam, at one point there were six or seven companies operating and competing in the Deliveroo or Uber Eats niche. They were undercutting each other all the time. If you set up a platform cooperative it would be very difficult to sustain it as a capitalist company without state intervention against the market leaders.

The research project Capital Architecture, led by Harald Trapp and Robert Thum together with photographer Immo Klink, examines the new working world of the algorithmic gig economy in London. Presented under the title Gig Space, the graphics, interviews (with Callum Cant, among others), and images create a platform for the "proletarians of the so-called fourth industrial revolution" (Harald Trapp) and document the space of Uber drivers, Amazon parcel couriers, and Deliveroo delivery drivers and their protest for better pay and fair working conditions.

Platform Cooperativism
Challenging the Corporate Sharing Economy

TREBOR SCHOLZ

It took a while to acknowledge that the *sharing economy* was really an on-demand service economy that set out to monetize services that were previously private. It is true that there are undeniable opportunities for students, educated workers between jobs, and everyone who owns a second home. Now, it's easier for college graduates to land a gig assembling furniture or renovating someone's house. Consumers, raised with a keen appreciation of low prices and uber-convenience above all else, welcome these upstarts. But should we understand the "sharing economy" as a road sign pointing to a better, more flexible future of work? What has this economy really brought us?

Welcome to the Potemkin Villages of the "sharing economy," where you can finally sell the fruit from the trees in your garden to your neighbors, share a car ride, or rent a tree house in Redwood Forest. Your friendly convenience is, for many workers, a low-wage, precarious trap. You are promoted to middle management, entitled to fire your driver. Companies even found a way to suck financial value out of your interactions with everyday objects, recruiting them as informants for surveillance capitalism.

Oh-so-cool labor companies like Handy, Postmates, and Uber revel in the fact that they launched their platform monopolies in the absence of a physical infrastructure of their own. They are running off *your* car, *your* apartment, *your* labor, *your* emotions, and importantly, *your* time. They are logistics companies that require participants to pay up to the middleman. We are turned into assets; this is the financialization of the everyday 3.0.

Occupations that cannot be offshored—the pet-walker or home-cleaner—are becoming subsumed under what is now called *platform capitalism*. Baby boomers are losing sectors of the economy like transportation, food, and various other sectors, to millennials who fiercely rush to control demand, supply, and profit by adding a thick icing of business onto app-based user interactions. They are extending the deregulated free market into previously private areas of our lives.

154

Platform Cooperativism

The "sharing economy" is not some isolated shrink-wrapped cube in "cyberspace"; it's just another reflection on capitalism and the massive atlas of digital labor practices. Consequently, we cannot have a conversation about labor platforms without first acknowledging that they depend on exploited human lives all along their global supply chains, starting with the hardware.

All the beloved Apple devices cannot be considered without first reminding ourselves of the labor conditions at what Andrew Ross called "Foxconn's suicide mills" in Shenzhen, China. Or take the rare earth minerals in the Democratic Republic of the Congo; it is essential to follow the supply chains that facilitate all those seemingly clean and glamorous digital life styles.

When responding to a political critique of the on-demand economy, some scholars pose that, well, the terrible results of unfettered capitalism are well understood; that whole Marxist spiel does not need to be asserted yet again. But perhaps, as McKenzie Wark claimed: "This is not capitalism, this is something worse." He suggested that "the mode of production we appear to be entering is one that is not quite capitalism as classically described."[01]

This isn't merely a continuation of pre-digital capitalism as we know it; there are notable discontinuities—new levels of exploitation and concentration of wealth for which I penned the term "crowd fleecing." Crowd fleecing is a new form of exploitation, put in place by four or five upstarts, to draw on a global pool of millions of workers in real time.

The current situation needs to be discussed at the fold of intensified forms of exploitation online and also older economies of unpaid and invisible work—think of Silvia Federici, Selma James, Brigitte Galtier, and Mariarosa Dalla Costa's "Wages for Housework" campaign and, in the 1980s, cultural theorist Donna Haraway discussing ways in which emerging communication technologies allowed for "home-work" to be disseminated throughout society.

Every Uber has an Unter

The "sharing economy" indicates a massive, global push in favor of "digital bridge builders." Platform capitalists insert themselves between those who offer services and others who are looking for them, thereby embedding extractive processes into social interactions. The on-demand economy indicates that digital labor is not a niche phenomenon. In 2015, 160,000 drivers were on the road for Uber, if you trust their numbers.[02] Lyft reported 50,000 drivers. TaskRabbit stated that it had 30,000 workers.[03]

In Germany, unions like ver.di concentrate their efforts on defending the rights of employees while in the United States, I see little chance for a return of the 40-hour workweek for those in the contingent sector. The question, then, becomes, how we can make it better for the one-third of the workforce that is not traditionally employed.

> This isn't merely a continuation of pre-digital capitalism as we know it; there are notable discontinuities—new levels of exploitation and concentration of wealth for which I penned the term "crowd fleecing."

"Whereas traditional employment was like marriage," legal scholar Frank Pasquale writes, "with both parties committed to some longer-term mutual project, the digitized workforce seeks a series of hookups."[04] Energetically projected myths about employment suggest that working as an employee means that you have to give up all flexibility and that working as an independent contractor somehow inherently means that your work is flexible. But this "innate flexibility" of low-income freelancers should be put to question. Using the language of entrepreneurship, flexibility, autonomy, and choice, the burden of the biggest risks of life—unemployment, illness, and old age—have been put onto the shoulders of the workers.

Who will be willing to offer employee–like rights for all freelancers, temps, and contract workers? Princeton economist Alan Krueger, among others, has suggested a third category of worker that is neither an independent contractor nor an employee: the independent worker.[05] This category of worker would receive many of the protections that came with employment.

Taking a step back, I argue that there is a connection between the effects of the "sharing economy" and the deliberate shockwaves of austerity that followed the financial crash in 2008. Tech billionaires jumped right in, riding on the back of those desperately looking for work, thereby not only increasing inequality but also restructuring the economy in a way that makes this new way of working, deprived of all worker rights, livable, survivable, or, as they would put it: "sustainable."

The "sharing economy" grew out of the lineage of Reagan and Thatcher who, in the 1980s, not only shut down the strikes of miners and flight traffic controllers, but also damaged the belief in the ability of unions to watch out for workers; they weakened the belief in the possibility of solidarity, and created a framework in which the restructuring of work, the cuts in welfare checks, and the decoupling of productivity from income became more plausible.

One in three laborers in the American workforce is now an independent contractor, day laborer, temp, or freelancer. Digital day laborers are getting up every morning only to join an auction for their own gigs. According to the economist Juliet Schor, the "sharing economy" increasingly provides access to low-level work for the educated middle class who can now drive taxis and assemble furniture in people's houses while simultaneously displacing low-income workers from these occupations.[06]

The software that is propelling the "sharing economy" is wrapped up in addictive interface design. On the screen, the ant-sized icon of a taxi approaching your location is as seductive yet dangerous as the Sirens who lured Odysseus; it's design for scale. On the business side, entrepreneurs and software engineers have created new markets. But is this innovation or is there a factory behind the playground? Should innovation be just about profits for the few while leaving in its wake a workforce that is predominantly without sufficient social protections? Is innovation geared for value extraction and growth, or is it about the circulation of this value between people?

Efficiency, in the same way, is not a virtue when it is, most of all, built on the extraction of value for shareholders and owners. It is in this sense of taking away value from people that labor companies like Amazon, CrowdSpring, and Taskrabbit are neither effective nor innovative. Platform capitalism, so far, has been highly ineffective in addressing the needs of the commonwealth. What initially looked like innovation, eventually cranked up the volume on income inequality.

Illegality as a Method

In the United States, illegality is a method of the "sharing economy," not a bug, and the Federal government, at least for now, is not intervening, leaving the field (and only hope) with the municipalization of regulation. Firms in the "sharing economy" failed to pay taxes and violated federal laws.[07] Their modus operandi follows a pattern. First, companies like Uber violate various laws—anti-discrimination laws, for instance—to then point to a growing and keen consumer base, demanding legal changes. Airbnb spent over $8 million to lobby in San Francisco when residents voted on regulating their operations. Uber spends more money on lobbyists than even Walmart. Significantly, both Uber and Airbnb are using their apps as political platforms that can be used to activate their clients to oppose any regulatory efforts against them.

There's some hope. In one recent decision, for example, a Federal judge found that an Uber driver was an employee and not an independent contractor.[08] Lyft and even Yelp workers are filing lawsuits to become recognized as employees.[09] In the fall of 2015, the city of Seattle opened the door for the unionization of Uber drivers. And around the same time, an unlikely coalition of startups and organized labor published a document outlining necessary social protections for workers that are needed for the digital economy to thrive.[10]

On the local and state level, some regulatory efforts are under way. In Montgomery County, for instance, the Maryland General Assembly decided to regulate Uber and Lyft by imposing a $.25 charge for each trip with those companies. The revenue will then be used to offer more accessible taxicab services for eligible senior citizens and low-income residents.[11] Mayor Bill de Blasio is working to curb the size of the Uber fleet in the streets of New York City.

Do we have to continue to rely solely on digital infrastructures that are designed to extract profit for a very small number of platform owners and shareholders? Is it really inconceivable to escape the likes of Uber, Facebook, and CrowdFlower?

A People's Internet is possible! What follows is a call to place the people at the center of virtual hiring halls and turn profits into social benefit. It's a call to city councils to consider running businesses like Airbnb themselves. Historically, American cities used to own and operate hotels and hospitals and some still do. It's time to revisit that history.

In her book *Collective Courage*, Jessica Gordon Nembhard describes the Black experience in cooperatives in the US as one of activism grounded in the experience of the struggle for human rights. In the mid-1960s in New York City, for example, it was Fluxus artist George Maciunas who started to form artist cooperatives motivated by his own precarious situation. In today's New York City, it is artists like Caroline Woolard who use the logic of art to transform their own living situation and that of others.

Worldwide, the solidarity economy is growing; cooperatives employ more people than all multinationals combined.[12] Today, co-ops employ 900,000 people in the United States.[13] The Japanese consumer cooperative union serves 31 percent of the nation's households and Mondragon, Spain's seventh largest industrial corporation, is a network of cooperatives that in 2013 employed 74,061 people. Emilia Romagna, an area in Italy that encouraged employee ownership, consumer cooperatives, and agricultural cooperatives, has lower unemployment than other regions in the country.[14]

The "sharing economy" increasingly provides access to low-level work for the educated middle class who can now drive taxis while simultaneously displacing low-income workers.

157

The Rise of Platform Cooperativism

Let's think about how the internet could be owned and governed differently and how solidarity could be strengthened in the process. My collaborator Nathan Schneider asked, "Can Silicon Alley do things more democratically than Silicon Valley?" Whether you are thinking about secure jobs, minimum wage, safety, health insurance, or pension funds—none of these issues can be addressed fundamentally without the reorganization of work, without structural change. None of these issues can be addressed effectively until we reinvigorate solidarity, change ownership, and introduce democratic governance.

Together we must redesign the infrastructure with democracy at its core. As part of this redesign, it is also worth re-examining the history of building structures for cooperativism and mutualism in the United States. Here, spiritual communalism and cooperative movements play a central role. The German Mennonites, including the Amish, started coming to the US as early as 1684. In the spring of 1825, Robert Owen opened the doors of the New Harmony community in Indiana. In the 1930s, The Nation of Islam as well as the Catholic Worker Movement set up hundreds of communal projects. The Catholic social teaching of distributism is influential in that context. It suggests that communities could co-own property and tools.

Since the first modern cooperative in Rochdale, England, in 1844, there has been enough time to talk about worker cooperatives, critics argue, and in their minds the evidence shows that the model isn't working. And partially, they are right; most worker-owned cooperatives in the United States did not succeed. But it is also worth keeping in mind, as the author John Curl observes, that

Platform cooperativism is about cloning the technological heart of Uber, TaskRabbit, Airbnb, or UpWork, but put it to work with a different ownership model. It is about structural change, a change of ownership.

"The very existence of cooperatives challenges corporations and capitalism; corporations have always worked hard to weaken, discredit, and destroy [cooperatives] through waging price wars, enacting legislation that undercuts their viability, labeling them in the media as subversive and a failure, and using several other strategems."[15]

One common objection to cooperatives is that they function within a capitalist context and are just as much bound to market pressures as any other capitalist enterprise, which make self-exploitation unavoidable. Co-ops are exposed to the pitiless competition of the market, but in the light of the 20 to 30 percent that companies like Uber are taking as profit, one approach would be for platform cooperatives to offer their services at a lower price. They could run on 10 percent profit, which could then be partially translated into the social benefit for workers. Here, workers control their own work in a fashion that contributes to their own wellbeing. Cooperatives, however small, can function as ethical, self-managed counterparts that provide a model for businesses that don't have to rely on the exploitation of their workers. Cooperatives can bring creativity not only to the consumption of products but also to the reorganization of work.

The concept of platform cooperativism has three parts:

First, it is about cloning the technological heart of Uber, TaskRabbit, Airbnb, or UpWork. It embraces the technology but wants to put it to work with a different ownership model, adhering to democratic values, so as to crack the broken system of the "sharing economy"/on-demand economy that only benefits the few. It is in this sense that platform cooperativism is about structural change, a change of ownership.

Second, platform cooperativism is about solidarity, which is sorely missing in this economy driven by a distributed, and sometimes anonymous workforce. Platforms can be owned and operated by inventive unions, cities, and various other forms of cooperatives, everything from multi-stakeholder and worker-owned co-ops to produser-owned platform cooperatives.

And third, platform cooperativism is built on the reframing of concepts like innovation and efficiency with an eye on benefiting all, not just sucking up profits for the few.

I am proposing ten principles of platform cooperativism that are sensible to the critical problems facing the digital economy right now.

Collective Ownership
Decent Pay and Income Security
Transparency & Data Portability
Appreciation and Acknowledgement
Co-determined Work
A Protective Legal Framework
Portable Worker Protections and Benefits
Protection Against Arbitrary Behavior
Rejection of Excessive Workplace Surveillance

The Right to Log Off

It is important to articulate such a vision, guided by such lofty principles. It will take us a very long time to get closer to this vision, which needs to be articulated. Our inability to imagine a different life, however, would be capital's ultimate triumph.

It will not come as a surprise when I say that platform cooperativism is also faced with enormous challenges, from the self-organization and management of workers, to technology, UX design, education, long-term funding, scaling, wage scales, competition with multinational corporate giants, and public awareness. Another challenge is that of worker mobilization: so-called independent contractors don't meet their colleagues during lunch break. They don't get to hang out in union halls. Instead they are, for the most part, isolated from each other. "If these people have to gain ownership and decision-making power, enhancement of their social networks must be part of the project," economist Paola Tubaro emphasizes in response to the idea of platform cooperativism.[16] The challenge remains: how do you organize distributed workers in the first place?

Toward a Typology of Platform Co-ops

Platform cooperativism is a term that describes technological, cultural, political, and social changes. Platform cooperativism is a rectangle of hope. It's not a concrete utopia; it is an emerging economy. Some of the models that I will describe have already existed for two or three years, while others are still imaginary apps. Some are prototypes, other are experiments; all of them introduce alternative sets of values.

Cooperatively Owned Online Labor Brokerages and Market Places

Quite likely, you're familiar with the model of the online labor brokerage. Just think of companies like TaskRabbit where you can schedule someone to assemble your IKEA furniture in 20 minutes. The app on your smartphone serves as an intermediary between you and the worker. With each transaction, TaskRabbit gets a cut of 20–30 percent.

In San Francisco, Loconomics is a freelancer-owned cooperative (in beta) where member-freelancers own shares, receive dividends, and have a voice in running the company. There is no bidding and no markup. Loconomics offers massages and other services that are locally in demand. A Loconomics membership costs $29.95 per month. The founders tested the app in the Bay Area and started to allow users from other cities in the spring of 2016.

In Germany, Fairmondo started as a cooperative alternative to Amazon and eBay. The site also promotes a smaller number of fair trade and ethically sourced companies. With its 2,000 members, it aspires to eventually become a genuine alternative to the big players in e-commerce, a decentralized global online marketplace that is collectively owned by all local co-ops.

Coopify is a student-built cash-pay labor platform that will soon serve low-income on-demand task workers. It was created by CornellTech's MBA program and financed by the Robinhood Foundation (NYC). Workers using Coopify will be comprised of low-income New Yorkers who are under- or unemployed and who do not have sufficient credit rating or documentation that would allow them to participate in the existing online markets. The platform, which has its own referral system and multilingual support, will also offer workers support with taxes and allow them to be paid in cash. The Center for Family Life (CFL), a social support agency in Sunset Park, NYC, is currently testing out Coopify.

City-Owned Platform Cooperatives

Now let me make a big leap and discuss public ownership. Janelle Orsi has detailed ideas about ownership and the internet. Corresponding to my proposal to clone and reconstruct "sharing economy" technologies with democratic values in mind, Orsi suggests a city-designed software/enterprise, similar to Airbnb, which could serve as an online marketplace owned and democratically controlled by the people who rent space to travelers. One such project is already underway in Seoul, South Korea, which is proposing to create a Cities Alliance for Platform Economy (CAPE) for the purpose of getting cities organized around such platform ideas. It is called Munibnb and could be created as a collaboration between a large number of cities that would pool their resources to create a software platform for short term rentals. These cities, then, could mandate that short-term rentals in their municipalities have to go through this portal. Fees could largely stay with the hosts or partly go to the city government, which could then use it to service the elderly or fix the streets, for instance. Orsi asks:

> "Why should millions of traveler dollars leak from our cities into the hands of wealthy corporate shareholders especially if it wouldn't be all that hard to run these operations through something like Munibnb?"[17]

Another app, suggested by Orsi, is called Allbnb and it would entail residents to be paid a dividend from the profits of such a rental platform. These apps seem ultimately feasible to implement; they would allow cities to not only play a role in the regulation of the on-demand economy; they could be actively shaping it.

Produser-owned Platforms

I am using the term produser, which is not a typo but a portmanteau of user and producer.[18] Produser-owned platforms are a response to monopolistic platforms like Facebook and Google that are luring users with the promise of the "free service" while monetizing their content and data. What if we'd own our own version of Facebook, Spotify, or Netflix? What if the photographers at Shutterstock.com would own the platform where their photos are being sold?

Sites like Stocksy and Resonate are a step in the direction of answering this question. They offer produsers the opportunity to co-own the site through which they are distributing their artwork. Produser-owned platforms allow artists to build careers by co-owning the platforms through which they are selling their work.

Berlin-based Resonate is a cooperative streaming music system owned by the people who use it. On Resonate, users stream a song until they own it, reflecting the process of converting casual listeners into dedicated fans. The first time they play a song, it costs 0.002 cents, the second time 0.004 cents, the price keeps doubling every time the same song is played until eventually by the ninth play, they will own it.

Stocksy is an artist-owned cooperative for stock-photography. The co-op is based on the idea of profit sharing and co-ownership with the artists who are contributing photos to the site. Artists can

Platform capitalism is getting defined top-down by decisions being made in Silicon Valley. What we need is a new story about sharing, openness, and cooperation; one that we can believe in.

apply to become members and, when accepted, license images and receive 50 percent commission on sales as well as profit sharing at the end of the year. The objective of the cooperative is to create sustainable careers for its members. By 2014, their revenues had reached $3.7 million, and since their founding they've paid out several million dollars in surplus to their artists.

The Platform as Protocol

Perhaps then, the future of work will not be dictated by centralized platforms, even if they are operated by co-ops. Perhaps peer-to-peer interactions can be facilitated solely by protocols. In Israel, for example, La'Zooz is a distributed peer-to-peer ride rental network. La'Zooz could be likened to the BitTorrent of ride sharing. Anyone driving around a city can earn crypto tokens by taking in fellow travelers. Compared to the system previously described, this one is entirely peer-to-peer, there is no central point, no HQ.[19]

Other possible types are union-backed labor platforms and cooperatives from within.

For All People

> "We must invent a new Web in the service of a viable macroeconomic model, rather than developing a completely ruinous economy of data."[20]
> – Bernard Stiegler

Right now, platform capitalism is getting defined top-down by decisions being made in Silicon Valley, executed by black box algorithms. What we need is a new story about sharing, aggregation, openness, and cooperation; one that we can believe in.

The co-operative movement needs to come to terms with twenty-first century technologies. The importance of platform cooperativism does not lie in "killing Death Star platforms."[21] It does not come from destroying the dark overlords like Uber. It comes from writing over them in people's minds, incorporating different ownership models, and then inserting them back into the mainstream. In the late 1960s and early 1970s, counterculturists formed utopian communities; they left cities to force their idea of the future into existence by living it in the mountains. Frequently, these experiments failed.

To successfully develop platform cooperatives, it does take more than practical wisdom and giddy enthusiasm. An anti-theory stance, a rejection of critical self-reflection, will—as we saw with American counterculture—become an impediment. We need to study the failures and successes of the past. We need to identify the areas in which platform cooperatives are most likely to succeed. We need to spread an ideology of felt mutualism, communitarian ideals, and cooperation that make all of this possible. Platform cooperativism can invigorate a genuine sharing economy. It will not remedy the corrosive effects of capitalism, but it can show that work can be dignifying rather than diminishing for the human experience.

Platform cooperativism is not about the next device or "platform"; it is about envisioning a life that is not centered on the shareholder enterprise. Making change is not always a dinner party, or writing an essay, or convening a conference; it's not so convenient. Platform cooperativism is also about confrontation.

We cannot waste any more time. Politicians and platform owners have been promising social protections, access, and privacy, but we are demanding ownership. It's time to realize that they will never deliver. They can't. But we must. Through our collective effort we will build political power for a social movement that will bring these ideas into existence.

This essay is an abridged version of the text "Platform Cooperativism: Challenging the Corporate Sharing Economy," edited by Stefanie Ehmsen, Albert Scharenberg, published by the Rosa Luxemburg Stiftung, New York Office, January 2016, reproduced with kind permission from the author.

01 McKenzie Wark, "Digital Labor and the Anthropocene," *DIS Magazine*, 2014, dismagazine.com/disillusioned/discussion-disillusioned/70983/mckenzie-wark-digital-labor-and-the-anthropocene (accessed January 25, 2018).
02 Rebecca Smith and Sarah Leberstein, *Rights on Demand: Ensuring Workplace Standards and Worker Security In the On-Demand Economy* (National Employment Law Project, 2015), www.nelp.org/content/uploads/Rights-On-Demand-Report.pdf (accessed January 25, 2018).
03 Ibid.
04 Frank Pasquale, "Banana Republic.com," *Jotwell: Cyberlaw*, January 14, 2011, cyber.jotwell.com/banana-republic-com (accessed January 25, 2018).
05 Seth D. Harris and Alan B. Krueger, "A Proposal for Modernizing Labor Laws for Twenty-First-Century Work: The 'Independent Worker,'" *The Hamilton Project*, December 2015, www.hamiltonproject.org/assets/files/modernizing_labor_laws_for_twenty_first_century_work_krueger_harris.pdf (accessed January 25, 2018).
06 See livestream.com/internetsociety/platformcoop/videos/ 105162259 (accessed January 25, 2018).
07 Frank Pasquale and Siva Vaidhyanathan, "Uber and the Lawlessness of 'Sharing Economy' Corporates," *The Guardian*, July 28, 2015, www.theguardian.com/technology/2015/jul/28/uber-lawlessness-sharing-economy-corporates-airbnb-google (accessed January 25, 2018).
08 Mike Isaac and Natasha Singer, "California Says Uber Driver Is Employee, Not a Contractor," *The New York Times*, June 17, 2015, www.nytimes.com/2015/06/18/business/uber-contests-california-labor-ruling-that-says-drivers-should-be-employees.html (accessed January 25, 2018).
09 Tim Cushing, "Judge Not At All Impressed By Class Action Lawsuit Claiming Yelp Reviewers Are Really Employees," *techdirt*, November 17, 2015, www.techdirt.com/articles/20150815/16091931969/judge-not-all-impressed-class-action-lawsuit-claiming-yelp-reviewers-are-really-employees.shtml (accessed January 25, 2018).
10 Cecilia Kang, "Coalition of Start-Ups and Labor Call for Rethinking of Worker Policies," *The New York Times Blog*, November 9, 2015, bits.blogs.nytimes.com/2015/11/09/coalition-of-start-ups-and-labor-call-for-rethinking-of-worker-policies (accessed January 25, 2018).
11 Martin Di Caro, "Taxi Regulations, E-Hail App Targeted By Montgomery County Council," *WAMU 88.5*, June 8, 2015, wamu.org/story/15/06/08/taxi_regulations_e_hail_app_targeted_by_montgomery_county_council_today (accessed January 25, 2018).
12 The statistics are taken from Marjorie Kelly's *Owning Our Future: The Emerging Ownership Revolution* (Oakland, CA: Berrett-Koehler Publishers, 2012).
13 E. G. Nadeau, *The Cooperative Solution*, 2012, 37, thecooperativefoundation.org/wp-content/uploads/2014/08/Cooperative_Solution_6x9-h_copy.pdf (accessed January 25, 2018).
14 John Logue, *Economics, Cooperation, and Employee Ownership: The Emilia Romagna model – in more detail* (Kent: Ohio Employee Ownership Center, 2006), community-wealth.org/content/economics-cooperation-and-employee-ownership-emilia-romagna-model-more-detail (accessed January 25, 2018).
15 John Curl, *For All the People: Uncovering the Hidden History of Cooperation, Cooperative Movements, and Communalism in America* (Oakland: PM Press, 2012), 350.
16 Paola Tubaro, "Discussing Platform Cooperativism," *Data Big and Small*, December 8, 2015, databigandsmall.com/2015/12/08/discussing-platform-cooperativism (accessed January 25, 2018).
17 Nathan Schneider, "5 Ways to Take Back Tech," *The Nation*, May 27, 2015, www.thenation.com/article/5-ways-take-back-tech (accessed January 25, 2018).
18 The term produsage was developed by Axel Bruns in *Blogs, Wikipedia, Second Life, and Beyond: From Production to Produsage* (New York: Peter Lang Publishing Inc., 2008).
19 Also in Israel but not a platform co-op, Google has released the Waze app, which links up passengers who want to get to their workplaces with drivers who have to make a similar trip. Drivers get paid depending on the distance they drove but the system is set up in the way that drivers cannot turn this into a business.
20 Sam Kinsley, "Stiegler on Daesh and 'the age of disruption,'" November 26, 2015, www.samkinsley.com/2015/11/26/stiegler-on-daesh-and-the-age-of-disruption (accessed January 25, 2018).
21 Neal Gorenflo, "How Platform co-ops Can Beat Death Star Platforms to Create a Real Sharing Economy," *Shareable*, November 3, 2015, www.shareable.net/blog/how-platform-coops-can-beat-death-stars-like-uber-to-create-a-real-sharing-economy (accessed January 25, 2018).

Politics of Data

"Concerns about the ownership of data are born out of a long overdue recognition that cloud platforms have absorbed many functions of modern states and that states themselves are co-evolving."

— Benjamin H. Bratton

Databodies in Codespace

SHANNON MATTERN
PHOTO ESSAY BY ANTOINE GEIGER

In late 2016, on a conference stage in Palm Springs, California, decision scientist Hannah Bayer made a bold declaration: "We're going to measure everything we can possibly measure about 10,000 people over the course of the next 20 years or more. We're going to sequence their genomes; track everywhere they go, everything they eat, everything they buy, everyone they interact with, every time they exercise."[01]

The "we" she is referring to is the HUMAN Project, born as a collaboration between two research labs at New York University—the Institute for the Interdisciplinary Study of Decision Making (a world leader in neuroeconomics) and the Center for Urban Science and Progress (a leader in urban informatics)—with startup funding from the Kavli Foundation. As you might suspect from those origins, the partners are less interested in defining the essential qualities of our species than in understanding how those qualities are operationalized. HUMAN, here, is the acronym of Human Understanding through Measurement and Analytics.

As the HUMAN Project is a scientific study, it needs a representative sample. Researchers started by crunching datasets to identify 100 micro-neighborhoods that embody New York City's diversity, and so they will contact randomly targeted households in those areas, inviting people to join the study, "not just as volunteers, but as representatives of their communities." With promises of payment and self-enlightenment, recruiters will try to turn 10,000 human subjects into *HUMAN*s.[02]

Let's say your family volunteers. To start, you might submit blood, saliva, and stool samples, so that researchers can sequence your genome and microbiome. You could undergo IQ, mental health, personality, and memory testing; and agree to a schedule of regular physical exams, where the researchers collect more biological samples, so they can track epigenetic changes. They might compile your education and employment histories, and conduct socio-political assessments of your voting, religious, and philanthropic activity.

In the photo series *SUR-FAKE* by Antoine Geiger, people merge with their smartphones, literally absorbed by the displays and transformed into zombie-like creatures, disconnected from the outside world.

Mona Lisa, 2014
70 × 70 cm

Databodies

Grande Galerie, 2014
70 × 70 cm

If you don't have a smartphone, they may give you one, so they can track your location, activity, and sleep; monitor your socialization and communication behaviors; and push gamified tests assessing your cognitive condition and well-being. They may instrument your home with sensors to detect environmental conditions and track the locations of family members, so they can see who's interacting with whom, when, and where. You may be asked to keep a food diary and wear a silicon wristband to monitor your exposure to chemicals. Audits of your tax and financial records could reveal your socioeconomic position and consumer behavior, and could be cross-referenced with your location data, to make sure you were shopping when and where you said you were.

With your permission, researchers could access new city and state medical records databases, and they could tap public records of your interaction with schools, courts, police, and government assistance programs. They could assess your neighborhood: how safe is it, how noisy is it, how many trees are there? Finally, they could pull city data—some of it compiled and filtered by the Center for Urban Science and Progress—to monitor air quality, toxins, school ratings, crime, water and energy use, and other environmental factors.

What does all this measuring add up to? The researchers assert, "for the first time ever we are now able to quantify the human condition." By investigating "the feedback mechanisms between biology, behavior, and our environment in the bio-behavioral complex," they aim to comprehend "all of the factors that make humans... human."[03] Of course, that requires a huge leap of faith. As Steven Koonin, the theoretical physicist who founded the Center for Urban Science and Progress, observes: "What did Galileo think he was going to see when he turned his telescope on the heavens? He didn't know."[04]

Now the telescope is turned inward, on the human body in the urban environment. This terrestrial cosmos of data will merge investigations that have been siloed: neuroscience, psychology, sociology, biology, biochemistry, nutrition, epidemiology, economics, data science, urban science. A promotional video boasts that the Human Project has brought together technologists, lawyers, ethicists, and "anthropologists, even!" to ask big questions.[05]

This is the promise of big data and artificial intelligence. With a sufficiently large dataset we can find meaning even without a theoretical framework or scientific method. As *Wired*-editor-turned-drone-entrepreneur Chris Anderson famously declared, "Petabytes allow us to say: 'Correlation is enough.' We can stop looking for models. We can analyze the data without hypotheses about what it might show. We can throw the numbers into the biggest computing clusters the world has ever seen and let statistical algorithms find patterns where science cannot."[06] HUMAN Project director Paul Glimcher says that collecting data on "everything we can think of"—at least everything related to

biology, behavior, and environment—will allow researchers to model every imaginable phenotype, or set of observable characteristics, both for people and the cities they inhabit.[07]

Apple recently announced that its Health app will allow users to access personal medical records. The company is also developing apps to aid studies, and even sponsoring clinical trials. Seemingly everyone is trying to break into the risky but lucrative health tech market, which offers ample opportunities for data harvesting. And many medical providers are happy to cooperate. A few years ago, Google's AI subsidiary Deep Mind and London's Royal Free Hospital partnered to develop new clinical technologies, but they didn't adequately inform patients about the use of their data, and were rebuked by the British government. More recently, Facebook has approached hospitals about matching anonymized patient data with social media profiles to find patterns that might inform medical treatment. Plans were paused when the Cambridge Analytica scandal came to light.

This is the promise of big data and artificial intelligence. With a sufficiently large dataset we can find meaning even without a theoretical framework or scientific method.

The blind faith that ubiquitous data collection will lead to "discoveries that benefit everyone" deserves skepticism. Large-scale empirical studies can reinforce health disparities, especially when demographic analyses are not grounded in specific hypotheses or theoretical frameworks. Ethicist Celia Fisher argues that studies like the HUMAN Project need to clearly define "what class, race, and culture mean, taking into account how these definitions are continuously shaped and redefined by social and political forces," and how certain groups have been marginalized, even pathologized, in medical discourse and practice. Researchers who draw conclusions based on observed correlations—untheorized and not historicized—run the risk, she says, of "attributing health problems to genetic or cultural dispositions in marginalized groups rather than to policies that sustain systemic political and institutional health inequities."[08]

We've seen such biases realized in other data-driven models, notably in law enforcement. Contemporary models of actuarial justice and predictive policing draw correlations between specific risk factors and the probability of future criminal action. Courts and police make decisions based on proprietary technologies with severe vulnerabilities: incomplete datasets, high error rates, demographic bias, opaque algorithms, and discrepancies in administration. Criminal justice management software packages like Northpointe's dramatically overestimate the likelihood of recidivism among black defendants.

These problems are compounded as datasets are combined. A Palantir software now used by some local governments merges data from disparate city agencies and external organizations, enabling police to collate information about suspects, targets, and locations. Key analyses, even decisions about where to deploy resources, are automated, which means that "no human need ever to look at the actual raw data."[09] Biology, behavior, culture, history, and environment are thus reduced to dots on a map. End users don't know which agencies supplied the underlying intelligence and how their interests might have shaped data collection. They can't ask questions about how social and environmental categories are operationalized in the different data sets. They can't determine whether the data reinscribe historical biases and injustices.

Environmental Epidemiology

While the neuroeconomists on the HUMAN project gather data on everything "that makes humans... human," their partners in urban informatics control a voluminous flow of information on what makes New York... New York. With special access to municipal data held by many offices and agencies, researchers at the Center for Urban Science and Progress have built "one of the most ambitious Geographic Information Systems ever aggregated: a block-by-block, moment-by-moment, searchable record of nearly every aspect of the New York City Landscape."[10]

The partnership with CUSP may give the HUMAN Project an advantage in the race to quantify health outcomes, but it is not the only such effort. The National Institutes of Health is building *All of Us*, a research cohort of one million volunteers with "the statistical power to detect associations between environment and/ or biological exposures and a wide variety of health outcomes."[11] The NIH receives data and research support from Verily Life Sciences, an Alphabet company. Sidewalk Labs, another Alphabet company (see Bianca Wylie, p. 124–129), recently announced Cityblock Health, which seeks to connect low-income urban residents with community-based health services, including clinics, coaches, tech tools, and "nudge" for self-care. Again, the precise targeting of individual patients and neighborhoods depends on a vast dataset, including in this case, Google's urban data.

All of these initiatives see public health through the lens of geography. The HUMAN Project even refers to its emerging databank as an atlas. Programs like Cityblock Health conceive the urban environment not just as a background source of exposure or risk, but as a habitat in which biology and behavior inform one another. The qualities of this habitat affect how people make choices about diet and exercise, and how bodies respond to stress or industrial hazards. What seems to set the HUMAN Project apart is that its researchers regard that habitat not as a given, but as something that can be rehabilitated or reengineered. Once researchers have identified relations between the city or neighborhood and the human condition, they can tweak or transform the habitat through urban planning, design, and policy. Their insights can also guide "the construction of future cities."[12] Individual phenotypes are mapped to urban phonotypes, databodies to codespaces.

Meanwhile, a group of HUMAN Project-affiliated researchers at Harvard and MIT are using computer vision to assign *Streetscores*, or measurements of perceived safety, to Google Street View images of particular neighborhoods. They then combine those metrics with demographic and economic data to determine how social and economic changes relate to changes in a neighborhood's physical appearance—its phenotype.[13] This work builds on the PlacePulse project at the MIT Media Lab, which invites participants to vote on which of two paired Street View scenes appears "livelier," "safer," "wealthier," "more boring," "more depressing," or "more beautiful." In such endeavors, Aaron Shapiro argues, "computer-aided, data-mined correlations between visible features, geographic information, and social character of place are framed as objective, if 'ambient,' social facts."[14] The algorithmicization of environmental metrics marks the rise of what Federico Caprotti and colleagues call a new "epidemiology of the urban."[15] The new epidemiologists echo the smart city rhetoric, but now the discourse is shaded toward the dual bioengineering of cities regarded as biophysical bodies, with their own circulatory, respiratory, and nervous systems—and waste streams.

> New epidemiologists echo the smart city rhetoric, but the discourse is shaded toward the dual bioengineering of cities regarded as bio-physical bodies, with their own circulatory, respiratory, and nervous systems.

In the mid-nineteenth century, as industrialization transformed cities and spurred their growth, physicians were developing new theories of infectious disease (e.g., miasma, filth), complete with scientific models and maps that depicted cities as unhealthy. City planners and health officials joined forces to advocate for sanitation reform, zoning, new infrastructures, street improvements, and urban parks. Healthy buildings and cities were associated with certain phenotypical expressions, although designers did not always agree on the ideal form. Frederick Law Olmsted's parks, Daniel Burnham's City Beautiful movement, Ebenezer Howard's Garden Cities, 1920s zoning ordinances, Modernist social housing projects and sanatoria: all promised reform, yet produced distinct morphologies. Today, initiatives like the World Health Organization's European Healthy Cities pro-

Man in the Street, 2014
70 × 70 cm

Sharing is Caring, 2014
70 × 46 cm

gram and New York City's Active Design Guidelines encourage the integration of health and planning. Now the focus is on designing cities that promote exercise and social cohesion, and that provide access to healthy food and quality housing. Given the rise of artificial intelligence in both health and urban planning, we might imagine a Streetscore for healthy neighborhoods, which could be used to generate an algorithmic pattern language for urban design: every healthy neighborhood has one playground, two clinics, lots of fresh produce, and a bicycle path.

Where do quantified humans fit in this new planning regime? China is preparing to use Citizen Scores to rate residents' trustworthiness and determine their eligibility for mortgages, jobs, and dates; their right to freely travel abroad; and their access to high-speed internet and top schools. "It will forge a public opinion environment where keeping trust is glorious," the Chinese government proclaims.[16] This is the worst case scenario: obedience gamified, as Rachel Botsman puts it, and humanity instrumentalized.

Self-Datafication as Civic Duty

The HUMAN Project study design envisions that participants will be motivated by payment and by the promise of insight into their own health and their families' medical histories. Data are currency. But there's a civic vision—and a civic aesthetic—behind this work too. Framing the project as a public service may help convince New Yorkers to share their most personal data. Contributors are assured that they will be more than mere research subjects; they will also be partners in governing the study, responsible for vetting proposals from researchers who want to use the databank. They'll receive newsletters and updates on research discoveries that their data has made possible, and they'll have access to visualization tools that allow them to filter and interpret their own data and aggregate data for the study population. Apparently, handing over bank statements and biometrics is a form of activism, too: "instead of giving [their] data for free, to corporations," they can "take [it] back," "bring [it] together as a community […] to make a better world."[17] Glimcher maintains that New Yorkers will see the potential to generate new knowledge, therapeutics, and urban policy and will understand "that this is a civic project of enormous importance."[18]

Offering oneself up as data, or as a data-collector, is often framed as an act of civic duty. Participation in US census and government surveys, for instance, has historically been regarded as part of the "social contract": citizens yield their personal information, and the government uses it for the public good. In the nineteenth century, philanthropists, researchers, and activists garnered support for social and industrial reforms by generating an "avalanche of numbers."[19] And in the early twentieth century, as the social sciences popularized new sampling methods, a swarm of surveyors and pollsters began collecting data for other purposes. According to historian Sarah Igo, these modern researchers "billed their methods as democratically useful, instruments of national self-understanding rather than bureaucratic control." Because they had to rely on voluntary participation, they manufactured consent by emphasizing "the virtues of contributing information for the good of the whole," for the "public sphere." Divulging one's opinions and behaviors to Gallup or Roper pollsters was a means of democratic participation—an opportunity to make one's voice heard. Pollsters, unlike newspaper editors and political commentators, were "of the people," and they argued that their methods were "even more representative and inclusive than elections."[20]

Modern survey methods, Igo says, "helped to forge a mass public" and determined how that public saw itself in mediated representations. Surveys shaped beliefs about normalcy, nationality and individuality. But like all methods of data-collection and analysis, those social surveys reflected and reinscribed biases.

This tendency continues today with the cutting-edge work being conducted at the Institute for the Interdisciplinary Study of Decision Making. The researchers' overarching goal, to link decision-making to social policy, is reflected in their motto: "from neurons to nations." Yet the extraction of neurons will never fully describe the individual subject, let alone the nation in aggregate. Even the myriad data sources collated by the HUMAN Project cannot capture "the human condition."

As Hannah Arendt observes, the disclosure of *who* one is "can almost never be achieved as a willful purpose, as though one possessed and could dispose of this 'who' in the same manner he has and can dispose of his qualities." *Who* one is, rather than *what* one is, is revealed to others through speech and action and physical identity.[21] Quantifying humans and habitats turns them into *whats*: into biometric entities and Streetscores. This ontological reduction inevitably leads to impoverished notions of city planning, citizenship, and civic action. Shapiro argues that because planning algorithms like Streetscore embed "indicators of deviance and normativity, worth and risk," they promote "normative and essentialist… aesthetics."[22] The computationally engineered city produces the urban citizens by measuring them. Then, Caprotti argues, "you're actually producing a subject for governance."[23]

> Surveys shaped beliefs about normalcy, nationality and individuality. But like all methods of data-collection and analysis, those social surveys reflected and reinscribed biases.

When civic action is reduced to data provision, citizens can perform public duties from the privacy of a car or bedroom. If convictions and preferences can be gleaned through an automated survey of one's browser history, network analysis of social media contacts, and sentiment analysis of texts and emails, one doesn't even need to go to the trouble of answering a survey or filling out a ballot. Yet citizens have no idea how an artificially intelligent agent discerns what kind of subject they are, how it calculates one's risk of heart attack or recidivism, or how those scores impact insurance premiums and children's school assignments. Likewise, the researchers who deploy that agent, like those now working with Palantir and Northpointe, have no need to look at the raw data, let alone develop hypotheses that might inform their methods of collection and analysis. In this emerging paradigm, neither subjects nor researchers are motivated, nor equipped, to challenge the algorithmic agenda. Decision-making is the generation of patterns that will translate into policy or planning initiatives and social service provision. This is a vision of the city—society—as an algorithmic assemblage.

And this is the world where we now live. All our bodies and environments are already data—both public and proprietary. So how can we marshal whatever remains of our public sphere to take up these critical issues? How can we respond individually and collectively to the regime of quantitative rationalization? How might we avert its risks, even as we recognize its benefits? We can start by intervening in those venues where pattern recognition is trans-lated to policy and planning. Wouldn't it be better to use algorithms to identify areas and issues of concern, and then to investigate with more diverse, localized qualitative methods? After the scores are assigned and hotpots are plotted on a map, we could reverse-engineer those urban pulses, dissect the databodies, recontextualize and rehistoricize the datasets that brought them into being.

Projects like NYU's and Alphabet's and the NIH's could yield tremendous improvements in public health. And even in their methodological and ethical limitations, they can teach us a few things about measuring a public and the spheres in which it is constituted. The methods by which publics and public spheres become visible—to one another and to the sensors that read them—reflect the interests and ideologies of their sponsors. At the same time, these databody projects remind us that public health is a critical precondition for, and should be a regular subject of debate within, the public sphere. They signal that the liberal subject has a physical body, one whose health and illness, pleasure and pain, affect and cognition, race and gender, class and sexual orientation, affect its ability to safely navigate and make itself seen and heard amidst the myriad publics that emerge across our digital and physical worlds.

A longer version of this article was first published by Places Journal. *Reproduced with kind permission of the author. More via https://placesjournal.org/.*

01 Hannah Bayer, "What If We Could Quantify the Entirety of the Human Condition?," TEDMED, Palm Springs, California, November 30–December 2, 2016.
02 See The Human Project, "Frequently Asked Questions," www.thehumanproject.org/faq, accessed November 21, 2018.
03 Kavli Foundation, "The HUMAN Project," www.kavlifoundation.org/kavli-human-project, accessed November 21, 2018, emphasis of the author.
04 Quoted in Aviva Rutkin, "Tracking the Health of 10,000 New Yorkers," *New Scientist* 228/3044 (2015): 20–21. Koonin was comparing the ambitions of the Human Project to the Sloan Digital Sky Survey, which "has transformed galactic-level cosmology from a small data science to a big data science and has catalyzed a renaissance in astronomy." See also Okan Azmak et al.: "Using Big Data to Understand the Human Condition – The Kavli HUMAN Project," *Big Data* 3/3 (2015): 173–88.
05 "The HUMAN Project (Long Version)," Vimeo, Video file, September 21, 2015. vimeo.com/139989450.
06 Chris Anderson, "The End of Theory: The Data Deluge Makes the Scientific Method Obsolete," *Wired*, June 23, 2008. www.wired.com/2008/06/pb-theory, accessed November 21, 2018.
07 Julie Anne Schuck, *Social and Behavioral Sciences for National Security: Proceedings of a Summit* (Washington, D.C.: The National Academies Press, 2017), 15–16.
08 Celia B. Fisher, "Will Research on 10,000 New Yorkers Fuel Future Racial Health Inequality?" *The Ethics and Society Blog*. August 30, 2016. www.ethicsandsociety.org/2016/08/30/will-research-on-10000-new-yorkers-fuel-future-racial-health-inequality.
09 Mark Harris, "How Peter Thiel's Secretive Data Company Pushed Into Policing", *Wired*, August 9, 2017. www.wired.com/story/how-peter-thiels-secretive-data-company-pushed-into-policing.
10 New York University Institute for the Interdisciplinary Study of Decision Making, *Kavli HUMAN Project – Preliminary Study Design* (New York 2015): 19.
11 National Institutes of Health, "All of Us" and "Scientific Opportunities," accessed November 21, 2018. www.allofus.nih.gov.
12 Philip Salesses, Katja Schechtner, and César A. Hidalgo, "The Collaborative Image of the City: Mapping the Inequality of Urban Perception," *PLOS One* 8:7 (2013). http://doi.org/f5bs55.
13 Nikhil Naik, Scott Duke Kominers, Ramesh Raskar, Edward L. Glaeser, and Cesar A. Hidalgo, "Do People Shape Cities, or Do Cities Shape People? The Co-Evolution of Physical, Social, and Economic Change in Five Major U.S. Cities," *National Bureau of Economic Research Working Paper Series*, Nr. 21620 (Oktober 2015); Edward L. Glaeser et al., "Big Data and Big Cities – The Promises and Limitations of Improved Measures of Urban Life," *National Bureau of Economic Research Working Paper Series*, Nr. 21778 (Dezember 2015): 11.
14 Aaron Shapiro, "Street-level: Google Street View's Abstraction by Datafication," *New Media and Society* (2017): 11. http://doi.org/cncx.
15 Federico Caprotti, Robert Cowley, Ayona Datta, Vanesa Castan Broto, Eleanor Gao, Lucien Georgeson, Clare Herrick, Nancy Odendaal, and Simon Joss, "The New Urban Agenda: Key Opportunities and Challenges for Policy and Practice," *Urban Research and Practice* 10/3 (2017): 367-78. http://doi.org/cncz.
16 Rachel Botsman, "Big Data Meets Big Brother as China Moves to Rate its Citizens," *Wired*, October 21, 2017, accessed August 14, 2019. www.wired.co.uk/article/chinese-government-social-credit-score-privacy-invasion.
17 "THE HUMAN Project (Long Version)," Vimeo, Video file, September 21, 2015. vimeo.com/139989450.
18 Eillie Anzilotti, "Quantifying Everything About Urban Life," *CityLab* (October 14, 2016).
19 Ian Hacking, "Biopower and the Avalanche of Printed Numbers," *Humanities in Society* 5 (1982): 279-95.
20 Sarah Igo, *The Averaged American: Surveys, Citizens, and the Making of a Mass Public* (Cambridge: Harvard University Press, 2008): 8, 119, 121.
21 Hannah Arendt, *The Human Condition*, 2nd edition (Chicago: University of Chicago Press, 1998): 159, 179.
22 Shapiro, Op. cit., 3, 10-11.
23 Quoted in Gregory Scruggs, "The 'New Urban Citizen' and the Dangers of the Measurable City," *Citiscope* (August 25, 2017), accessed November 23, 2018. www.archive.citiscope.org/story/2017/new-urban-citizen-and-dangers-measurable-city.

A Wall of Data Points

DENNIS HÄUSLER, JOHANNES REBSAMEN,
MATTHIAS VOLLMER

A dam wall is a monument to the way in which humans deal with water as a force of nature. In the Alps, water is stored in glaciers and groundwater streams, and is gradually fed into rivers. Climate change is slowly erasing the image that characterizes the Swiss landscape.

In 2015, MediaLab, together with students from the Department of Architecture at ETH Zurich, began to investigate this landscape-shaping phenomenon using the example of the Morteratsch Glacier. The dams at Punt dal Gall and Ova Spin are representative of the massive human intervention in the ecosystem. Radical changes were made to the natural environment and its appearance in the 1960s to advance the country's participation in the electricity market. In addition to the two dams, the network of the Ova Spin pumped-storage power plant includes a first power plant built on the Ova Spin wall, water catchments, an extensive branched network of underground pipes and caverns, and other facilities located in the valley. This sweeping infrastructure is only sporadically visible; much is hidden deep below the surface or behind thick concrete walls. Where the walls seem to butt against the cliffs, the complex branches out further into the mountain. The concrete underground channels and pipes that feed the river with strictly controlled amounts of water end where the natural flow of the river begins. The technical infrastructure mixes with the natural system; the boundaries between the two are blurred.

In the spring of 2017, we began surveying this system with laser scanners, acoustic recording devices, and photo cameras. Laser scanners work with a light-based measuring method in which millions of pulses are emitted at fixed angles in all directions. Exact coordinates in the space are determined by measuring the amount of time it takes for the reflected light to be detected by a sensor. The scanning device is set up at various positions and the resulting data coordinates are analyzed by a computer program to identify their spatial relationships. The model is gradually built from each position along the wall, moving through rooms, corridors, staircases, and caverns. In addition, the data points are colored using photographs. The result is a model of colored points that shows the geometry and texture of the surfaces without having a geometry itself; it consists only of information on position and color. There is also no distinction among the various elements. Walls, ceilings, rocks, snow, vegetation— they are all equally scanned and displayed. Together they comprise a "point cloud" whose origin lies in reality, and whose production and use changes our perception. The model remains forever incomplete, the complexity of reality unrivalled.

Spöl Valley at Ofen Pass road, with the Punt da Gall Dam
(above) and the Ova Spin Dam (below).

Data Points

We seem to more willingly accept this incompleteness of the point clouds— the gaps in the surfaces that occur when there are large distances between points—than we would accept it in conventional digital models. The resulting transparency can be seen as a benefit: a simultaneity of spatial levels is created, which enables otherwise impossible views, similar to an anatomical representation, and allows us to grasp spatial relationships. With the movement in the model, in digital space, this representation is constantly changing and thus allows for new and unexpected experiences of a place whose dimensions play only a subordinate role. There is a fluid transition from a territorial view to the detail of a screw, challenging our familiar notions of scale.

The visual work is complemented by the parallel recording of geopositioned sound and its location in the point cloud model. It returns a sense of temporality to the environment frozen in time. The sound complements and heightens our perception of the place by adding materiality and a spatial experience. The resulting model transfers our perception of the landscape into a dimension in which the surfaces become transparent while views and sound penetrate the walls and floors. In the process of audiovisual composition, the prepared sound recordings are precisely positioned in the point cloud model and the digital avatar is carefully maneuvered through space and time. It is a search for a new aesthetic that allows a subjective, physical experience without sacrificing accuracy.

All scanning positions at Ova Spin, in different colors.

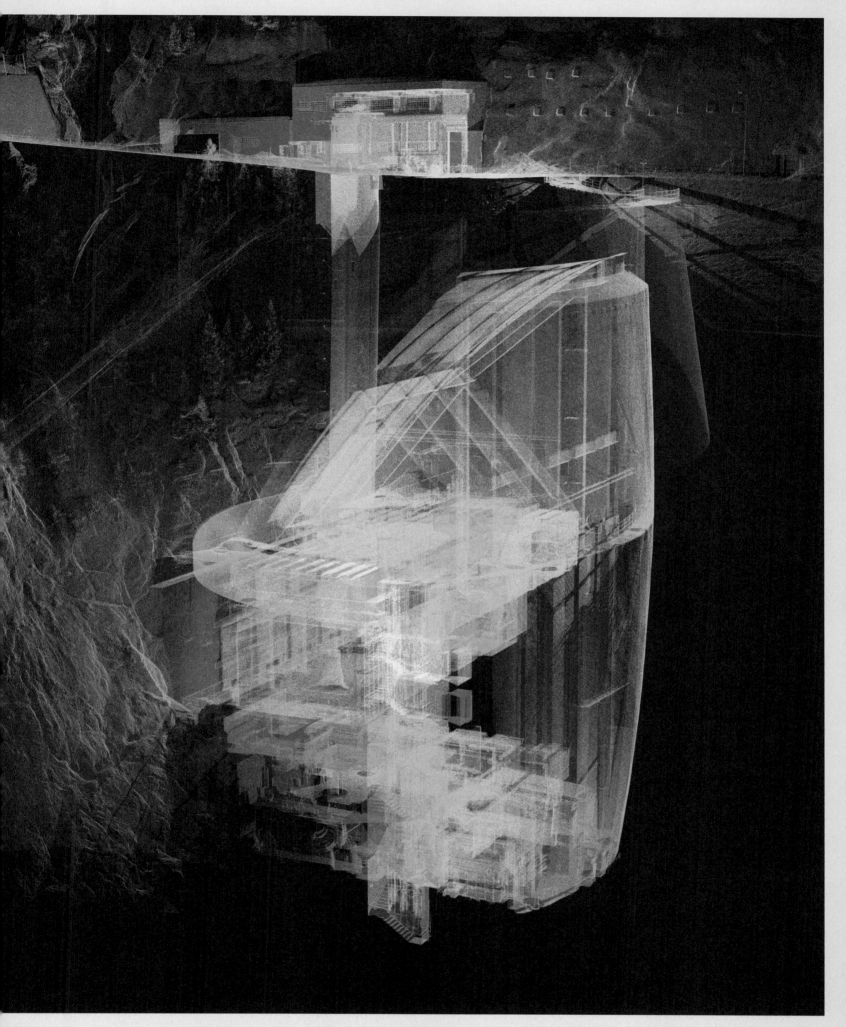

Frontal view of the Ova Spin Dam with underground facilities.

Section through the Punt da Gall Dam.

Access tunnel to the throttle chamber next to the Punt da Gall Dam. Visible in the foreground are photogrammetric models by the students Julius Henkel and Noé Lafranchi.

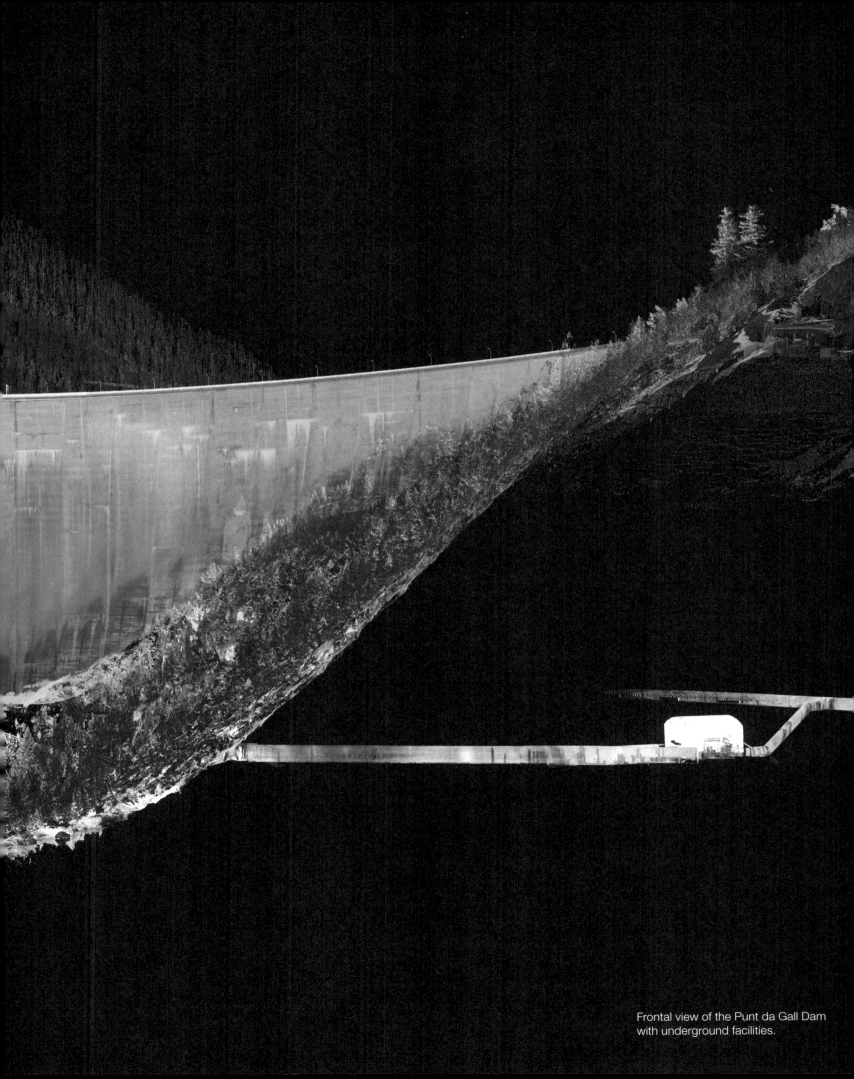

Frontal view of the Punt da Gall Dam
with underground facilities.

Agency in the Age of Decentralization

JAMES BRIDLE IN CONVERSATION WITH
MICHAELA FRIEDBERG AND OLAF GRAWERT

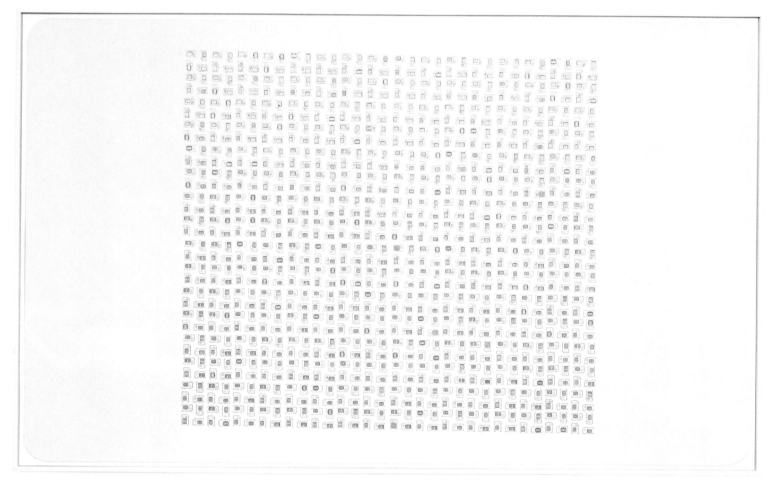

For *The Possibility of an Army,* produced in 2016 by Constant Dullaart, the artist formed an army of thousands of fake profiles on Facebook that took a stand against social media, with its "like" economy. The fake identities were based on phone-verified accounts (PVA) from various countries, which have now been largely removed by Facebook. The only physical remains, the SIM cards, were arranged by Dullaart into abstract images.

Constant Dullaart: *PVA Composition (Tilt),* 2016, forex rigid foam board, aluminum, sim cards, 117 × 182 cm.
Courtesy of Constant Dullaart

The analogue world that surrounds us as well as the digital spheres in which we move on a daily basis are becoming increasingly complex. Despite our possessing ever more data, it is becoming increasingly difficult for us to understand the mechanisms that track and analyze us and predict our behavior. Nevertheless, many people hold to the idea that more data, technology, and digitalization are enough to create a better world. In his work, James Bridle exposes simple assumptions, resentments, and unquestioned conventions that have become deeply ingrained in our everyday behavior and thus in the technologies we use. Michaela Friedberg and Olaf Grawert spoke with the writer, artist, and curator about spaces of agency in the "New Dark Age."[01]

OLAF GRAWERT: *In late 2018, you curated an exhibition at Nome Gallery in Berlin, titled* Agency. *What was the idea behind it?*

JAMES BRIDLE: *Agency* presents artists who are actively and specifically engaging with the situation they are describing. Their works are not works of documentation, but works that try to reconfigure an existing situation in some meaningful way. In many cases, this means telling stories rather than documenting something directly, because, more often than not, the stories that are handed down to us are written by the same people who created these situations, technologies, and devices. What some of the artists in this show have done is to rewrite the narratives that we have been told. They are re-telling stories through the same objects, processes, and systems but with radically different outcomes.

OG: *What is your understanding of agency in a moment when people seem to increasingly feel at the mercy of new concentrations of power, especially within the technological sphere and the web?*

JB: For me it is essential to keep in mind that agency is something different than mastery. There is a very common belief that as things become more complex you need to gain an understanding at every possible level in order to be able to act. I increasingly think that this is not possible anymore. No one can have this kind of totalizing overview of the system. Even people or entities who one thinks are in control have very little agency overall. So, the question one should ask oneself is: What is required to act under any particular circumstances? That is what I think of as agency. It is about figuring out one or two actions or interventions that can be performed and recognizing that they are taking place in a much larger system. It is not about striving for mastery but looking for smaller entry points, smaller things that can be twisted and that might have wider systemic effects.

MICHAELA FRIEDBERG: *Despite the invisibility of the systems you address, in your own artistic work you often draw a connection to a tangible material output. In doing so, you imply that no immaterial process can ever be absolved from producing a physical footprint. In a time when everyone thought brick-and-mortar would become obsolete, tech companies are again investing in physical assets at the scale of infrastructure and urban planning. How do you see your work fitting into this binary of material and immaterial, virtual and real?*

JB: I think we all suffer from this bias towards the physical because we are still using our fairly basic mammalian brains to understand the world, so things that aren't at our fingertips are harder to understand. One strategy for producing critical techno-political analysis is to point at the concrete aspects of the internet: to look at data centers as spatial entities, trace the cables under the ground, or look at sites of extraction where things are mined to make iPhones. This strategy makes the virtual a little more tangible and easier to understand. It makes it easier to pinpoint the politics of technology that are so often physically difficult to encounter.

This is needed to prepare the ground for critiquing those same technologies as we encounter them on a daily basis in cities and architecture. If we don't do this, these architectural and urban schemes might escape criticism in the same way that the application of so many technologies have escaped criticism in the past, which have been neglected because they are seen as politically neutral. We often think of the internet as some sort of magical faraway place where stuff just happens and then gets beamed down to us, but in many ways the internet is quite physical. There are big buildings at the edge of cities filled with computers generating a lot of heat and consuming huge amounts of electricity. There are countless cables that run along the ocean floor and connect everything together. If you look at the map of where the internet fiber optic cables go around the world, you will see that they trace out completely the routes of former empires. All the fiber optic cables from Africa still root back to their former colonial powers. A lot of the ones from South America still go back to Spain. This is because imperialism did not end with decolonization; it moved on to the level of the global infrastructure.

Agency

The artist Trevor Paglen documented the transatlantic fiber optic cables and the coastal regions where they meet the mainland. The photographs are supplemented by nautical charts and documents from the NSA and collaborating companies, leaked by whistleblower Edward Snowden, which reveal the surveillance methods and espionage techniques of the secret service on these channels.

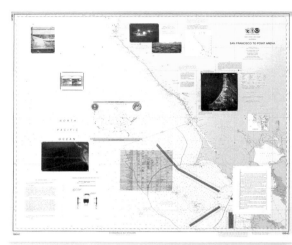

NSA-Tapped Fiber Optic Cable Landing Site, Miami Beach, Florida, United States, 2015, c-print and mixed media on a navigational chart, 122 × 157 cm and 122 × 148 cm.

NSA-Tapped Undersea Cables, North Pacific Ocean, 2016, c-print, 122 × 183 cm.

NSA-Tapped Fiber Optic Cable Landing Site,
New York City, New York, United States, 2015,
c-print, 122 × 52 cm.

Columbus III NSA/GCHQ-Tapped
Undersea Cable Atlantic Ocean, 2015,
c-print, 122 × 152 cm.

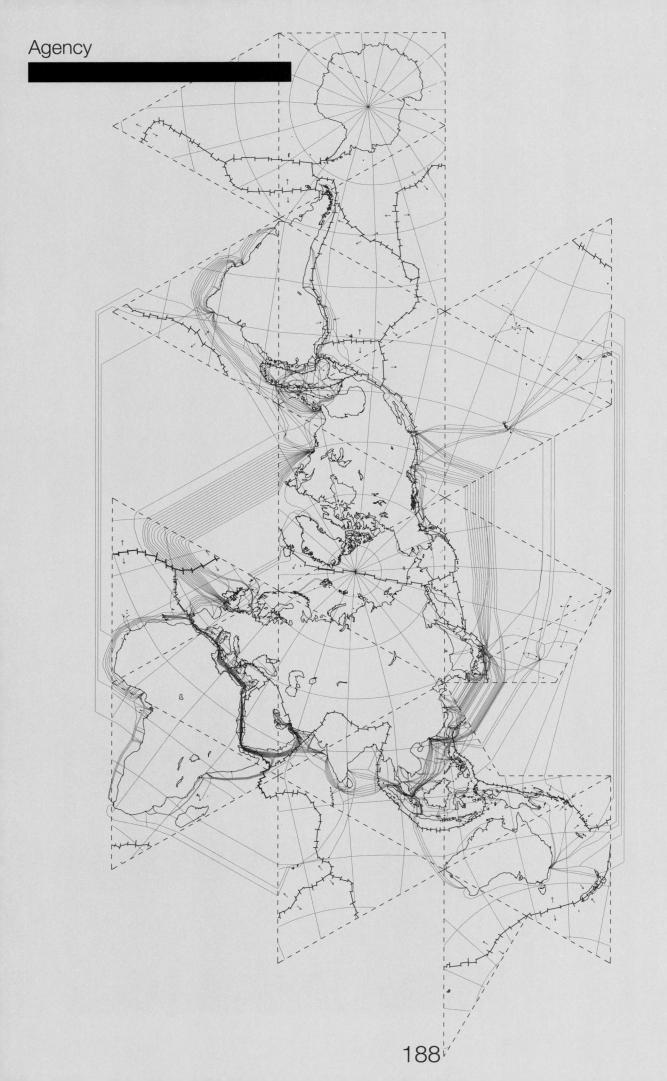

Michel Kessler: Dymaxion map of
the global undersea cable network.

Illustration: Damian Ineichen

© Michel Kessler

If you look at the map of where the internet fiber optic cables go around the world, you will see that they trace out completely the routes of former empires.

If you can see the infrastructures behind the technologies, you can work out where the power still lies. Once people confront the physical dimension of technology they can start to get down to the roots of the problems. They can move from a mere critique of technology towards a deeper understanding of the actual distribution of power that underlie the flows of capital.

MF: *We are constantly hearing the assumption that technology is neutral. Yet such arguments make it easier for technology to penetrate all aspects of our everyday lives. What exactly are the implications of this assumption?*
JB: I was in a talk a few years ago where Eric Schmidt, the former CEO of Google, spoke about this idea of technology as neutral, as a kind of rising tide lifting things that are inherently good. In the course of that speech he talked about the genocide in Rwanda, and said that if there would have been mobile phones in Rwanda in the early 1990s the genocide would not have happened. This is emblematic of the belief that the application of more technology—particularly of technologies of vision and surveillance, but also the gathering of situation-specific information in the form of data—is intrinsically positive. This is fundamentally and dangerously untrue. There were plenty of eyes on Rwanda at that time. There was satellite imagery, reports and radio recordings. There was an immense amount of media attention. The problem was not that we did not know what was going on. The problem was a lack of political will, as well as inability, to act for many reasons.

But it is also dangerously wrong because the technology Schmidt described in such positive light, the mobile phone, has been shown to make things worse

in many situations. For example, the violence that flared up in Kenya during the last elections was heavily driven by information spreading over social networks, so one could argue that mobile phones also brought huge amounts of violence. Facebook recently admitted it played a role in the genocide in Myanmar. It certainly wasn't Facebook's fault, or mobile phones' fault, but the idea that the application of technology alone is somehow neutral or good is deeply wrong and incredibly dangerous to promote. Still, it's something that is deeply embedded in the culture of Silicon Valley, which is why it needs to be constantly challenged.

OG: *As architects we have a relatively limited skill set for addressing many of today's technical developments. For example, when it comes to the implementation of "smart" technologies at the scale of architecture and infrastructure, we can approach programmers, computer scientists, and developers and have productive conversations with them. But this does not change the fact that we ourselves lack the necessary technical expertise. As someone that studied computer science and therefore has insight into both worlds, what would you say is the agency of people working behind the scenes of these major tech companies?*
JB: So often we are concerned with our own lack of agency, even when we become politically aware of these technologies and start realizing that there are people behind them with their biases. It is fairly easy to imagine those people as being more powerful than us, but that is very rarely the case. The people who build these things don't necessarily have more agency than anyone else, and if they do they very rarely recognize it because they lack the overview, just as everyone else does. The transdisciplinary perspective is still incredibly rare. The people who develop a technology rarely give too much thought to the political or social outcomes of it, which is why I say that expertise or mastery of technology itself is not the simple answer to fixing this. Educating people to be better at technology does not necessarily produce some kind of higher conscious-

ness. In general, people are mostly defined by the context in which they are working, and the context, in my opinion, is not that you are a programmer but that you work for a large company with shareholders, which is realistically the driving mindset behind your work. So, when we talk about domains of agency: yes, there is educational work to be done at all different levels, but it is the broader framework that sets the direction in ethical matters, and right now the direction is mostly set by the returns anticipated by companies and their investors.

MF: *What roles can people with specialized technical knowledge take outside of the corporate context? If we are aiming for a more integrated, transdisciplinary perspective of the whole system, then could you imagine specialists, including yourself, taking on a more conventional role in a governing body? As a politician?*
JB: I think that I have a political role already, as does everybody else. If you're asking if I would put myself up for election under a party system, that seems fairly unlikely, but there are many other ways to actively shape society. If we understand governance as the assumption of responsibility, then this should be the goal.

MF: *In the case of the genocide in Rwanda, you framed the problem as a lack of political will to intervene, which suggests the need for alternative organizations to deal adequately with such catastrophic developments. If conventional political structures do not take on the task, are there other methods, such as technological management, which might work better?*
JB: Representative democracy is not the worst form of government. We need people to tackle the tasks at hand, and it is all the better if truly competent people are chosen to do so. We obviously don't live within a perfect version of representative democracy right now, but there is growing awareness of the importance of infrastructure, which forms the basis for many of our activities. And this is something that I think is as relevant to architecture and its physical questions as it is to digital ones. When we are building

189

Agency

In their *terra0* Research project, Paul Seidler, Paul Kolling, and Max Hampshire investigate whether natural ecosystems can own and manage themselves using decentralized blockchain networks. For a piece of forest in Brandenburg, a "smart contract"—a program stored in the blockchain—defines the conditions of its management, for example, when and which trees may be felled. The licensing process is automated by means of digital data collection. © terra0

things, we rarely think about the shape of the infrastructure on which it's constructed, and how that affects its outcome. I am thinking of things like open-source software. For example, when it comes to video conferencing tools most people still use Skype, which is based on a deeply centralized system. Every Skype call travels through a data center owned by Microsoft, so you are compelled to trust that company. But Skype is not the only video conference tool. There are many other vendors in this area, so you can have the conversation with another software just as well. By using those alternative tools you are radically changing the shape of the network, expanding and boosting it, making it increasingly attractive to other users.

There are fundamentally different ways we can design and build things, which are also based on different profit models and methods. I don't mean that we should completely abandon centrally organized companies or representative democracy altogether, but that we can produce a shift by thinking differently about how things are shaped, how they communicate across networks, and how they produce very different effects on a much wider scale just by the way they are constructed. This is a possible design challenge, and an architectural challenge, but it is not just thinking about the surface aesthetic of these things, it's thinking about how they are systematically constructed.

MF: *For all the empowering aspects decentralization promises, there is also the loss of legal entities that can be held accountable for their actions. In other words, when you decentralize power, you also decentralize responsibility. Are you arguing for stronger decentralization?*
JB: There is a lot of discussion about over-centralization of power on the web today. At the same time, we have gone through an incredible phase of decentralization of media and communication technologies over the last 20 to 50 years, to the extent that now we don't know whom to trust anymore. Politicians, media—these traditional gatekeepers of the truth within society—I think that it is absolutely essential that these existing forms of power are questioned and that we build some other ways of discussing the truth. That applies in a broader sense to the idea of centralization and decentralization. Decentralization is democratizing to the point where it meets education and engagement. The agency happens in the middle. It is not enough to radically decentralize without people having the power to have an informed opinion. We have gone through all these decentralizing processes but we have been disempowered at the same time because we don't understand the technologies that we are using. Decentralization must therefore be accompanied by educational measures relating to the tools we use on a daily basis. This concerns software, for example, but can also be applied to architecture and urban planning. Currently these tools are designed to make everything invisible, and therefore not subject to criticism. All these magic, advanced, complex, extraordinary tools—whether it is chat apps or maps— are all hidden behind little icons on our smartphones. We don't think about them. There are ways to build these tools so they are also educational in their use, so that you don't just access them blindly but learn how they work and how to use them thoughtfully.

OG: *The Berlin-based group terra0 Research has tried to develop a system of decentralized ownership based on blockchain technology and designed for a forest so it can own itself. There is also a historical case in Germany: the Cologne Cathedral. The cathedral is owned by the Hohe Domkirche zu Köln, meaning it owns itself. It is represented by the Domkapitel (the cathedral chapter), a board of humans that acts in its interest, albeit only for its maintenance, and with no profit interests. What can we learn from such examples?*
JB: I know that there is a river in New Zealand which has obtained legal personhood. In the corporate sector, this possibility has existed for a long time. I don't know enough about the Cologne Cathedral to say for sure, but what I understand is that it's not about giving agency to the cathedral itself, but about creating a situation where it shares agency with humans. It is the board, the cathedral chapter, which acts in its interest. When we talk about a self-owning forest I get a bit nervous because I think that if a forest is self-owning, then in classical economic terms, it is put in competition with other forests, or even with people. The incentive to cut it down could then become even greater. What is interesting, on the other hand, is the shared responsibility of space, in which they form a kind of community with common interests and care for one another. I think that the terra0 project is good but mostly as a critique of the idea that you can somehow magically separate anything from humanity, or society, or politics by the application of technology.

It's the so-called Oracle Problem: all these models are ultimately based on "smart contracts," which use external data sources—the "oracle"—to make automated decisions and forecasts. The use of this data is problematic because it is used to decide on how the contract responds to future external inputs (the if-then conditions). If you rely on a central oracle that outputs incorrect data, this compromises the smart contract, and any benefits you would have gained from decentralized decision-making are lost. What happens at the edge of any one of these technological systems? How does it interface with the world? How do you get data from the "real" world into this supposedly magic, imperfect system? I may be proved wrong about this in the long term, but I think the Oracle Problem is essentially insurmountable. That problem is never going to go away. The only response, for me, is the notion of mutual responsibilities between parties. This turns the question from how do we lay down some kind of perfect network of control to a question of stewardship: How do we manage things in the best interests of everyone in the present where the means will define the ends?

01 James Bridle, *New Dark Age: Technology and the End of the Future* (London: Verso, 2018).

New Trees

A PHOTO ESSAY BY ROBERT VOIT

Yuma, Elks Lane, Arizona, USA, 2006.

All images © Robert Voit: *New Trees*, 2004–14.

Norscot, Johannesburg,
Gauteng Province, South Africa, 2006.

Cuckfield, Haywards Heath, West Sussex,
England, 2004.

Mobile Home Park, Las Vegas,
Nevada, USA, 2006.

Riseley, Bedfordshire, England, 2004.

Industrial Drive, Flagstaff, Arizona, USA, 2006.

New Trees 2004–14

Over the course of more than ten years, Robert Voit photographed the "new trees" of our mechanized society in Europe, South Africa, the United States, and South Korea: camouflaged cell phone masts made of steel, fiberglass, and plastic, which emit electromagnetic waves beneath artificial tree crowns. They can be found in meadows and car parks, along motorways, and on the edge of housing estates, and are usually fenced in and surrounded by technical installations. While some are arranged in groups, they mostly dominate the landscape as solitary objects, up to 30 meters high. Depending on the location, they stretch up into the sky like Central European deciduous and coniferous trees and shrubs, spread their pointed thorns like cactuses in the barren desert landscape of Arizona, or tower above US or South African housing settlements like coastal palms. The harmonious, camouflaged insertion of these trees into their respective local contexts aesthetically reflects what they were designed to do and what their actual purpose is: to create a seamless, interference-free mobile phone network.

194

Scottsdale, Arizona, USA, 2006.

Mono Lake, California, USA, 2006.

Luxury and Paranoia, Access and Exclusion

On Capital and Public Space

ANASTASIA KUBRAK, SANDER MANSE

No-fly zones for drones in the Netherlands.
© Ministerie van Infrastructuur en Waterstaat, 2017

We get into an Uber, whose route, calculated by GPS, takes us past the Kremlin. However, when we arrive, the charge is three times higher than usual. Why? We check the route: according to the navigation app, we have driven to an airport outside of Moscow. Impossible!
We check more closely: the moment we approached the Kremlin, our electronic location suddenly jumped across to Vnukovo Airport. As I later discover, this glitch in our GPS position was due to a phenomenon known as geofencing. An invisible wall surrounds the Kremlin, throwing GPS sensors into confusion so as to prevent unwanted drone overflights.

A GPS fence around the Moscow Kremlin aims to protect against drone attacks. © Anastasia Kubrak/Sander Manse/Apple Maps

New forms of urban zoning

Daily life in cities has been increasingly augmented with new technologies. Equipped with a plethora of sensors and signaling devices—Wi-Fi networks, Bluetooth devices, GPS apps—we can navigate the city more easily. At the same time, this makes our own location knowable at any given moment. Today, these technologies are mainly deployed by platform businesses, giving them increasing influence over how cities function. Above all, this is about capitalizing on the information generated by the so-called augmented city.

For some years now, a great jumble of virtual borders has been laid out across our cities, including private air routes, no-fly-zones for drones, and geofences. Traditional urban zoning laid down rules for land use in particular city areas, allocating spaces to housing or commerce, for example. But today a location can belong to several virtual zones at once, while being occupied and used by a variety of actors. Contemporary technological advances mean zoning is no longer restricted to the regulation of matters like building height or usage. It now also extends to new, physically intangible spaces.

These new zones allow giant digital corporations to tap into new markets and colonize virtual land outside traditional jurisdictions, thus taking advantage of current legal grey zones. These companies capitalize patterns of individual movement, monetizing the data extracted and the so-called behavioral surplus generated by surveillance technologies. Services previously offered by state institutions—ranging from security and energy management to public transportation—are being privatized and optimized by the platform economy, enabled by network technologies and big data. The augmented city is a source of profit for Google, Amazon, Facebook, Cisco, Siemens, IBM, and similar firms.

The platform economy is profoundly disturbing our material world. Airbnb brings new gentrification effects in its wake while Uber disrupts traditional modes of transport (or at least claims to do so). Platform capitalism's business model is based on aggressive growth—profitability, in the first instance, plays no role here—in the collection and exploitation of freely available user data, as well as on a dismissive attitude to laws and legal processes. Default implementation of new services by platforms, without user approval, allows citizens and governments only to raise objections in retrospect. People first come to enjoy the convenience of the new services; only later do the contradictions and conflicts they bring with them become clear.

But what is life like in the privatized city, as structured by this new vertical zoning? How can citizens profit from the increasing use of sensor technologies, data processing algorithms, incessant tracking devices and parasitic mapping interfaces? Instead of simply exploiting urban structures, can the forced verticality of platform capitalism somehow enrich them? Maybe cities deserve a truly augmented reality—a literal expansion of reality within urban space, which could benefit inhabitants by creating fairer social alternatives. How can augmented zones be actively reshaped and used for needs other than servicing capital?

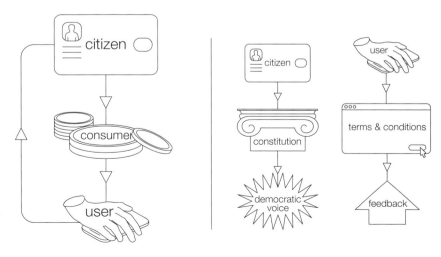

Citizen or user: How do decision-making processes and power relations shift when citizens are reduced to consumers? © Kristof Croes/Brandlhuber+ Team

Following the Asian financial crisis in 1997–98 and the SARS outbreak in 2002–03, the Singapore government launched an economic program with tax incentives for investors. A typical project from that time is the Sentosa Cove residential enclave, which is located on reclaimed land off the coast of Singapore.

Functions of zones

A stroll through London, Berlin, or Singapore reveals just how directly developers, investors, and the private real estate market can influence a city's appearance. Legislation and public policy have allowed capital and public space to bleed ever more closely into one another. Virtual zones render this relation increasingly complex and intensive, as shown by examples such as Dubai's Media City or the special economic zones in the Chinese city of Shenzhen. In her book *Extrastatecraft: The Power of Infrastructure Space*, Keller Easterling describes the history of these special zones, whose predecessor phenomena include Export Production Zones (EPZ) and classic free trade zones, which allowed for efficient, rapid economic exchange.

The earliest free trade zones, which at first applied only to the storage and distribution of goods, sprang up along the major trade routes, before spreading to airports, commercial areas, and container ports between the 1950s and the 1970s; in the 1990s, offshore banking quarters and office parks were added to the mix. The zones developed into small cities, later even into megacities. Shenzhen, the first of China's special economic zones, was established in 1980. In the decades that followed, its population has grown from 30,000 to well over 12 million.

The idea of EPZs was first developed in the mid-20th century as a way of boosting developing economies and allowing them access to the global market. However, "it did not dissolve into the general business and industrial climate of its host country, but rather became a persistent yet mutable instrument, transforming as it absorbed more and more of the general economy within its boundaries."[01] Easterling's analysis shows how these zones, originally considered a means to a particular end, came to exert strong influence on human beings, resources, and capital far beyond their actual borders. The impact of the zones, in other words, radically diverged from their advertised intent. Rather than making the host country richer, the zone pulls in labor from the domestic hinterland, while profits go to colonialist multinationals, usually acting in a parasitic way.

Today, zones like this are increasingly built from scratch, located outside existing cities, on the periphery of national territories, even on off-shore islands recovered from the sea. As an island, the zone is like a blank sheet of paper, a field of experimentation beyond the reach of existing legislation.

Luxury and paranoia

A special kind of city has emerged from the symbiotic relationship between politics and the real estate market, which is perfectly tailored to the special economic zones. This ready-made city is a kind of spatial product: it can be bought as a total package, right down to door handles and sensors, and reproduced at any location on Earth. An archetypal example is Songdo, a "smart city" or "ubiquitous city" located in Incheon, a South Korean free trade zone. Songdo's infrastructure is entirely digitally networked, using hardware and telecommunications systems by the likes of Cisco, IBM, Arup, and 3M. The city was completed in 2015: it resembles a thinly populated high-tech utopia, in which streets and buildings come with built-in computing capacity. Inhabitants enjoy access to Cisco's TelePresence system, fully automated trash collection by the Envac Group, as well as security measures like Smart Keys, which give access to certain spaces and public services. The digitally equipped city promises a life of pleasant convenience; at the same time, the whole city becomes a kind of gated community.

In this case, however, exclusion is achieved by infrastructure, not by walls. When new zones are carved out of the earth, technology companies rapidly move in to directly develop the urban architecture. But the effect of their hardware and software is to exclude certain population groups, in this way drawing new boundaries. In a place developed specifically for economic activity and capital generation, the population becomes an economic variable, judged by the added value they can bring to the city. Local, low-paid workers are driven out by high property prices. Within traditional cities, there are also an increasing number of separated urban enclaves, serving to perforate the city's existing social fabric. The privatization of urban landscapes has impacts on universal human rights associated with spaces, including basic, physical rights of way: luxury outlets and guarded residential areas already prevent entry to the poor and marginalized. What does it mean for a city when citizens can be scanned and analyzed more and more easily, when it is increasingly simple to exclude them on the basis of status or credit-worthiness?

This development can also be observed on Facebook, for example, where targeted advertising allows the application of indirect discrimination. By now, Facebook can target user profiles to exclude entire social groups from seeing certain offers.[02] Uber has different prices for consumers from richer or poorer neighborhoods.[03] This speculative valuation, made possible by collecting huge quantities of data, creates new forms of informational inequality, with platforms observing users as if through a police two-way mirror.

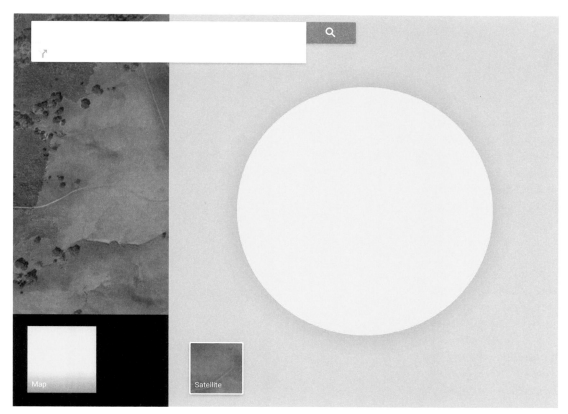

Map software influences our movement in space and what we do and don't perceive. To regain control of the city, Anastasia Kubrak and Sander Manse propose that government institutions define spaces that are exempt from the collection and exploitation of user profiles and related data. These "free spaces" should then be rendered unrecognizable on Google Maps and other platforms. © Arthur Röing Baer

Jumping from zone to zone

As they seek to introduce increased automation through technologies like self-driving cars and delivery robots and drones, the big technology companies have repeatedly faced regulatory obstacles and even defeats. What these companies want is more freedom, more flexible political conditions, and more data extraction—in essence a state of exception, a zone where law itself is set aside.

Silicon Valley has a long-standing libertarian dream of a laboratory of lawlessness, an island in international waters beyond legal systems and their national laws. For new technologies, this space would offer an atmosphere akin to the Burning Man festival: "a safe space where you can try out new things and test their impact on society,"[04] as Larry Page has repeatedly put it. While Burning Man is a temporary quest for freedom in the Nevada desert, the famous, notorious Seasteading Institute wants to see

floating startups throw off the yoke of legality once and for all, its drive to populate the oceans underpinned by its libertarian ideas. "When seasteading becomes a viable alternative, switching from one government to another would be a matter of sailing to the other without even leaving your house,"[05] said founder Patri Friedman, the grandson of neoliberalism's key thinker Milton Friedman, at his first annual Seasteading Conference in 2008.

If every seasteading settlement could choose a legal system as it sees fit, industry could ruthlessly pursue its own interests. On ethical questions, companies would escape the political yoke of national and supranational institutions, including limits on genetic transformation, cloning, or animal testing.

The promise of flexible citizenship is based on assumptions that each individual has, without exception, their own appropriate

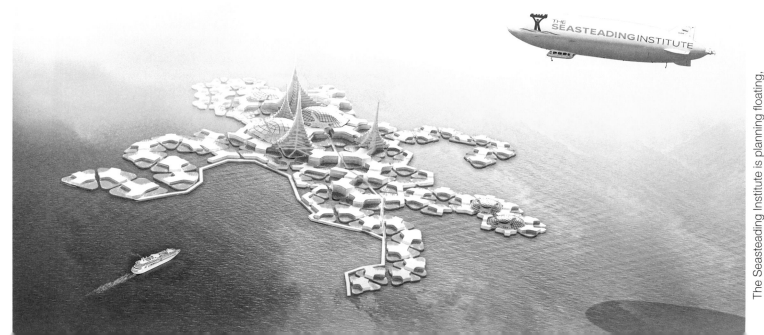

The Seasteading Institute is planning floating, legally autonomous island states in the open sea.
© The Seasteading Institute

zone. According to Seasteading claims, this would lead to improvements for the poor, but so far, the plans appear to address mainly a more privileged audience: advertising images show reconditioned high-seas cruise ships and luxury yachts anchored offshore at the first floating islands. If seasteading is the ultimate libertarian-capitalist utopia, what would its socially-inclusive counter-model look like?

New counter-spaces

The establishment of classical counter-spaces—such as abortion centers in international waters—has been closely connected with the existence of territorial boundaries and the legal partitioning of the surface of the earth. A temporary sojourn in a zone outside the ruling legal system—for example on a floating offshore island—could allow new applications of human rights, opening up new opportunities for minorities. Digital vertical zoning could allow these exceptional spaces to be located anywhere, with users granted access to various systems while never having to change their location.

What we then might imagine could be a kind of counter-space laid out across the existing city, taking advantage of the temporal limitations of new spatial zoning practices. The verticality of this type of zone could allow it to change form and size according to the circumstances. These could be elastic zones: fleeting, flexible, and stackable.

Enclosures

When the platform economy takes cities hostage, governments must look for new ways to counteract this privatization through legal means. The geofence around the Kremlin, described at the beginning of this article, sends false coordinates to all navigation apps within central Moscow, disrupting the operations of Uber and Google Maps. White patches on the map like this are generally pre-coded by platforms into their spatial representation software; they can exclude certain technologies and any possible influence by them from a particular geographical location. In a reversal of how free economic zones work, democratic institutions could win back control over the city by establishing these kinds of spaces, removed from all possibility of exploitation. There could be clear boundaries demarcating certain zones: Uber-free areas, neighborhoods invisible to the Airbnb platform, districts in which data and user profiles cannot be gathered for use.

However, this kind of consistent boundary creation does not rectify the problem of segregation: prohibiting certain services in one urban area can lead to unforeseen consequences in others. The protection of a few select buildings or neighborhoods could lead to even more elitist, gentrified zones with limited access. But could there also be cleverer possibilities for zoning, ones which do not erect virtual fences in public space? Because of their vertical organization, zones might be laid over one another at a specific location, leading to a genuine form of augmented reality: a reality that expands on what was already available. The following examples are an attempt to show how zoning could serve as a counterweight against the aggressive behavior of platform capitalism.

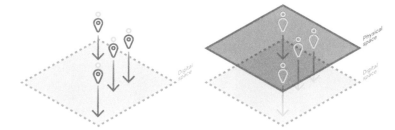

The ad-based business model of most tech companies rests on the assumption that users generate value in a "digital vacuum." But users are real people who occupy physical place in the analogue world.

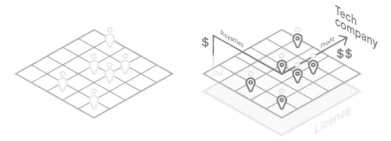

If platform users are the resource of the information economy, what if tech companies had to pay in order to use the value (data and attention) that users generate?

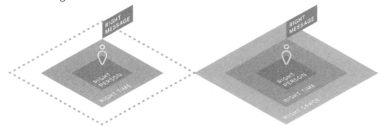

Georeferenced data enables tech companies like Google to place personalized ads with the advertiser's target group at opportune moments based on algorithmic calculations: the right message for the right person, at the right time, in the right place. This could allow Google to further improve its prediction algorithm to extend its influence on physical space.

Reinvention of zones

The platform economy cashes in on citizens' behavior patterns in public space. What if zoning allowed citizens to take control over data extraction systems? *Google Urbanism*,[06] a final project by students of the Strelka Institute in Moscow, put forward a model where added value created by the platform—in their example created by Google—can flow back into public spaces. In other words, value can move back into the spaces from which it is ordinarily siphoned off. Local governments could sell exclusive licenses to companies, giving them the right to extract data at particular locations; in return, the companies would have to invest part of their profits in taking care of public space. Currently, individual cities have few if any ways to force Google into a potential partnership between platform and citizens. However, it may be possible for authorities to take back control over their streets: a variety of legal measures could be tested and introduced, representing new mechanisms of value creation.

Vertical zoning may come to change the very manifestation of capital itself. The Bristol Pound[07] is one example of a local currency, introduced to keep value created in Bristol within the city. The local pound is accepted by an impressive number of local businesses and is used for monthly wage and tax payments. Bristol pounds are still a paper-based currency, but recently there has also been a global spread of blockchain-based community currencies: the Colu Local Digital Wallet can be used in Liverpool, East London, Tel Aviv, and Haifa, for example.

To prevent smart technology taking over completely, as in Songdo, a new zoning of the city could enable citizens to organize services for themselves. The ideal platform of the future would belong to and be controlled by users themselves: it would be available as a social service, in which all would invest and from which all could profit [see the essay on platform cooperativism by Trebor Scholz in this issue]. But the full development of models like these has at times brought with it substantial problems. It is particularly difficult to attract the necessary critical mass of users: without this, any platform will lack the necessary resources and will fail to achieve network effects. Ultimately a platform only offers its users value if it has enough participants. For this reason, we can imagine a different approach, entirely practical and pragmatic, which would make use of the existing platforms of large companies and their networks. Then, even if the platform profits from user activities, the users could begin to draw new and unintended value from the business, while also getting to know alternative social functions within augmented urbanity.

Vertical future

The examples discussed in this article show how vertical zoning can have a concrete impact on the city: Google Urbanism allows capital to flow back into the city, while the Bristol Pound strengthens local value creation. In the future, this kind of soft zoning may offer counter-mechanisms to platform capitalism, enabling citizens to become active on their own behalf, while making use of the very resources and methods that technology giants have used to siphon off so much value.

Previously, users profited from the easy user experience and convenience of platforms, but in this way they delivered themselves up to their monopolistic tendencies. Now, through active participation in vertical zoning, the same users could become mature citizens, exercising political power and becoming more conscious of their right to alternative models. Using vertical zoning, political institutions can offer citizens greater value, while resisting the contemporary dogma of the neoliberal smart city, which is based on information exploitation and unfair treatment of platform users.

When you walk through a city, it quickly becomes clear that every patch of ground you stand on is more than just a point on a map. We are balanced on a large number of different, vertically overlapping grids. Although platforms like to seek out new unpopulated terrain to colonize, people on the ground should create active spaces which will enable alternative functions within the digital infrastructure that surrounds us all. It is a question of discovering new forms of regulation, exchange, and habitation, as well as developing non-capitalist social relations between these activities. What we must demand are new, temporary, flexible, autonomous zones, not in order to secede from the state, but rather to rethink its role in today's world.

01 Keller Easterling, *Extrastatecraft: The Power of Infrastructure Space* (London: Verso, 2014), 29.
02 Alvin Chang, "How the Internet Keeps Poor People in Poor Neighborhoods," *Vox*, December 12, 2016, accessed November 12, 2018, www.vox.com/2016/12/12/13867692/poor-neighborhoods-targeted-ads-internet-cartoon.
03 Eric Newcomer, "Uber Starts Charging What It Thinks You're Willing to Pay," *Bloomberg*, 19 May, 2017, accessed November 12, 2018, www.bloomberg.com/news/articles/2017-05-19/uber-s-future-may-rely-on-predicting-how-much-you-re-willing-to-pay.
04 Larry Page: *Google I/O 2013: Keynote*, May 15, 2013, accessed November 12, 2018, www.youtube.com/watch?v=9pmPa_KxsAM.
05 "Seasteading: Cities on the Ocean," *The Economist*, December 3, 2011, accessed November 12, 2018, www.economist.com/node/21540395.
06 googleurbanism.com, accessed November 12, 2018.
07 bristolpound.org, accessed November 12, 2018.

Google Urbanism is a project of Strelka's New Normal program. It examines the influence of platform-based companies on the production of space using Google as an example and, from this, develops future scenarios for the use of public space.

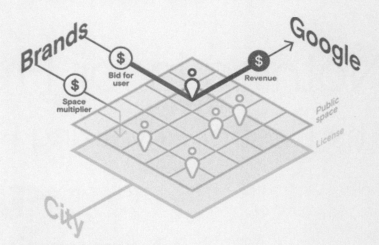

SCENARIO 1: LICENSING
In order to access user data and extract it at specific locations, companies must pay license fees to local authorities. This enables part of the profit to flow directly back into the maintenance of the public space and thus to the users' benefit.

SCENARIO 2: GOOGLE MAPS PLATFORM
Through a new expanded platform, Google simplifies the process of license acquisition and allocation, aggregating urban stakeholders and providing them with new mechanisms for value creation.

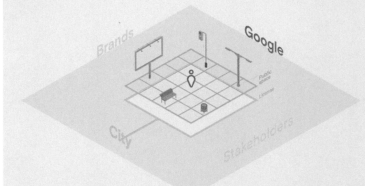

SCENARIO 3: GOOGLE URBANISM
Google becomes the preferred partner for smart city concepts and is displacing all other competitors, because the focus of new city models is now on "human behavior" instead of infrastructure. The monopolization of the market in both the physical and digital realms is leading to the next generation of global tech conglomerates.

Nothing is for Free
The Cost of Privatizing Public Services

MICHAELA FRIEDBERG

LinkNYC media station.

In 2013, crowds of people watched as New York's last silver payphone booths were removed from its streets. Since their debut in 1905, these once ubiquitous metal vessels became places of mafia film backdrops, ad-hoc work spaces, and temporary shelters for the lost or homeless—veritable icons of the New York cityscape. But with the introduction of private service providers and cell phone technology, fewer and fewer people were using payphones.[01] They were increasingly vandalized, used for crime, and occupied by the homeless, making them a financial burden for the city. After years of the payphone's slow decline, the Department of Information Technology and Telecommunication (DoITT) put out a solicited Request for Proposals (RFP) on how to redesign the outdated machines.

The winning design, LinkNYC, proposed a slender black tower equipped with large digital interfaces, eerily reminiscent of the monolith from Stanley Kubrick's *2001: A Space Odyssey*. On its main face, next to headphone jacks and USB charging plugs, an Android tablet lets users access Google maps, city data, video calling, and emergency helplines. Covering each side of the tower are 55-inch screens, which function as digital billboards for advertising and public service announcements.

At a public press conference, Dan Doctoroff, now CEO of the Alphabet subsidiary Sidewalk Labs, and then Deputy Mayor for Economic Development in New York, declared the integration of new technologies into daily life as an important task for the city.[02] During his presentation of the project, Doctoroff spoke of digital inequality and emphasized the importance of internet access in order to remain competitive in the free market.

As a first step towards this mission, Link kiosks were installed with conventional Android tablets that let users browse the internet without a time or data limit. Within months, users of different demographics began using the "Links." Tourists charged their cell phones in between sights, business women used the 1 GB/sec network to send presentations, teenagers congregated to watch music videos after school, and the homeless were able to receive their monthly fill of TV.

This democratization of the internet was made physical through new dynamics on the public sidewalks. A second layer of ad-hoc infrastructure began to appear throughout the city as a means of long-term browsing. Mailboxes were turned on their side to become communal benches, stacked delivery boxes served as temporary stools, and old office chairs were dragged up to Links to create home cinemas. The rules of the sidewalk began to change, reverting to the characteristic chaos of New York in the 1990s: unpredictable and shared, replacing what had become sterile and uniform.

But rather than seeing these public browsing events as a success of the new infrastructure, the operator, CityBridge, was concerned with the project's overuse and public image, and therefore disabled internet browsing after the first year, weakening the city's promise of equal access. The inequality between users continued to expand from the digital to the geographic; of the 7,500 planned Links in New York City, only 700 were assigned to the Bronx—the borough with the least amount of broadband-equipped households.[03] This uneven distribution reflects the economic motives behind LinkNYC, which ultimately helped the project succeed in the restricted tendering procedure in 2014.

In order to convince the city of its proposal, CityBridge developed a funding plan that would cost the city, and its tax payers, no money. Instead, the consortium proposed to fund the entire construction and maintenance of the machines by raising approximately $83 million per year through advertising.[04] With its 12-year contract, CityBridge will earn approximately $1 billion—well over the $200 million it graciously offered to pay for the initial construction costs. Of its total earnings, CityBridge is obligated to give 50% to the city, making LinkNYC profitable not only to the consortium, but also to the government.

Improvised seating in front of a LinkNYC station.

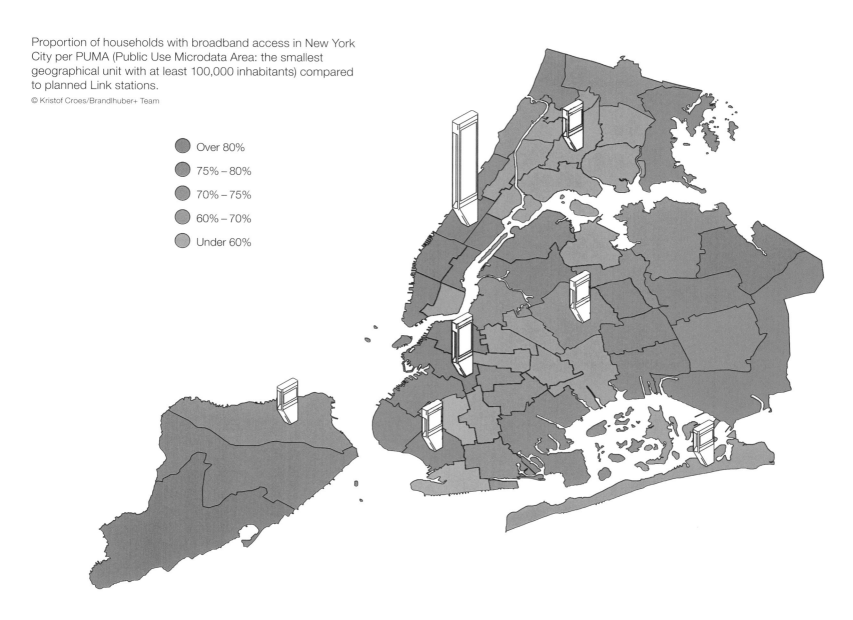

Proportion of households with broadband access in New York City per PUMA (Public Use Microdata Area: the smallest geographical unit with at least 100,000 inhabitants) compared to planned Link stations.
© Kristof Croes/Brandlhuber+ Team

Over 80%
75% – 80%
70% – 75%
60% – 70%
Under 60%

Whereas in the past, infrastructure was largely publicly funded, today private companies are increasingly taking over tasks that were previously in public hands. Capitalizing on the weakness of the state, companies approached the fragile socioeconomic moment as an opportunity for investment, operating under what Naomi Klein aptly identifies as "disaster capitalism." In a desperate act to uphold the market, urban land was sold in bulk to developers and global tech companies. As the real estate market rose again, private actors found themselves in a new position of power; with their large urban plots, companies that once existed solely in virtual space were able to expand into, and capitalize on, the real.

This phenomenon finds expression in the new building complexes touted by the big tech companies: "Amazonia," as Amazon's headquarters in Seattle is known, Facebook's campus in Menlo Park (noted as the largest continuous office space in the world), and Sidewalk Toronto, Alphabet's plan for a smart city in Toronto. The financial crisis spurred an unprecedented privatization or economization of urban space, which has made its mark on myriad elements of the urban fabric, from sprawling campuses to the names of subway stations.

In 2009, for example, the New York City Metropolitan Transportation Authority (MTA) sold the naming rights of the Atlantic Avenue subway station to the British bank, Barclays, which at the time was building a new sports arena nearby. The bank acquired the rights for $4 million and renamed the station Atlantic Avenue–Barclays Center. Forest City Ratner, the developer of the Barclays arena, agreed to pay the MTA $200,000 per year for the next 20 years—a welcome income given its $25.5 billion debt.[05]

Other cities began doing the same. In 2012, for example, the city of Madrid launched a partnership program where private telephone companies could temporarily rename the metro stations for a fee. The first partnership was a one-month contract with Samsung, in which the Sol metro station was renamed Estacíon Sol Galaxy Note, enabling the city to fund renovation work on its public transport system. Unlike New York, which permanently sold the naming rights of one of Brooklyn's oldest subway stations to a foreign bank, Madrid opted for a temporary approach.

Working at the scale of infrastructure, these new privatized elements impact the daily lives of city dwellers; they are omnipresent. If this infrastructure is truly intended for public use, then its

207

LinkNYC

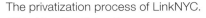

The privatization process of LinkNYC.
© Kristof Croes/Brandlhuber+ Team

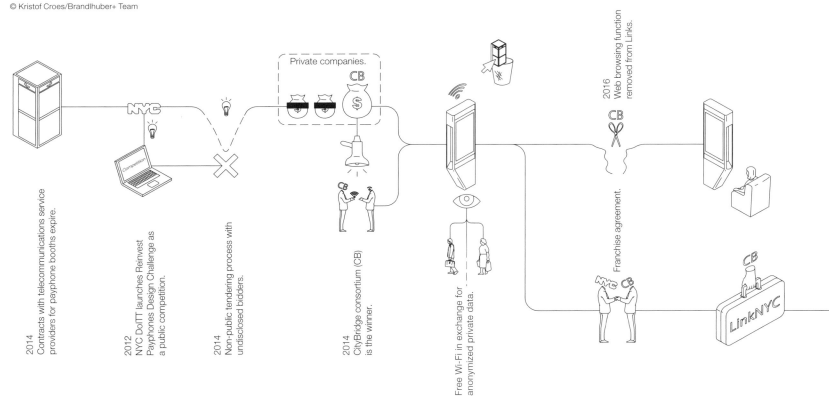

design should take into account people's physical nature and fluid behavior. Here, a conflict arises between its large scale, which requires standardization and reproducibility, and social complexity, which requires it to be flexible in different scenarios. In this sense, the truest public projects are those which can be configured and adapted for different bodies, contexts, and uses. If this is the real meaning of public design, architects and urbanists should instead commit themselves to a discursive mission rather than to the profit-oriented projects of private companies. As architects and planners, we must define and construct possibilities to sustain good design in an age of privatization and tech fetishes. This mission should exist outside the spheres of art and academia, as structural systems and rulesets for protecting the independent designer.

PUBLIC INTERESTS IN PRIVATE HANDS

In 2012, the New York City DoITT launched a public design challenge to collect ideas on the new infrastructure. The "public" release of the Rethink Payphones Design Challenge took place at the 2012 NY Tech Meetup, a weekday event in Manhattan with an entrance price of $10 per person. In order to apply for the challenge, designers were encouraged to work in teams, formed through the provided startup website, CollabFinder. Although categorized as a public competition, the rhetoric around the event

worked to target applicants from the tech startup industry, visibly influencing the end results of the submissions.

Of the 125 proposals submitted to the design challenge, six were selected as finalists, none of which were LinkNYC. Rather than selecting a winner from the public design competition, the city translated the hundreds of idea submissions into a private Request for Proposals (RFP), in which they directly contacted a number of undisclosed companies to solicit a proposal. On November 17 2014, it was announced that CityBridge—a consortium of Qualcomm, Comark, and Intersection, three of the wealthiest tech companies in the industry—had "won" the RFP. The Request for Proposals was not a design competition, but rather a proposal for a new franchise agreement to assume the entire management of the old payphones. Therefore, the jury that selected LinkNYC as the winning entry was neither a design nor entrepreneurial jury; instead, the proposal was approved by the City's Franchise and Concession Review Committee (FCRC), which has no resident architect or urbanist on its board. Without the regulation of public commissions, architectural, spatial, and urban decisions fall back on the free-market, transforming the built environment into a reflection of the most economic industries and ideologies. How can we regulate the increasing privatization of general public services?

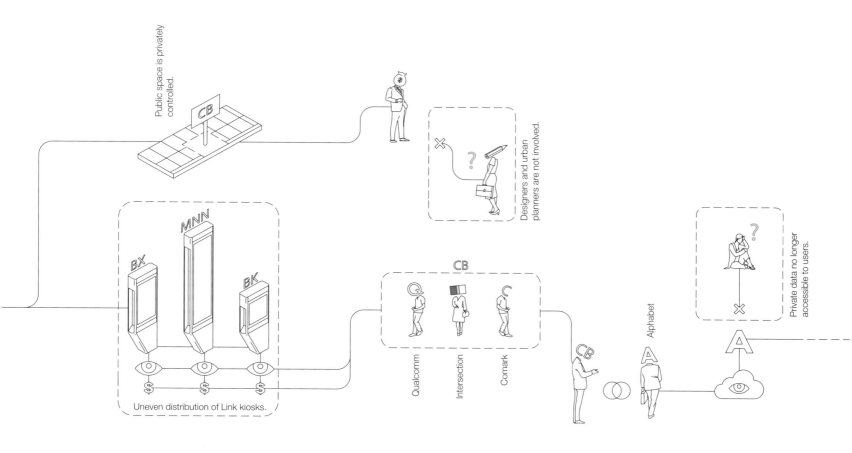

Public space is privately controlled.

CB

Designers and urban planners are not involved.

MNN

BX

BK

Uneven distribution of Link kiosks.

CB

Qualcomm

Intersection

Comark

Private data no longer accessible to users.

Alphabet

While motives of profit are standard for private corporations, the complete enmeshment of public and private becomes a threat to the basic organization and ethics of governmental bodies. In December 2014, the City of New York approved a franchise agreement with CityBridge that gave the consortium the rights and control over the design, maintenance, and use of the Link kiosks.[06] Rather than working with the designers from the first phase, CityBridge drew up a comprehensive 30-year business plan, characteristic of today's largescale development projects, in which architects and even government agencies become marginalized. Similarly, in the case of Toronto's waterfront project, the City of Toronto quickly amended its privacy policy to match the plans of Sidewalk Labs.

With these types of totalizing design plans, every decision—spatial and political—becomes outsourced to a single private organizer rather than an elected public body. In handing off the management and operation of the entire LinkNYC network, the municipality excuses itself of any accountability around the project's political and ethical responsibilities. Rather than being designed and governed by public interest, which protects the rights of human users, the Links are instead managed by their private owners, which prioritizes economic gain as a for-profit enterprise.

The global shift from public to private fundamentally weakens political and architectural responsibility alike. Where once the governing ethics of the state were decisive, now corporate interests have the last word, with the aim of collecting increasing amounts of data to target consumers and turn as high a profit as possible. Finding ourselves in the position of relying ever more on private capital, we have to ask ourselves: At what cost?

01 See Renée Reizman, "What Killed the Pay Phone?", *The Atlantic*, February 2, 2017, accessed August 16, 2019, www.theatlantic.com/technology/archive/2017/02/object-lesson-phone-booth/515385.
02 "Google City: How the Tech Juggernaut is Reimagining Cities," Dan Doctoroff in conversation with Jessica Lessin at The Information Subscriber Summit, April 5, 2016, accessed September 8, 2019, vimeo.com/161980906.
03 See Robert Wirsing, "LinkNYC Installs Free Wi-Fi Hotspots in the Bronx," *Bronx Times* September 11, 2016, accessed August 17, 2019, www.bxtimes.com/stories/2016/37/37-linknyc-2016-09-09-bx.html.
04 See Christopher Robbins, "Brace For

the 'Fastest Internet You've Ever Used' at These Free Sidewalk Kiosks," *Gothamist*, January 5, 2016, accessed August 30, 2019, web.archive.org/web/20161001055640/http://gothamist.com/2016/01/05/linknyc_wifi_2_fast_2_furious.php.
05 See Ciara Linnane, "NY MTA Fiscal Crisis Due to High Debt Costs: Report," *Reuters*, April 9, 2009, accessed August 30, 2019, www.reuters.com/article/us-newyork-mta-report/ny-mta-fiscal-crisis-due-to-high-debt-costs-report-idUSTRE5386CB20090409.
06 New York City Department of Information Technology & Telecommunications, *LinkNYC Franchises*, accessed August 30, 2019, www1.nyc.gov/site/doitt/business/linknyc-franchises.page.

The City as Enemy

HANNES GRASSEGGER

One can only understand the form and nature of the struggles in Hong Kong— and also the message of the protesters— by understanding that they are taking place in a smart city.

The smart city is often discussed as a model for the future. As if it were a vague plan, a structure yet to be built, somewhere far away. In fact, most of us already live in a smart city, at least in the digital sense. In nearly every major city around the world, including Hong Kong, projects have been underway for years to sensorize the infrastructure; to network with residents' sensor-filled mobile devices and to merge and then intelligently analyze the various public data sources. The goal is an adaptive city, a city that reacts, or even anticipates.

This is exactly the fear of the protesters in Hong Kong, that their smart city is being used by a pro-Chinese government against its own citizens. That the smart city is actually a weapon being directed against its citizens. This is why Hong Kong protesters are at war with the smart city. The smart city is their enemy.

This became clear to a larger audience when, in August of 2019, photos and video clips started circulating on social media showing a group of people gathering around a lamppost on a sunny day, holding umbrellas.

Umbrellas had been a symbol of the resistance movement in Hong Kong in 2014. The "umbrella protests" is what people called the 11-week blockade of downtown Hong Kong when tens of thousands demonstrated against the ongoing expansion of mainland China's stronghold over Hong Kong. The umbrellas were a telling sign of the nature of police violence being used against protesters,

serving to protect against pepper spray, the police force's weapon of choice. Today the umbrellas have reappeared, again as a shield. But this time against a new weapon, that of surveillance.

In one clip from 2019, sparks were seen flying from an electric saw that someone had brought along and started to use on the lamppost. Then a rope was thrown around it, and the umbrella protesters began to pull. To the cheers of those around them, it fell over and onto the street.

The lamppost was part of the smart city, one of 50 "smart lampposts" that had been installed that summer; a total of 400 of them are planned for Hong Kong's inner city area. The smart city infrastructure aims to make citizens "happier, healthier, smarter, and more prosperous," as stated in the city government's *Smart City Blueprint*, published in 2017.[01]

The lampposts, which are supposed to support traffic control, integrate a variety of functions, according to a document from the city administration. Each post serves as a 4G/5G antenna and a Wi-Fi hotspot, and is equipped with Bluetooth detectors, panoramic and thermal imaging cameras, and fracture sensors that measure humidity, temperature, wind speed, and solar radiation. They can also transmit location signals to devices in their vicinity.

The city administration has repeatedly assured that the lampposts do not operate facial recognition software, that they will not be used to monitor the population, and will not pass on any data to mainland China. But the citizens are losing confidence in the city government. They want proof.

Hong Kong has been part of the People's Republic of China since being handed over by its former British colonizers. However, until the end of the 50-year transition period in 2047, it remains a hybrid: a special administrative region with democratic elements, its own laws, and its own legislature consisting of elected politicians, representatives from the financial sector, and representatives of the People's Republic of China appointed by the mainland. Beijing

Protesters attack a smart lamppost. Hong Kong, 2019. Photo: © Pierfrancesco Celada

City as Enemy

Protesters use umbrellas to shield themselves from surveillance cameras as well as from physical abuse by the police, such as water cannons and tear gas. Hong Kong, July 2019.
Photo: © AP Photo/Kin Cheung

Protesters pulling down a smart lamppost during a rally. Hong Kong, August 2019. Photo: © AP Photo/Kin Cheung

also decides on the head of government, and appointed Carrie Lam as Hong Kong's current Chief Executive. When Lam proposed a bill in February 2019 that would allow the extradition of Hong Kong citizens for trials in other states, including mainland China, protests started flaring up early last summer and then grew explosively. Protesters were incensed that the head of their government no longer wanted to protect her citizens from prison camps and social credit systems. Lam, and the smart city infrastructure she had pushed so hard for, became the target of the demonstrations.

The protesters dismantled several of the felled lampposts and posted the parts they found inside them online. They wanted to find out the resolution of the cameras, whether facial recognition technology had been installed, and whether the lampposts could read the RFID chips that are in the cards we all carry in our wallets, which would make it possible to identify passers-by. The issue is a sensitive one for people in Hong Kong, who are well aware that sensors are all around them. What they don't know is where these sensors are and what they are technically capable of. This has led to a distrust of the built environment.

Ticket machines and the turnstiles installed at entrances to the subway have come under suspicion. Many Hong Kong residents use the Octopus Card to pay for public transportation; this anonymous e-cash card is also accepted in selected shops and fast-food chains. But the fact that it can be reloaded using a credit card at the terminals located in many of the transport stations offers possibilities for deanonymization. Fearing that their movement patterns will be tracked, protesters refrain from using the card, instead preferring to use cash. Since the subway turnstiles are not equipped to handle cash, many of them have been intentionally damaged. Sometimes, the cash equivalent of the entrance fee is conscientiously left on top of the barriers by silent supporters of the protesters. This in turn has led to the curious sight of piles of cash piling up in the metro stations. The protests themselves rely on public transport, as they are organized according to the flash mob principle. In order to avoid security forces, entire demonstrations change locations via metro and unexpectedly reappear elsewhere. "Be water" is the name of this strategy, alluding to a famous slogan by Hong Kong's martial arts star Bruce Lee. This too, is a consequence of the ever-increasing surveillance possibilities in the digitized city.

Meanwhile, various myths are forming around smart city technologies. On the online forum Reddit, for example, it was claimed that the surveillance systems used in Hong Kong were the same as those used as in Xinjiang, where the Uighur territory stands under total surveillance, and where the existence of concentration camps has recently been revealed. The flood of speculation about the smart lampposts led the news agency Reuters to publish a fact check on them. However, their examination did not yield any clear results as to their ability to recognize faces or where the data is sent. The Shenzhen-based lamppost manufacturer stopped supplying them, allegedly due to personal online threats its employees had received.

In the meantime, however, people in Hong Kong are asking themselves where else sensors might still be installed. Many demonstrators are wrapping their smart cards and their new state-issued, chip-equipped electronic ID cards in aluminum foil. And during demonstrations, they switch their phones to flight mode, deactivate location tracking, Wi-Fi, and Bluetooth, or even remove their batteries. Others use disposable phones that do not contain any data, in the case of arrest. For this reason as well, some demonstrators deactivate their smartphone's facial recognition function. Police officers have been known to simply hold the phone in front of the arrested person's face to gain access to their device.

Protesters' concerns about others identifying or pulling data from their devices stems from uncertainty about what the state might do with that information in the future. Although there are still decades to go before the transition to mainland China's judicial system, many Hong Kong citizens already work in nearby China or with Chinese companies. Consequences could therefore arise at the next border crossing, or even at their workplaces.

Of course, Hong Kong has data protection laws. However, these include exceptions for the prosecution of offences. In addition, police forces have so often disregarded the rules pertaining to demonstrations that a violation of data protection rules is hardly unimaginable.

The clothes worn by the protesters, at least by the most dedicated ones, almost resembles a knight's armor. In addition to using umbrellas as a shield, many wear protective headgear and glasses or a gas mask, and are dressed all in black. The aim is not only physical protection, but also anonymity. They are anonymous, and they are legion. Laser pointers have become their „swords," wielded against surveillance and police cameras. During marches, they have pointed to hidden cameras installed in the buildings of mainland Chinese companies. This is what cyberpunk looks like, agreed William Gibson, the science fiction writer who coined the term, in a recent Twitter conversation that showed protesters fighting police with laser pointers.[02]

A central feature of the protests in Hong Kong is the simultaneity of the digital and the physical. It is the first Internet of Things battle in an environment where bits and atoms have merged. A good example of this is the constant filming of street battles. Hong Kong's demonstrations are also performances that harness the global publicity of the digitized public space. This is one of the reasons why fire plays such an important role. Not necessarily because of its destructive power, but because a burning Molotov cocktail draws online attention. It is also apparent that many Hong Kong protesters are addressing the West in their protests. They publish content on digital platforms used in the West, such as Twitter, which is otherwise not very popular in Hong Kong itself. Unlike mainland China, where Facebook and Google are blocked, Hong Kong is not behind the Great Firewall. The archaic nature of some of the protesters' "weapon systems" is also revealed when one con-

> People in Hong Kong are well aware that sensors are all around them. What they don't know is where these sensors are and what they are technically capable of.

Even your ears will be evidence to arrest you.

We also use spray paint to blind the cameras.

Two video stills from a WSJ video report show counter-strategies by protesters in Hong Kong against surveillance technologies. 2019. © Wall Street Journal

In 2014, thousands of Post-It notes scribbled with messages were left on the walls of the Legislative Council in Hong Kong (an action referred to as the "Lennon Wall"). During the 2019 protests, new Lennon Walls appeared in numerous locations across Hong Kong, particularly in subway stations.

siders that all of the components needed to build a catapult, for example, can be ordered online without appearing conspicuous to the authorities.

Essentially, the protests in Hong Kong reveal two strategies to cope with technology. One is post-digital, and ranges from the destruction of metro hubs, to the coordination of demonstration routes by means of widely shared hand signals, to the so-called Lennon Walls—walls at public hubs covered in Post-Its full of news, a kind of bulletin board or newsfeed made of paper.

The counter-strategy is the creation of self-controlled sovereign digital territories. For instance, a popular technological tool that emerged early on in the protests was a crowd-sourced map of the city with a live view of all police movements. Now separate spaces have also been created where people share the latest news. Many demonstrators use Telegram groups to keep up to date. Not only does this messaging app bypass the publicly searchable internet, it also allows for closed groups with administrator controls. Apps such as Bridgefy, Twitch, and FireChat go even further by linking the phones of app users to create so-called mesh nets, information networks that are beyond state control because they work independently of the internet. Apps like these forward messages from sender to receiver via Bluetooth networked devices, without the need for a network-based connection. So even shutting down the internet would be of no avail for the state in this case.

But the essential digital tool for the protesters has become the bulletin board LIHKG. Bulletin boards are digital message platforms where users can easily post texts and images. LIHKG is special in that only users with a Hong Kong IP address or an email address from a Hong Kong university can register with it. This prevents mass infiltration by trolls of the so-called 50 Cent Army, paid for by China, who try to influence online discussions. In addition,

most contributions are written in Cantonese, the main language used in Hong Kong, and not Mandarin, the dominant language used by the trolls from mainland China. LIHKG is therefore considered a safe environment where Hong Kong residents can exchange ideas. As simple as the forum is, it enables a kind of crowd intelligence. This is where demonstration routes, changes of direction, and activities are decided. Registered users can post suggestions anonymously, and if they receive enough upvotes, the posts will appear on the front page of the bulletin board. But LIHKG also functions as an armory of the resistance. For example, personal data for doxxing attacks on pro-Chinese activists and security forces are collected here. Thousands of times in recent months, personal details about opponents and information that could be used to discredit them have been published on the bulletin board. LIHKG also collects money for costly measures: this is how the full-page "Open Letter" was funded, which protesters in Hong Kong had published in numerous leading Western newspapers. LIHKG thus helps to coordinate a movement that tries to function without a leader. With LIHKG, a separate, intelligently acting urban online space has therefore emerged from concerns about the many possibilities of internet misuse and of smart city infrastructures implemented in the urban space. It is an autonomous infosphere that belongs to its inhabitants: a real smart city, born from the fight against the official smart city.

01 Hong Kong Smart City Blueprint, "Mission," accessed March 11, 2020, www.smartcity.gov.hk.
02 William Gibson (@GreatDismal), "If it's not, what is?" Twitter, August 1, 2019, 10:34 a.m., accessed March 11, 2020, twitter.com/GreatDismal/status/1156845729748377601.

A Political Forum for a Digital Public

LUDGER HOVESTADT IN CONVERSATION
WITH ARNO BRANDLHUBER

What is the agency and influence of global technology companies that are currently massively investing in real estate and urban planning? Does this pose an even greater challenge to the architect's role as innovator and visionary than the commodification of the city and rural areas in the past decades? What approaches can foster the self-empowerment of digital citizens?

As part of his research and design project station+, Arno Brandlhuber, Professor of Design and Architecture, spoke with Ludger Hovestadt, Professor of Architecture and CAAD. Both teach at the Department of Architecture at ETH Zurich.

ARNO BRANDLHUBER: *I would like to start with a quote of yours. During a summit on the future of the Swiss Federal Institute of Technology Zurich (ETH) you said: "Most of our international competitors in education are companies. They are smart, rich, fast, and flexible—they are aggressive. If we play their game, as a democratic institution we can only lose."*[01] *Who are these competitors, and what role do they play in the discussion on innovation?*

LUDGER HOVESTADT: As an architect working in the field of artificial intelligence—teaching and researching at a public, state-funded university—the current discussion about the role and task of an institution like ours causes me great concern. It always revolves around the question: what is the subject of our research and how can we adjust it in order to get ahead of the field? The

Investment volume in research and development by companies compared to the total budget of universities.
Amounts in billion US dollars (fiscal year 2017).

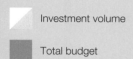

Investment volume

Total budget

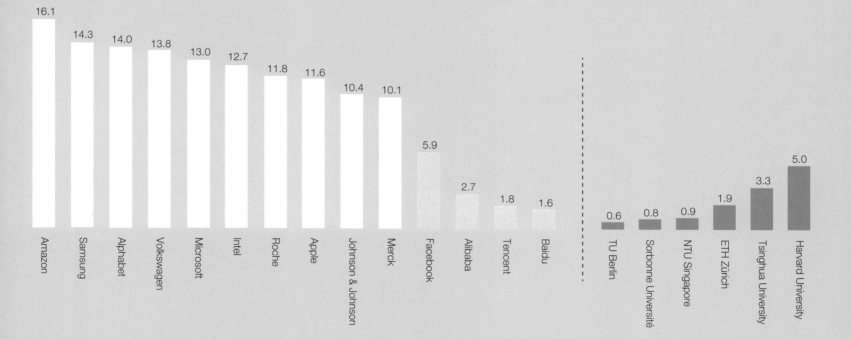

The top ten companies worldwide in terms of investment volume.

Facebook ranks 22nd, with Chinese tech giants Baidu, Alibaba, and Tencent further down the line.

Sources: Investment volume according to PwC Strategy&: *The 2018 Global Innovation 1000 Study.*
Total university budgets according to official figures from the respective universities.

annual budget of ETH Zurich is about 1.8 billion Swiss francs, or approximately 1.65 billion euros.[02] But this is nothing compared to what companies like Alphabet or Amazon are investing in research and design. If we want to continue researching and investing in areas such as artificial intelligence, we need to look at these figures. Even inside the country, investments by tech companies are much higher than ETH's overall budget, which is not a lot when compared to Switzerland's gross domestic product of around 670 billion Swiss francs in 2017. This imbalance needs to be acknowledged. That's one of the reasons we are discussing economics and fighting for every million, even though we should actually be discussing politics if we want to achieve something on a global level.

AB: *When Switzerland was established in its present form in 1848, it was decided to invest one third of the budget in the ETH because technology and the natural sciences were considered as being "neutral." Given the shift in power you described, from educational institutions to private companies: instead of lamenting the brain drain, shouldn't this development be seen as an opportunity to bring politically literate people into the industry, or to integrate industry into the institutions?*
LH: There is growing interest and investment in new private educational institutions, such as the Singularity University founded in Silicon Valley, which is financed by companies such as Google, Nokia, Autodesk, and others. These institutions don't have professors, but are run with artificial intelligence. In terms of optimization they are far ahead of us, but they lack any degree of reflection. Students learn the technology, but they

never reflect on what they are doing. It's similar to the military, where orders are followed without question. If we want to change this lack of self-criticism, we have to "civilize" technology, meaning we have to understand and integrate it into our civil society. Civilization means nothing other than educating people. While the United States and China are currently at the helm of AI, Europe could take on an intermediary position, linking private tech companies (in the US) with centralized state governments (like China). This could be a good role because of our European history and culture. It's also another reason why we must acknowledge the scale of the developments we are talking about and realize that we are at a turning point comparable to the Copernican turn.

AB: *For a number of years now, we have been witnessing the worldwide phenomenon that global tech companies, which previously made their money with business models based on the exploitation of data, are now putting their capital into urban planning; the city is a new source of data and capital for them. Does the civilizing process you mentioned indicate a shift of responsibility back from private enterprise into public hands?*
LH: Only if we don't assume that it's a technical issue, but understand the intellectual challenge as such. People who are educated on the topic will begin to speak and act politically. This means you have to move beyond the economic aspects of the discussion. I see the main task as being to build a political forum, a platform or institution in which people can participate and reach out to a wider audience, in order to domesticate and civilize alienating technologies.

Otherwise, only private companies like Google will dominate the discourse, because they already have the agency to do so and know this world better anyway. The only way we can avoid being manipulated by these technologies and companies is by anticipating their tricks, which means we need to increase our digital literacy.

AB: *How can we create a common ground in order to civilize technology, and how should this political forum be structured? What role could architects play in this context?*
LH: Since architects and urban planners have a profound knowledge of the public, private, and organizational aspects, they have the necessary tools to tackle spatial problems. However, they have no access to the tools of artificial intelligence. But this access must not be left only to specialists; it has to be developed by people all over the world—we must democratize it. To stabilize the use of digital space, we need a kind of global platform that defines rules on how to negotiate conflicts that may arise in this digital realm. And when these conflicts cannot be resolved among ourselves, we need a globally recognized institution such as the United Nations. We need to operate in an environment that is based on rules, which is not the case at present.

AB: *You propose a kind of "digital citizenship" as part of this new order. How would you define the civilization that comes with it? Would it still be based on nation states?*
LH: I think there is no way around the traditional forms of territorialized citizenship. But I also think there should be another, digital level—namely digital

We need a kind of global platform that defines rules on how to negotiate conflicts that may arise in the digital realm. And when these conflicts cannot be resolved, we need a globally recognized institution such as the United Nations.

citizenship. By this I don't mean owning a digital passport or digitizing the infrastructure and bureaucracy, but rather protecting the integrity of your online persona. Because the main reason for legal problems in the virtual world is the fact that no one—no state or authority—is protecting you in that respect. As a single digital person, I am powerless at the global level. This is why we need to develop reliable systems and rules, and we need institutions that can enforce the law at the international level.

AB: *Wouldn't it require complete transparency in order to regulate identity on a global scale? In other words, a counter-model to the darknet, which operates beyond regulation or jurisdiction: a "whitenet" where transparency is guaranteed? Or could this idea be implemented within the existing infrastructure?*
LH: That would be too simple, too much of a black-and-white view of things—which does not exist in architecture, urban planning, politics, or questions of citizen-

ship. If we look at our current situation, the internet is already very transparent for companies and states—all our activities are recorded. However, it is far from transparent for users and we can only hope that we are treated fairly when it comes to surveillance. If you don't want this transparency, the darknet offers you an option, which is also outside of all regulatory constraints. Our task, however, is to define sets of rules, standards, and principles that are subject to public control and thus provide security, but at the same time allow for control by the individual.

AB: *You are addressing a structural problem. Who should set these standards? Is that why you are connecting the idea of digital integrity with the nation state, especially with Switzerland?*
LH: Switzerland could provide the right framework for thinking about something like digital citizenship. The country stands for values such as neutrality and integrity. And the Swiss are very skilled at negotiating and keeping things in balance. There are many international institutions in Geneva and Zurich. People would be more likely to trust Switzerland to protect them through a democratic setup rather than they would a private company. In my view, it would be a good opportunity to use and build on the existing image of Switzerland in order to establish a global discourse and knowledge about artificial intelligence and related topics.

AB: *How would the creation of such digital citizenship be financed?*
LH: The idea is that people, no matter where they come from, would pay a reasonable amount of money for their

new digital citizenship; it could be a monthly payment, like a tax. With these revenues, not only could the rights of digital citizens be protected, but a global digital civilization could be built. I'm certain that it would be cheaper to do this not in the private sector, but either as part of the UN or as a newly established forum.

AB: *Would this be a new form of community as well?*
LH: No, digital Swiss citizens would not be a community. The idea of community was corrupted by platform capitalism. It would simply be a group of people who care about cultivating the digital planet, and who asks the question: how do we want to manage the changes we are facing—intellectually, economically, legally? Digital citizenship should be an act of domestication of the digital planet. It would be a kind of voluntary constitution that we would have to negotiate and implement on a global scale. Somebody has to do it!

01 "ETH plus, 100+ and the Missing Political Profile of ETH," letter to the professorship of ETH Zurich in response to the ETH Summit in Lucerne, November 17, 2017. The document is available to the editorial staff, but is not publicly accessible or viewable.
02 *Annual Report 2018*, ETH Zurich, accessed September 3, 2019, ethz.ch/en/the-eth-zurich/information-material/annual-report.html.

BAT vs. GAFA

BAIDU

DuerOS
Baidu Shopping
Baidu Wangpan
Baidu Maps
Baidu
Baidu Wallet
Baidu Mobile Assistant
Baidu Duer
Baidu Music
Baidu Browser
Raven Tech
Baidu Raven
xPerception
Hao123
iQiyi

TENCENT

Tencent Cloud
Tencent Maps
Soguo
WeChat Pay
QQ Wallet
Tenpay
Tencent MyApp
Tingting
QQ
WeChat
QQ Games
Tencent Games
Qzone
Tencent Weibo
QQmail
Foxmail
Xiaowei
QQ Browser
QQLive
Tencent Video
Tencent AI Lab
Tencent YouTu Lab
Tencent Pictures
Tencent Music
QQ Music
KuGou
KuWo

ALIBABA

AliOS
Tmall
Taobao
Alibaba Cloud
Shenma
PP Assistant
Tmall Genie
Dingtalk
AliGenie
Xiami Music
YouKu
Ciaoniao
AutoNavi
Amap
Ant Financial
Alipay
Alibaba Pictures
AliHealth
AliSports
South China Morning Post
Ele.me
UCWeb
UC Browser
Alibaba.com

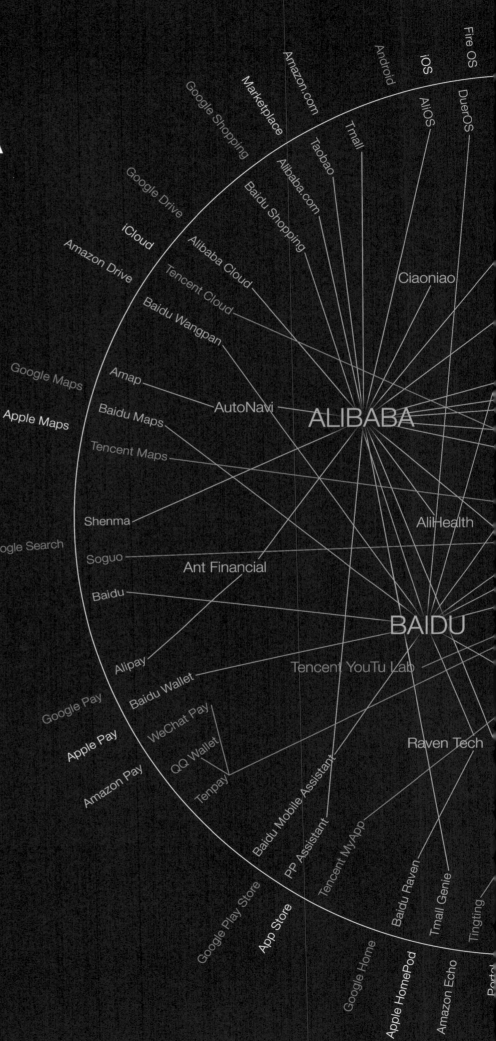

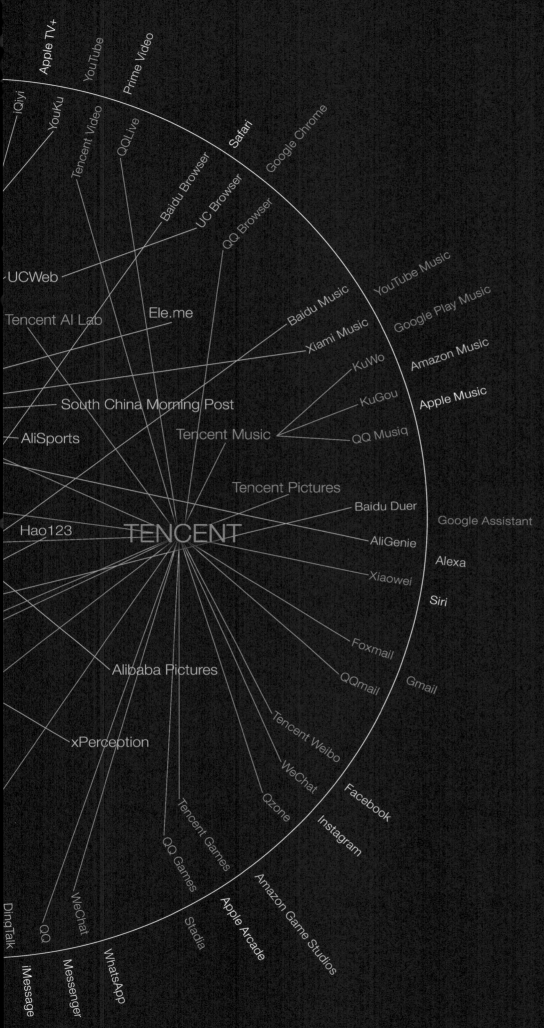

ALPHABET

Android
Google Shopping
Google Drive
Google Maps
Google Search
Google Pay
Google Play Store
Google Home
Stadia
Gmail
Google Assistant
Google Play Music
YouTube Music
Google Chrome
YouTube

APPLE

iOS
iCloud
Apple Maps
Apple Pay
App Store
Apple HomePod
iMessage
Apple Arcade
Siri
Apple Music
Safari
Apple TV+

FACEBOOK

Marketplace
Portal
Messenger
Whatsapp
Instagram
Facebook

AMAZON

Fire OS
Amazon.com
Amazon Drive
Amazon Pay
Amazon Echo
Amazon Game Studios
Amazon Music
Prime Video
Alexa

Three of China's most valuable tech companies—Baidu, Alibaba, and Tencent (BAT)—and their subsidiaries in comparison with the US technology giants Alphabet (formerly Google; Alphabet has served since 2011 as the parent company of Google and its subsidiaries), Apple, Facebook, and Amazon—also known by the acronym GAFA.

An Update on *The Stack*

"The whole age of computer has made it where nobody knows exactly what's going on."

BENJAMIN H. BRATTON

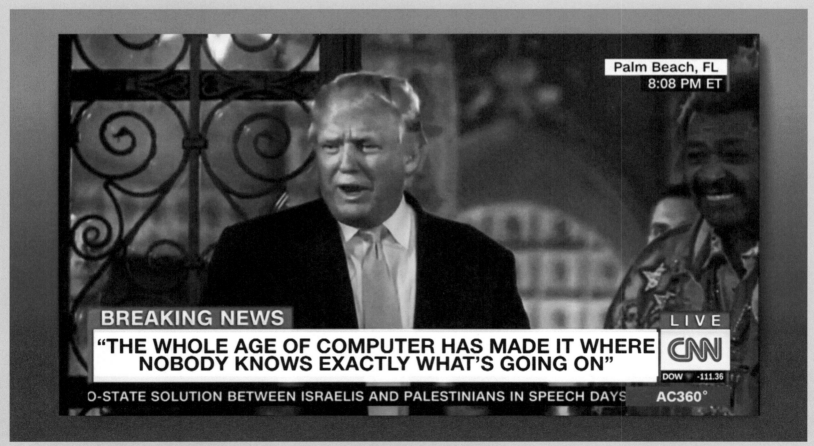

Still from an interview with US President Donald Trump, broadcast on CNN on December 29, 2016.

In the summer of 2016, in the period after the Brexit vote and before Trump's election, I wrote, "In the exact spot where a viable future should be, something insufferably backwards fills it in. A psychotic simulation of mediaeval geopolitics burning as bright as creepy clown hair." Or as Donald Trump put it, "The whole age of the computer has made it where nobody knows exactly what's going on."[01]

The rise of ethnonationalist and neotraditionalist populism is a global phenomenon with global causes. From Manila to Milwaukee, we see the same demographic voting patterns of urban, highly educated cosmopolitans vs. rural, less educated, monocultural nationalists and/or national monoculturalists. Even as globalization has de-linked sovereignty from geography in uneven ways, we try to deal with this phenomenon one eighteenth century jurisdiction at a time.

As idiocratic global politics put so many things in question, including the future and design futures, it does not however change the reality of the system-scale problems that we face. While there are many reasons to hold in suspicion those whose main entitlement is to stand earnestly against the real, we may do the same for those whose primary alibi is simple futurism. Among the main reasons for this is that the conventional definition of the future—in the means of design thinking—is 10 to 50 years from now. The year 2050, for example, is not the future. We are already designing 2050 today and doing so rather poorly for the most part. The alternative alibi, of presentism—that addressing the "real world" requires the most myopic forms of stakeholder utilitarianism only, without further abstraction—is perhaps precisely what makes the deferral into weak futures or pasts possible in the first place.

That said, it's certain that having the time to think long-term is increasingly a privilege. It is not that I criticize the need of addressing immediate problems, but doing so doesn't always add up to what it wants to add up to. Presentism and shallow futurism conspire to validate an intuitive sense of cause and effect bound within an autobiographical tempo of life and death and wish fulfilment. Against the present moment, the job remains still towards our successive generations. In contrast with the smugness of human-centered design, we should presume that subjective user experiences of cause and effect are necessarily flawed, and insufficient. The Copernican turn in design that I would champion focuses on intelligence as an emergent effective matter, and of material technologies. The world itself is a model open to design and designation, not by false mastery, but because our planet uses humans and other things to know itself and to remake itself. We are the medium, not the message.

The Stack

I will introduce a few ideas that add on to my book *The Stack: On Software and Sovereignty*, from 2016. The book makes two key arguments: one is that what we call planetary scale computation has both distorted and deformed traditional Westphalian logics of political geography, and in doing so, has created new territories in its own image. Two, that these various genres of planetary scale computation—such as smart grids, cloud platforms, mobile apps, smart cities, internet of things—can be seen as forming a kind of coherent whole. These technologies align layer by layer into something like a vast, incomplete, pervasive, irregular, accidental megastructure called the Stack that is both a computational apparatus and a new governing architecture. Within the Stack, sovereignty is contested and produced at each one of the layers, and not always in ways that are recognizably political. How sovereignty is created by each layer of the Stack—Earth, Cloud, City, Address, Interface, User—plays out quite differently.

The Earth layer is mostly about energy and mineral flows, and about the ways in which energy infrastructures determine social relations. The primary problems of sovereignty at the Earth layer largely have to do with the fact that the necessary structures of actors and plural agencies that would be necessary for massive carbon remediation, carbon taxation, carbon pricing, the rewilding of landscapes, etc., don't exist. We have the technologies but we don't have the institutions to deploy them.

The Stack

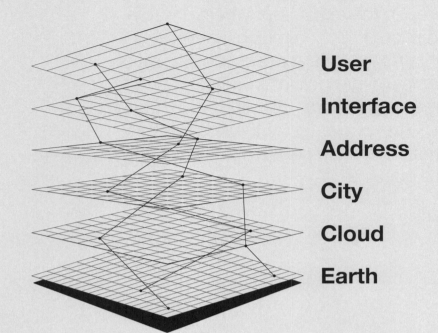

User

Interface

Address

City

Cloud

Earth

A program analyzes the facial expressions of the
exhibition visitors and then searches its constantly growing
image archive for photographs of faces
with similar expression patterns.

Moritz Wehrmann: *Face to Face – Interface* 2016, 28 monitors,
server, camera, 320 × 520 × 47 cm. Installation view,
at the exhibition *+ultra, gestaltung schafft wissen (design
creates knowledge)*, Martin-Gropius-Bau, Berlin, 2016–17
© Moritz Wehrmann

The Cloud layer is where cloud computing spurs various platform economies creating virtual geographies in its own image, sometimes absorbing traditional core functions of the state, and vice versa, where states evolve into cloud platforms. Cities forming vast discontiguous networks as they weave their borders into enclaves, exclaves, and escape routes.

The City layer is where diverse practices are played out in multiple and overlapping assemblages of everyday life. It is where metropolitan singularities and networks of quasi-sovereign city-states hold recursive relationships to their own national host territories. The city may be the capital of a territory, or the territory may be its extended jurisdiction. The countryside, as Rem Koolhaas puts it, is where the cloud actually lives: in data centers, in the logistics archipelagos, and in other megastructures, which form an urbanism of a different sort.

At the Address layer, we have multiple ontologies of nomination and classification, and mutual accountability compete for things that can be known or unknown. For an entity to participate in the broader stack architecture, it must be known to the entity. It must be enumerated and named by an address. For ubiquitous computing and an internet of things, almost everything is included in a landscape of addressable objects. Ultimately, the scale and complexity of the landscape can exceed the limits of human control or knowledge. Increasingly we see a bifurcation of different addressing systems, a forking of network ontologies.

The Interface layer is where a user makes sense of the rest. It's how one part of one system sees the others. It's where governance and bio-semiotics collaborate. While the form of these interfacial regimes become more standardized, the content is untethered from the real on behalf of motivations of self-reinforcing micro-mythologies. It is where often dangerously symbolic relations are freely substituted for causal ones. Interfaces are not only something users look through at the world, it is also the layer through which the world looks at itself.

The fragility of agency, and the boundaries between agents, are drawn at the User layer, including, but not limited to, the status of humans. Individuation, collectivization, encapsulation, prosthetization, and the polyphony of imaginaries for AI and evolutionary robotics may be trained here; so does the standardization of corporeal cultures that are projected onto a common virtualization. Here, we may also see the proliferation of new co-agencies that are

The Stack is both a computational apparatus and a new governing architecture. Within the Stack, sovereignty is contested and produced at each one of the layers, and not always in ways that are recognizably political.

unaccountable by industrial-era political economic theory, and where contestations and identity are sometimes fought one idea at a time.

Users both human and non-human populate this tangled apparatus, this accidental megastructure we call the Stack. There is no one layer where the interplay of software and sovereignty is more truly and properly located, radiating out from there. Sovereignty is contested and produced at each layer and not only in ways that are recognizably "political." This multiplies the complexity of mapping, because the fundamental problems of governance—such as replication, recursion, and enforcement—are now more widespread. Instead of thinking of these new territories as something developing in opposition to the Westphalian states, we see that the states are themselves producing new territories. The state is actively re-spatialized as a stack system, whose relative continuity may span from hard enclosures within a bounded territorial domain to atmospheric encapsulations that happen through informational securitization and monetization.

Hemispheric stacks

What we see emerging here is not one global stack, but a mitosis of the stack genera into a regime of multipolar hemispherical stacks in which the sovereign steerage of states, even if unbounded by Westphalian borders, is paramount. Three of the most clearly drawn multipolar hemispherical stacks are recognizable as those of China (called the BAT stack: standing for Baidu, Alibaba, and Tencent), the Euro-American stack (defined by GAFA: Google, Amazon, Facebook, Apple) including not only Europe and North America, but also Australia, New Zealand, and Israel for example; and finally, the Russian stack, also including the CIS countries. The Russian stack doesn't have a nice acronym like the other two, but it's defined by Mail.ru, Yandex, VK, and Telegram. Then of course there are also others, like the Latin American, the African, the Middle Eastern, and the Japanese stack. Clearly nationalism in linguistic homology plays a role here, but it doesn't explain the whole picture alone.

In the Euro-American stack, recent scandals related to data privacy breaches and misuse, both real and imagined, have amplified calls to take our data out of the hands of opaque global corporations and to make it more public. "Public" of course could mean a lot of different things. "Take back our data!" Yes, we're supportive of this, but ultimately who do we mean by we? And what is this data? These questions may be the start of a rather important transformation in the understanding of the role of algorithmic systems as governing mechanisms, but they also open up much more difficult questions than some of our early answers about the Stack are capable of addressing. First of all, data is not like a physical resource. You don't gather data like you pick strawberries. The act of modelling data produces data in the first place, and so in many cases, the most interesting data of course is the derivative data that is produced, not the raw data. There is a lot to discuss here about what models for an algorithmic governance we should constitute and pursue. There aren't simple answers to this, and I don't propose them. Concerns about the ownership of data are valid and real. They are born out of a long overdue recognition that cloud platforms have absorbed many functions of modern states and that states themselves are co-evolving. The implications for politics and geopolitics are profound to say the least, but the conversation to date has failed to directly address what this "new normal" really means. In order to get there, we need to rethink some basic assumptions. Instead of re-imposing old political maps directly onto platforms, we need to measure what has shifted to imagine and design what comes next, including new boundaries of public and private in a platform.

In Europe, many people are now debating the terms of inclusion or exclusion in a Euro-American stack and what in fact those norms of inclusion may be. General Data Protection Regulation (GDPR) laws are the ones that would identify and codify the legal status of EU data, drawing lines from data center to data center regardless of where those are located. The EU digital single market, including right of erasure, pseudonymization, data portability, etc., all quite sensible, may in time take on a gravity similar to that which was once afforded to the Euro and the ECM. But while on this side of the Atlantic it might seem that all of this is being fought in response to American dictates, on the other side, in North America, serious policy discussions were of course scrapped in favor of

Concerns about the ownership of data are valid and real. They are born out of a long overdue recognition that cloud platforms have absorbed many functions of modern states and that states themselves are co-evolving.

telecom companies. Some programs that fight at the forefront of the "take back our data movement"—which to be clear I am supportive of—thematize their work in terms of making data more public, arguing that citizens are the core actors. "Citizens' data for citizens," but citizens of what? Do the boundaries of citizenship align well to the boundary of data flows? Given the benefits of mobility and the controversies of migration, why should we refortify the legal border between citizen and non-citizen as the basic condition of such rights and responsibilities? At any moment, cities are full of non-citizens and non-residents, and so the model of how algorithmic governance may work needs to include them too in order to recognize their access to infrastructure, and vice versa.

In the US and Canada, after all the Facebook scandals, the winds now blow for more state oversight of private cloud platforms to ensure that the information carried is not biased or socially malicious. This is not such a dumb idea, but there is a much longer and more complicated discussion behind algorithmic governance, and, for what I have seen so far, there is a clear sign of a myopically Western perspective: a rush to measure the pros and cons of state oversight of the Euro-American stack as if the Chinese stack were not available as a relevant comparison.

The Chinese stack

The Chinese stack is not only a system that is composed of different platforms, it is also increasingly the means by which this data structure is kept protected from other platforms, tools, and applications that are not part of its prescribed territory. So, for example, Skype is blocked in China, LinkedIn is blocked in Russia, and you can't buy Huawei or Xiaomi phones in the US. These are the ways in which hemispherical stacks are increasingly being weaponized.

On one hand, there are the projects of social credit, both real and imagined, which are China's way of developing a credit score system, which includes data on your positive or negative participa-

Chinese communist party apps, which are evaluated by the government, available in the Chinese app store.

tion within society, rating content that you and your friends post online that may be critical of the party and which might drive your score down. And then there is the emergence of QR codes and facial recognition, which are essential features of the urban-scale structure of these kinds of systems; a kind of evolutionary response on the behalf of the synthetic environment of the city to the presence of a new species: that of the camera. There is a conversation going on between the app and this coded surface that doesn't require us to be a part of. I think there is something rather profound in that kind of dynamic: the city itself is very clearly instrumentalized as one of the key mediums of the BAT stack. Not only what happens in the glowing glass rectangle of the mobile phone, but a real technical evolutionary dynamic towards a distributed form of urban AI. Anyone who would unproblematically recommend the Full Court nationalization of stack systems and data systems should spend a little bit of time perusing the various party apps that you can get in the Chinese app stores—of which there are hundreds, and which give you daily homilies of dedication reminding you to do things that would be beneficial to the performance of your dutiful citizenship.

The Chinese stack is not just about end-user applications, but also about logistics and material production. It is about the global movement of objects and the automation of those assemblages that move the objects around the world. One of the things that makes this stack particularly interesting is the ways in which it operates at the environmental and urban scale.

For example, this speculative megastructure called the Belt and Road Initiative, which is kind of like Superstudio's Continuous Monument: both real and unreal at the same time. The Belt and Road Initiative is an enormous interlocking network of networks facilitating the flow of goods between China and Eastern Africa, Russia, and Europe, like a huge new Silk Road. If you take all of these different ports and roads as a single meta-machine, it would be the biggest work of design happening to date. A lot of the roads and workways would go through former Soviet republics like Turkmenistan, Tajikistan, and Kazakhstan, producing a huge shift within Eurasian geopolitics. China's relationship with India is also at stake, India being the country that is most against the Belt and Road Initiative, partially because China is making so much investment in Pakistan. Regardless of this, China still includes India as being part of the Belt and Road Initiative because it allows them to add another billion participants to the story. Ultimately, the Belt and Road doesn't exist. It is a narrative about a hyperstitional infrastructure. There is this port and that road, and if you imagine them all as one big machine then it is a giant structure, and of course this narrative of the mega-infrastructure mobilizes capitalization, mobilizes participation and investment. It is state-scale speculative design at infrastructural scale. In many respects it has become a convention to think about the futures of these systems in a stack-level Cold War between the GAFA and the BAT stack—but of course, it is not all that simple.

The Russian stack

Russia, of course, has its own different version of this: its own speculative megastructures. There are a lot of rhetorics around the Russian stack that seem to be drawn around issues of contamination, of keeping things in and out, like for immunological models. What we are beginning to see in Russia is a kind of retroactive

Superstudio: *The Continuous Monument: On the Rocky Coast*, 1969, collage, 47 × 46 cm.
Courtesy of Museum of Modern Art (MoMA), New York. Donation by the Howard Gilman Foundation.

firewall. But while China circumscribed its barrier locations within its Westphalian borders and produced very specific strategic checkpoints by which the packet inspection works well, Russia's attempt to do this retroactively has not had a lot of success.

For example, Russia tried to shut down Telegram, the dominant messaging app in Russia by far. Only after it moved out of the country did the Russian federal government try to shut it down. Telegram then moved their location from Google service to Amazon service, but meanwhile the government was trying to shut down those servers—accidentally also shutting down Google Docs structures that the whole country works on. Pavel Durov, the CEO of Telegram, who knows how to play the game of Russian social media, took up the challenge and started the famous social media campaign where people threw paper airplanes out the windows. Then something interesting happened: people in Russia taught each other how to use VPNs—the use of VPNs in Russia quadrupled in about two weeks.

Facebook

Today, many bad metaphors are crashing down around Facebook, and perhaps the worst one is that of community. Community is not what Facebook does, nor are actual communities always so great in the first place, especially as idealized models for larger social forms. Communities can be quite lovely, but they can also be petty, and small, and normalizing. Facebook is a private company and a public utility with neither the accountability nor the sovereignty to execute its own policy, it nevertheless tries to do so in a de facto way in multiple jurisdictions. Its function as an amplification machine for idiotic populism is obvious. At the same time, scapegoating is also a way of forestalling the more difficult discussions about what painful changes are necessary. I think the original sin of Facebook was designing a social network with the individual as the fundamental unit of analysis and composition. The presentation of the self as the lens for the interactions that we make, see, and perform has led directly to the echoing cascade of recursive narcissism and apophenia that we find there today. However, I find it ludicrous for the popular press to sound the alarm on how the social media landscape creates narrow worldviews and echo chambers filled with moral panic feedback loops. That is to say quit Facebook and cancel your account, but it also means to quit the tabloid politics, the hate clicking, and the soft-focus conspiracy theories.

Many kinds of social good require data in order to work, health data being one example. It is not only about privacy but also about communalization. It is not just about surveillance, it is also about the responsibility of the archive.

Besides, the internet as a whole is not just about social media. Social media is the thing we see ourselves reflected in, but most of the internet is not about us, so we should not fool ourselves into thinking that by deleting one's account we are also removing the platform's operations, impacts, protections, and privileges.

For networks like Facebook, the problem is not only that they do bad stuff but that they take up the place where the good stuff should happen. Their harm is not only what they cause but also what they prevent. There are other ways of thinking about big data beyond the premature optimization of existing interfaces and systems. Many kinds of social good require data in order to work, health data being the most obvious example. It is not only about privacy but also about communalization. It is not just about surveillance, it is also about the responsibility of the archive. Ultimately, what is at stake is the governance, not just of data itself, but of the value that the information signifies.

Reterritorialization

Currently, there is an ongoing reterritorialization of bounded geographic hemispheres, which are not necessarily the same as the Westphalian borders, but more like remodeled quasi-sovereign interlocking platforms. Their borders are defined by the circumscription of the data that each of these stacks is able to sense. The tendency of any complex system at this level is to attempt to reduce reality to the level of complexity that the control system is capable of thinking with. So, almost inevitably, each of these hemispherical stacks as a model system becomes based upon a certain type of Potemkin ontology, a way in which it believes the world to work through its premises regardless of how fragile they in fact may be. Assuming that the arcs of human migration are unstoppable, we

The Stack

Estonia is the first country to offer e-Residency, which allows foreigners to register a virtual residence and start a business online.

In 2017, US President Donald Trump had eight prototypes built for the border wall between the USA and Mexico. The artist collective MAGA launched a petition to preserve the prototypes as a national monument to the current sociopolitical state.

© MAGA/Bjarni Grimsson.

recognize that borders don't only split but, like all interfaces, they have a generative function as well. Which designs on interiorization versus exteriorization matter most for the future of political geography?

Currently, we observe both secessionist withdrawal into traditional territories and the consolidation of much larger hemispherical domains. We see the continuing expansions of de facto sovereignties of cloud platforms, as well as the reformation of traditional states into regional platforms. Estonia's social democratic models of algorithmic governance or e-residence program may be interesting, not because they allow you to pay taxes in a Baltic state that you've never been to, but because they suggest that there is no imperative link between the distributed provision of state social services and legal state jurisdictions. The geographic walls and fences that separate citizens from non-citizens become taller and wider as they become less and less necessary. These are fundamental questions one must address, for example, when discussing any universal basic income program. In fact, there is a real danger that as wealthy jurisdictions will start to offer universal basic income, the prophylactic divisions between who is in and who is out will become more stark, portending transgenerational partitions of tiered levels of citizenship, like in Italy, where the Five Star Movement proposed its own version of universal basic income based on an "Italians first" logic. Instead of alleviating the extreme disparities of wealth, universal basic income, if misapplied as welfare chauvinism, may lock them in or even accelerate them.

That said, what some call techno-optimism, I think, is rightly criticized for its breathlessly positive investments of faith in quick technological fixes to complex conditions and painful histories. The amalgamation of states' vertical integration in the cloud's power is steering toward fundamentalist sovereignties in a narrowing of the political discourse. But this outcome is not inevitable. Its vision of how things work is inaccurate and vulnerable. It holds that internal relations of a social body precede in time and value any external or transitive relation that the polity may enter into in some subsequent place. Instead, we should see the productive function of membranes to give shape and form to a new poly-polarity of cultures that are always in motion. In this way we would spend less time attending to an overdetermined placefulness than to the trophic cascades of discontiguous polities located not in one location at a time but across sites and situations. This reactionary moment also stems from an inability of the West to account for the entropic forces that

> It holds that internal relations of a social body precede in time and value any external or transitive relation that the polity may enter into in some subsequent place. Instead, we should see the productive function of membranes to give shape and form to a new poly-polarity of cultures that are always in motion.

it helped to set in motion, but which have now far less need of its privileged steerage.

Provincializing the West

What is coming next may be horrible, authoritarian, catastrophic, or it may be far better than what we have now, but it will not necessarily be Western in character, and it may decisively unlink universalism from its European vernaculars. "Provincializing Europe," to quote Dipesh Chakrabarty[02], is something the left can find as difficult to fathom as the right, though for different reasons. I suspect, and hope, that the current wave of consolidation around legacy territories is a transitional interruption of the longer arc towards truly planetary polities, and that whatever form we take as humans, we should always remain an unapologetically migratory species. Territories defined by very recent occupation, geologically speaking, can always be fortified, but to what end?

Recently, I spoke to someone who is involved in an ongoing project of theorizing the Anthropocene and I was alarmed by some of the inverse conclusions that were in fact taken for granted. He repeated quite joyfully that the root causes of our ethical and ecological malaise were opaque, mystical, planetary, hyper-objects and conspiratorial hyper-processes. For him, the work of art and design under such circumstances is to re-render these sprawling systems at a phenomenologically intuitive human scale so to rebind ecology not only with socio-historical time, but even with psychological time. "This is what localism means," he said. The purpose of doing so is not only that people can understand them, but also that their abominably inhuman scope can be reformed. We can heal the anthropogenic predicament by descaling its unnatural complexities back to graspable, proximate, organic norms. This approach is symmetrically opposite to the one I would suggest. In my opinion, an approach that may provide some uncannily practical paths out of the Anthropocene is absolutely not one in which the vast, impersonal, temporal, and spatial scale of global systems is brought down to intuitive, neurological, and emotional comfort zones. To think and design in other ways and at other scales is not only theoretically defensible, it is a necessity. Design must be scaled to the scope of the real, not down-sampled to the digestible.

The Anthropocene

Anthropogony is the study of human origins, of how something that was not quite human becomes human. It considers what enables and curtails us today such as tool making, prehensile grasp, the development of the prefrontal cortex, the ability of abstraction, figuration, war, mastering fire, culinary chemistry, plastics, metals, agricultural urbanism, etc. Given that Darwinian biology and Huttonian geology are such new perspectives, we may say that scientific anthropogony is only recently possible. Human emergence was and is still considered through the distorting lens of various folklores and creation myths, both sacred and secular. When Hegel was binding the history of the world to the history of European national self-identity, it was assumed among his public that the age of the planet could be measured in only a few millennia. The means by which we get outside our prejudicial intuitions about how the world works may also be the very means by which we undermine the ecological substrate upon which we depend.

Finding oil was and is an impetus for the excavation of the Earth. It is the ongoing project that turns up sedimentary layers of fossils and that provides evidence of an old Earth, allowing us to conceive of deep time, of geological time. If not for the comprehensive disgorging of fossil fuels since the late nineteenth century we would not have the Anthropocene, and if not for the economic

> Earth is roughly 4.6 billion years old. A confident figure for the age of the Earth came as late as 1953. We are the medium through which the planet thinks. We, the Earth's digestive residue, were able to discover the planet's own duration.

incentive to look below the earth's crust we might have never been confronted with the utter discontinuity between anthropometric time and planetary time. Mining made geology possible, and geology made the unthinkable abyss of deep time a fundamental truth. So, even though deep time is one of the ways that we learn to delink social phenomenological time from planetary time, the Anthropocene does in fact now make ecological time run on the clock of social time, as Dipesh Chakrabarty and others have put it. In other words, we dig for oil because we think the planet runs on our time, while doing it we learned that this is not true, however, by doing so, we made it true.

Earth is roughly 4.6 billion years old. A confident figure for the age of the earth came as late as 1953. We are, as Nikolai Fyodorov wrote a century ago, the medium through which the planet thinks.[03] We, the Earth's digestive residue, were able to discover the planet's own duration. But was this project in which the Earth formulated a biochemical intensity—humans—that would prove capable of knowing its own age worth the cost? A Faustian bargain to top them all! Was discovering this fundamental truth worth exhuming hundreds of millions of years of pre-Mesozoic bio matter—merely enough for a two-century fuel supply—and thus inaugurating the age of mass extinction? Or maybe better: what would make it worth it? Must the accomplishment of a Copernican epistemic disenchantment destroy which it knows a necessary outcome? Or is it only provisional damage that will make for a more durable relationship between knower and known? The answer isn't given in advance. It must be designed and designated. Here and then, there and now.

Benjamin H. Bratton presented his thoughts as a keynote lecture at project bauhaus Werkstatt/Datatopia Summer School *on September 1, 2018 in Berlin. In his presentation he shared an update to the theses in his book* The Stack: On Software and Sovereignty *(Cambridge, MA: MIT Press, 2016).*

01 Jeremy Diamond, "Trump, the Computer and Email Skeptic-in-Chief," *CNN* online, December 30, 2016, accessed March 23, 2020, https://edition.cnn.com/2016/12/29/politics/donald-trump-computers-internet-email/index.html.

02 Dipesh Chakrabarty, *Provincializing Europe: Postcolonial Thought and Historical Difference* (Princeton, NJ: Princeton University Press, 2000).
03 Ibid.

Trilobites are arthropods from the early Paleozoic
era and are preserved in large numbers as fossils.
Because of their geologically short life span,
they are a reliable indicator for dating the stones
in which they are found.

© Rocks and Gems Canada

The series *Metamorphism* by the artist Julian Charrière consists of electronic waste such as main circuit boards, hard disks, processors, and memory cards, which are melted together to form new anthropogenic primordial matter.

Julian Charrière: *Metamorphism XVII*, from the series *Metamorphism*, 2016.

Julian Charrière: *Metamorphism XVII*, 2016.

Julian Charrière: *Metamorphism XXXI*, 2016.

Contributors

CHRISTIAN VON BORRIES
(* 1961) is a musician, artist, activist, and filmmaker. In his films, including *The Dubai in Me* (2010), *MOCRACY—Neverland in Me* (2012), and *IPHONECHINA* (2014), he addresses the forms and mechanisms of the capitalist production of space. His works have been shown at the Lucerne Festival, Kunstfest Weimar, Volksbühne Berlin, Kampnagel Hamburg, and documenta 12. In 2017, von Borries curated the technology art fair, *A BETTER VERSION OF YOU,* in Seoul. He is currently working on another film series on the future of the city in collaboration with the Daimler Project Future division.

ARNO BRANDLHUBER
(* 1964) is an architect and urban planner. In 2006, he founded the collaborative practice Brandlhuber+ in Berlin. His work includes architectural and research projects, exhibitions, publications, and political interventions. His research about the idea of legislation in architecture and urban design resulted in two movies, *Legislating Architecture* (2016) and *The Property Drama* (2017), produced with artist and director Christopher Roth. Brandlhuber has been associate professor of architecture and design at ETH Zurich since 2017. In 2019, he co-initiated *2038*, an interdisciplinary team to represent Germany at the 17th International Architecture Biennale 2020.

BENJAMIN H. BRATTON
(* 1968) works in the fields of philosophy, art, design, and computer science. He is a professor for visual arts at the University of California, San Diego, where he also directs the Center for Design & Geopolitics. He is also program director of the Strelka Institute for Media, Architecture and Design in Moscow, professor of digital design at the European Graduate School, and a visiting professor at the Southern California Institute of Architecture and at NYU Shanghai. In his current research project, *Theory and Design in the Age of*

Machine Intelligence, he addresses the challenges that artificial intelligence poses to design: from machine vision to synthetic cognition and perception, and from the macroeconomics of robotics to everyday geoengineering. He is the author of *The Stack: On Software and Sovereignty* (2016).

JAMES BRIDLE
(* 1980) is a London-based artist and writer. His work has been published in various magazines, journals, and newspapers, including a regular column on technology in *The Observer* from 2011 to 2015. His concept of the "New Aesthetic" describes a new visual language that blends the virtual and physical worlds, influenced by digital technologies and the internet. In his book *New Dark Age: Technology and the End of the Future*, published in 2018, he examines the relationship between technology and knowledge, and points out that as technology progresses, our understanding of it diminishes.

CALLUM CANT
(* 1994) is a social researcher and doctoral candidate at the University of West London, where he is investigating class composition and self-organized activism in the UK through workforce surveys. He is editor of the socialist online magazine *Notes from Below.* He has written on strikes and social movements for publications including *The Guardian, Vice, The Independent,* and *Novara Media.* He presented his research findings in the book *Riding for Deliveroo: Resistance in the New Economy* (2019).

EGBERT DRANSFELD
(* 1962) studied spatial planning at the University of Dortmund and compared for his PhD thesis property market systems in Western Europe. He is co-founder and managing director of the Institut für Bodenmanagement in Dortmund, where his research focuses on property- and space management, land law, building

plot strategies, land policies, urban development contracts, real estate, and leasehold.

MICHAELA FRIEDBERG
(* 1993) is an architectural historian and designer based in Berlin. She received a master's in architecture from Princeton University, where her research focused on typologies and politics in the contemporary American suburb and the impact of new technologies on architectural form. Friedberg has worked for Brandlhuber+, MOS Architects, and Stan Allen Architects, and is co-founder of *Rumor,* an online platform for architectural criticism.

RENÉE GAILHOUSTET
(* 1929) is an architect and former chief urban planner of the Paris suburb Ivry-sur-Seine; she developed its master plan together with Jean Renaudie. Both of them independently designed numerous housing estates in Ivry, most notably their terraced apartment buildings. Gailhoustet taught at the École Spéciale d'Architecture in Paris and has published numerous books and essays. In 2019, she received the Grand Art Prize of the Academy of Arts Berlin for her lifetime achievements.

MIRKO GATTI
(* 1987) studied architecture in Milan, and completed a master's at the Center for Research Architecture at Goldsmiths University, London, as well as a research fellowship at ETH Zurich. While his interest in architecture encompasses such fields as critical theory and political activism, his approach remains highly practical. Since 2014, Gatti is based in Berlin where he works as a freelance architect, carpenter, curator, as well as editor at ARCH+. He co-curated the exhibitions *An Atlas of Commoning* (2018) and *1989–2019: Politics of Space in the New Berlin* (2019).

ANTOINE GEIGER
(* 1995) is an artist and currently studying architecture at the École nationale supérieure d'architecture Paris-Malaquais. His photo series

SUR-FAKE has been featured in *Vice, Spiegel online,* and *ZEIT online,* among others.

MARISA GONZÁLEZ
(* 1945) is an artist based in Madrid. Her work *Ellas filipinas* was part of the 13th Venice Architecture Biennale, curated by David Chipperfield.

HANNES GRASSEGGER
(* 1980) is a journalist and economist. He is a regular contributor to *Das Magazin, The Guardian,* and *Buzzfeed.* His investigative reports about Cambridge Analytica (with Mikael Krogerus), Facebook's secret censorship team in Berlin (with Till Krause and Julia Angwin), and the meme war against George Soros received international attention. His book *Das Kapital bin ich – wie wir im Kapitalismus unsere Souveränität sichern können* (I Am Capital: How to Ensure our Sovereignty in Capitalism) was published in 2014.

OLAF GRAWERT
(* 1987) studied architecture and urban planning in Innsbruck and Berlin where his research focused on architecture theory and urbanism. He has been a guest lecturer at the Joint Master of Architecture Suisse program, at the Accademia di Architettura Mendrisio, both in Switzerland, and at the Chicago Architecture Biennial. He is co-editor of WIA (whatisarchitecture.cc), has worked with Brandlhuber+ since 2015, and has been a research assistant at the Department of Architecture at ETH Zurich since 2017. In 2019, he co-initiated *2038*, an interdisciplinary team to represent Germany at the 17th International Architecture Biennale 2020.

ANGELIKA HINTERBRANDNER
(* 1992) studied architecture at Graz University of Technology (TU Graz) and at the Chinese University of Hong Kong. She has worked for MVRDV, Buchner Bründler Architekten, and as a project and research assistant at

TU Graz. From 2018 to 2019 she was an editorial assistant at ARCH+. Since then she has been working for Brandlhuber+ and is studying Leadership in Digital Innovation at the University of the Arts in Berlin. Her research interests include the social and political aspects of architecture as well as current trends in technology and communication.

FLORIAN HERTWECK
(* 1975) is an independent architect (Studio Hertweck) and director of the master program Architecture, European Urbanisation, Globalisation at the University of Luxembourg. He was the curator of the Luxembourg Pavilion at the 2018 Venice Architecture Biennale together with Andrea Rumpf. Since 2018, Hertweck is leading, together with Milica Topalovic from ETH Zurich, a consortium of researchers and planners for the development of a territorial design strategy for Greater Geneva 2050. Among his publications are *Architecture on Common Ground – The Question of Land: Positions and Models* (2020), *The Dialogic City – Berlin wird Berlin* (2015, with Arno Brandlhuber and Thomas Mayfried), *The City in the City – Berlin: A Green Archipelago* (2013, with Sébastien Marot).

MARKUS HESSE
(* 1960) is a geographer, spatial planner, and professor of urban studies at the University of Luxembourg. One of his current research projects focuses on fast-growing, highly internationalized cities and their relation to global economic processes, as well as to consequences of land use and real estate. He is member of the German Academy of Spatial Research and Planning. sustaingov.blogspot.lu.

LUDGER HOVESTADT
(* 1960) is a professor of architecture and computer aided architectural design (CAAD) at ETH Zurich. In 1994, he received his PhD from the Technical University of Karlsruhe under Fritz Haller on the subject of *Digital Construction: A Model for Extensive Computer Support of the Design, Construction, and Operation of Buildings.* The current focus of his work is in the areas of generative design, digital production, and building intelligence. He is the inventor of the digitalSTROM® chip and founder of several spin-off companies in the field of smart building technology. In addition to numerous scientific publications, he is the author of the foundational book *Jenseits des Rasters: Architektur und Informationstechnologie – Anwendungen einer digitalen Architektonik* (Beyond the Grid: Architecture and Information Technology – Applications of Digital Architectonics, 2009).

IMMO KLINK
(* 1972) is a photographer based in London. He is known for his genre-crossing visual language, taking documentary approaches into fashion and using commercial aesthetics in documentary, art, and political campaigns. He has exhibited at FOAM in Amsterdam, Sala Rekalde in Bilbao, and the Victoria & Albert Museum and National Portrait Gallery in London. His works have been published in *Adbusters, Another Magazine, Dazed, Exit, i-D, L'Officiel, The New Yorker, The New York Times Magazine, Süddeutsche Zeitung Magazin,* and *ZEITmagazin.*

ANASTASIA KUBRAK
(* 1993) is a designer based in Rotterdam. Her work deals with the socio-political implications of new technologies. Kubrak holds a master's in Visual Strategies from Sandberg Instituut in Amsterdam. She is currently working as a researcher at the Het Nieuwe Instituut, and is teaching at the master's program Social Design at Design Academy Eindhoven.

NIKLAS MAAK
(* 1972) is a journalist, architectural critic, and editor at the *Frankfurter Allgemeine Zeitung*, in Berlin. He was a visiting professor for the history and theory of architecture at Städel Schule in Frankfurt, and teaches at the architecture department of Harvard University. His publications include *Eurotopians* (2017, with Johanna Diehl), *Living Complex – From Zombie City to the New Communal* (2015), and *Le Corbusier – The Architect on the Beach* (2011).

SANDER MANSE
(* 1991) graduated in 2014 from the Design Academy Eindhoven, is currently writing his master's in Philosophy, Art and Critical Thought at the European Graduate School, and works for the Office for Metropolitan Architecture (OMA) in Rotterdam.

SHANNON MATTERN
(* 1976) is a professor of anthropology at the New School in New York. Her research focuses on spaces and infrastructures for data and media and their influence on architecture and the city. She is involved in various public (design) projects, teaching, and exhibition formats (wordsinspace.net), and writes a regular column on urban data and media infrastructures for *Places Journal*. Her books include *The New Downtown Library – Designing with Communities* (2007), *Deep Mapping the Media City* (2015) and *Code and Clay, Data and Dirt – 5000 Years of Urban Media* (2017).

MEDIALAB ETH ZÜRICH
is a project led by Professor Christophe Girot. It addresses issues of landscape perception through audiovisual media and how these can alter and expand our perception. The focus is on the combination of sound, photography, and laser scanning and how these respective techniques can highlight specific aspects. The MediaLab team, which includes Ludwig Berger, Laura Endres, Dennis Häusler, Johannes Rebsamen, and Matthias Vollmer, specializes in various disciplines of audiovisual composition. The use of laser scanners has become an important tool in all areas of the department and is being continuously developed.

OKSANA MIRONOVA
is a researcher and writer. She co-founded the New York City Real Estate Investment Cooperative (NYC REIC) in 2015. Her writing about cities, alternative economies, and public space has appeared in *Urban Omnibus, Metropolitics,* and other publications.

ANH-LINH NGO
(* 1974) is an architect, author, and ARCH+ editor-in-chief and co-publisher. He co-founded the international initiative *project bauhaus*, which critically examined the ideas of the Bauhaus (2015–19). He served as a member of the Art Advisory Board of ifa (Institut für Auslandsbeziehungen) (2010–16). He is a member of the curatorial board for IBA 2027 Stadtregion Stuttgart. In 2018, he co-initiated and co-curated the ifa exhibition *An Atlas of Commoning,* which is now touring worldwide. In 2019, he co-curated the exhibition *1989–2019: Politics of Space in the New Berlin* at Neuer Berliner Kunstverein. In 2020, he received, together with Nikolaus Kuhnert and ARCH+, the Art Prize Berlin awarded by the Academy of Arts Berlin for his contribution to the discipline of architecture.

RAQUEL ROLNIK
(* 1956) is an architect, urban planner, and professor at the Faculty of Architecture and Urbanism at the University of São Paulo. She was director of the planning department of São Paulo (1989–92), national secretary for Urban Programs of the Brazilian Ministry of Cities (2003–07), and UN special rapporteur on adequate housing (2008–14).

CHRISTOPHER ROTH
(* 1964) is an artist and director. His movie *Baader* was selected in the competition for the Golden Bear at the Berlinale in 2002, and was awarded the Alfred Bauer Prize. In recent years, he directed

Contributors

Hyperstition (2015) with Armen Avanessian, *Legislating Architecture* (2016) and *The Property Drama* (2017) with Arno Brandlhuber. He is currently working on three thematic TV stations, together with Studio Brandlhuber at ETH Zurich (station.plus), with KW Institute for Contemporary Art in Berlin (realty-v), and with the Haubrok Foundation (42). In 2019, he co-initiated *2038*, an interdisciplinary team to represent Germany at the 17th International Architecture Biennale 2020.

WOLFGANG SCHEPPE
(* 1955) is an interdisciplinary philosopher based in Zurich and Venice, where he directs the Arsenale Institute for Politics of Representation. His research project *Migropolis* is considered a standard work on the theme of the globalized city. He curated a series of theory installations at the Staatliche Kunstsammlungen Dresden about the relation of ethnology to nationalism and world trade. Other exhibitions have dealt with the scientific-ideological etiology of racism and, on the occasion of the 2017 Venice Biennale, with Hegel's thesis on the end of art.

TREBOR SCHOLZ
(* 1969) is an activist and associate professor for culture & media at the New School in New York, where he founded the Platform Cooperativism Consortium. His publications include *Ours to Hack and to Own: The Rise of Platform Cooperativism, a New Vision for the Future of Work and a Fairer Internet* (2017, ed. with Nathan Schneider), *Uberworked and Underpaid: How Workers Are Disrupting the Digital Economy* (2016), and *The Internet as Playground and Factory* (2013, ed.). www.platform.coop

PATRIK SCHUMACHER
(* 1961) is an architect and has been a partner of Zaha Hadid Architects since 2002. Schumacher is considered to be the theoretical

mastermind of parametrism, which is based on the consistent use of digital design techniques. He teaches at the University of Innsbruck, co-directs the Design Research Laboratory of the Architectural Association (AA) in London, and is a member of the Royal Institute of British Architects (RIBA) and the Academy of Arts in Berlin.

MANUEL SHVARTZBERG CARRIÓ
is an architect and scholar based at the Graduate School of Architecture, Planning, and Preservation, Columbia University in New York, where he runs the thesis for the master's program in Critical, Curatorial, and Conceptual Practices in Architecture (CCCP).

DEANE SIMPSON
(* 1971) is a professor at the Royal Danish Academy of Fine Arts (KADK) where, together with Charles Bessard, he runs the Urbanism & Societal Change master's program at the School of Architecture. His research focuses on topics as demographic change, social and ecological sustainability, and the securitization of public space. He is the author of *Young-Old: Urban Utopias of an Aging Society* (2015) and co-editor of *The City between Freedom and Security: Contested Public Spaces in the 21st Century* (2017) and *Atlas of the Copenhagens* (2018).

DOUGLAS SPENCER
(* 1962) is author of *The Architecture of Neoliberalism* (2016). As a critical architecture critic, he contributes regularly to *The Journal of Architecture, Radical Philosophy, Architectural Design, e-flux, AA Files, New Geographies,* and *Volume.* He teaches at the Architectural Association and at the University of Westminster in London.

NICK SRNICEK
(* 1982) is an author and lecturer of Digital Economy at King's College, London. Among is publications are *Inventing the Future* (2018 with

Alex Williams) and *Platform Capitalism* (2016). Together with Helen Hester, he is currently writing *After Work – The Fight for Free Time*, expected to be published in 2020.

ROBERT THUM
(* 1966) is professor for computational design in architecture and heads the Architecture Department at Trier University of Applied Sciences. He studied architecture in Vienna, Stuttgart, Phoenix, and London. From 2006 to 2013 he was director of the master's program at the University of East London. Together with Harald Trapp, he is currently working on the research project *Capital Architecture*, about the connection between Karl Marx and the production of space and architecture.

MILICA TOPALOVIĆ
(* 1971) is an architect and assistant professor of architecture and territorial planning at ETH Zurich, where her research focuses on territorial urbanization, in particular the relations between cities and their hinterlands. She is author/editor of *Belgrade. Formal/Informal: A Study of Urban Transformation* (2012), *The Inevitable Specificity of Cities* (2014), *Architecture of Territory. Beyond the Limits of the City: Research and Design of Urbanising Territories* (2016). She is currently working on the forthcoming book *Hinterland: Singapore Beyond the Border.*

HARALD TRAPP
(* 1960) is a sociologist and architect. He co-curated the Austrian Pavilion at the Venice Architecture Biennale in 2014 and teaches at the Vienna University of Technology, where he completed his PhD in 2013. He was head of the Master of Architecture program at the University of East London from 2015 to 2018. Since 2017, he has collaborated with Robert Thum on the research project *Capital Architecture*, and in 2019 co-founded Akt, an architecture collective in Vienna.

HANS-JOCHEN VOGEL
(* 1926) is a politician and member of the German Social Democratic Party (SPD). He was mayor of Munich, member of the Bundestag, and federal minister for Regional Planning, Construction and Urban Development. As governing mayor of West Berlin, he dealt, in particular, with issues of housing vacancy and squatting. He then went on to become leader of the SPD in the Bundestag as well as party chairman. He has published numerous essays on urban development issues.

ROBERT VOIT
(* 1969) studied fine art and photography at the Academy of Fine Arts in Munich and the Academy of Art in Düsseldorf, where he graduated as a Meisterschüler (master student) under Thomas Ruff. From 2011 to 2013 he was a visiting professor at the Academy of Fine Arts in Nuremberg. His books *New Trees* (2014) and *The Alphabet of New Plants* (2015) were awarded the silver German Photo Book Prize.

BIANCA WYLIE
(* 1979) is a senior fellow at the Centre for International Governance Innovation (CIGI) in Waterloo, Canada. There she works on the Canadian government's data policy and technology strategy and its compliance with consumer protection regulations and basic democratic principles. She is co-founder of Tech Reset Canada, an advocacy group for the nonprofit expansion and deployment of new technologies. She is a regular contributor to publications such as *Huffington Post Canada, The Globe and Mail, Medium,* and *Vice/Motherboard.*

Since 1968, ARCH+ has been a leading publication
for discourse in the fields of architecture and urbanism.

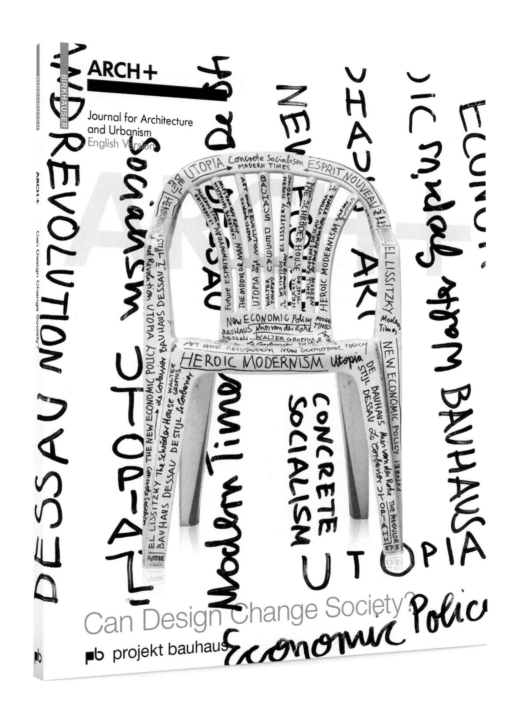

Projekt Bauhaus:
Can Design Change Society?

We are interested in the Bauhaus from a contemporary perspective.
Our focus lies less on Bauhaus' actual output, and more on the school's
ambitions and methods. In the interests of a reflective modernism,
we examined and critically reflected on the history, impact, and development
of the historic Bauhaus, as to learn from its mistakes and impasses.
It is only in and with society, and together with other social actors that
we will be able to change society.

ARCH+

2019, 240 pages
EUR 25.95 / USD 29.99 / GBP 23.50
archplus.net   birkhauser.com

As of 2019, ARCH+ and Birkhäuser are
jointly publishing and distributing an English
edition of the architecture journal ARCH+.

Imprint

ARCH+
Journal for Architecture and Urbanism

PUBLISHERS
ARCH+ / Birkhäuser Verlag GmbH

EDITOR
ARCH+ Verlag GmbH
Friedrichstr. 23a, 10969 Berlin, Germany
Phone: +49 30 340 467 19
verlag@archplus.net

EDITOR IN CHIEF
Anh-Linh Ngo

EDITORIAL TEAM ARCH+
Mirko Gatti, Christine Rüb

GUEST EDITORS
Arno Brandlhuber, Olaf Grawert,
Angelika Hinterbrandner

ART DIRECTION
Mike Meiré

DESIGN
Charlotte Cassel, Julia Pidun
Meiré und Meiré

ENGLISH LANGUAGE EDITOR
Alisa Kotmair

GERMAN TO ENGLISH TRANSLATIONS
Gareth Davies (pp. 70–77), Brían Hanrahan
(pp. 198–203), Richard Humphrey (pp. 16–35),
Gerrit Jackson (pp. 66–69), Alisa Kotmair
(pp. 1–3, 60–65, 174–83, 192–97, 210–15),
Rebecca van Dyck (pp. 48–51)

PROOFREADING
Cameron Cook

PREPRESS
max-color, Berlin

PRINTING
Medialis Offsetdruck GmbH, Berlin

Direct orders ARCH+ English editions
archplus.net/english-publications
degruyter.com/view/title/572122

Subscriptions to the magazine ARCH+
in German: archplus.net/kiosk

This publication includes key features from
ARCH+ 231 – *The Property Issue*,
Spring 2018, ISBN 978-3-931435-45-5;
ARCH+ 236 – *Posthumane Architektur*,
Autumn 2019, ISBN 978-3-931435-53-0.

EDITORIAL TEAM ARCH+ 231 –
The Property Issue: Anh-Linh Ngo,
Nora Dünser, Mirko Gatti, Christian Hiller,
Max Kaldenhoff, Alexander Stumm.
GUEST EDITORS: Arno Brandlhuber,
Olaf Grawert (station+, DARCH, ETH Zurich).
EDITORIAL ASSISTANTS: Ilkin Akpinar,
Nils Fröhling, Angelika Hinterbrandner,
Alexandra Nehmer, Lorenz Seidl,
Jan Westerheide (ARCH+); Annalena Morra,
Anna Yeboah (Brandlhuber+).

EDITORIAL TEAM ARCH+ 236 –
Posthumane Architektur: Anh-Linh Ngo,
Nora Dünser, Mirko Gatti,
Christian Hiller, Angelika Hinterbrandner,
Alexandra Nehmer, Christine Rüb.
GUEST EDITORS: Arno Brandlhuber,
Olaf Grawert (station+, D-ARCH, ETH Zurich).
EDITORIAL ASSISTANTS:
Frederick Coulomb, Dorothee Hahn,
Melissa Koch (ARCH+); Kristof Croes,
David Djuric, Jakob Eden, Annalena Morra,
Peter Richter (Brandlhuber+);
Michaela Friedberg, Anna MacIver-Ek
(station+, DARCH, ETH Zurich).

The topics in this issue were developed
in parallel to the films *The Property Drama*
(2017) and *Architecting after Politics* (2018)
by Brandlhuber+ and Christopher Roth
as well as the accompanying travelling
exhibition of the same name.

Many of the considerations reflected in
ARCH+ 236 evolved in discussion
with students participating in the design
studios *Real Virtuality* (Fall 2018) and
Architecture as Argument (Spring 2019) as
part of the teaching program by station+
(DARCH, ETH Zurich).

The charts "Alphabet World" (pp. 116–17)
and "BAT vs. GAFA" (pp. 220–21) were
compiled and designed by Kristof Croes
and David Djuric.

Bibliographic information published
by the German National Library:
the German National Library lists this
publication in the Deutsche National-
bibliografie; detailed bibliographic data
is available online at dnb.dnb.de.

Library of Congress Control Number:
2020937306

ISBN 978-3-0356-2106-8 (Birkhäuser)
ISBN 978-3-931435-57-8 (ARCH+)